BARACK OBAMA

BARACK OBAMA

CONSERVATIVE, PRAGMATIST, PROGRESSIVE

Burton I. Kaufman

CORNELL UNIVERSITY PRESS
Ithaca and London

First published 2022 by Cornell University Press

Printed in the United States of America

Library of Congress Cataloging-in-Publication Data

Names: Kaufman, Burton Ira, author.
Title: Barack Obama : conservative, pragmatist, progressive / Burton I. Kaufman.
Description: Ithaca [New York] : Cornell University Press, 2022. | Includes bibliographical references and index.
Identifiers: LCCN 2021037172 (print) | LCCN 2021037173 (ebook) | ISBN 9781501761973 (hardcover) | ISBN 9781501761980 (pdf) | ISBN 9781501761997 (epub)
Subjects: LCSH: Obama, Barack. | Presidents—United States—Biography. | African American politicians—Biography. | United States—Politics and government—2009–2017.
Classification: LCC E908 .K38 2022 (print) | LCC E908 (ebook) | DDC 973.932092 [B]—dc23
LC record available at https://lccn.loc.gov/2021037172
LC ebook record available at https://lccn.loc.gov/2021037173

For Jane

Contents

Preface

Barack Obama's keynote address at the Democratic National Convention in Boston in 2004 vaulted him into national promise and four years later, into his election as President of the United States. Having watched the speech, I decided to learn more about this intriguing young leader, who became the nation's first Black American president. Over the years, I have read extensively on his life and political career, including his memoirs and those by other senior administration officials as well as his speeches and public papers, newspapers, magazines, and contemporary journals.

What became clear about the forty-fourth president's life was his commitment to a multiracial, multiethnic, and multicultural society. Obama was, however, also an economic conservative, something more generally ignored in the existing literature, which emphasizes instead his pragmatism and progressivism. His conservativism explains why he became so criticized both by Democrats on his political left and Republicans on his political right and accounts in part for the congressional deadlock that he encountered throughout much of his administration after the congressional election of 2010. In this biography I seek to explain and elaborate on this conservative aspect of his political views. I also try to explain why and how Obama made the decisions he did throughout his life, but especially during his presidency.

I do not deal at length on the background for each of the important decisions that Obama made, although I attempt to provide enough context for the reader to understand the issues he faced. I focus, for example, on why in 2009 he decided against the advice of many White House officials, to make passage of the landmark Affordable Care Act (ACA) his highest domestic priority and why he responded so enthusiastically to the so-called Arab Spring beginning at the end of 2010 despite the outbreak of violence, the overthrow in Egypt of a long established government and ally of the United States, and the civil wars taking place in Libya and Syria that accompanied the Arab Spring.

While I have sought not so much to pass judgment on the Obama presidency as to understand it, I make clear throughout the book and, more explicitly, in my conclusion my belief that future historians and biographers will evaluate Obama as one of the nation's best post–World War II presidents along with Harry Truman and Dwight D. Eisenhower.

BARACK OBAMA

Introduction

Barack Obama's commitment to a multiracial, multiethnic, and multicultural society traced back to his teenage and young adult life when, as the son of biracial parents growing up in Indonesia and Hawaii, he encountered many different cultures and societies and searched for his own racial identity.

What is most striking about his presidency, however, was his economic conservatism. His purpose was to maintain the nation's existing free enterprise system rather than replace it with a more powerful centralized government being proposed by a more radical wing of his party. He believed strongly in supporting and rewarding entrepreneurship, in individual responsibility, and in a broad middle-class society.

What differentiated his administration from others before him were his efforts to expand opportunities to enter the middle class for those he regarded as not yet part of it. To the extent he believed the federal government had to play an important role in opening the gates of opportunity, he was fully prepared to use the force of his presidency. But because he believed in individual responsibility and achievement and thought a good education was essential for entering the middle class, he always emphasized the need for Black fathers to fulfill their parental obligations by helping raise their children, especially by taking an active interest in their education.

Obama's commitment to conservative values materialized in other ways as well. Two of his greatest accomplishments as president were the passage of the Affordable Care Act (ACA) in 2010 and keeping the nation's worst economic recession since the Great Depression of the 1930s from devolving into another depression. At the time of these achievements, loud voices from the political left of the Democratic Party were calling for drastic measures, including a program of national health insurance or some other kind of national option to replace the nation's existing health system based on private insurance. Opposition to the ACA also came from the political right, which opposed any expansion of the government's role in providing health insurance beyond Medicare and Medicaid, approved during the Lyndon Johnson administration in 1965.

As for the economic recession that Obama inherited when he became president, most economists attributed it to the collapse of an overextended housing boom caused by easy borrowing, complex financial instruments known as derivatives, and lax regulation of the nation's largest financial and banking institutions, which dominated this sector of the economy. Those to the political left of the president called for breaking up these banks and institutions and creating, in their places, a more regulated but decentralized system of finance and banking. They also wanted more federal money used to prevent foreclosures on homes whose values had tanked because of the housing collapse and whose owners found themselves unable to meet their monthly mortgage payments. Instead, the president propped up the existing system by infusing hundreds of billions of federal dollars into it, at the expense, according to the president's critics, of homeowners who lost their homes as a result of foreclosures and bankruptcies.

Another result of the nation's economic recession was the near collapse of its automobile industry, in particular General Motors (GM), which was about to declare bankruptcy, and Chrysler, which also bordered on bankruptcy. Instead of allowing the collapse of this vital economic sector, which critics of the president were prepared to do in order to spur on greater industrial competition, Obama concluded that the collapse of GM and Chrysler would mean too great a loss of jobs by those employed by the auto giants or those who produced parts for them to allow their bankruptcy. Instead, his administration loaned billions of dollars to GM and Chrysler and helped arrange a sale of Chrysler to the Italian auto giant Fiat Industries.

For the most part, those who have written about the former president have either ignored or not pointed out adequately his conservative values even though they are foundational to his political outlook and the way he governed as president. Instead, these writers have emphasized his pragmatism and his progressivism. Indeed, Obama was a pragmatist and a progressive. He was pragmatic in the sense that he was more concerned about results than the means to achieve them. Although his presidency was always known for its candor and lack of scandal as compared to previous presidents and his successor as president, Donald J. Trump, Obama could also be ruthlessly pragmatic in achieving his goals.

Obama was also progressive in the sense that his goal was always a more perfect union, knowing that a perfect union was not achievable. His efforts to broaden entry into the middle class was one example of his progressivism. So was the ACA, which allowed millions of Americans who lacked health insurance to receive it. A third example was his executive order allowing children brought into the country by illegal immigrants to be granted permanent residency status.

Even in his conduct of foreign policy Obama was at the same time a pragmatist, a progressive, and a conservative. His pragmatism was evident in his expanded use of drones, first used by his predecessor, George W. Bush, to behead the international terrorist movement by assassinating its leaders. His progressivism was apparent in his efforts to confront the growing world problem of climate change and in his support of the so-called Arab Spring in the Middle East, in which millions of Egyptians and Arabs from other countries took to the streets to establish democratic institutions in the region. Rejecting revolution in which force was used to overthrow autocratic regimes, Obama advocated peaceful regime change through the ballot box and, when necessary, the application of US pressure to assure the results of the elections. Although rejecting Bush's Wilsonian doctrine of "making the world safe for democracy," he also envisioned a region predicated on the same principles of liberalism, free enterprise, and competition as those that existed in the United States.

The fact that Obama was a conservative as well as a pragmatist and progressive is important in understanding why he came under such heavy criticism, not only by Republicans who opposed his progressive values and expansion of government, but also by Democrats who wanted him to take more radical measures in response to the economic crisis he inherited as president and the delivery of health care in the country. There were other reasons why the majority of his achievements came within the first two years of his administration, when the Democrats controlled both the House and Senate as well as the White House. These included his failure to develop close relations even with his own congressional leadership, and the strength of the so-called Tea Party, a grass roots conservative movement that was instrumental in the Republican landslide victory in the congressional elections in 2010 and still remains a powerful force on Capitol Hill. All that said, the fact that Obama remained a conservative as well as a pragmatist and progressive explains why he alienated both the political left and the political right and, in part, why he was able to get so little done in Congress after 2010. Increasingly, he resorted to the use of executive orders to accomplish what he otherwise could not accomplish on Capitol Hill.

Even on the racial divide that has burdened the nation since the United States' original sin of slavery and that became a dominant issue in his second administration with the Black Lives Matter movement (BLM), Obama angered many Black leaders because of what they regarded as his indifference to racial issues and his failure to do more for his Black constituency. As the president acknowledged, even though he was born in 1961, he was never sympathetic to the more radical fringe of the civil rights movement of the 1960s, and he always opposed violence as a means to resolve racial issues. Until the eruption of sometimes violent street demonstrations beginning with the killing of two young Black men, Trayvon Martin in June 2013 and Michael Brown in August 2014, he paid relatively little attention to issues of race relations after he became president. And while he endorsed the Black Lives Matter movement, he placed much greater emphasis on "My Brothers Keeper" (MBK), his alternative to BLM.

In contrast to the street demonstrations associated with BLM, which had the potential for violence and offered little substantive in confronting the hardships that people of color faced in their lives (other than to restore Black pride and make the privileged aware of the needs of the underprivileged), MBK was a mentoring program helping young men of color from deprived backgrounds improve their lives by filling the opportunity gaps they encountered. It was part of the president's effort to open the middle class to those not already part of it.

CHAPTER 1

Roots

Barack Hussein Obama Jr. was born in Honolulu, Hawaii, on August 4, 1961, less than eight months after John F. Kennedy's inauguration as the nation's thirty-sixth president. By the time he left his adopted city of Chicago twenty-seven years later to attend Harvard Law School, Obama had already lived an extraordinary life. Growing up in Indonesia and Hawaii, he and his mother, Stanley Ann Dunham (Ann), had been abandoned by his Kenyan father, Barack Hussein Obama Sr. After she got remarried to an Indonesian businessman, Lolo Soertoro, Ann chose to pursue her own fulltime career in Indonesia, leaving it to her parents in Hawaii, Madelyn and Stanley Dunham, to raise Barack (Barry). Notwithstanding the love he received from his mother and grandparents, he often felt lonely and abandoned by both his parents. Complicating matters was his sensitivity to being biracial. Much of his young adult life was spent on a redemptive search for his roots and his own sense of racial identity. Although he left for Harvard still conflicted about issues of race, he no longer felt rootless. Quite the contrary. For someone his age, he was already unusually well grounded with a clearly defined sense of purpose and confidence in his own ability to achieve the goals he set for himself.

Childhood

At the time of Barack Jr.'s birth, the United States was enjoying the greatest prosperity in its history. Jobs were plentiful and the number of college attendees and graduates was growing at record levels. Even working-class families could look forward to a better life for their children. The civil rights movement, which had begun during the 1950s, was gaining momentum and social mobility was increasing. As a result, a transformation of thinking was taking place among many young African Americans. By the 1970s, things that had been unimaginable in the 1950s seemed possible.

Yet what characterized the 1960s was not widespread optimism but pessimism about the soundness and stability of the US economy, about the gains of the civil rights movement, about the lack of opportunities for those entering the marketplace, and even about the United States' place in the world. Kennedy had been elected on a campaign promise to get America "moving again." This was a thinly veiled reference to the widespread belief that President Dwight Eisenhower, while still enormously popular, had allowed the country to stagnate economically and militarily. He had also permitted its most dangerous adversary, the Soviet Union, to spread its influence almost to the shores of Florida by providing large amounts of economic and military aid to the Communist dictator of Cuba, Fidel Castro. There were even references to a "missile gap" in Moscow's favor. Rumors spread that the Soviet Union was building missile bases in Cuba with rockets powerful enough to launch a nuclear strike against targets along the Atlantic and Gulf coasts and to strike most major cities east of the Mississippi River. Eisenhower was personally depicted as a lackluster president whose administration was actually run by his secretary of state, John Foster Dulles, or by his chief of staff, Sherman Adams.[1]

Barack's mother, Stanley Ann Dunham, shared these views of Eisenhower and the 1960s and was an admirer of John Kennedy.[2] In 1956 she wore a campaign button for the Democratic nominee, Adlai Stevenson. In 1961 she was attracted to Kennedy's idealism, sense of purpose, and commitment to making the world a better place through such proposals as the Peace Corps, which matched her own values and overriding commitment to working with the world's poor.[3]

At the time Ann gave birth to Barack, she was living with her husband, Barack Obama Sr., a Black student from Kenya, in a small apartment in Honolulu. Born on November 29, 1942, she was only eighteen years old at the time of her marriage. Growing up, Ann had been, in many ways, a typical adolescent. She always had a close group of friends, participated in youth groups, enjoyed her share of slumber parties and record hops, and took pleasure in sometimes annoying her parents, especially her overprotective father whom she liked to tease.[4]

There was, however, an entirely different side of Ann that became even more pronounced as she grew older. She has often been described, even by her own son, as naively idealistic—almost as a flower-child of the 1960s. She was, indeed, a romantic and a dreamer, but these were not her most defining characteristics. More accurately, she was deliberative, disciplined, and targeted. She was also bookish, witty, curious, and opinionated. As an indication of just how smart she was, she won early admission to the University of Chicago; but she had to turn down the offer because her father thought she was too young to leave home.[5]

Most notably, though, Ann was unconventional. She liked jazz, refused to babysit, shared the wanderlust of her parents, and regarded education as the key to her future. Her friends at Mercer High School in a mostly affluent suburb of Seattle regarded themselves as being on the cultural cutting edge. The fact that she married a Black man, who was the first African exchange student at the University of Hawaii, at a time when miscegenation was still a crime in many states, was the strongest indication of her willingness to defy convention. Even in Hawaii's polyglot culture a Black and white couple was an oddity.[6]

An only child, Ann had already lived a nomadic life. After he married her mother, Madelyn, in 1940, and then served in the army, her father, Stanley, had moved his family from Wichita, Kansas, to California, where he attended the University of California at Berkeley before dropping out and taking a job as a furniture salesman in Ponca, Oklahoma. Always in pursuit of better opportunities, he went from job to job, first to Vernon, Texas, then to El Dorado, Kansas, then to Seattle, Washington, and, finally, to Honolulu, where he retired. He died in 1992. Madelyn was the real breadwinner of the family. Even though she never went to college, she held a number of responsible administrative positions and eventually retired as a vice president of the Bank of Hawaii. She died on November 4, 2008, on the eve of the election of her grandson as the nation's forty-fourth president.[7]

Despite being one of the nation's most conservative states, Kansas had always had a progressive streak going back to the Farmers' Alliances and Greenback Movement of the last third of the nineteenth century. In their beliefs and outlook, Stanley and Madelyn Dunham reflected this progressive stream in Kansas politics. Although they were not especially political, they came from a background that scorned the more traditional and conservative values of the state. Stanley's ancestry included antislave settlers and his great-grandfather was a veteran of the Union army. Following the suicide death of his mother, he was raised by his grandparents. Former teachers who were secular and worldly, they surrounded Stanley with great literature and took him and his older brother Ralph to Civil War battlefields and places like Yellowstone National Park. Although Stanley struggled through high school, he appreciated and valued good books and placed a premium on education.[8]

Born in the small farming community of Peru, Kansas, near the Oklahoma border, Madelyn came from a more traditional background than Stanley. Yet even her parents were not typical of most farm families in Kansas. A Roosevelt Democrat in the 1930s, her mother passed that leaning on to her children. Although she and her husband went to church on occasion, they were only nominally religious and placed no religious strictures on Madelyn and her two siblings.[9]

Madelyn yearned, nevertheless, for the amenities of modern life. Her wish was partly met when her father took a job in the oil industry in Augusta, a town just southwest of El Dorado, which claimed to have the best neon-lit movie theater west of the Mississippi River. Madelyn, however, wanted more and often traveled with friends to Wichita, about thirty miles due west of Augusta, where she loved to jitterbug at one of the city's many dance halls. Although she was in the top tier of her class in high school and yearned to go to college, her parents could not afford the expense. At the time she graduated, she seemed destined for some menial employment in rural Kansas.[10]

When Madelyn had the opportunity to escape her surroundings by marrying Stanley, she grabbed it. She had met him while he was working on a construction crew in Augusta. Tall and handsome with wavy brown hair, he swept her off her feet with tales of ventures to California and claims that he had written plays and scripts for Hollywood. Four weeks after meeting Stanley, she married him over the objections of her parents and friends.[11]

Their marriage of nearly fifty-two years was often rocky and strained, in part because they always lived in financial straits and in part because they had conflicting personalities. Stanley never seemed satisfied with his life. He was opinionated, stubborn, argumentative, and prone to fits of anger. Sometimes he exploded when Ann's teasing became too much for him. In contrast, Madelyn was proud of her success as a bank vice president, less complaining of the money she earned, and wiser, more focused, and responsible. Even though she began to drink heavily, she was the one who put food on the table, paid the bills, and disciplined Ann.[12]

If Stanley was disappointed with his life, however, he hid it under a veneer of mirthfulness and good humor. A doting father, he enjoyed being with Ann and her friends, amusing them with the tales he told, some woven from whole cloth. Although his stories and pretensions with her friends sometimes embarrassed Ann, she inherited his imagination, curiosity, opinionated views, sense of longing, and even verbosity. In contrast, Ann looked to Madelyn as her rock of stability in her otherwise chaotic life, moving as she did from town to town and denied by another of her father's searches for Eldorado from the fulfillment of her dream to attend the University of Washington.[13]

At first, Madelyn and Stanley had difficulty adjusting to the fact that their daughter had married a Black man from Kenya and had given birth to a biracial son, especially at such a young age. For the most part, however, they were racially tolerant, especially for their times. While living in Vernon, for example, they came face-to-face with Texas's system of segregation. Once, after Stanley gave his attention to a Black couple during regular store hours, he was instructed to do business with "coloreds" only at the end of a day after white customers had left the store. Another time, after Ann played with an African American child, Madelyn was told by a school principal and group of white mothers that her daughter should not play with Black children. Both Stanley and Madelyn were repelled by this treatment of Blacks as second-class citizens. Stanley even claimed he left the state because he and his wife could not put up with its racial intolerance.[14]

Ann had married Barack Obama Sr. in part to explore the world and get away from her strong-willed parents. But she had also been attracted to his racial and cultural background, his deep intellectualism, and his charismatic personality. He charmed people with his self-confidence, friendliness, and obvious intelligence. Ann also found him good looking, similar in appearance to the Black singer Nat King Cole.[15]

By all accounts Obama Sr. was a remarkable student who was determined to complete his education in the United States and then to serve in an influential position in Kenya in economic development or international trade. Unfortunately, he was also unreliable. He enjoyed partying, drinking, and frolicking. He was also a serial liar. He skipped from job to job, mostly because he had been fired from the previous one. Privately, he could be arrogant, domineering, and mentally abusive. At the time he married Ann, he was already married and had a child living in Kenya. Obama was a member of the Luo tribe in Kenya, which allowed polygamy. But he lied when he told Ann that he had divorced his Kenyan wife.[16]

After two years at the University of Hawaii, Barack Sr. was accepted with a scholarship into the PhD program in economics at Harvard University. He did not, however, have enough money to take Ann and their son to Cambridge. Although he promised Ann, who had already left the islands to enroll at the University of Washington in Seattle, that he would send for her and Barack Jr. as soon as he could save enough money, he never did. He would not see them for the next nine years.[17]

Unable to make it on her own financially, Ann returned to Honolulu to be with her parents, who helped raise Barack while she completed her degree in anthropology at the University of Hawaii. In 1964 she divorced Obama. While still married and working on her degree, she had met Lolo Soertoro from the Indonesia island of Java who, as a civilian employee working for the Indonesian army, had been sent by the army to obtain a master's degree at Hawaii's newly established East-West Center. Unlike Obama Sr., Soertoro was a responsible person who was also easygoing, kind, patient, and amusing. In March 1965 he and Ann married. Three months later, he received his master's in geography. For the next year he remained in Hawaii, but following an attempted coup in Indonesia in the fall of 1965, he was ordered home by the army along with all other students studying abroad on government grants. A year later, in 1967, Ann and Barack joined him in Jakarta after she completed her degree.[18]

Ann embraced the mixed and varied cultures of Indonesia and the tapestry of villages that made up Jakarta. She often dressed in the colorful skirts of Indonesia. Because Lolo had been conscripted into the military and was earning a low salary, Ann, Lolo, and Barack, whom she came to calling "Barry" (the more common American name), lived at first in one of Jakarta's more undesirable neighborhoods with unpaved streets, open sewers, and spotty electricity. But after Lolo completed his service, he took a job in the Jakarta office of the Union Oil Company. By the 1970s he was earning enough that they were able to rent a three-bedroom house in an upper-middle-class neighborhood. The owners of the house lived in a large home on the same grounds with a full staff of servants, who cleaned, cooked, and shopped for the Soertoros and even cared for Barry.[19]

Freed of most domestic duties, the career-minded Ann was soon able to find employment. After a couple of years in a job she did not like supervising a group of Indonesians teaching English, she took a more responsible and innovative position working for a private nonprofit management training school started by a Dutch priest. On August 15, 1970, shortly after Barry's ninth birthday, she gave birth to Maya Kassandra Soertoro.[20]

Even before then, Ann's marriage to Lolo had begun to fall apart. Much of the problem was work-related. Although an important part of Lolo's job was to socialize with oil company executives and their wives, Ann begged off going to these functions, where she was expected to converse with people whom she found boring and inane. "They are not my people," she told an increasingly angry Lolo, who also resented the fact she refused to conform to his cultural expectations. He started drinking heavily and barely spoke to Ann. Though she remained married to Lolo until 1980 when she divorced him, she was lonely in the marriage and spent most of her time working and living apart from him.[21]

In addition to her increasing concern over her estranged relationship with Lolo, Ann grew worried about Barry's education. Indonesian schools were notorious for providing their students with a poor education. The government controlled the curriculum and the teachers were inadequately trained. To give Barry a better and more varied education, Ann sent him first to a Catholic school and then to a government-funded Muslim one. After work, she went over his homework, and in the morning, she woke him early to tutor him. She always encouraged him to read books.[22]

By the time Barry reached the age of ten and was about to enter the fifth grade, Ann felt she had to send him back to Hawaii to get a proper education. Although Barry did not stand out as a student, she thought he was gifted and had unlimited potential. In 1971, she put him on an airplane to live with his grandparents and to attend the Punahou School in Honolulu, a prestigious private preparatory school where many of Hawaii's elite sent their children. The school was also within walking distance of the Dunhams' apartment. Ann promised Barry that she and Maya would be joining him soon in Hawaii. Although she came back the next year, she left three years later to return to Indonesia.[23]

Even before passing her qualifying exams for a PhD in anthropology from the University of Hawaii, Ann found employment with the Agency for International Development (AID). As part of her job, she conducted research on rural credit for women in cottage industries in the villages surrounding Yogyakarta, a city about 320 miles southeast of Jakarta. She later used her research as the basis of her dissertation. In the field, she spoke the local dialects, ate the native food, and followed local customs while making many friends. The work she did—serving as an adviser to small-scale craft industries, all the while building trust by being sensitive to the way local businesses were conducted—was similar to the work her son would do later in Chicago as a community organizer.[24]

Barry, meanwhile, continued to live with his grandparents while completing his high school education at the Punahou School. By the time he graduated in June 1978, he had gone through a set of experiences unusual even for someone twice his age. He had been uprooted by his mother. He had moved from Hawaii to Indonesia where he had lived in two economically different neighborhoods and had gone to two culturally and religiously different schools. He was biracial as was his half sister Maya. Although his father visited in 1971 to spend Christmas with him (a visit that did not go well) and occasionally wrote him letters, he had mostly abandoned his son.

His mother loved him dearly and often visited him during the holidays and his summer vacations, but she was absent most of the time.[25]

Early photographs of Barry living in Hawaii reveal a happy child with a big smile, posing with his grandfather, walking barefoot along Waikiki Beach, playing in the sand, and riding a tricycle with red, white, and blue streamers dangling from the handlebars. His life in Indonesia, however, was different. Although he still maintained his happy disposition, he was chubby with big ears that stood out. More important, he was light-brown-skinned with brown eyes, and black curly hair common to children of African descent. As a result, he was constantly teased and picked on by Indonesian children, who, like their parents, scorned Blacks. Once a classmate asked him if his "father ate people," and he constantly had to endure racial epithets. Although he did not give much thought to his own identity until he returned to Hawaii and entered his teenage years at Punahou School, he was sensitized to his race at an early age. While he was an eager and intelligent student, who in the second grade was put in the first of four sections and who tried to fit in, he always sat in the back row and felt like a misfit who did not belong.[26]

Living most of his first ten years in Indonesia, Barry was bound to be influenced by its culture, which placed a great premium on self-control and self-sufficiency. He also learned as a young boy growing up in a foreign land to be culturally aware and adaptable. At the same time, he found that life was complicated and disparate and could be unpredictable and cruel.[27]

His iconoclastic mother was the one, however, who had the greatest influence in shaping his values and understanding of the world. Commitment, determination, empathy, resiliency, a strong work ethic, the value of education, and a love of books were some of these values he learned from his mother. She also taught him to be respectful, polite, and courteous but not to be intimidated by the racial epithets he constantly had to endure. At home, she even tutored him about his racial heritage, playing recordings ranging from Mahalia Jackson to Sam Cooke and reading books to him on Martin Luther King Jr. and other prominent Black figures. Believing that Barry should have a sense of obligation, she also worked to instill in him ideas of public service. "If you want to grow into a human being," Obama recalls her telling him, "you're going to need some values."[28]

Over the next seven years, Barry's grandparents reinforced the belief system that their grandson had begun to develop while living in Indonesia. Once they accepted the facts of an interracial marriage and a biracial grandson, they accepted Barack Sr. into the family—or at least as much as they could for a son-in-law whom they regarded as being untrustworthy.[29]

As for Barry, they gave him their unconditional love. Having grown up and gone to school in Indonesia and having only seen his grandparents on holidays and during the summer, he felt at first as if he were living with strangers. But that quickly changed as they showed their love for him in different ways. Stanley, whom Barry called "Gramps," was constantly at his side. Later he introduced Barry to his many friends. Madelyn, who was called "Toot" or "Tutu," the Hawaiian term for "Grandparent," played the same responsible role as parent as she had with Ann. Believing that Barry was intellectually gifted, she paid for his expensive education at the Punahou School.[30]

As Barry spent the next seven years living with Gramps and Toot, he sensed the tension in his grandparents' marriage. He also felt his grandfather's disappointment with his career. One reason Gramps had moved to Hawaii was his conviction that the newly established state's beaches and weather would attract a migration from the west coast and open up new opportunities for him to sell furniture. When that did not happen, he decided to sell insurance, but with no better luck. "As he was unable to convince himself that people needed what he was selling and was sensitive to rejection," Obama later wrote, "the work went badly. Every Sunday night, I would watch him grow more and more irritable [as he tried] to schedule appointments with prospective clients over the phone." When he was able to arrange an appointment or sell a policy, his mood changed. He would come into Barry's room smiling and tell him stories from his youth or read a joke from *Reader's Digest*. Sometimes, he even showed Barry a book of poems he had started to write, or a sketch of a painting he planned to paint, or the plans of a house he intended to build.

Barry sensed the anguish his grandfather continued to feel. Although he feigned delight at Gramps's plans and encouraged him to complete them, he understood that Stanley's romanticizing about the future was his expression of regret about the present. Just as he had learned from his mother to dream about the future, he learned from his grandfather's experience to approach tomorrow not as a blind-eyed romantic but as a realist and pragmatist.[31]

Barry adjusted quickly to life with his grandparents in their small, cramped, but well-kept apartment near both Waikiki Beach and Punahou School. Years later, as he matured into adulthood, Obama developed a number of unattractive characteristics, including peevishness, prickliness, and even ruthlessness. But these were not apparent while he grew up in Hawaii. Despite the melancholy of his grandfather, his grandmother's growing drinking problem, the ongoing bickering between Gramps and Toot, and the absence of his mother, he had learned even as a young child to adjust to changing circumstances. He also had been taught by his mother and his experience in Indonesia the virtue of self-control, a trait which only strength-ened his naturally serene personality. He fit in easily, therefore, with the laid-back culture of his school with its imposing lava rock buildings, tree-covered hills, and verdant lawns.

As a teenager at Punahou, Barry seemed little different from most of the rest of his classmates. In fact, what stands out about Barry's teenage years was how little he stood out. He was a good but not outstanding student. Some of his teachers thought he did not live up to his academic potential. A few even commented that he was a deep thinker, but this was not the consensus.[32]

Nor was Barry a class leader. Athletics rather than student government consumed his interest. As he later wrote, "for the world beyond my family—well what they would see for most of my teenage years was not a budding leader, but rather a lackadaisical student." In his freshman year at Punahou, he played football, but his real passion was basketball. He tried out and made the basketball team at Punahou, which, in his senior year in 1979 won the state championship, but he was a benchwarmer rather than a starting player. He grew to be 6'1" tall, but he became thin as he grew taller, and he lacked both the height and the brawn of a standout player to whom Division I col-leges normally gave athletic scholarships. He worked hard to be a good defensive player. But he lacked quick moves and was weak on both offense and defense.[33]

Unlike his mother, who chose to associate with the more intellectually oriented and culturally nonconventional students at Mercer High, Barry selected as his friends at Punahou mostly his basketball teammates, who, like the rest of the student body, were almost all white. When not on the bas-ketball court, they were often on the beach drinking beer, smoking cigarettes and pot, and engaging in teenage talk about sports, girls, and music. Barry even experimented with cocaine, but except for that, he seemed typical of most high school students.[34]

As he was going through adolescence, however, Barry began to wrestle with the issue of his own racial identity. Gramps introduced him to one of his Black friends, who had long talks with him about racial matters. He also had intense discussions with a Black teammate, who emphasized the preva-lent nature of racism in society, something that Barry doubted at first but on which he began to reflect. He was deeply affected by a story his grandfather told in which Tutu asked Stanley to drive her to work the next day because she had been annoyed by the presence of a panhandler while waiting for a bus to take her to work. What bothered Barry was the emphasis that Toot placed on the fact that the panhandler was Black. "Never had they given me reason to doubt their love," Obama later wrote. "I doubted if they ever would. And yet I knew that men who might easily have been my brothers could still inspire their rawest fears."[35]

Although loving his grandparents and later describing his childhood and adolescent years in Hawaii as idyllic—a place where he would vacation every year even as president—Barry missed the counsel his absent father might have given him on racial matters. He rebelled against his mother, who fearing that her son might wind up like her father, scolded him for not living up to his academic potential and being irresponsible even in applying to college. He went through the inner turmoil and confusion that teenagers often experience as they mature into adulthood, except that his issues were compounded by the fact that he was biracial. While often ignoring or skimming class assignments, he immersed himself in Black literature, reading such authors as Ralph Ellison, James Baldwin, Richard Wright, W. E. B. DuBois, and Malcolm X. He grew a thick Afro, and in his senior year, he criticized his basketball friends for playing a "white" style game. He also became annoyed by the obvious discomfort of two of his white friends while attending a mostly Black party.[36]

In its curriculum, the Punahou School stressed multiculturalism, but by his senior year, Barry concluded that Hawaii was too insular and isolated to find the answers to the questions he was asking about his racial identity. What did being biracial mean? Was he more Black than white? Did it matter? Should it matter? Were all whites inherently racists? These were some of the questions with which he wrestled.[37]

Although Hawaii was known for its multicultural population and racial tolerance, its African American population was small. At Punahou School, Blacks constituted only 5 percent of the student population. Much like his venturous mother, he wanted exposure not only to a larger African American population but to other ethnicities and to the variety of experiences offered mostly in cities much larger and more diverse than tourist-oriented Honolulu. He wanted to go to a big city on the mainland for his college education.[38]

Occidental College (Oxy), in Los Angeles seemed ideal. Widely rated as one of the best small colleges in the country with a highly respected faculty and rigorous academic programs, it attracted students from throughout the nation and abroad. Since it was located on the west coast, Barry was closer to home than he would have been had he chosen to study at a more inland or east coast institution. Although the campus was located in a predominantly white suburb, it was not far from the downtown area in a city made famous by its film industry but also known for its economic and cultural diversity. But according to Obama the decisive reason why he chose Occidental over other colleges that accepted him was to be near a girl he had met while she was vacationing in Hawaii. She had first told him about Occidental.[39]

Collegiate Years

At Oxy Barry began to change from the lax, indifferent student he was at Punahou, whose interest were more on the basketball court than in the classroom. He still could be found in a pickup game on Occidental's basketball courts or, at night, at the student union. Photographs continued to show him with the broad smile that would become famous. But they also displayed a cocky young man wearing a straw hat with a colorful band of stripes around the rim, a bomber jacket, white shirt, and tight-fitting black jeans, dragging on a cigarette and blowing out puffs of smoke. Although the bomber jacket and black jeans would stay staples of his wardrobe through Harvard Law School, he pulled away from the foolishness of high school, cut back his big Afro, and started to reinvent himself. His first year at Occidental, he later wrote, had been "one living lie, hampered by self-consciousness and insecurity." He sought to change that.[40]

While Barry could still hardly be accused of working too hard, he read more extensively and broadly than he had at Punahou. It was embarrassing for him, he later wrote, "to recognize the degree to which my intellectual curiosity those first two years of college paralleled the interests of various women I was attempting to know." Yet he also studied and thought about politics and world events. He became interested in social movements and was inspired by the "young leaders of the civil rights movement—not just Dr. King but John Lewis and Bob Moses, Fannie Lou Hamer and Diane Nash." Nighttime discussions with his friends became heated. Often focused on the United States' role in the world, they revealed also Obama's increasing ability to comprehend the complex patterns and nuances of global politics.[41]

The courses Barack preferred were those in political science, history, and literature. Influenced in particular by one of his professors, Roger Boesche, who held a distinguished chair in the political science department, he read many of the classics on political theory and philosophy. A testimony to the impact Boesche had on him was the fact that after he became president, he invited the professor and his wife to the White House, where Obama announced that Boesche had "taught me all I know about politics." Then he added, "But he gave me a 'B' on a paper!"[42]

Obama also took in more of the life around him. He fully embraced the multiculturalism that had been such an integral part of his life. He decided to be called by his given name, "Barack" instead of "Barry." He chose as his friends politically active Black students and Chicanos, but he found foreign students to be the most interesting. He lived in his first year with a student from Pakistan, and his closest friends and subsequent roommates came from South Asia. He also displayed his developing talent as a writer by publishing two poems in the campus literary magazine, and, in what may have been his first political speech, he spoke out at a demonstration against the college's practice of investing in South Africa's apartheid regime.[43]

Yet Barack never became radicalized even on matters of race. He was Black. Of that he was certain. He grew annoyed by how fast and thoroughly minority students on campus assimilated into Occidental's predominantly white culture. But he continued to struggle with the question of what being Black meant. Despite reading such radical writers as Malcolm X, who impressed him more than other writers for the poetry of his words and his belief in Black pride and assertiveness, he thought Malcolm X went overboard in his view about white deviltry. He was taken aback especially by Malcolm X's statement that he wished he could expunge the white blood that ran through his veins, a position biracial Barack could never accept.[44]

Obama's transient and multicultural upbringing pointed him in the opposite direction. He had difficulty understanding how people learned to hate, and he longed for order and community. He saw no inconsistency between taking pride in his race and wanting to live in a multiracial, multiethnic, and multicultural world. His identity might start with the reality of his race "but it didn't, couldn't end there," he believed.[45]

By the time Barack decided to leave Occidental College in 1981 to attend Columbia University, he had become involved in the anti-apartheid movement and other causes dealing with Latino and African American students. In doing so, he burnished the personal skills that later powered him into politics. He left Occidental because most of his friends were either leaving or transferring to other colleges and universities. Like them, he found Occidental to be too small, too white, too apathetic, too limited in its curriculum, and too inaccessible to the city without a car. As a learning experience, he felt he had gotten all he could out of the college. "What I needed," he wrote in *Dreams from My Father*, "was a community." He was attracted to Columbia, which had a transfer program with Occidental, because of its size and the diversity of its student body, faculty, and curriculum. At Columbia he would have the opportunity to choose courses taught by some of the nation's most respected academic minds at one of the world's most prestigious universities. He also wanted to live in and explore one of the world's major cultural centers and the nation's most populous and diverse city.[46]

Yet Obama never availed himself of the opportunities that Columbia and New York offered him. Although he roomed his first year with a friend from Occidental near the campus on the city's Upper West Side, he failed to participate in Columbia's campus life or take full advantage of the city's cultural scene. A jazz fan since high school, he went to nearby night spots featuring jazz. He attended what he referred to as "socialist conferences" at Cooper Union college in the city's East Village and to African cultural fairs in Brooklyn and Harlem. He also wandered the city aimlessly as he continued to cope with issues related to his racial identity and as he thought increasingly about his future. He even kept a detailed journal, in which he recorded his observations, including the economic disparity that he witnessed. But he had little money to spend in an expensive city, and he became more withdrawn and bookish than he had been at Occidental. In *Dreams from My Father*, Obama barely mentioned Columbia, and only a few of his classmates could later remember anything about him.[47]

During the summer between his junior and senior years, Barack visited his mother and half sister, who were living in an exclusive area of Jakarta reserved for officers of the Ford Foundation with whom Ann had landed a position as a program officer. Her expertise in small-scale economies helped her win the job. In Jakarta, he was able to reconnect with his mother, who had been writing him almost every day and proudly boasted to friends about his brilliance, and Maya, who was attending a highly regarded international school.[48]

After a pleasant but uneventful visit with his mother and half sister, Obama flew to Pakistan where he stayed with two of his friends from Occidental, Wahid Hamid and Hasan Chandoo, both from the upper economic strata of Karachi. At Oxy, Barack had bantered with them about their indolent lifestyle even as they spoke out against the wrongness of wealth inequality. During his three weeks in Pakistan, Barack witnessed both abject poverty and enormous wealth as he saw the hovels of Karachi and visited the mansions and estates of Chandoo's and Hamid's relatives and friends. Even more than his experience as a child in Indonesia, he was deeply disturbed by what he saw. The harmful effects of the income inequality he witnessed in Karachi remained permanently burned into his mind. He committed himself to what he called "a regimen of self-improvement" that he "never entirely shed."[49]

Back in New York, Barack moved to the Upper East Side, over two miles from Columbia where he roomed with Sohale Sidiqqi, a Pakistani whom he had met at Occidental. Once settled in his apartment, Barack sought to take more control of his future. He envied his high school and Pakistani friends, whose futures seemed secure in the sense that they were either headed into the business world or, as he put it, "toward the mainstream." "Caught without a class, a structure, or tradition to support me, in a sense the choice to take a different path is made for me," he later reflected. "The only way to assuage my feeling of isolation are [*sic*] to absorb all the traditions [and all the] classes; make them mine, me theirs."[50]

News that his father had been killed in a car accident in Kenya after several earlier crashes involving his consumption of alcohol only underscored his sense of loneliness and his need to take control of his life. He read and reread Ellison's *Invisible Man*, which, as one of his Pakistani crowd remembered, "became a prism for his self-reflection." He also began to run more, stopped using marijuana (but not smoking because he feared he would gain weight if he did) and ate more healthy foods. Sidiqqi even called him "a bore."[51]

A political science major, Obama was interested primarily in international relations. He even wrote articles for *Sundial*, the college's weekly news magazine, including one, "Breaking the War Mentality," in which he said that students across the United States were trying to "enhance the possibility of a decent world."[52]

Although receiving mostly As in his major and an overall 3.7 average, Obama did not stand out as a student. Unlike most of his graduating class in 1983, he had no plans to go to graduate or professional school or to begin a career with some high-powered firm. Instead, he took employment as a research assistant for a firm, Business International Corporation (BI), that collected and analyzed business statistics. The quality of the reports he prepared so impressed management that it promoted him to the position of financial writer with his own tiny office and a substantial salary increase.[53]

Gap Years

While working at BI and now living on the Upper West Side, Obama had a lengthy affair with a white woman, Genevieve Cook, an Australian who, like Obama, had grown up in Indonesia. Earlier he had had an affair with another white woman, Alexandra McNear, an undergraduate friend from Occidental, who was living in New York over the summer. In both cases the women expressed their deep love for Barack, even keeping journals of their relationship with him. Barack expressed similar feelings, often in long letters to them. Whether with them or in his letters he engaged in a type of wide-ranging but dispassionate discourse about the arts, literature, racial identity, and purpose of life that made the women realize they could not get past his aloof personality during the most existentialist stretch of his life. Eventually the women and he drifted apart.[54]

Adding to Barack's problems in his relationship with Genevieve was the fact that he became bored by the routine of his job with BI. He found no satisfaction in helping wealthy clients become more wealthy. He had an aversion to accumulations of wealth in the control of the few at the expense of the many. He referred to his job as "working for the enemy."[55]

Although Obama was not even able to describe to other students what the job entailed, he had decided to become a community organizer while he was still a student at Columbia. Comparing himself to "a salmon swimming blindly upstream," he concluded that the conservative administration of Ronald Reagan was guilty of "dirty deeds," that Congress was "compliant and corrupt," and that top-to-bottom change in Washington was needed. Change would only come from "a mobilized grass roots." [56]

As a graduating senior, Barack had applied for a position with civil rights and social service organizations throughout the country, but without any luck. He took the job with BI because he needed an income and wanted to build up his savings, knowing all the time that his future lay in grassroots organizing and aware of how little organizers were paid. But he did not decide to resign until after he received a call from his half sister in Kenya, Auma Obama, about the death of their half brother, David, in a motorcycle accident. Following the call, he left his office for the day and wandered the streets of Manhattan. Auma's call, he later said, changed his life. It reignited his search for redemption by becoming a community organizer. A few months after the call, he resigned from BI and began looking in earnest for an organizing job.[57]

The search was not easy. Barack was offered a position in New York, which involved organizing and facilitating conferences on drugs, unemployment, and housing. But he felt the job was not grassroots enough. He needed to be "closer to the streets." He also took a few temporary jobs. While waiting for the "right" job to come his way, he depleted his savings. He was, he recounted, down to "eating soup from a can," when he received a call from an organizer in Chicago, Jerry Kellman, who had placed an ad to fill the position of a community organizer in the South Side of Chicago. Was Barack still interested in the position? he asked. After Obama expressed an interest, they agreed to meet each other the following week in New York.[58]

Kellman had reservations about hiring Barack. He was impressed by his intelligence, and he wanted someone for the position who was Black. But he was concerned that Obama might be too young, too elitist (being a graduate of Columbia), and too inexperienced for the position. Never having lived in the city, he knew nothing about Chicago and its ward-based politics. Weighing these factors, Kellman decided, nevertheless, to take a chance with him.

He offered him the position at $10,000 a year (a major decrease from what he had been earning at BI) plus a $2,000 travel allowance to be used to purchase an automobile.

Obama had his own reservations about Kellman, whom he found to be brash. Obama also drove a hard bargain. "He questioned me on whether we could teach him anything," Kellman remembers. "He wanted to know things like 'How are you going to train me?' And 'What am I going to learn?'" But after some thought, he decided to accept Kellman's offer.[59]

He had been to Chicago when he was ten years old. He remembered it as being cold and gray. This time he was struck by how pretty it was. More important, he was attracted to the nation's second largest city by the fact that it had recently elected its first African American mayor, Harold Washington, who defeated the incumbent Jane Byrne. A progressive, Washington had served in both houses of the state legislature and in the US House of Representatives, where his most notable achievement was helping win an extension of the Voting Rights Act. By promising to address the problems of Chicago's inner city, Washington had racked up insurmountable majorities among Blacks in Chicago's South and West Sides. Obama was so excited at Washington's victory that, shortly after his election, he applied (unsuccessfully) for a position with the administration.[60]

He took quickly to his new job in the nation's largest concentration of African Americans. His main responsibility was growing the newly formed Developing Communities Project (DCP), a church-funded effort to help residents of the Altgeld Gardens housing project on Chicago's South Side get needed improvements from the city. He also worked to establish a college tutoring and preparatory program, a jobs-training program for laid-off steelworkers, and even a tenants' rights organization. His efforts at Altgeld Gardens were his first immersion into a Black community. "It was the best education I ever had," he later recounted. "I fell in love with the city."[61]

Obama chose not to live close to the people with whom he worked. Instead, he took a small, dumpy apartment in Chicago's more upscale Hyde Park area, near the University of Chicago. Outside of work, he continued to lead an austere life, never inviting anyone to his apartment, looking and acting more like a graduate student than a community organizer, and mostly spending his free time reading biographies and books on subjects like theology. His chosen lifestyle underscored one of the great paradoxes of his entire career. He became a politician and ultimately reached the highest office in the land. He did so partly by his charm and great mass appeal. But he disliked politics and much preferred contemplation and quiet to back-slapping.[62]

Also known as "Alligator Gardens" to the police who had to deal with its drug trade, Altgeld Gardens was located in the remotest regions of the South Side. Housing some of Chicago's poorest residents, it was built in the 1940s for Blacks with wartime jobs in the nearby steel mills. Forty blocks from the nearest train station and miles from the Sears Tower in downtown Chicago, it looked like a military camp with row after row of two-story mud-brown brick apartments.[63]

Not only did Altgeld's residents lack adequate public transportation, half of them did not own automobiles. This made it extremely difficult for them to find jobs even if jobs were available. But most of the steel mills had closed, and the rest were cutting back their operations. Soot remaining from the mills continued to penetrate buildings and people alike. Many residents were single young mothers on public assistance. Job skills were limited. Drugs were big business. The project recycled poverty and dependence.[64]

Obama's responsibility was to break this vicious chain. Kellman was a disciple of the highly controversial sociologist, Saul Alinsky. Widely regarded as the founder of community organizing, Alinsky was criticized by his conservative opponents as a radical provocateur for his outspoken public support of leftist organizations and movements and for his views calling for so-called have-nots to gain political power by organizing against entrenched power. Like Alinsky, Kellman believed that power at the top could be toppled by organization at the bottom.[65]

Successful organization, however, required professional organizers to mobilize the community around immediate, and winnable, issues. Its ultimate object was to bring about social reform and a democratic revival. Since churches attracted the loyalty of their adherents, one of Alinsky's strategies was to gain the support for his agenda of a community's religious leaders. Given the fact that much of the life of African Americans centered around their churches, Kellman expected his new hire to establish close relationships with the clergy of the Altgeld community.[66]

As Obama quickly discovered, developing a close working relationship with the community's religious leaders proved difficult. Alinsky—and Kellman—assumed that they would be united in their grievances. After all, the organization that Kellman headed consisted of a group of Latino churches. What might have worked elsewhere, however, did not work in the poverty-stricken Black community to which he was assigned. Religious leaders in the Altgeld community defended their turf. They also questioned Obama's name, youth, and lack of religious affiliation, and mistrusted the fact that the parent organization of DCP was Catholic and that his offices were in the rectory of a Catholic church.[67]

Obama became frustrated at the negative reception he received from these pastors and ministers, who pointed proudly to their own social and educational programs and openly disputed the need for another layer of bureaucracy that might undo what they had already accomplished. Of the leaders he visited, only one, a Baptist minister, Reverend Alvin Love, who was new to the community and young like Obama, agreed to work with him.[68]

Of the Altgeld residents he met, a few were openly hostile to someone they regarded as an outsider. Most were either uninterested, afraid, or had no time to become part of any movement. But three middle-aged women, Yvonne Lloyd, Loretta Augustine, Margaret Bagby, all of whom resided just outside the Altgeld projects but were members of the DCP board, were impressed by the sincerity of the gangly young person they met. They were also surprised by his knowledge of the South Side and by his honesty in admitting that he knew nothing about community organizing. Despite his Ivy League education and outsider status, they agreed to join him in organizing residents of the Altgeld community.[69]

Obama remained at DCP for three years. He learned from his failures and grew on the job. As a new organizer, he made a number of mistakes, including calling the religious leaders together in a failed effort to get them to agree upon a common agenda. The meeting annoyed, rather than united, the church leaders. The only thing they agreed upon was that they did not need some young, inexperienced outsider representing an organization they did not like interfering in their daily lives. Obama left the poorly attended meeting feeling rejected and demoralized in a way that he had never experienced.[70]

Realizing the need for a different approach, he turned to the Reverend Love and to Bagby, Lloyd, and Augustine, whom he found to be the most dependable of the three women, to knock on doors and persuade the community to come to DCP meetings. They also convinced the city to open a branch office of the Mayor's Office of Employment and Training (MET) and persuaded Obama's idol, Mayor Washington, to attend the ribbon cutting ceremony. Being told by Love that he might better connect with the community by belonging to a church, he joined the large Trinity United Church of Christ after hearing its pastoral leader, the Reverend Jeremiah A. Wright, speak on faith's power to inspire underdogs.[71]

In attempting to organize the Altgeld community, Obama adopted an Alinksy-style strategy of rallying the community around a single issue that would outrage the public and embarrass city hall. When he learned that there was asbestos in the Altgeld project, he launched a public relations campaign that brought to the community the city's top public housing official, Zirl Smith. Like all meetings in which he was involved, he prepared meticulously for this meeting with scripted roles for the participants. Much to his regret, the large and increasingly impatient crowd of about seven hundred became unruly after Smith arrived seventy-five minutes late in his chauffeur-driven city car and then appeared to give the gathering the brush-off by his snide comments. The meeting left him once again deeply dispirited and despondent. But it served the purpose of making Smith appear indifferent to community needs and forced the city to begin the process of removing asbestos from all Altgeld's buildings.[72]

By his third year in Chicago, Obama could point to a record of accomplishment sufficient to have his salary doubled to $20,000 a year. He was also attracting the attention of powerful figures within Chicago's political circles. He had even persuaded a group of younger pastors to make their churches members of the DCP. But he was not happy. Although he had gotten the city to begin the process of removing asbestos from the Altgeld's buildings, the project would not be completed until after he left Chicago to attend law school. Getting the city to make such basic repairs in the apartment as fixing toilets and furnaces also proved slow and tedious.[73]

The Kellman-Alinsky organizational approach of confrontational politics and Alinksy's radical agenda and language, moreover, did not comport with his own style of mediation and conciliation in search of a common ground. More important, he concluded that while grassroots organization might achieve limited objectives, it could not bring about the type of systemic change that Kellman and Alinsky believed it made possible. What was needed was the building of a community culture and a long-term vision.[74]

Instead of a career as a community organizer, Obama reflected on the possibility of a career in law and politics. To effect fundamental change, even on the most local level, he felt he had first to obtain a law degree at a top law school, which would provide him with more skills and give him entry into the corridors of power. As an additional benefit, becoming a lawyer would put him on the road to the economic security his father never had.[75]

When Obama decided to become a politician is not entirely clear. In December 2016, he stated in an interview that the decision to become a politician was not the result of one transformative event, but began when he became more socially conscious as a student at Occidental. It was also mixed with his search for his racial identity. If there was no transformative event that bent him toward a political career, however, Harold Washington's successful career as a politician deeply affected him. Although Washington's mixed record of accomplishments in his more than four years as mayor disappointed him as it did others who backed the mayor, his success in motivating Chicago's Black community and even some of its liberal, socially conscious white community on Chicago's upscale North Side inspired him. So did Washington's promise to uplift the lives of the city's poor through the political power he wielded. Obama may even have considered becoming the city's mayor someday.[76]

Having decided to pursue a law degree, he applied and was accepted to Harvard Law School. Even as he prepared to leave Chicago for Harvard, he made clear he intended to return to the city with the skills he still lacked to effect change. Previously he had felt lost and alone. Now he had a home and a purpose. "I would learn about interest rates, corporate mergers, the legislative process," he later reflected, "knowledge that would have compromised me before coming to Chicago, but that I could now bring back [to the city] like Promethean fire." Meanwhile, he would bring to Harvard a restless and probing mind along with a deep internal equanimity that would act as ballast against the type of radical thinking of Malcolm X, Saul Alinsky, and Jerry Kellman.[77]

Before entering Harvard, Obama toured Europe and visited Kenya, the home of his father. He wanted to see and explore the ancestral roots of Obama Sr., and his own. He also wanted to visit with his grandmother, half siblings, and numerous aunts and cousins he had never seen. By visiting Kenya and returning to the place where his father grew up, he hoped to better understand his own identity as well as his father's. By learning more about his father's motivation in coming to the United States, he hoped also to learn more about what motivated his own actions. In these ways, his trip to Kenya would be as much one of self-exploration as of exploration.[78]

Touring Europe, Obama felt uncomfortable and ill at ease. Europe, he said, was beautiful, the churches and historic places he saw imposing. But after a week, he felt that as a Black person conscious of his racial identity and searching for his roots, his decision to come to Europe had been a mistake and that he was "living out someone else's romance." The "incompleteness of my own history," he added, "stood between me and the sites I saw like a hard pane of glass." His European stop was also "just one more means of delay, one more attempt to avoid coming to terms with the Old Man."[79]

In Kenya, Barack was embraced by family. The emptiness he felt in Europe was washed away by familial ties and the welcoming spirit he received wherever he visited. Members of his large, extended family opened their homes to him. Aunts, uncles, half brothers and half sisters, a step-grandmother Sarah (known as "Mama" Obama) and his cousins peppered him with questions about his life and experiences. They also wanted to know more about the US and Harvard. Most knew little about one of the world's most prestigious universities other than that Barack's brilliant father had gone there. They also understood the value of education in bettering one's position in life. By going to Harvard, Barack would be honoring his father's memory.[80]

His visit to Kenya was redemptive. "How tempting," he reflected, "to fly away with this moment intact. To have this feeling of ease wrapped up . . . and take it back with me to America to slip on whenever my spirits flagged." At the same time, he resented the fact that in public facilities, like bars and restaurants, locals were treated in a condescending manner while wealthier tourists from Europe received first-class treatment. Once Auma, who was studying German at the University of Heidelberg and would later receive her PhD degree from the University of Bayreuth, walked out of a restaurant in a fit of anger after servers ignored her and Barack. Outside, he kept his poise and tried to make light of the incident. But like his half sister, he deplored the treatment that they had received in contrast to the first-class treatment extended to tourists from what he referred to as "imperial cultures."[81]

From his visit to Kenya, Obama gained a number of insights about his father and himself that he would take back to the United States. Throughout his visit, for example, he tried to understand why his father had abandoned him and his mother in order to return to Kenya. He found his answer in the concept of "family"; in effect, his father had left his family in the United States to join his larger and needier family in Kenya. But he concluded that family for his father meant more than the immediate or extended family. As in concentric circles, it meant an ever-extending community of Kenyans. This reinforced his own view of the interconnectedness between family and social obligation and between community organization and his belief in community as a lever of political power.[82]

Auma provided this insight when she explained why she returned from Germany to Kenya. In Germany, she found stability and security, a modicum of which she was still able to retain in Kenya because her training assured that she would always be able to find employment. Still, she faced familial strife over issues such as whether Obama Sr. had left an inheritance and, if so, who was entitled to it. Even more of a strain was the obligation she felt to support her relatives, even those who had a job, on a salary barely sufficient to meet her own needs. "I feel like they are all just grabbing at me and that I'm going to sink," she told her half brother. Yet she stayed.[83]

Auma's account of her Kenyan life affected her half brother emotionally and led him to pose new questions about his own familial and social obligations. "Now I was family . . . now I had responsibilities," he wrote in his memoir. "But what did that mean exactly?" "For the first time in my life," he continued, "I found myself thinking deeply about money: my lack of it, the pursuit of it, the crude but undeniable peace it could buy." But he also realized that a career in pursuit of wealth was not for him. He would, he said, experience a "perverse survivor's guilt . . . if I ever did try to make money and had to pass the throngs of young Black men on the corner as I made my way to a downtown office." The only way to prevent others from being left behind, he concluded, was to transfer power from an economic elite to "a group larger even than an extended family."[84]

Although Obama's visit to Kenya was redemptive, it was also dispiriting. If he expected to experience an epiphany in visiting his father's homeland, he was disappointed. What he found in Kenya "were the same maddening patterns" he experienced wherever he had lived or visited—wealth and poverty, social inequality, political and economic elites determined to hold on to power, an overriding loss of heart about the possibility of peaceful change.[85]

As Obama looked at the shanty towns of Nairobi, observed the despair of Auma and the other relatives he visited, witnessed the tribal divisions that still existed in Kenya, and saw firsthand the lack of electricity or any infrastructure in the small villages that dotted the country, he developed doubts about what he could accomplish. "I'd come to Kenya thinking that I could somehow force my many worlds into a single harmonious whole," he later wrote. "Instead the divisions seemed only to have become more multiplied."[86]

Toward the end of his stay in Kenya, he visited his father's grave in the small village of Kogelo, about 435 miles from Nairobi near the coast of Lake Victoria. It was a highly emotional experience for him. When he saw the site, he realized that his father's effort to escape from his roots in an isolated village in rural Kenya and become an influential figure in his homeland had failed. He wound up buried in the same remote area where he was born and raised. "To discover that he remained trapped on his own father's island with its fissures of anger and doubt and defeat, the emotions still visible beneath the surface, hot and molten and alive," horrified him. "For a long time," he recounted, "I sat . . . and wept."[87] He saw that his "life in America—the Black life, the white life, the sense of abandonment [he had] felt as a boy, the frustration and hope [he had] witnessed in Chicago—all of this was connected with this small plot of earth an ocean away."[88]

Returning to the US to attend Harvard Law School, Obama came back more uncertain about his future and more conflicted about issues of race, class, culture, and identity than when he began his trip to Kenya two months earlier. But his roots were now firmly established in two continents with ties of family and home both in the United States and Kenya and with a mother and half sister living in Indonesia, another ocean away. [89]

Notwithstanding the doubts the future president may also have had about bringing meaningful change to a community like the Altgeld Gardens or to nations like Indonesia, Kenya, or the United States, he continued to lean toward pursuing a political career based on his conviction that change was possible. Key to success was an inspiring leader like Harold Washington and the rallying of voters on a community or grassroots level. Obama had developed these views under the forceful guidance of his mother and the protective guidance of his grandparents. They had been refined through a broad menu of reading and his experience as a student at Punahou, Occidental, and Columbia, and as a community organizer in Chicago's South Side. Now he was about to take them with him to Harvard.

CHAPTER 2

From Organizer to Politician

Barack Obama attended Harvard Law School from 1988 to 1991. On his entrance at age twenty-seven, he was several years older than most of the 548 students in his class, the majority of whom were recent graduates of Ivy League schools or other well-respected private and public colleges and universities.[1]

What struck faculty and staff was how much more mature and self-confident he seemed than the rest of the students. Almost from his first days at Harvard, when classmates became both friends and rivals in the highly competitive atmosphere of the law school, his calmness and rationality set him apart from the largely high-strung, often ideologically driven, and ambitious class. Although he shared some of these qualities, he was able to balance ambition, commitment, and drive with confidence, modesty, and dispassion. His ability to reconcile these seemingly conflicting characteristics would define his entire political career, but not before resulting in his only electoral defeat. His years at Harvard through the beginning of his political career also revealed a natural conservativism in his political nature.[2]

Harvard Law School

Obama had several mentors while at Harvard. Among them was Laurence Tribe, who held the title of University Professor, awarded only to faculty who had done groundbreaking work across multiple disciplines. In the spring semester of his first year, Obama came by Tribe's office to ask for a position as his research assistant. His request took Tribe by surprise because he was known for not hiring first year students. But he was so impressed by Obama's intelligence, personality, and demeanor that he hired him as his primary research assistant.[3]

At the time, Tribe was preparing an essay arguing the need for judges to apply Albert Einstein's theory of relativity to the law. Just as Einstein argued that the very act of observation altered phenomena, Tribe maintained that judicial decisions altered social relations. Contrary to claims by strict constructionists, he argued that the law was not passive in its relationship to society.[4]

Instead of giving his research assistant mechanical assignments like checking articles in law reviews, Tribe got together with him periodically, sometimes to walk along the Charles River in order to discuss the article he was writing and to exchange ideas on the relationship of the law to society. He also had him assist on a book, *Abortion: The Clash of Absolutes* (1990) in which Tribe argued that the judiciary's proper role was "to preserve those human rights and other principles to which our legal and political system is committed." He later said that he regarded his assistant "much more as a colleague than a student."[5]

Obama had entered Harvard with the intent of learning about the nature of America's power structure, which he planned to apply politically, probably by running for office, after he returned to Chicago. While at law school, new ideas also came to shape Obama's thinking and personality. "Here was an opportunity for me to read and reflect and study as much as I wanted," he later recounted. Having spent much of his time reading while a student at Occidental and Columbia, he was no stranger to the world of ideas. With the exceptions, however, of Black authors like Ralph Ellison and Malcolm X influencing his identity as an African American and some of Saul Alinsky's ideas on community organization, they were not formative in the way they became while at Harvard. [6]

During that time, the legal profession was going through a period of great division and intellectual ferment. Orthodoxies of the law, like original intent and strict construction, were being challenged by newer persuasions of legal realism, particularly critical legal studies, which rejected the very concept of a consistent jurisprudence. The debate over whether the Constitution had unaltered meaning or was a living document subject to changing interpretation was an old one. But critical legal studies, whose adherents shared the view of the Constitution as a living document, took increasing hold on law school campuses as faculty and students fell under the influence of new theories drawn from such academic disciplines as history, philosophy, psychology, and women's studies. In history, for example, an earlier emphasis on the importance to the founding fathers of liberty, defined as protection of personal rights including property rights, was challenged by a new emphasis on the influence of equality and civic virtue on them. Similarly, philosophical pragmatists, Freudians, and feminist theoreticians pried the Constitution away from its foundation in natural rights and natural law.[7]

Although Obama never wrote an essay spelling out his legal views, he was clearly a proponent of critical legal theory, except that he was more optimistic than some critics of the legal establishment, who argued that since the law was written and interpreted to preserve existing power structures, it was impossible to change the status quo. His own experience as a community organizer and his belief that politicians like Harold Washington could make a difference, led him to believe otherwise. Knowledgeable in history and a student of the Constitution, he accepted the latest interpretation by historians that the founding fathers emphasized republican concepts of equality and civic virtue rather than liberty.[8]

Not only did he reject the notion of absolute truths in the law, he adopted the principles of philosophical pragmatism first propounded by Charles S. Peirce, William James, and John Dewey in the early years of the twentieth century. Like them, he rejected the view that pragmatism should be grounded on the idea that an action was justified solely by its success. Instead, he believed it should be based on weighing the consequences of that action on society. It should subordinate goals, policies, and objectives to the general welfare. It should incorporate an ongoing process of evaluation to determine whether they remained workable and achievable. It should emphasize the plasticity of society. It should be premised on the need for consistent adjustment to meet changing societal needs, and it should embrace democratic inclusion.[9]

In his second year at Harvard, Obama enrolled in Tribe's courses in constitutional law. Tribe later referred to him as an "incandescent intellectual [who had a] deep appreciation for history and for the impossibility of fully appreciating its unfolding while in the process of being made," an acknowledgment of Obama's awareness of the ongoing dialogue among historians over the original intent of the founding fathers in formulating the Constitution. According to Tribe, his student focused especially on that part of the preamble that spoke of the nation's commitment "to form a more perfect union," which, he maintained, would always be, "an unfolding narrative— never completed, much less perfected." Together, he became convinced that critical legal theory, philosophical pragmatism, and civic engagement pointed the way toward resolving societal differences.[10]

By the time Obama began the spring semester of his second year, he had achieved what few others in his class were able to accomplish. Because of his academic performance and the quality of the essay he had written as part of his application to be an editor of the *Harvard Law Review*, he was selected as one of eighty members of its board of editors.

As a member of the board, he won the respect of other board members who barely coexisted in what was one of the most fractious faculty and student bodies in the nation. In addition to advocates of critical legal studies, these included proponents of more centrist liberalism and more conservative free-marketers known as Federalists. Even these groups were splintered into subgroups like ones on the political left concerned with feminist jurisprudence or racial discrimination and others on the political right concerned with original intent or free market economics. Finally, there were divisions on issues of race. Some conservative editors questioned the selection process to be a board member, which they believed favored minority applicants by not basing selection solely on the basis of academic records as had been the case until the 1970s when an alternative essay was incorporated into the process.[11]

Former students and faculty from all sides of the political spectrum later recalled Obama's efforts to reconcile these warring factions and to lower the heat of argument by encouraging a fair hearing of all viewpoints. As an editor on the *Law Review*, he purposely avoided taking sides in these highly charged discussions. As a number of his instructors and classmates at Harvard later pointed out, he understood nuance and complexity and did not think he had a monopoly on truth. This was one reason why he later hated presidential debates in which he was expected to give brief answers to questions on complex issues. As a student, he preferred, instead, to play the role of mediator and conciliator, a characteristic he would continue to follow throughout his political career and for which he would later be criticized.[12]

Friends encouraged him to run for president of the *Harvard Law Review*, something he was already planning to do. Being president of the *Review* was normally a path to a clerkship with a high-ranking federal judge, followed by a clerkship with a justice of the Supreme Court, and then a position with a major law firm or law school. Even as he prepared to run, he knew that this was not the course he was going to follow. Because he had gone deeply into debt to pay for his $25,000-a-year Harvard education and wanted to pay off this debt and accumulate some savings, he planned after graduation to work for two or three years in a corporate law practice before returning to Chicago where he now had more clearly in mind running for political office, possibly with the goal of becoming the city's mayor.[13]

He realized that being the first Black president of the *Harvard Law Review* would attract national attention and open avenues of opportunity for him to help the Black community in his adopted city. He was also aware that as president of the nation's most influential law journal he could influence the course of legal debate in the country and break racial barriers. He would become a model for other aspiring minorities. He also thought he could bring practicality and good management skills to running the *Law Review*.[14]

Just before the deadline for applying to be president, Obama submitted his application after a conversation with one of his friends. Eighteen other *Law Review* editors, including three other African Americans, also applied. The election process was long and complicated. Involving frequent voting by all the editors not seeking the position or eliminated in earlier ballots, it lasted in Obama's case for seventeen hours of fractious debate along ideological lines. By the end of the process all his conservative opponents had been eliminated and the choice came down to a contest among the liberal candidates.[15]

In the final ballot Obama was chosen because the conservative editors believed he would be the liberal candidate least tied to ideology and most open to listening to them. As described by Brad Berenson, a conservative member of the board, in the final round of balloting *"en masse* the conservative vote swung over to Barack. There was a general sense that he didn't think we were evil people, only misguided people, and he would credit us for good faith and intelligence."[16]

His election as the first Black president of the *Harvard Law Review* attracted national attention. To the many newspapers and magazines that interviewed him including the *New York Times*, the *Associated Press*, *Daily Mirror*, and *Vanity Fair*, he gave the same answer when asked about the significance of his election: he viewed it as more an accomplishment for American Blacks and minorities than as a personal success. He also left many in disbelief when he stated that after graduation he intended to forgo a clerkship with the US Supreme Court followed by a well-paying position with a major law firm. "One of the luxuries of going to Harvard Law School," he said, "is it means you can take risks in your life. You can try to do things to improve society and still land on your feet."[17]

By the time of his election as president of the *Law Review*, he had entered into a romantic relationship with his future wife, Michelle Robinson, whom he met while interning during the summer between his first and second years at *Sidley & Austin* (now *Sidley Austin*), one of Chicago's leading corporate law firms. Tribe had not been the only faculty member impressed by

Obama's first year performance at Harvard. Another was Martha Minow, the daughter of Newton Minow, a partner at *Sidley & Austin*, who had served as chairman of the Federal Communications Commission (FCC) during the Kennedy administration. Minow recommended to her father that he hire Obama, referring to him "as the best student" she ever had. When offered the chance to intern in Chicago, he grabbed at the opportunity.[18]

Hired a year earlier by *Sidley & Austin*, Michelle was assigned to mentor Obama while he interned at the firm. A graduate of Princeton University (1985) and Harvard Law School (1988), she grew up in Chicago's South Side. Her parents, Fraser Robinson III and Marian Robinson, made great sacrifices to educate her and her older brother, Craig. Even though Fraser Robinson suffered from a debilitating case of multiple sclerosis that would eventually kill him, he worked for thirty years for Chicago's water department where he rarely took a sick day and eventually rose to the position of foreman.[19]

Marian, who had been a housewife while raising their children, returned to secretarial work when she felt the children were able to fend for themselves after school. Fraser and Marian were determined to give them the best education possible no matter the cost. They even turned the living room of their small one-bedroom apartment on the top floor of a two-story bungalow into two bedrooms and a communal study area so that both children could have their own room and a place to do their homework. They also paid their children's tuition with borrowed money.[20]

From the first day he arrived at *Sidley & Austin*, Obama was struck by Michelle's commanding appearance. "She was tall, beautiful, funny, outgoing, generous, and wickedly smart—and I was smitten almost from the second I saw her," he later wrote. Nearly six feet tall, always well-dressed, and attractive, she had the toned body of an athlete. Within a few days after beginning his internship, Barack asked Michelle out for a date. She declined. Career-oriented, she thought it would be inappropriate to date an intern under her supervision, who was still in law school even though he was three years older than her. For over a month she turned him down notwithstanding the fact that he sent her flowers and called her regularly. She was attracted, nevertheless, to Barack, whose life story she found fascinating and whose intelligence was obvious. After being impressed during a church meeting in the Altgeld Gardens by his ability to communicate with people from the South Side like herself, she agreed to go out with him for lunch and a movie. Soon thereafter, she was dating him on a regular basis.[21]

As much as Michelle was interested in Barack, he still had to pass the litmus test of playing basketball with her brother, Craig, also a graduate of Princeton who had twice been named Ivy League Player of the Year and was an investment banker with a Wall Street firm. As Craig explained, Michelle had had a number of suitors before Barack. Setting high standards for herself she had turned most of them down after only one or two dates. The few who gained her interest she invited to her home to meet her parents and to play basketball with her brother, who believed that a basketball game revealed a player's true character. Craig later wrote that Obama passed the litmus test with flying colors. "He's very confident without being cocky," he reported to his sister. For the rest of the summer Michelle and Barack became inseparable.[22]

The relationship continued after he returned to Cambridge. In November, he spent Thanksgiving with Michelle and her family. Around this time, he told her parents that he was planning to run for president of the *Law Review*, something he had discussed with Michelle before returning to Cambridge. They were impressed. He also told them that he was biracial, a fact they had trouble absorbing but which they eventually accepted.[23]

During Christmas break Michelle and Barack went to Hawaii where Michelle met Barack's family for the first time and was welcomed warmly. Barack's grandmother, Toot, reportedly told Barack to aim after graduation at serving on the Supreme Court while his mother, Ann, said that he should target the White House. As a result of the visit, Michelle understood where Obama got his confidence.[24]

Back at Harvard from his vacation in Hawaii, Obama kept in daily touch with Michelle. Once elected president of the *Law Review*, he made plans for the next summer, when he expected to return to Chicago as a second-year intern, but not with *Sidley & Austin*. Although the firm was anxious to have him back and was intending to offer him a lucrative position after graduation, he had his own plans. As much as he had enjoyed his summer with *Sidley & Austin* and appreciated the firm's liberal leanings, he did not want to work for a mainly corporate law firm.[25]

Instead, he was attracted to a much smaller firm, *Davis, Miner, Barnhill & Garner*, with about a dozen lawyers who dealt primarily with civil rights and employment discrimination cases. The senior partner at the firm, Justin Miner, had worked as Harold Washington's corporate counsel. Hoping he could attract to his firm such a promising prospect as Obama, he met with him several times for lunch while conducting business in Boston. During one of these luncheons he convinced Barack to intern with *Davis, Miner* the following summer. Having to divide his time between his obligations as *Law Review* president and as a summer intern, all the while continuing his romance with Michelle, Obama's summer of 1990 was complicated even more when he accepted an offer to write his memoirs for an immediate advance of $40,000 and another $85,000 to be paid to him as the book was completed. [26]

His first task as president of the *Law Review* was selecting the masthead editors who would work with him daily in making the many editorial and managerial decisions and assignments involved in putting together and publishing eight numbers of the *Law Review*. Almost immediately, he alienated a number of Black and liberal members of the editorial board, many of whom had been his strongest backers and expected him to name them to top positions on the *Review*. Despite his reputation for open-mindedness and inclusion when discussing cases in class and as a member of the board of editors, they felt betrayed when Obama passed them over in favor of more conservative board members. [27]

Obama worked fifty to sixty hours on the *Law Review*, often having to miss class in order to do so. By most accounts, he did his job well, especially in balancing the articles accepted for publication and in managing personnel. Typically, he tried not to interfere with the work of the masthead editors and welcomed their different points of view. They were the people who would be running the country in some form, someday, he told a reporter. "If I'm talking to a white conservative who wants to dismantle the welfare state," he added, "he has the respect to listen to me and I to him. That's the biggest value of the *Harvard Law Review*. Ideas get fleshed out and there is no party line to follow." [28]

Poised and confident, he never got ruffled even when he had to reject articles by some of Harvard's most prominent faculty members or on the occasions when he had to differ with one of his top editors or writers or do a final copyediting of their work, to which they often objected. They were always impressed by his coolness and thoughtfulness in trying to explain the reasons for his decisions. [29]

He was not above criticism. The most serious one—one that would be made about his presidency—was that, as editor of the *Law Review*, he was not transformational. While several of the articles in the *Review* reflected his commitment to civic engagement and philosophical pragmatism, he so excelled in navigating the scorched waters of ideological battles that he avoided setting forth his own ideological point of view. Concerned with building consensus, he also never established any new direction for the *Review*. Although aware of the opportunity he had, for example, to affect legal debate on race by selecting articles or book reviews that dealt with issues of racial inequality, he chose not to go in that direction. Except for one article dealing with racial discrimination in retail car sales, there were no other articles or reviews of books on racial inequality. Instead, the articles he and the board accepted for publication and the books they chose for review ran the gamut from criminal justice and constitutional law to corporate and labor law. Other than the fact that he was the *Law Review*'s first Black president, which benefited him more than the *Review*, he failed to make his mark on the journal.[30]

While Obama was occupied mainly with editing the *Review* and attending classes when he could, Michelle stayed busy in Chicago working for *Sidley & Austin*. She became increasingly unhappy, however, finding corporate law unfulfilling and wanting more challenging assignments. In contrast to Barack, she was impatient and made known her unhappiness to her superiors. Although they responded by trying to give her what she wanted, she remained distraught.[31]

Following the death of her roommate at Princeton, who had always told her that the most important thing in life was a sense of fulfillment, and then the unexpected and devastating death of her father from complications of his illness, she also decided to give up corporate law in favor of giving back to the community. Recalling that her father found happiness without the trappings of wealth, she was willing to trade her $120,000 salary as a corporate lawyer to accept a $60,000 position on the staff of Mayor Richard Daley. Before being offered the job, she was interviewed by Daley's deputy chief of staff, Valerie Jarrett, who was destined to become one of Michelle's and Barack's closest friends and a senior adviser to President Obama.[32]

By the time of her interview, Michelle had become engaged to Barack, who had been reluctant to get married. As Michelle later explained to the *New Yorker* magazine, "We would have this running debate throughout our relationship about whether marriage was necessary. It was sort of a bone of contention." But at dinner one night at a restaurant, after an argument that Barack purposely initiated over ever getting married, he surprised a flustered Michelle with an engagement ring. They were married on October 3, 1992.[33]

Early Political Career

Back in Chicago after graduating *magna cum laude* from Harvard Law School, Obama reached out to leaders of the African American community with whom he made contact as a community organizer. Among these people were the Reverends Jeremiah Wright and civil rights icon, Jesse Jackson, whose sister, Santita, had been Michelle's closest friend as a teenager and was a bridesmaid at her wedding.[34]

The new lawyer also became a founding board member of Public Allies, a recently established nonprofit organization whose purpose was to train young and talented minorities to work in the nonprofit sector in the hope that they would become future public leaders. He also put off his legal career for six months to head a registration drive, *Project Vote*, for Democratic candidates running for office in 1992, most notably Bill Clinton for president and Carol Moseley Braun for the US Senate. Established in 1982 for the purpose of mobilizing underrepresented minority communities throughout the country, *Project Vote* had begun to branch out from its headquarters in Washington, DC, into other major cities with large minority populations. In Chicago, where it had not yet established a local office, its efforts to register voters had been largely through donations to Harold Washington's own organization, which helped get him elected mayor of the city. Following Washington's death, its still limited efforts failed to bring minority voters to the polls. Relying on the traditional machine established by his father, Richard J. Daley, Richard M. Daley was elected mayor in 1989, and held the office for the next twenty-two years.[35]

Officially nonpartisan, *Project Vote* aligned closely with the Democratic Party because of the party's historical support of minorities, including minority candidates. In 1992, the Democrats had a good chance to wrest the White House from twelve years of Republican control and to elect an African American to the US Senate following Braun's primary victory over the incumbent, Alan Dixon. Key to victory would be getting out the minority vote in Chicago (Cook County), which often made the difference in the battleground state of Illinois.[36]

To accomplish this objective *Project Vote* hired Obama as director of its operation in Chicago. He was hired not only because he had flourished at Harvard and gained national attention as the first Black president of the *Law Review*, but because of the influential network he had already established within Chicago's political circles. By the time he graduated Harvard, people like Newton Minow, Judson Miner, the Reverend Jeremiah Wright, and Valerie Jarrett, who had met and taken an immediate liking to him, had begun to spread the word about this promising young star with political aspirations. "I was asking around among community activists in Chicago and around the country, and they kept mentioning him," the founder of *Project Vote*, Sandy Newman, commented after the election.[37]

In the six months that Obama served as director of *Project Vote* more than 150,000 African Americans were added to the voting rolls. For the first time in Chicago's history, voter registrations in the city's nineteen predominantly Black wards outnumbered those in the city's nineteen predominantly white wards. Almost every local pundit attributed that historic development to Obama's organizational skills and political acumen. "He helped train 700 deputy registrars, out of a total of 11,000 citywide. And he began a saturation media campaign." reported Gretchen Reynolds for *Chicago Magazine.* The organization's slogan, "It's a Power Thing," filled the airways, and posters with the slogan were plastered throughout African American neighborhoods. Minority-owned businesses, including Black-owned McDonald's franchises, became registration sites, and the owners donated radio time to *Project Vote.* Labor unions and the Clinton campaign provided funding for the drive.[38]

Chicago Magazine called *Project Vote* the "most effective minority voter registration drive in memory." As a result of it, Braun, who had been in trouble during the campaign, was elected the first US African American woman senator, and Clinton, who had watched his lead against his Republican opponent, President George H. W. Bush, fade, won Illinois on his way to being elected the country's forty-second president.[39]

Obama became an instant political star. *Chicago Business* named him to its annual "40 under 40" list and wrote that he had "galvanized Chicago's political community, as no seasoned political had before." Influential friends helped get Obama appointed to the Woods Charitable Fund and the Lugenia Burns Hope Center, both of which promoted organization among African Americans on the South Side through small grants to local activist entities. He also got appointed as chairman of the board of directors of the Chicago Annenberg Challenge, whose purpose was to raise funds to improve Chicago's school system. By serving on these organizations, he was honoring his lifelong commitment to community service, while laying the basis for a political career.[40]

Obama remained coy about his political ambitions. He maintained that it was too early for him to run for political office, but he had already mentioned to Michelle while courting her that he could see himself "running for office." He warned that if politicians on the local and state levels were not responsive to the needs of the African American community, he would "work to replace them" and that he would run if he felt he could accomplish "more that way than agitating from the outside." He also told Federal Judge Abner Mikva of the DC Circuit Court, a former liberal activist in Chicago politics and a friend, whose offer of a clerkship Obama had turned down, that he hoped soon to run for political office.[41]

Even though he retained a commitment to community organization, he had by now fashioned a political identity for himself that ran contrary to some of the basic rules for a community organizer as set forth by Alinsky in his seminal book, *Rules for Radicals.* In the book Alinsky rejected the concept of leadership and agendas from the top down in favor of local leadership with local agendas. The role of organizers, he maintained, was to identity local leadership and promote the self-interests of the communities in which they worked, *not* to create a movement based on their own personal leadership. To the contrary, organizers needed to draw a clear distinction between their work and that of the political world.[42]

For Obama, however, the political world was where meaningful change took place. To be successful, politicians needed to "undergird their efforts [with] a systematic approach to community organization." It was, however, charismatic leaders, like Harold Washington and Martin Luther King Jr., winning political office or leading mass movements with vision and clear political agendas who could achieve change. As much as community organization was important to success, moreover, even more crucial was the network of power brokers with the money, workers, and volunteers needed to win an election. Instead of the slow change that Alinsky and his disciple, Jerry Kellman, believed was the route to success, Obama was convinced that change, while still incremental, would happen quicker by a combination of charismatic leaders carrying with them a political agenda and a message of hope.[43]

Michelle proved to be an indispensable partner to her husband. After only a few months on the job, Valerie Jarrett, whom Mayor Daley selected to head the city's Department of Planning and Development, appointed her as the city's economic development coordinator. In that capacity she worked daily with the leaders of Chicago's business community. Among them was billionaire Penny Pritzker, who helped bankroll Obama's quest into politics. They also included powerful voices within the African American business community such as John W. Rogers Jr., who founded Ariel Capital Management, the largest Black-owned firm of its kind, and Martin Nesbit, who played basketball with Craig Robinson and ran a highly profitable airport parking company that Pritzker helped finance. Rogers later served as chairman of Obama's 2009 Inauguration Committee. Nesbit became one of his closest friends and an unofficial adviser throughout his political career.[44]

Following the election, Obama began working for *Davis Miner*. In addition, he accepted a part-time position as visiting law and government fellow at the University of Chicago Law School. He was offered the position based on a recommendation from Michael W. McConnell, a conservative member of the mostly conservative law faculty, who had been impressed by the editorial suggestions Obama had made on one of McConnell's articles when he was president of the *Harvard Law Review*.[45]

Obama's positions at *Davis Miner* and the University of Chicago gave him ample time to establish the groundwork for a political campaign. At his law firm, Miner, who was white, and another managing partner, Allison Davis, who was Black and had close ties to the African American business community, assigned Obama to a team of lawyers. At no time was he a court lawyer. Mostly he prepared briefs and depositions. At the University of Chicago, where he received a small stipend and office, he was given only light teaching assignments. As a result, he was able to use most of his time at the law school writing what became *Dreams from My Father* and getting ready to run for office.[46]

He threw his hat into the political arena in 1994 after the popular and progressive African American state senator from his predominantly Black district, Alice Palmer, decided to run for Congress in a special election to fill a vacant seat and backed Obama for her seat. With her support and his well-funded political network, he seemed likely to win the election.[47]

The situation changed dramatically when Palmer lost the 1995 primary for the Democratic nomination to Jesse Jackson Jr., the son of Jesse Jackson. Encouraged by her supporters and with the support of Jackson Jr., Palmer decided to run again for reelection. Her backers asked Obama to withdraw his name, arguing that he was young and had a promising political future, but that he had to wait his turn. He refused, maintaining that Palmer had promised him she would not run against him even if she lost the primary. He also said that he had spent too much time and effort gathering the needed signatures to appear on the ballot, raising funds, and building a ground organization to withdraw from the race.[48]

Although there were three other persons besides Obama and Palmer trying to get on the Democrat ballot in 1996, he realized that Palmer was his strongest opponent and that he would have an uphill battle if he had to run against her. He also knew that in Chicago an office seeker often challenged the signatures of potential opponents on ballot petitions, frequently with success.[49]

He decided to follow that course. Suspecting Palmer had not had sufficient time to get enough valid signatures to be on the ballot, he sent lawyers and volunteers to examine her petition lists. They found enough invalid signatures to disqualify Palmer and the others from running. Unopposed in the Democratic primary, Obama went on to a lopsided victory in the November general election in his heavily Democratic district. He was easily reelected to two four-year terms in 1998 and 2002.[50]

As he was preparing to run for office, his mother, Ann, was diagnosed with ovarian cancer that had metastasized. When he first learned that his mother was ill, he flew to Honolulu where she was living with his grandmother Toot. Taking an apartment in the same building where they resided, he helped Ann while she underwent chemotherapy treatments. When her health seemed to improve, he returned to Chicago. Just as he was about to launch his campaign, however, his mother took a turn for the worse. In November 2005, she died at the age of 52.[51]

Obama relationship with his mother had always been complex. He always understood the love his mother had for her children, the importance she attached to education, and the values she worked so hard to instill in him. One of his biggest regrets, he would later admit, was that he did not acknowledge fully the crucial role she played in shaping his character and the support she gave him throughout his career. In 2006, after he had been elected to the US Senate and was contemplating running for president, he dedicated his second book, *Audacity of Hope*, to Toot and to his mother whose "spirit still sustain[ed] him."[52]

In *Audacity*, Obama also described his mother as "an unreconstructed liberal," whose political and cultural views were defined by the 1960s. Reflecting his own conservative values, he said that he could never identify himself with the radicalism of the decade. But he also acknowledged his progressivism by noting his fascination with the period and making clear that his mother's rebelliousness against the status quo rubbed off on him. "If I had no immediate reasons to pursue revolution," he wrote, "I decided nevertheless that in style and attitude I, too, could be a rebel unconstrained by the received wisdom of the over-thirty crowd."[53]

In his postpresidential memoir, *A Promised Land*, the former president called his mother "forever the architect of her own destiny" and described the last months of her life in a way that once more made clear his deep love for her. Knowing that she had been diagnosed with uterine cancer and that her prognosis was not good, he remarked that "at least once a day, the thought of losing her made my heart constrict." He also pointed to the strength of will she maintained even knowing that she was ill with terminal cancer. "I'm not going anywhere until you give me some grandchildren," he quoted her as saying, and remarked that, given her state of health, he asked his mother's approval before deciding to run for the state senate. He even suggested that Ann come to live with him in Chicago, an offer she declined, preferring to live out the rest of her life in the familiar and warm surroundings of Hawaii.[54]

In portraying her in this way, however, Obama ignored the other side of the relationship. While Ann loved her son and Maya as most mothers loved their children and was ambitious for Barack, believing he had unlimited potential, motherhood was not her highest priority in the way that Michelle's mother, Marian, made Michelle and Craig her primary concern. Rather, she was an itinerant, fascinated by other cultures, who gave her career and work most of her attention. Although she tried to reunite with Barack several times a year, she was willing to let her parents raise him during his formative years while she spent most of her time in Indonesia pursuing her career. In contrast to Michelle's mother, Ann did not provide her children with structure and stability.[55]

Obama never completely forgave his mother for the vacuum she created in his life. It may even have been one reason why he chose to focus his first memoir, *Dreams from My Father*, on his father. Not surprisingly, Ann, who had long felt that Barack's move to Chicago and his assumption of a strong Black identity was his effort to distance himself from her, was crushed at how little attention she received in *Dreams from My Father* and by his unflattering remarks in it about her.[56]

Nevertheless, the telephone call from his half sister, Maya, informing him of his mother's death, affected him more deeply than one might have expected from a person known for being stoic and aware that his mother was dying from a painful disease. Hit hard by news of his mother's death, which he later referred to as "the worst day" of his life, he flew with Michelle to Honolulu, where a private memorial was held for Ann. After spending a few days with Toot, they flew back to Chicago where Obama carried on the campaign that led to his victory the next year to the state senate.[57]

All the while he was teaching at the University of Chicago Law School, where he taught mostly required courses in constitutional law and elective seminars on matters involving issues of race and civil rights. As an instructor, he employed the Socratic method common at Chicago, Harvard, and most other law schools in which the instructor engages students with an ongoing series of probing questions on an unending search for truth. But his style was open-minded rather than intimidating. For assignments he prepared packets of documents and opposing readings instead of assigning whole books.[58]

Obama developed a reputation as being an excellent instructor with a cool and friendly demeanor and middle-of-the-road classroom approach, who made students understand the complexities of the law including its moral and political implications. He even developed his own following among students. Although starting as a lecturer, the academic equivalent of an adjunct faculty member, he was promoted in 1996 to senior lecturer, a title usually reserved for those not seeking a tenure track position and equivalent to that of a professor.[59]

In 2008, when he was the leading candidate for the Democratic presidential nomination, his course materials and exam questions became public record. According to a number of legal experts from different sides of the political spectrum who examined them, they were well thought out and demonstrated a subtle and sophisticated command of the law. Unlike other faculty members teaching constitutional law, he also did not require students to agree with a position he espoused since he tried to avoid taking a particular point of view in the classroom.[60]

Several of the legal experts criticized Obama's syllabi and exam questions, however, because they thought they were too conventional and did not confront such contemporary issues as the war on terror, which he would also face as president. Nor did they reveal any insights into how he thought Supreme Court doctrine could be improved. Despite Obama's lifelong interest in multiculturalism and interracial relations, one expert even pointed out that his course materials on racism and the law were limited almost exclusively to issues involving Blacks and whites. Only one session was devoted to the unique issues of Native Americans.[61]

As these experts pointed out, even as an instructor Obama remained reluctant to interject his views into the classroom. He wanted his students to be open-minded in approaching the law and to think and argue like a lawyer. His assigned readings for a course he taught on racism and the law included such diverse figures as Robert Bork, Martin Luther King Jr., and Malcolm X. He saw his role in the classroom to be one of getting his students to be probing, to consider even the moral and ethical dimensions of the cases he assigned, and to hone and refine their responses to judicial decisions. Similarly, his exam questions were designed to ferret out his students' understanding of the law. As in the classroom, he remained ideologically neutral in evaluating their performances.[62]

Contrary to those who criticized him for not dealing with controversial issues, he required students for his course on racism and the law to make an hour-long group presentation on such contentious matters as immigration policy, interethnic tensions, reparations, hate speech, and welfare and reproductive freedom. Although he did not impose his own views in the classroom or in evaluating exams, he continued to be guided by the principles of critical legal theory, philosophical pragmatism, and civic republicanism in the readings he assigned and the questions he asked.[63]

An offshoot of critical legal theory becoming prominent in major law schools like Chicago was critical race theory (CRT), most closely associated with Derrick Bell, an African American law professor at Harvard when Obama was there. Bell maintained that racism was so engrained in the fabric and system of American society that it perpetuated the marginalization of people of color. As a student, Obama greatly admired Bell for his principled stand on the lack of minorities and women on the law school faculty. At a 1990 protest meeting in support of Bell, he even hugged him. For his course on racism and the law at Chicago, he assigned a seminal article by Bell outlining CRT. During Obama's campaign for reelection as president, Bell's influence on him was blown far out of proportion by the right-wing media, which showed a video of him embracing Bell in 1990 to illustrate how he was being manipulated by left-wing extremists in 2012 with their un-American agendas.[64]

Just as Obama rejected the pessimism inherent in critical legal theory, however, he rejected the even more pessimistic assumptions of CRT. His assigned readings included many critics of CRT and reflected his more optimistic view that economic and social uplift were possible starting with organization at the community level and continuing through the election of dynamic leaders able to bring about social and economic change. His selection, for example, of Martin Luther King Jr.'s essay, "Where Do We Go from Here: Chaos or Community," suggested his optimism about the nation's future even on matters of race relations and the nation's political process. Rather than advocating CRT, his syllabi encouraged students to pursue a pragmatic and political approach to the issues they would be confronting after they graduated.[65]

Toward the end of the campaign, the candidate took time off to attend the "Million Man March" in Washington, DC, organized by followers of the Black nationalist and anti-Semite, Louis Farrakhan. Even though he would later be criticized by his right-wing opponents for participating in the gathering, he justified his participation by pointing out that many of the issues the march was intended to highlight, such as higher than average incarceration rates, levels of poverty, and rates of unemployment for African Americans, were ones on his mind. After returning to Chicago from the nation's capital, he rejected both Farrakhan's racist and anti-Semitic remarks and the march's organizers' lack of "a positive agenda, a coherent agenda for change."[66]

Political Victory

In less than five years Obama had gone from being a newly minted graduate of Harvard Law School to an Illinois state senator. Almost as soon as the election was over, political pundits began to speculate on whether he would remain content with this office or had higher political ambitions, perhaps as mayor of Chicago or even as a United States senator. Whatever his political aspirations, he had become an important political force in Chicago with a powerful political network that crossed racial lines and needed to be included in any calculus involving Chicago politics.[67]

His election as a state legislator revealed a side of him that had not been apparent earlier; the extent of his ambition and his determination to win. He first showed his ambitious side when he decided to run for president of the *Harvard Law Review* in 1989. But he became president of the *Review* because his moderation, patience, and willingness to consider all sides on issues convinced conservatives to vote for him. What stood out in his first election to public office, however, was his impatience and commitment to winning regardless of the cost. As a result, his opponents accused him of being little more than a callow newcomer and ruthless opportunist bent on furthering his own political ambitions even if that meant steamrolling over his opponents.[68]

Although they misunderstood Obama, there was more than a grain of truth in what they said. Like most politicians he always justified his actions by the larger goals he sought to achieve, in his case elimination of the decay and dolefulness he found throughout Chicago's South Side. Unlike many of these same politicians, who wrapped their political ambitions in campaign platitudes and sloganeering, his commitment to bettering conditions in the South Side went back to his years as a community organizer in Chicago. His idealism was what continued to stand out in his district. He was a man on a mission. But that did not negate his personal ambition and determination to win.[69]

There was also an arrogant side to his personality. Throughout his adulthood he had been singled out for his brilliance, confidence, and charm. So many important figures who came into his life had told him so often that he had the talent and the ability to effect change for the public good that he believed it. He was so certain about his abilities and the righteousness of his ambition that he sometimes became callous toward those who seemed to stand in his way.[70]

In Springfield, the state's capital, Obama paid a political price for ousting Palmer. A cadre of rivals and friends of Palmer harassed him on the senate floor, even mocking his name. While it was a common practice to make newly arrived legislators go through the ritual of being questioned brutally on the floor by more seasoned veterans, they maintained a visceral dislike for Obama throughout his eight years in the senate.[71]

At one point, he almost got into a physical brawl with Rickey Hendon, an African American senator representing Chicago's West Side, who may have regarded Obama as a potential threat to his own ambitions. Repeatedly, Hendon ridiculed Obama's surname calling him "Yo Mama." He also ridiculed him on legislative matters he was pushing. Finally the usually placid Obama decided he had enough and confronted his antagonist just outside the senate floor, almost leading to a fist fight.[72]

His election and subsequent legislative responsibilities also took a toll on his young marriage. Michelle had played an important role in connecting Obama with a number of Chicago's power players, but she had always been skeptical about his ambition to run for political office. "I married you because you're cute and you're smart, but this is the dumbest thing you could have ever asked me to do," she said to him after he decided to run for Palmer's senate seat.[73]

Growing up on the South Side, Michelle had witnessed the power of the Daley machine and the seamy side of Chicago politics. She understood that her father owed his job with Chicago's Water Department to the fact that he was a volunteer precinct captain for the Democratic Party. As Chicago's economic development coordinator, she saw firsthand how favors were dispensed and deals made between the mayor's office and those with whom she worked every day. Having left the corporate world to serve the public interest, she found herself serving special interests. She was ready, therefore, for a change. After only two years at city hall, she resigned her position and took another one as chief executive of the Chicago operations of Public Allies.[74]

Despite her dislike for politics, Michelle played a prominent role in Obama's campaign. As in future elections, she felt that if her husband was going to run for office, she would be a partner in helping him win. Accordingly, she did everything in the campaign from going door-to-door collecting the signatures needed to put her husband on the ballot to keeping open her political connections with the power brokers she trusted. But she disliked the idea of being the wife of a career politician, who would often be away from home. What she wanted was a comfortable income, children, and a husband who would be an equal partner in raising them.[75]

Michelle's concerns about being a politician's wife became real after her husband assumed office in January. When the legislature was in session, he was in Springfield, able to come home only for long weekends. Even then, his time was stretched between his teaching duties at the University of Chicago and his lawyerly responsibilities at *Davis Miner*. Even when the legislature was not in session, he had to tend to his constituency, often going to nighttime meetings and social events. Complicating matters was the birth in 1998 of the Obamas' first child, Malia Ann. "How full of joy the months that followed were!" he later wrote. "I lived up to every cliché of the expectant father, attending Lamaze classes, trying to figure out how to assemble a crib, reading the book *What to Expect When You're Expecting* with pen in hand to underline key passages."[76]

His frequent absences because of his responsibilities as a state senator, however, meant that Michelle was often alone with the baby. Increasingly, she felt neglected by her husband. "Shuttling between mothering and work, [she was] unconvinced that she was doing either job well." The former president also commented about the strains in his early marriage. "We began arguing more, usually late at night when the two of us were thoroughly drained."[77]

Making the situation even worse was the financial stress Michelle felt. Both she and Barack had borrowed heavily to attend law school. Had they pursued careers in corporate law, their financial plight might have been different. But Michelle gave up a career in corporate law and Barack never pursued one. He also lost the remainder of the $125,000 advance he was to receive for his memoirs because of his failure to deliver a manuscript on time. He was able to secure another contract with a much smaller $40,000 advance and to complete the manuscript two years later, but he did so only by isolating himself from Michelle. Reviewers gave the final product, *Dreams from My Father*, excellent reviews, but it sold only about 9,000 of the 12,000 copies printed before he rocketed to national fame in 2004. Even though the Obamas were still able to put together a comfortable annual income of around $250,000, they found themselves in enough debt for Michelle to worry about their financial future.[78]

As a state senator, Obama practiced what he preached. Through legislation he sought to build community. At first, he had only limited success. In a Republican-controlled body with a group of African American senators determined to get payback from him for taking Alice Palmer's seat, he was unable even to get through the senate a minor bill that would have established a registry of local job openings for community college graduates. Even senators who bore no grudge against him found him to be too aloof, too policy driven, and too overly intellectual.[79]

By the end of his second term in the senate, however, the networking Obama had already done before his election began to pay dividends and boosted his career in a major way when the Democrats, already in control of the house, took over all branches of the state government in 2002. The leader in the senate after 2003, Emil Jones Jr., was another African American from Chicago. In contrast to Obama, Jones already had a long political career in which he had worked himself up from a patronage job as sewer inspector for Chicago to senate majority leader. As a machine politician, he sought not only to pass progressive legislation but to steer state money to his constituency and provide well-paying jobs for his family.[80]

Despite the help Jones gave Obama in the 1980s in securing a state grant, Obama thought Jones was the type of hack politician who did not belong in Springfield. In *Dreams from My Father*, he even referred to him as an "old ward heeler." For his part, Jones, who had known Obama since he was a community organizer a decade earlier, was leery of him and other community activists who, he believed, liked to manipulate and criticize politicians to further their own ambitions.[81]

Once in the senate, however, Obama added Jones to his network of power brokers. In an early meeting with the minority leader, the newly elected senator told him that he was prepared to work hard and hoped he would hand him "tough assignments on legislation." Jones was receptive. United States senator Paul Simon, widely regarded as one of the most progressive and principled members of the Senate, who had taken a liking to Obama for a brief he had drafted while working at *Sidley Austin*, recommended him to Jones. So did Newton Minow, the senior counsel in the firm's Chicago office and Abner Mikva, a former congressman, federal judge, and White House counsel to President Bill Clinton, who had known Obama since he was a law student.[82]

Jones agreed with their assessments. He saw in the young legislator what he had never been; a handsome, articulate, and dynamic political figure whose potential for higher office was unlimited. Like Minow, Mikva, and so many others in Obama's career, Jones took him under his wing and became his unofficial mentor, teaching him the intricacies of the legislative process and assigning him to a bipartisan task force to draft an ethics reform bill. With Jones and one of his career staffers, Dan Shomon, who became his legislative aide, by his side, the state senator learned the ropes of Illinois politics.[83]

He also softened his image, playing golf with his colleagues and displaying his skills in poker during a regular game when the senate was in session. He even began to make friends across the aisle. His ability to adjust to new circumstances bore results. In 1998, he was key in getting an ethics reform measure, which the house had already passed, through the senate. In subsequent years, he also worked successfully to establish a state version of the earned income tax credit, was instrumental in persuading Republicans to soften their positions on adding a new work requirement to the state welfare laws, and successfully championed a requirement that police videotape interrogations in capital cases.[84]

Political Defeat

He remained frustrated, however, by the power of the special interests in Springfield. Even more important, he never intended to spend his career as a state legislator. His ambitions ran higher than that. Over the objections of most of those closest to him, including Michelle, who would have been happy if he gave up politics entirely, he decided sometime around the end of 1997 to run against the incumbent congressman for his district, Bobby Rush. He reasoned that Rush, a former member of the Black Panthers, whom Mayor Daley had badly defeated in the recent Democratic primary for mayor, was vulnerable, especially in white districts where he received only 13 percent of the vote. Because of the political network he had established, he also believed he could capture the white vote in the district while gaining enough of the majority Black vote to defeat Rush. Although he did not have Rush's financial resources, he was able to raise enough money through his political network to run a respectable campaign even before he officially announced his candidacy in the spring of 1998.[85]

Ambition—and hubris in believing that a first-term and relatively unknown senator could defeat a three-term, popular, and progressive US congressman supported by most of the Democratic political establishment in Washington, including President Bill Clinton and Illinois senator Dick Durbin—was the major reason why he decided to oppose Rush. But it was not the only one. He also believed that Rush served just the interests of the Black areas of his district and that he sent the wrong message to young people—that one could gain enough fame as a gun carrying revolutionary threatening to kill white people to later gain a seat in Congress. What kind of incentive did that give kids, he wondered, to behave and earn their way to public office through hard work and a sense of social obligation? His heroes, like King and Washington, offered hope rather than despair and reform rather than revolution. In taking this position, he overlooked the fact that Rush had renounced his past and became a strong advocate of gun control and an ordained Baptist minister with two master's degrees.[86]

During a primary debate, Rush attacked his opponent for being an outsider and a Harvard "educated fool" whose "eastern elite degrees," he said, would not impress his constituency. His opponent fired back. "When Congressman Rush and his allies," attack me for going to Harvard and teaching at the University of Chicago, they are telling Black kids that "if you're well educated, somehow you're not keeping it real."[87]

Rush's attacks on Obama proved effective. His campaign was even able to mobilize on his behalf two of the most influential groups in Black districts, ministers and funeral directors. At a "Clergy for Rush" rally, one hundred Black ministers stood in front of a banner that declared "We are sticking with Rush." In speeches at the rally, they pointed to the seniority that Rush would gain if he was returned to the nation's capital. They also remarked on how much the congressman had already achieved for his district, including saving an Amtrak ticket center and helping write legislation creating a tax on long-distance carriers to be used to fund the wiring of Illinois schools and libraries. For the South Side alone, he had obtained funds to create a new post office building and to resurface an important thoroughfare.[88]

Responding to attacks on him for once being a gun carrying member of the Black Panthers, Rush emphasized how the situation had changed since the 1960s and how he now championed gun control. Turning on its head the Obama campaign's criticism of him for being a Black Panther, his campaign argued that instead of talking the talk in the 1960s, he was proud that he had walked the walk at a defining period in the nation's history.[89]

As for the Obama campaign, everything went wrong, including even a personal tragedy for Rush when in October 1999, his twenty-nine-year-old son was shot to death, forcing Obama to suspend his campaign and creating a wave of sympathy for Rush. In December, while he was vacationing with Michelle and Malia in Hawaii, he missed a vote in Springfield on gun control, a key issue in the campaign, and the measure went down to defeat by only five votes. Although he defended his failure to show up for the vote on the grounds that he was tending to his sick daughter, his missed vote became an important issue in the campaign. Even his strategy of getting the congressman to debate him backfired. Rush was able to keep Obama, who seemed pedantic and distant, on the defensive.[90]

Underestimating Rush as a bland figure and an obscure congressman, and overestimating his own personal appeal and political skills, he was surprised by just how wily Rush was. Believing that the First District, which Rush represented, was ready for a generational change, he missed the point that in the district Rush remained a hero of the civil rights movement and proof that a Black man could succeed. Only toward the end of the campaign did Obama realize that he was going to lose the election. When the votes were counted, Rush had defeated him by a margin of 31 percent. Only in the white parts of the district did he do well against the congressman, but even there he won only one ward.[91]

His defeat was a low point in his life. His political career seemed over. After the election, a Chicago political reporter asked on the air, "Is Obama dead?" It seemed that way. The state senator did not want to remain a legislator in Springfield, but having been defeated so badly by Rush, there seemed nowhere to go in terms of elective office. If he had dreams of being mayor of Chicago, those were shattered by the overwhelming Black vote against him. He did not have the personal resources to seek statewide office, and he was uncertain whether his political network would back him if he decided to run again.[92]

When he flew to Los Angeles to attend the Democratic convention and tried to rent a car, his American Express card was declined until he got the credit company to increase his credit limit. His embarrassment was compounded when he was denied a floor seat at the convention hall and had to settle for a seat in the stands even though he was a state senator. Returning to Chicago, he was in a "dark mood." "I was almost forty, broke, coming off a humiliating defeat and with my marriage strained," he later recounted.[93]

As he stated, his marriage was going through a rocky time. Never having wanted him to run for office, Michelle had strongly opposed his decision to run against Rush, believing it would drain what resources they had and keep him away from home. Despite their income, bills continued to pile up. Malia was now a toddler. She needed a father, and Michelle, who had given birth on June 10, 2001, to a second daughter, Natasha Marian ("Sasha"), needed a full-time husband. She offered Barack a choice between becoming a full-time partner with her in raising their family or staying in politics without her being involved. Together they even sought marriage counseling.[94]

After the election Obama had an opportunity to become head of the Joyce foundation, which funded community projects in Chicago and would have paid him a handsome six-figure salary plus two club memberships. It was a dream opportunity that would have assured the family life and security that Michelle so desperately wanted. He thought seriously of taking the position if he were offered it, but his political ambition prevailed. In 2002, he ran again, this time unopposed, for the state senate.[95]

He found an alternative, however, to Michelle's demands on him that satisfied her. He would not seek a fourth term as a state senator. He would continue his positions at *Davis Miner* and the University of Chicago Law School. He would become a better father and husband. But a seasoned and chastened politician now, he would make one more stab at elective office. If he won, he would remain in politics. If he lost, he would give up his political career and become a full-time attorney able to command a sizable income.[96]

Perhaps because she did not think Barack could win a statewide contest and also understood how important political office was to her husband, Michelle agreed to his proposal. She was even prepared once more to become Barack's political partner in what she considered the impossible goal on which Obama had set his political future—election in 2004 to the United States Senate. Her husband proved her wrong. Five years later, he was elected President of the United States.[97]

The years 1988 to 2000 were as formative for Obama as had been his earlier years, from the time he grew up in Indonesia and Hawaii until he became a community organizer and then decided to go to law school. During these years, his views on how to bring about change in his adopted city of Chicago crystallized, and he launched his political career. What stands out in this period was that the future president was a pragmatist, who believed in the art of compromise, yet could be ruthless in pursuit of his goals and ambitions. He was also a middle-of-the-road progressive *and conservative*, who rejected extremist views, either from the left or the right of the nation's political center. What was still to become clear was his belief that the road to a more perfect union was through the expansion of the middle class.

CHAPTER 3

The Presidential Run and the Earthquake of Iowa

Obama's decision to run for the United States Senate was the first step in a journey that culminated on November 8, 2008, with his election as the forty-fourth president of the United States. Whether he was thinking that far ahead when he officially announced in January 2003 that he was running for the US Senate is unclear, although a number of persons who knew him were already predicting that he might become the nation's first African American president. Whatever his intention, in the five years following his announcement that he was running for the US Senate, he became the transcendent figure in national politics. What continued to stand out about him was his intellect, his commitment to principle, his pragmatism, his ambition, and his drive. He was also a progressive on a journey of heart and mind central to which remained the establishment of a shared multiethnic, multicultural society. Beyond that, he was a political and economic conservative bent on expanding the nation's middle class.

Winning the Democratic Senate Nomination

Obama may have briefly considered running for the US Senate as early as 1998 after he was elected to the state senate and while deciding to challenge Bobby Rush for his congressional seat in 2000. In early 1998, his legislative aide, Dan Shomon, a seasoned political operative who had served previously in Springfield as a legislative aide to Democratic leader Emil Jones Jr., took him on a week-long golf outing at a resort in the rich farmland of southern Illinois. Although Shomon had been reluctant to work with Obama, whom he found to be overly ambitious and starry-eyed at what he thought he could accomplish as a newly elected state senator, he changed his mind after having dinner with him. After just one meal, he left committed to his political future. Like others who came to know Obama, he was struck immediately by his sheer brain power and appealing personality. Not only was Obama a community activist and organizer, he had a keen intellect with a demeanor to match.[1]

Still viewing Obama as politically naïve and uninformed about the vast regions of Illinois south of Chicago and its suburbs, Shomon proposed the trip downstate to give him a better idea of the largely conservative makeup of the state's small town and rural regions and a more realistic sense of what he could hope to accomplish in a government controlled by Republicans representing these constituencies.[2]

Despite the color of his skin and the fact that he was a liberal Democrat from Chicago, known for its lawlessness, broken homes, crime, and secular values—the very antithesis of what most downstate voters valued—Obama was struck by how well he was received at a number of stops along the way, "whether we were at a county fair or a union hall or on the porch of someone's farm." Because Shomon was well known and respected in Springfield and Obama was a state senator who had established friendly relations with a number of his Republican colleagues from the region, Shomon was able to arrange small gatherings of local farmers and merchants and rounds of golf and one-on-one meetings with local officials in the towns he visited, including a number of downstate liberals and graduates of elite institutions like himself. Among these was the state's senior US senator, Richard Durbin of Springfield, who later became one of the first national figures to urge him to run for president. Wherever he went, he was greeted respectfully. Returning to Chicago, he was pleased by the reaction he received downstate. "These folks could vote for me—I mean these folks could help me—they could support me," he later remarked. "I think it was a revelation to him that he had a lot of appeal as a politician," his aide added.[3]

Obama's visit to downstate Illinois also convinced him that the state and the nation might not be as divided as the media and pundits proclaimed and that by running for the US Senate, he might be the person who could heal whatever divides there were. "If . . . a campaign could somehow challenge America's reigning political assumptions about how divided we were," he wrote, "well just maybe it would be possible to build a new covenant between its citizens."[4]

Soon after his defeat for Congress, he began to organize his campaign for the US Senate. In July 2002 he established a campaign committee to run for the Senate in 2004 against the first-term Republican incumbent, Peter Fitzgerald. A renegade, who spent millions of dollars of his own fortune to defeat another first-term senator, Democrat Carol Mosely Braun, Fitzgerald had alienated even his own party's leadership by his opposition to measures they supported.[5]

As a result, most political observers considered Fitzgerald's seat highly vulnerable to a challenge even from within his own party. Facing opposition from six Democrats, including Obama and three formidable Republicans, Fitzgerald announced on April 3 that he would not seek reelection. After he made his announcement, Mosely Braun also made clear that she did not intend to try to get her seat back—that she was preparing instead to run for president of the United States. With Mosely Braun out of the race, Obama reasoned he could capture most of the state's Black vote. Having done well among white voters in his bid against Rush and having been well received in his first trip downstate in 1998 and in a number of follow-up trips afterward, he also reasoned that in the primary he could win enough white votes, which, together with the Black vote, would carry him to victory in the primary.[6]

As a largely unknown state senator who had been handily defeated for Congress in 2000, he was regarded by most political pundits as a long shot to gain the Democratic nomination. Among the Democrats running to replace Fitzgerald, the most prominent were the state comptroller, Daniel Hynes, and the multimillionaire businessman and stock investor, Blair Hull. A member of a prominent Chicago political family, whose father, Tom Hynes, had been president of the Illinois state senate and Cook County assessor, Hynes brought to his campaign name recognition, political connections, an ability to raise large sums of money, and a reputation as a capable officeholder. Hull shared none of these qualities with Hynes but he was prepared to spend a considerable portion of his personal fortune, estimated to be around $300 million, on his campaign.[7]

Luck played an important role in bringing Obama from underdog status to a decisive victory in the Democratic primary in March 2004. For most of the campaign, Hull had been the front runner, largely because of the millions of dollars he poured into promoting his candidacy and gaining name recognition. But as the campaign drew to a close, he was forced to release divorce papers showing that his ex-wife, a Chicago real estate broker, had obtained two restraining orders against him and that there had been a physical fight between him and his former wife.[8]

Luck alone, however, cannot account for the fact that, by the end of February 2004, Obama had jumped from being an obscure state senator with little name recognition and no apparent source of funding into second place with significant funding just waiting to be used in a media blitz to vault him to a landslide victory in March. What accounted for his success was that he never wavered from his original strategy of sweeping the Black vote in Chicago and gaining enough of the white vote in the suburbs, in the wealthy North Shore of Chicago along Lake Michigan, and in downstate, to win the primary.[9]

Although Hull denied the charge of physical abuse, his campaign was never able to recover from the revelations. When the primary was held in March 2004, Obama won a landslide victory capturing 53 percent of the vote, nearly 29 points ahead of his nearest opponent, Comptroller Hynes, who picked up 24 percent of the vote with Hull badly trailing in third place with just 11 percent of the electorate. The other candidates were in single digits. [10]

If there was any surprise in the outcome, it was how well Obama was able to do among white voters. This was made possible, in part, by two other strategic moves he made. One was to hire as his media specialist David Axelrod, and the second was to continue to build upon the network of wealthy donors and political insiders he had been developing even before he first ran for office in 1996. A University of Chicago graduate and one-time city hall bureau chief and political columnist for the *Chicago Tribune*, Axelrod had left the *Tribune* in 1984 to help run the successful campaign for the US Senate of Paul Simon.[11]

A liberal and political idealist, Axelrod became attracted to politics by the idealism of Bobby Kennedy during his 1968 campaign. As a media specialist, he enjoyed great success in getting Black candidates elected to office and had a long list of clients that included the Black mayors of Philadelphia, Cleveland, Detroit, and Chicago. His strategy employed heavy reliance on the life story of his clients.[12]

Axelrod came to regard Obama as a potential Bobby Kennedy. He first heard about him in 1992 while he was organizing *Project Vote*. A Democratic activist, Betty Saltzman, urged him to meet with Obama. "I think he will be our first Black president," Saltzman told him. Meeting with Obama shortly thereafter, he also was impressed with the Illinois senator. "Without displaying any arrogance," he later wrote, "Barack spoke with the wisdom and earnest self-assurance of someone much older. . . . He was clearly ambitious, but those ambitions seemed less about doing well than about doing good." [13]

In the ensuing years prior to Obama's successful campaign for state senator, Axelrod did not have much contact with him. Once he ran for office and got elected to Springfield, the media specialist started to follow his career more carefully, especially since now retired Paul Simon spoke so favorably about him. What impressed Axelrod was Obama's packaging of idealism and toughness. "This thoughtful and polished young man had a competitive edge," he wrote about his 1995 campaign for the state senate. "Clearly he could be tough, unsentimental and even bruising when the situation demanded it."[14]

Not until Obama challenged Bobby Rush for his congressional seat, however, and called Axelrod asking for his help in his coming campaign against the congressman, did he begin to establish the close relationship with him that would carry both of them to the White House in 2008. Although Axelrod advised him against challenging Rush and turned down his request to run his media campaign because he was a consultant to Mayor Daley, whose machine politics Obama opposed, he did give the state senator the names of other consultants he might call and offered to provide him with informal advice.[15]

Having decided to make a last effort at public office by running for the US Senate in 2004, Obama turned again to Axelrod for help in the coming campaign. The media consultant remained reluctant. "Wait till Rich Daley retires and then run for mayor," he told the state senator after a luncheon meeting. After more meetings, however, Obama was able finally to convince Axelrod to be his media consultant and help run his campaign for the US Senate. Several polls showed that while name recognition was still a major problem for him, if voters were made aware of his life story, including the fact that he was the first Black president of the *Harvard Law Review*, Obama could win the Democratic primary. That was enough to persuade Axelrod. "Barack personified the kind of politics and politician I believe in," he later stated.[16]

On Axelrod's advice, Obama replaced Dan Shomon as his campaign manager with Jim Cauley, a seasoned political operative. No one had been closer politically to him since he was first elected to the state senate in 1996 than Shomon. Since 1996 he had managed every one of his political campaigns. But in a display of how hardened and unsentimental Obama could be, he concluded after conferring with Axelrod that Shomon did not have the organizational and policy skills to run a statewide campaign. As painful as it was to him, he also moved his campaign treasurer, Cynthia Miller, to a position with the state because of the distraction he believed her membership in the Nation of Islam would cause to his campaign.[17]

One of the first issues that Obama and Axelrod took up after Axelrod agreed to become his media consultant involved a little-known speech Obama had made in 2002 opposing United States' involvement in a war in Iraq to oust its dictator, Saddam Hussein. The talk would become pivotal to his senatorial campaign and remain one of the most important issues of his whole journey to the presidency.

Up to this point, he had not spoken publicly about Iraq or, for that matter, about most other foreign policy issues. But as someone who had lived overseas much of his life, had studied European political thought while at Occidental College, majored in political science with an emphasis on international relations at Columbia, and envisioned a multiracial and multicultural world, he took a keen interest in the rest of the world.[18]

This was apparent in his reaction on September 11, 2001, to the terrorist attacks on the Twin Towers in New York City and at the Pentagon. As he began to explore the meaning of these attacks, he laid out what would become a hallmark of his foreign policy in the Middle East—a determination to pursue relentlessly and to destroy completely terrorist networks while at the same time reaching an understanding of the root causes of terrorist activity. "We must be resolute in identifying the perpetrators of these heinous acts and dismantling their organizations of destruction," he stated. "We must also engage, however, in the more difficult task of understanding the sources of such madness."[19]

In the late summer and early fall of 2002, the immediate issue facing the candidate was Iraq. Claiming that Hussein possessed weapons of mass destruction (WMDs), including nuclear weapons, President George W. Bush threatened to take unilateral military actions against him. In September 2002, Saltzman asked Obama to speak at an antiwar demonstration she was organizing as the US Senate prepared to take up a resolution approving military intervention in Iraq. Like other liberal progressives, the state senator opposed military intervention. Not only did he believe it would divert attention and resources from a failing economy at home, he did not think Hussein posed an imminent threat to the United States. He had no misconceptions about the Iraqi dictator. He was ruthless and his possession of WMDs posed a threat to stability in the Middle East. He also had not cooperated for many years with UN inspectors sent to Iraq to examine his stockpiles of weapons. But Obama was still convinced that additional diplomatic pressure short of war could force Hussein to open his stockpile of weapons for international inspection.[20]

He was inclined, therefore, to join other speakers at the antiwar rally. At the same time, he was concerned about the impact his remarks might have on his campaign for Senate. "I mulled over the question for a day or so and decided this was my first test," he later commented. Polls indicated that there was strong support for the war resolution. He wanted Axelrod's input on how seriously he would be hurt if he spoke out against the war. After consulting with other advisers, Axelrod responded that he should participate in the rally.[21]

In a short speech he gave in Chicago in October before a crowd estimated as high as several thousand, Obama startled his audience by making clear that he did not oppose all wars. He thought, for example, that the Civil War was a war worth fighting and pointed out that his grandfather had fought in George Patton's army during World War II. He was "not opposed to all wars," he then said in what became a refrain throughout his speech and another tenet of his foreign policy as president. He was "opposed to dumb wars." Similarly, he suggested that if President Bush wanted a fight, he should battle "against ignorance and intolerance. Corruption and greed. Poverty and despair." His speech was so well received by the crowd that Axelrod later regretted he had not taped it for later use in the campaign.[22]

In a radio interview in November, he amplified on his views about military intervention in Iraq. First, he expressed his satisfaction about President Bush's recent decision to seek a UN resolution calling for "aggressive inspections" of Iraqi weapons stockpiles. Then he raised a number of issues that characterized the way he would approach making major foreign policy decisions. What would be the costs of the intervention? he asked. What did it mean to rebuild Iraq, and how did the United States stabilize and make sure that the country did not "split into factions between the Shias and the Kurds and the Sunnis?" Finally, he stated that he was against giving "carte blanche to the administration for a doctrine of preemptive strikes that [he] was not sure would set a good precedent." If he had had to vote up or down on an Iraq war powers resolution, he would have voted against it.[23]

By coming out against intervention in Iraq, he separated himself from the rest of the candidates running for the US Senate. His refrain that he was not opposed to all wars, just dumb wars, showed again how pragmatic and genuine Obama could be at the same time. It also made for good oratory. For the tens of thousands of voters still strongly opposed to intervention, he became their only candidate.[24]

A strong message that was barely covered in the media and failed to reach a large audience, however, was of little value. The candidate's problem was how to spread his message and attract enough white voters in Chicago and downstate, while winning an overwhelming majority of the Black vote. Former senator Moseley Braun's announcement that she would not seek her old job back cleared the way for Obama to win the Black vote by the margins he needed to win the primary; had Mosely Braun decided to seek the nomination, he would have withdrawn from the race.[25]

As for the white vote, his opposition to US intervention in the war assured strong support from antiwar progressives living along Lake Michigan's North Shore and in Chicago's white suburbs. He still had to increase his share of the white vote elsewhere, however, where his opposition to the war was unpopular and where he was still an unknown figure.[26]

Obama's intellectual gifts and personality stood out in winning over these voters. Even when voters disagreed with him on specific issues, they were won over by his freshness, earnestness, and clarity in explaining his position on these matters and by his engagement with them. When he spoke, his answers were fluent and knowledgeable. As he told his life story, moreover, he emphasized his grandparents' roots in Kansas rather than his father's roots in Kenya. Addressing Black audiences, he could be Black. Addressing white audiences, he could be white. "It's like he's talking to you, and not a crowd," one local downstate politician remarked. "That's the thing about him," David Axelrod added. "He has the ability to walk into any room and connect with anybody. I think it's because of who he is—the many different cultural strands that are part of him."[27]

He was also able to project a message of optimism and hope and of inclusion and not exclusion. He made his audiences feel proud to be Americans. Speaking directly on the question of racial differences, he declared, "We have shared values, values that aren't Black or white or Hispanic—values that are American, and Democratic." After following him on the campaign trail, William Finnegan of the *New Yorker* called his ease before white crowds "a source of wonderment."[28]

Throughout the primary and the general election Obama tried to avoid racial issues. This was, of course, good politics since the premise of his campaign was attracting a large enough white vote, which, when combined with his almost certain monopoly of the Black vote, would assure his nomination and then his election to the United States Senate. But he avoided bringing race into his candidacy for more than political calculation. A predicate of his campaign was his lifelong commitment to a multicultural and multiethnic nation devoid of issues like race. Taking pride in the great strides of the civil rights movement of the 1950s and 1960s, he sought, nevertheless, to transcend that movement, which had pitted the supporters of civil rights against its opponents, sometimes in violent confrontation, often through lesser acts of civil disobedience. Even though Obama embraced the goals of the movement, he rejected its confrontational politics.[29]

Instead, he sought to be a bridge-builder—a unifier rather than a divider. He saw no inconsistency between diversity and his pride in his own race and in wanting to live in a postracial, postethnic, and postpartisan world. Unlike the liberals of the 1960s, Obama did not even intend to rely primarily on government organization to achieve his agenda. While he felt government had an important role in advancing infrastructure projects, public education, and dynamic communities in which even poor children had the opportunity to rise and succeed, he believed strongly that individuals had to earn their own success. As much a product of a middle-class upbringing and an elite education as a community organizer working (but not living) in the poorest areas of Chicago's South Side, he sought to return to an America that was ever expanding its middle class. Ironically, his political and economic conservatism was foundational to his belief on how progress was achieved in the US.[30]

Obama spent eighteen months on the campaign trail going from small town to small town throughout Illinois. "I was having fun," the former president recalled. He enjoyed going into ethnic communities and speaking at Black churches. But increasingly he just listened. He raised enough funds to sustain the primary campaign, mostly from smaller donors, including the network of supporters he had been building since he entered politics a decade earlier. Because Axelrod chose to hold back most of these funds for a television blitz in the last month of the campaign, he could only reach a relatively small number of Illinois voters. A poll conducted one month before the primary showed Obama with still just 15 percent of the vote.[31]

About three weeks before the March primary, Axelrod unleashed the funds the campaign had been raising and he had been hoarding. In a data-driven media campaign, he spread the story throughout the state about the gifted and talented candidate from Chicago with a biography that included both a midwestern and international upbringing, president of the *Harvard Law Review*, experience as a community organizer, knowledge about national issues, and skillful in getting state measures passed in Springfield. The campaign also featured both Obama talking about his life and the endorsement of Paul Simon's daughter, Sheila. In addition, it emphasized how he represented the politics of hope and promise at a time when the nation was in the first throes of an ill-conceived war abroad and an economic downturn at home. For the first time, he employed the phrases "Yes We Can," and "Change We Can Believe In," which became the themes of his 2008 presidential campaign. Combined with the collapse of the Hull campaign, the result was his overwhelming victory in the March primary in which he gained a majority of the vote and more than doubled the vote of his nearest rival, Dan Hynes.[32]

Election to the US Senate and the Keynote Address

As in the Democratic primary, Obama faced a formidable Republican opponent, Jack Ryan, in the general election in November. Though Ryan had
never run for office, he managed in March to win a decisive victory over a
number of strong Republican rivals. Handsome with movie star looks, Ryan
had been married to a movie and television star, Jeri Ryan, with whom he
had a son. A graduate of Harvard Law School with an MBA from Harvard
Business School, he had been a wealthy investment banker at Goldman Sachs
before giving up his career on Wall Street to teach at an all-Black Catholic
school for boys in Chicago's South Side. In his campaign he appealed directly
to African American voters. Charismatic and personable, he had a personal
attraction rivaling Obama's appeal.[33]

Obama maintained a sizable lead against Ryan in the early polls, but
the electorate was divided evenly between Democrats and Republicans,
the Republican Party had a sizable war chest that it was prepared to use to
hold onto Fitzgerald's seat, and its candidate took a stand on the issues that
enjoyed widespread support downstate. Unlike his Democratic opponent,
Ryan supported the Iraq war. He also took a pro-life position on abortion,
opposed gun control, and was a fiscal conservative. Had Ryan stayed in the
race, the voters would have been offered a clear choice between the two
candidates.[34]

As in the March primary, however, a nasty divorce involving his opponent
worked in Obama's favor. In 1999, Ryan's wife had divorced him. To protect their young son, the couple had the court records involving his custody
sealed. During the primary the *Chicago Tribune* and a local ABC affiliate filed
successfully to have the records unsealed, and when they were opened, they
revealed that Ryan's ex-wife had accused him of making her go to sex clubs
in New York, New Orleans, and Paris. Although Ryan denied the accusation,
the media storm that followed forced him to leave the race at the end of July.[35]

Even though Obama profited from the revelations, this type of mass-
appeal journalism genuinely disgusted him. It was one reason why he did
not like journalists or debates that required short answers to what he considered complex issues requiring lengthy and sometimes nuanced answers.
"So much of our culture is caught up in celebrity and sensationalism," he
remarked in response to the unsealing of the records. "It's an unfortunate
aspect of our culture generally, and our politics ends up taking on that same
flavor."[36]

After the Republicans failed to find a candidate within the state willing
to challenge Obama so late in the race, they turned to a well-known African

American activist from Maryland, Alan Keyes, who had earlier run for president and the US Senate. An arch opponent of abortion and gay marriage, he had a volatile personality and outspoken conservative views on a large agenda of social issues, which left him outside the mainstream of American politics. Characterizing Obama's views on abortion as "the slaveholder's position," he added separately that "Jesus Christ would not vote for Barack Obama because Barack Obama has behaved in a way that is inconceivable for Christ to have behaved."[37]

Ryan's withdrawal from the race and the choice of Keyes to replace him turned what promised to be a close race into a romp. When the votes were counted in November, Obama won by a margin of 70 percent to Keyes's 27 percent, the largest one in the state's history. He also carried 92 of the state's 102 counties.[38]

It was not, however, just good fortune again coming to Obama's assistance that accounted for the size of his victory over Keyes. Not taking the bait of his opponent's outrageous statements against him, he continued to campaign hard and not let Keyes's remarks distract him. Nor was it only good fortune that turned an opportunity given to him by Massachusetts senator John Kerry, the likely Democratic nominee for president in 2004, to deliver the keynote address at the party's national convention in Boston in July into the springboard for his own presidential bid in 2008.[39]

Kerry decided to give the Illinois senatorial candidate the keynote spot because of the personal buzz surrounding him as a result of his decisive, come-from-behind victory in the March primary. Party leaders regarded the Illinois seat as one they could take back from the Republicans in November and realized Obama's broad appeal among voters. Not only would he become the only Black member of the Senate, they were aware of his growing reputation among all those who met or heard him speak as one of the party's brightest, most articulate, and most promising future leaders.[40]

Kerry was also personally impressed by the Illinois lawmaker and candidate for the US Senate. Although he hardly knew him before coming to Chicago after the primary for a big fund-raising event, he was impressed by Obama's charismatic personality, oratorical skills, and ability to rouse an audience. Kerry had a similar impression of him as he campaigned with him the next day at a job-training site in the city's West Side. "We believe he represents the future of the party," Stephanie Cutter, the communications director for the Kerry campaign, remarked in explaining Kerry's choice of Obama.[41]

Once Obama was told he would be named the keynote speaker, he seized the opportunity given him. Even before he got word that Kerry would give him a national spotlight, he began to think seriously about what he would say if he were given the opportunity. He intended to write his own speech. "I know what I want to say," he told Axelrod. "I want to talk about my own story as part of the larger American story." "I want to talk about who we are at our best." [42]

"The words came swiftly," the former president later recalled, "a summation of the politics I'd been searching for since those early years in college and the inner struggles that had prompted the journey to where I was now. My head felt full of voices: of my mother, my grandparents, my father; of the people I had organized with and folks on the campaign trail."[43]

Obama did not deliver his speech without engaging in a dispute with campaign officials who objected to the speech's length and some of its phraseology. The final draft that Obama gave the Kerry campaign was timed at almost thirty minutes even though campaign officials had allotted him just eight minutes. Obama was upset. If the campaign insisted on a short speech, he told Axelrod, he would give up his spot entirely. After several rounds of negotiations, he was able to reach an agreement with campaign officials by which he was allotted seventeen minutes for his address.[44]

Another problem between Obama and the Kerry campaign involved what became one of the most memorable sections of his address. A young Kerry official, John Favreau, who would later become his chief speech writer, asked him to strike out from his draft a phrase having to do with an alleged divide between red and blue states. The official claimed that Kerry had a similar phrase in his acceptance speech. Again, Obama became furious. After he cooled down, Axelrod convinced him to cut the phrase, arguing that his sacrifice of a few words was worth speaking before millions of people.[45]

Despite never having spoken before an audience of fifteen thousand delegates and visitors, much less millions more watching on television, despite never having used a teleprompter (which he rarely looked at since he had memorized his speech), and despite being fully aware that he was a Black man doing what had always been a white person's business with his political future on the line, Obama remained composed and unflappable throughout his address. His highest priority was generating enthusiasm for Kerry's campaign against his Republican opponent, President George W. Bush. Like the other speakers at the convention, he did this by first comparing the failures of the Bush administration with Kerry's qualifications to be president. But instead of a frontal attack on the president like these other speakers, he never even addressed Bush by name. Rather, he spoke artfully of the urgency of the situation facing the nation and used a recurring phrase "more work" that needed to be done. "More work to do for the workers I met in Galesburg, Illinois who are losing their union jobs at the Maytag plant that's moving to

Mexico," he remarked. "More to do for the father that I met who was los-ing his job choking back the tears, wondering how he would pay the $4500 a month for the drugs his son needs without the health benefits he counted on." "These individuals and thousands like them were not looking for a gov-ernment handout," he added. "They know they have to work hard to get ahead, and they want to."[46]

Pivoting away from the bad judgment and mistakes of the Bush admin-istration, he then spoke about Kerry's commitment to public service from the time he was a young naval officer patrolling the dangerous waters of the Mekong Delta during the Vietnam War to his present role as a US senator from Massachusetts and chairman of the Senate Foreign Relations Commit-tee. Next, he outlined what the senator intended to do as president. This part of the speech could have been a traditional laundry list of promises, but what made it so effective was his cadence, his powerful voice, his grow-ing confidence before an increasingly cheering audience, and his repetitive use of a few key phrases. "John Kerry believes in an America where hard work is rewarded," he stated. "John Kerry believes in an America where all Americans can afford the same health coverage our politicians have for them-selves. . . . John Kerry believes in energy independence."[47]

The most memorable part of his speech was his portrayal of the United States as a nation united rather than divided and of optimism rather despair. As he neared the end of his remarks, he speeded up his delivery and his voice burst with energy. Employing all the tactics he had used throughout his ear-lier remarks, including reference to his own life story, alliteration, anecdotes, contrasting imagery, and short repetitive phraseology, he portrayed an Amer-ica different from that often described in the media. "There is not a Black America and a White America and a Latino America and Asian America—there is the United States of America," he stated. "The pundits, the pundits like to slice-and-dice our country into Red States and Blue States," he con-tinued. "Red States for Republicans, Blue States for Democrats. But I've got news for them, too. We worship an 'awesome God' in the Blue States and we don't like federal agents poking around in our libraries in the Red States." His final words were those of "hope," using shorter, quicker sentences. "Hope in the face of difficulty, hope in the face of uncertainty. The audacity of hope!" The response in the convention hall to Obama's address was electric. Stand-ing up throughout much of the speech, the delegates waved banners and shouted chants of "hope" and "Obama."[48]

Afterward, some critics argued that Obama's remarks actually hurt the cause of the civil rights movement by its emphasis on the unity of America, thereby allowing white Americans to ignore the racial and other divides that still plagued the nation. For these critics, Obama remained "not Black enough," a charge that had been made against him earlier and one with which he would have to deal during his campaign for the presidency.[49]

Those critics, however, represented a small ripple in the sea of approval that greeted his speech. Most major media outlets hailed his address as one of the greatest speeches ever delivered at a presidential convention. Some even speculated on the possibility that he might someday be president of the United States even though he had not yet even been elected to the US Senate. "A great speech brings together three aspects—the right speaker, with the right message, at the right time," one analyst commented. "Obama's speech covers all three aspects and you are left with the impression that he is a man whose message was right, whose delivery was right and whose time had come."[50]

Obama denied that he had anything in mind following his convention speech other than being elected to the Senate and helping Kerry get elected to the White House in November. Throughout the months following the Democratic convention he campaigned for the Democratic nominee and for himself while refusing to speculate about his future beyond his election to the US Senate. Given the extent of the media coverage already being given to him, however, it would have been impossible for him to have ignored the widespread speculation about an Obama presidential candidacy, possibly as early as 2008, if Kerry lost in November. [51]

The idea of running for president was almost certainly on his mind even as he labored over his speech in Boston. While remaining an idealist, his determination to advance up the ladder of success—a constant in his career—meant that he always kept his eye on the prize and worked with all the skill, determination, and cold calculation needed to achieve that goal. Having been successful throughout most of his career and having been told all the while that he could become the first Black president of the United States, he had enough confidence in himself to believe that goal was achievable.[52]

From Capitol Hill to the Iowa Caucuses

With Obama's overwhelming election to the US Senate and Kerry's defeat for the presidency, a new round of speculation began over whether he would run for president in 2008. In news interviews, he repeated over and over that he had no plans for the future other than to be a good senator on Capitol Hill. Throughout 2005, he turned down almost all speaking engagements outside of Illinois and, indeed, devoted most of his time to his senatorial duties. Minority Leader Harry Reid (NV) and Dick Durbin, his second-in-command

and Obama's political friend, gave the new senator special attention, introducing him to what Obama later described as "the old bulls of the Senate"—Ted Kennedy (D-MA), Robert Byrd (D-WV), Orrin Hatch (R-UT), and John Warner (R-VA).[53]

As a new senator, and because Democrats were in the minority, Obama had little input on the legislation that came before the upper chamber, mostly establishing a reputation as a hardworking, smart, Democratic loyalist with presidential ambitions who, as a member of the Senate Foreign Relations Committee, traveled extensively abroad. About the most noteworthy event of his four years in the Senate was a public clash with Senator John McCain (R-AZ), who accused him in 2006 of reneging on a promise he made to work on a task force on rules governing lobbyists.[54]

In January 2006 Obama made an unequivocal statement on the Sunday news show *Meet the Press* that he would not run for president in 2008. The same month he made that statement, however, he formed a political leadership PAC, "The Hope Fund." In a little over a year, he managed to raise $4.4 million for his PAC, one of the largest amounts ever raised so quickly by a member of Congress. With these funds, he was able to support a major political operation including experienced staff members like Robert Gibbs, who had signed on to be his communications director just before he gave his keynote address and who later became his White House press secretary, Jennifer Yeager, who had been his cofinance director during his campaign for the US Senate and would serve as a finance director during his presidential campaign, and David Axelrod, whose firm, AKP, sent camera crews videotaping virtually every one of his public activities. In 2007 Axelrod used this footage to produce a five-minute online video for Obama's announcement on January 16 that he was running for president. [55]

Besides supporting his own political operation, Obama was able to contribute $562,000 to candidates running for federal office and another $110,000 to local, state, and national parties and committees. As the most sought-after Democratic speaker among the party's rank-and-file, he also began in 2006 to travel throughout the country raising money for his PAC, promoting his new book, *The Audacity of Hope*, and speaking at political events in support of Democratic officials and candidates for office. In these ways, he built up his donor base, won over volunteers, and gained political capital if he decided to run for president.[56]

Wherever he went, he was greeted by an outpouring of emotion usually reserved for entertainers. "For our generation he is kind of the lighthouse, the hope," explained one nineteen-year-old student from the University of Chicago. "He's changing the face of government in America." In Chicago, where he began his book tour, people lined up before bookstores for as long as three hours in the rain for a chance to have him autograph their copies of *The Audacity of Hope*. Very quickly, it became the nation's number one best-selling nonfiction book. *Dreams from My Father*, which had sold fewer than ten thousand copies when it was first released in 1995, was re-released, and it, too, became a number one best seller. The royalties he received from the sales of both books made the Obamas comfortable enough to buy a large home in the upscale neighborhood of Hyde Park near the University of Chicago.[57]

The Audacity of Hope lacked the introspective quality or lyrical prose of *Dreams from My Father*. Instead of *Dreams'* poignant reflection on an unusual life, he intended *Audacity* as a political autobiography written at a time when he had just been elected to the US Senate. In the book, Obama spelled out his latest thinking on most every policy issue facing the nation. Not surprisingly, he called for a progressive, multicultural, postethnic, postracial world. In doing so, he spoke out against doctrinaire thinking, criticized such organized evangelical groups as the "Moral Majority" and "the Christian Coalition," and wondered why anyone would spend their evenings watching conservative "sour-pusses" like Sean Hannity and Ann Coulter. "I find it hard to take them seriously," he wrote. "I assume they must be saying what they do primarily to boost book sales or ratings."[58]

At the same time, he took the Democratic Party to task for not understanding the importance of religion to Americans and for being the "party of reaction" rather than the party of hope and reform. "In reaction to a war that is ill conceived, we appear suspicious of all military action. . . . In reaction to religious overreach, we equate tolerance with secularism, and forfeit the moral language that would help infuse our policies with a larger meaning." [59]

Finally, Obama explained why he was a Democrat. "Sometimes we need both cultural transformation and government action," he wrote. "The state of our inner-city schools is a case in point. All the money in the world won't boost student achievement if parents make no effort to instill in their children the values of hard work and delayed gratification." He was a Democrat, he continued, because his party believed in "the idea that our communal values, our sense of mutual responsibility and social solidarity, should express themselves not just in the church or the mosque or the synagogue; on the blocks where we live, in the places where we work, or within our own families; but also through our government." Concluding, he added, "Like many conservatives, I believe in the power of culture to determine both individual success and social cohesion. . . . But I also believe that our government can play a role in shaping that culture for the better—or for the worse."[60]

By the summer of 2006 Obama was clearly thinking of a White House bid. He had been deeply affected by the ineptitude of the Bush administration in responding to Hurricane Katrina the previous August. The hugely destructive storm overwhelmed the levees in New Orleans, led to the destruction of whole sections of the city (most of which were predominantly Black), left hospitals without backup power and emergency workers without supplies, and caused misery to families sheltered in the leaky Superdome. Over five hundred thousand people were displaced as a result of the hurricane, and eighteen hundred more died. According to Michelle Obama, her husband's visit to New Orleans after the storm "kindled something in him, that nagging sense he wasn't yet doing enough."[61]

In September, the senator accepted an invitation to be the keynote speaker at the annual steak fry of Senator Tom Harkin in the early caucus state of Iowa—his strongest indication yet that he was contemplating running. In a return appearance on *Meet the Press* in October, he walked back his earlier statement of January that under no circumstance would he be a candidate for president in 2008. At the same time, he refused in his public appearances to commit himself to serving out his six-year term as senator or to pledge that he would not run for president in 2008.[62]

Following a decisive Democratic victory in the congressional elections the next month in which Democrats gained control of both houses of Congress, Obama assembled his closest advisers, including two new members of his political team, Peter Rouse and David Plouffe. Erstwhile chief of staff to former senate majority leader Tom Daschle before Daschle's recent defeat for reelection in South Dakota, Rouse became Obama's chief of staff. Plouffe, who had a sterling reputation as a campaign strategist and manager, had been Axelrod's partner since 2003, but he had not been heavily involved in Obama's race for the US Senate. He would later become his campaign manager in his race for president.[63]

The meeting's purpose was to discuss an Obama presidential candidacy. A number of those in attendance advised against running, pointing out to him the need for him to wait in line and first gain more experience on Capitol Hill, and the difficulty of defeating such Democratic heavyweights as Senator Hillary Clinton of New York, whom political pundits regarded as having a virtual lock on the party's nomination should she decide to seek it, and John Edwards, Kerry's vice presidential candidate in 2004, who remained popular among the party's more progressive wing.[64]

Obama thought differently. Earlier he had been advised against running for Congress and then had been advised against running for the US Senate. Both times he had let his own instincts and reading of the political map override the advice he received, but not this time. "I've never been a big believer in destiny," he commented as a former president. Still, he knew "by the spring of 2006, the idea of running for president in the next election, while still unlikely, was no longer outside the realm of possibility." Minority Leader Reid even took him aside and urged him to consider running, telling him that ten more years in the Senate would not make him a better president and that he motivated people, especially young people and minorities and even middle-of-the-road white people. Senator Kennedy also encouraged him to run, remarking, "you don't choose the time. The time chooses you." Before moving further, however, Obama waited until after the big Democratic victory in the 2006 congressional elections.[65]

At his meeting with his advisers, the senator directed them to develop a preliminary plan for winning the Democratic nomination. At the same time, he instructed them to examine the obstacles to winning and the impact on his family of a run for the presidency. If he determined they were too much against him or that a campaign for the presidency would be too harmful to his family, he was prepared to give up any thought of running. Later, he also asked the staff to look closely at the strengths and weaknesses of his likely opponents.[66]

Even after these early meetings, a few of his advisers, including Plouffe, were not convinced that he would become a candidate for president in 2008. "I still believed that the undertaking was largely a theoretical exercise," Plouffe later wrote. But he also acknowledged that "Obama was more serious about running than [he] had anticipated." The Illinois senator was aware of how difficult his march to the presidential nomination, much less to the Oval Office, would be. He was untested and unforged in a national campaign, lacked experience on Capitol Hill, and was without the resources or organization of Clinton, who enjoyed her own star power.[67]

Driven by his own restless ambition and motivated by confidence—almost cockiness—in himself as an agent of change at a time of growing partisanship and loss of optimism about the nation's future, the senator believed he could win his party's nomination and the election with his message of hope. The conservative tide in the country was coming to a close, he thought, and the American people yearned for a new and different type of politician like himself. As the political writers of Newsweek wrote, he "understood that he had become a giant screen upon which Americans projected their hopes and fears, dreams and frustrations."[68]

Before he could make a final decision, however, he still needed Michelle's approval. He knew that she had serious reservations about making the race. "Her initial instinct was to say no," Obama recalled. She had accepted only reluctantly his decision to run for the US Senate. She feared he might be killed by an assassin determined not to have a Black president in the Oval Office. As the mother of two young children and the wife of a career politician, she was also aware of how disruptive the campaign would be for her children and herself. Never comfortable on the public stage, she dreaded even the thought of having to speak at routine campaign events. And if Barack was elected, she was concerned that Malia and Sasha would not be able to have normal childhoods.[69]

For the first time in their lives, the Obamas did not have to worry about money. Besides her husband's income as a new US senator and the royalties from his two books, she had recently taken a new position with a handsome six-figure salary as vice president for community and external affairs at the University of Chicago's Medical Center. She enjoyed the semblance of a regular family life, her children were in school, and she had a close network of friends. She realized that if her husband ran for president, they would become subject to a grueling presidential campaign that would last eighteen months, test the endurance of their marriage, open every facet of their lives to close scrutiny, and almost certainly subject them to racial epithets and scurrilous accusations.[70]

Obama understood the difficult position in which he placed his wife and even questioned his own motives for running. "Why would I put her through this?" he asked himself. "Was it just vanity? Or perhaps something darker—a raw hunger, a blind ambition wrapped in the gauzy language of service? Or was I still trying to prove myself worthy of a father who had abandoned me, live up to my mother's starry-eyed expectations of her only son, and resolve whatever self-doubt remained from being born a child of a mixed race."[71]

Despite the difficult position in which he placed Michelle and his self-doubts about why he was running for president, Obama was unable to "close the door" on a presidential run, and Michelle threw her full support behind him. Accepting the fact that she was the wife of a career politician who set high, seemingly impossible, goals for himself, she was persuaded that if their marriage was to succeed, she needed to support him. The fact that she frequently changed jobs, always with increasing responsibilities, also suggested a certain restlessness and ambition on her part. Most important, she shared her husband's goals and believed he could win and break through the partisanship and deadlock that gripped Capitol Hill. Like her husband she wanted stronger regulation of big business and big banks, universal health care, tax cuts and rising wages for lower- and middle-class Americans, and stronger efforts to deal with climate change. She was certain her husband could deliver on these and other promises he made to the American people and restore confidence in the US system of government. "In the end," she later wrote, she approved of Obama's candidacy for president "because I believed that Barack could be a great president."[72]

With Michelle's approval, Obama announced on February 10, 2007, on the stairs of the state capitol in Springfield, where Abraham Lincoln had begun his political career, that he was running for president of the United States. Despite temperatures in the single digits, a gathering estimated at more than sixteen thousand people crowded the blocks below the capitol to hear Obama deliver an impassioned speech in which he invoked the name of Lincoln and spoke of a new generation of Americans who had formed into a movement committed to bringing about change in Washington. By running for president, he was offering to lead that movement into the seats of power. "Each and every time, a new generation has risen up and done what's needed to be done," he remarked. "Today we are called once more, and it's time for our generation to answer that call.".[73]

Having framed his candidacy as one of a new leader for a new generation of Americans and having adopted a message of hope and confidence about the future, Obama still faced the huge problems of developing an electoral strategy and an organization for taking his message to the people of the US. Recognizing that he remained far behind the overwhelming favorite to win the Democratic nomination, Hillary Clinton, both in terms of organization and fund-raising, and reflecting his background as a community organizer, he was convinced that the successful strategy for winning the nomination was to build support from precincts to counties to states and then the nation. His strategy was similar to President Jimmy Carter's in the 1976 campaign in which Carter realized that the first state primary took place not in New Hampshire, the traditional start of the primary season, but in Iowa. In the Hawkeye State the process of choosing delegates to the national convention was started in January of the election year with the holding of a complex system of local caucuses in schools and other public buildings.[74]

Obama's commitment to a grassroots campaign coincided with Plouffe's and Axelrod's view of the race not as a national campaign but as a series of state races starting with Iowa in January and continuing through Montana and South Dakota on June 3. In 2004 Edwards had come in a close second to Kerry in Iowa both in terms of votes and delegates. If Obama won in Iowa in 2008, he would not only strike a blow at Clinton and build momentum going into the New Hampshire primary, but he would also replace Edwards as the leading challenger to the New York senator.[75]

In choosing to run a series of state races rather than a single national campaign, Plouffe and Axelrod challenged the tradition-bound strategy of the Clinton campaign, which called for concentrating on the states with the biggest blocks of delegates, like New York, California, the industrial states of the Midwest, Texas, and Florida. In making their decision on an alternative, grassroots national strategy, they were influenced by the 2004 presidential campaign of Governor Howard Dean of Vermont and the 2006 gubernatorial campaign of Deval Patrick in Massachusetts.[76]

A little-known governor from a small rural state, Dean shook the political world in 2004 when, for a short while, he emerged as a front-runner in the campaign for the Democratic presidential nomination. The strategy that Dean employed was to tap into the still relatively new internet to raise large sums of money and, in the process garner campaign volunteers, through a successful appeal to small donors of $5 to $50. Also little known at the time he decided to run for governor, Patrick was an African American businessman and civil rights lawyer who had run the Civil Rights Division of the Justice Department during Bill Clinton's administration. He managed to win the election by a campaign using the internet to organize and communicate with local supporters and get voters to the ballot box on election day.[77]

Using the Dean and Patrick campaigns as models, Plouffe developed a technology-driven campaign structure that made it possible for Obama to stay in touch with supporters throughout Iowa and get them to the polls for the January caucuses. The technology was more sophisticated than any used in previous campaigns. Its usefulness, however, was effective only to the extent to which it supported the hundreds of young, idealistic volunteers who, having been motivated by Obama, poured into the state to support him. Going door-to-door, they reminded those whom the technology had identified as his supporters to go to the caucuses to vote.[78]

Even before Obama declared his candidacy for president, speculation had begun to grow that he would soon make it official. In April, he announced that he had raised $24.8 million during the first quarter of 2008 for his campaign, more money than any other Democratic candidate except for Clinton, much of whose funding was designated for the general election rather than the primaries. He also began to draw large crowds at his rallies.[79]

The pressure of the campaign began to take its toll on him. His cool, dispassionate, and unflappable public face started to show signs of cracking. He bridled at the constant pressure of cable news to break a news story. As he told *Newsweek*, he resented what he believed was its pressure for him to show his "toughness" on the war on terrorism by stating that he "want[ed] to bomb the hell out of someone." He grew annoyed at the desire of crowds to touch him, and his hands became numb from all the handshaking he had to do. Because of the unusually large number of racial death threats on him, he was provided with extra secret service protection, which limited his activities. He began to snap at his campaign staff, such as when a low staffer issued a press release mocking Clinton as "D-Punjab" because of her ties to alleged supporters of India. "I don't want you guys freelancing and, quote, *protecting me*, from what you're doing," he warned his staff.[80]

Eight candidates sought the Democratic nomination for president. Besides Obama, Clinton, and Edwards, the most prominent were former governor Bill Richardson (NM) and US Senators Joe Biden (DE), and Chris Dodd (CT). Although the candidates agreed to a series of party-sanctioned debates beginning with the first one at South Carolina State University in Orangeburg on April 26, 2007, in March they held an earlier face-off at a health-care forum in Las Vegas. Even Obama was displeased by his performance in these debates. "It's worse than I thought," the candidate told Axelrod, who agreed that Clinton had crisper, better prepared answers. He seemed remote to reporters, many of whom found him chilly and guarded. In contrast to their editors, they did not like him. Unlike former president Bill Clinton, who had the gift to simplify complex issues in a way audiences could easily understand, Obama also tended to be long-winded in explaining similar issues.[81]

In May, he reflected at length on why he was not living up to his own standards as a candidate. "Part of it is psychological," he told his aides. "I'm still wrapping my head around doing this in a way that I think other candidates just aren't. There is a certain ambivalence in my character that I like about myself. It's part of what makes me a good writer. . . . It's not necessarily useful in a presidential campaign." Even though aware of his problem, he continued to be distant and detached throughout the months preceding the Iowa caucuses. A staffer, Betsy Myers, the sister of Bill Clinton's former press secretary, Dee Dee Myers, even expressed disappointment that after returning to Chicago from a campaign trip, he preferred to use the gym rather than come to headquarters to mingle with the staff. [82]

After a short time, however, the senator began to loosen up and be more comfortable on the campaign trail, speaking to small and large groups. Addressing a Black crowd in South Carolina (an early primary state that would vote soon after Iowa and New Hampshire), he began to riff and speak with the cadence of a Black preacher, soliciting cheers and "Amens!" from the audience. In Aiken, he brought a rally to its feet by retelling the story of how a local city council woman, Edith Childs, had "fired up" a small crowd of only thirty attendees in a dismal rainy day by chanting repeatedly, "Fired Up! Ready to Go!" Then he introduced Childs to the audience, whom she led in the chant. Very quickly it became a part of the campaign. Volunteers carried signs and wore shirts with the slogan printed on them. Childs was even interviewed by CBS News.[83]

At the most important event of the early primary season, the Jefferson-Jackson dinner in Des Moines on November 10, which the campaign had already packed with Obama supporters, he lighted up the large gathering with his best speech since announcing he was running for president. Because the speakers were not permitted to use teleprompters, he spent hours memorizing the speech and perfecting its delivery. Talking for about thirty minutes, the candidate employed many of the same elements as his keynote address of 2004, alliteration, repetition, short phrases, and an increasingly more rapid delivery that built to a crescendo at the end. Mixing opposing elements of contempt for the Bush administration and his own confidence in the future, he spoke about the president's failures of leadership at home. He also attacked him for "using fear and falsehoods" in leading the United States into an unwarranted war in Iraq and for not having any plan for bringing the troops home. In contrast, he emphasized his own opposition to the war and made clear that if elected president, he intended to withdraw all troops within sixteen months.[84]

Also taking potshots at Hillary Clinton, Obama pointed out that she had voted for the Iraq War. Without mentioning her by name, he mocked her for basing her campaign on the latest polling. He wanted, he said, a "party that offers not just a difference in policies, but a difference in leadership. A party that doesn't just focus on how to win but why we should. A party that doesn't just offer change as a slogan, but real, meaningful change—change that America can believe."[85]

Like his keynote address, his speech at the dinner was singled out by journalists as the outstanding event of the night. The reporter, Garance Frank-Ruta, remarked that he "finally gave the speech his supporters have been waiting for him to give all year. If anyone comes out of this dinner with The Big Mo," she said, "it will be him." "The excitement generated by Obama's fiery but disciplined speech is a reminder of what it means to convince someone," the commentator Ana Marie Cox, added.[86]

In contrast to the Obama campaign, the Clinton campaign never caught fire in Iowa. While Mrs. Clinton came to the debates with a firm grasp of the issues and, almost always, was on point in responding to questions, on occasion she tripped up or was caught off guard by her opponents. On one particularly bad night, she danced around a question by Tim Russert about whether she supported New York governor Elliot Spitzer's plan to give driver's licenses to undocumented workers. This allowed her opponents to trounce on her for her indecisiveness on the issue of illegal immigration.[87]

The leadership of the Clinton campaign seemed to be in denial about the earthquake that was about to take place in Iowa or about the impact of Obama's speech at the Jefferson-Jackson dinner on the coming caucuses. Mark Penn, Mrs. Clinton's chief pollster and strategist, whom Axelrod described as "dark, brooding [and] smugly self-assur[ed]," commented after the dinner that Obama's supporters "look like Facebook," while Mandy Grunwald, a veteran consultant and adviser to the New York senator, remarked, "Our people look like caucus-goers and his people look like they are eighteen."[88]

Many of his supporters in Iowa may have been only eighteen or just a few years older; indeed, some were only seventeen since Iowa permitted seventeen-year-olds who would be eighteen by the November election to vote in the caucuses. But when they took place a month later, Obama won a resounding victory, capturing 38 percent of the vote while Edwards eked out a narrow victory over Clinton gaining 29.8 percent of the vote to Clinton's 29.5 percent. What was astonishing about his victory was that 239,000 Iowans turned out to vote compared to just 124,000 in 2004. As polls confirmed, a large percentage of the turnout consisted of new registrants, who were under the age of thirty and voted for him. They were attracted by his charismatic personality and his change-oriented message. Like him, they also believed that his victory represented, "a defining moment in history."[89]

Immediately after the caucuses, Dodd and Biden dropped out of the battle for the Democratic nomination. Richardson remained in the contest, but was given almost no chance of surviving the New Hampshire primary a week later. The contest for the nomination had been whittled down to one between Obama, Clinton, and Edwards. Obama had gone from being an underdog in the race to being the favorite. Edwards still had a chance of winning, but Clinton, who had been the clear frontrunner, looked as if she could be knocked out if she lost in New Hampshire even though she still had a formidable national organization and a sizable war chest at her disposal.[90]

It was a momentous time for Obama. Practically unknown to the American public in 2004, when the presumptive nominee for the Democratic nomination delivered his keynote address in Boston, he introduced himself to the American people as a new kind of politician for a new generation of Americans. A unifier rather than a divider, he rejected the status quo in favor of change, arguing that change was possible, but only through shared responsibility and collective action within the context of the nation's existing political system. America's best times, he said, lay not in the past but were yet to come. There was also a subtext to his message. Politics and smart government were not mutually exclusive. Joined together, they could bend the arc of history toward a more just, moral, and humane society.

This was a set of beliefs that Obama had always maintained since his years as a community organizer in Chicago's South Side. It was one he brought to the political arena when he first ran for the Illinois state senate in 1996, and it guided his actions in the state legislature. Until he delivered the keynote address in 2004, however, he had not had the opportunity to champion his beliefs before a national audience. His message resonated with the American people. In the Iowa caucuses, it created a seismic event that elevated him to within grasp of the Democratic nomination. All eyes turned to New Hampshire to watch if that primary would knock Senators Clinton and Edwards out of the race and all but assure that Obama would be the presumptive Democratic nominee in 2008.

CHAPTER 4

From Iowa to President-Elect

Following Obama's decisive victory in the Iowa caucuses, political commentators speculated on the likelihood that the Illinois senator would wrap up the Democratic presidential nomination quickly. He left Iowa heavily favored to win the New Hampshire primary over Hillary Clinton and John Edwards. Two weeks after New Hampshire, South Carolina held its primary. A victory in the Palmetto State, with its high percentage of Black voters, could seal the nomination for him even before Clinton could test her big-state strategy. The New York senator, however, surprised Obama in New Hampshire, leading to a protracted battle for the Democratic nomination that was not finally decided until the last days of the primary season in June.

Obama viewed his defeat in New Hampshire as a disappointment rather than as a major setback to his campaign. More than Clinton and Edwards, he understood the complex Democratic rules that provided for selection of two sets of delegates to the Democratic nominating convention in Denver: the first, superdelegates, mostly Democrats holding high elected office: the second, elected delegates. By gaining enough elected and superdelegates even in the states he lost, his campaign reasoned he would secure enough delegates to win the party's nomination in July.

Despite losses to Clinton in key states like Ohio, Pennsylvania, New York, New Jersey, and Texas, the strategy worked remarkably well. Although Clinton continued to refuse to cede the nomination to the Illinois senator until after the final primary was held in Puerto Rico in June, Tim Russert of *Meet the Press*, the dean of Washington commentators, announced a month earlier that Obama already had enough delegates to be the presumptive Democratic nominee for president. By the time the Democrats assembled in Denver to nominate their presidential candidate, the only remaining question was whether Hillary Clinton would insist on a divisive roll call vote of the delegates or cede the nomination to the Illinois senator without a vote. Clinton split the difference by asking for the vote but calling soon after the roll call began for his nomination by acclamation.

Obama won the nomination by continuing to frame the contest as one between the politics of the past represented by Clinton and the politics of the future, which he represented. In contrast to Clinton, he presented himself as the agent of change. In a bipartisan manner he promised to resolve the major issues facing the nation from the economy, health care, and failing education, to the Iraq War, Afghanistan, and the Russian threat in the Crimea. In making the primaries a referendum between Clinton and himself, he raised unrealistic expectations of what he could accomplish as president, a fact that later came back to haunt him. In the process, he revealed far more about himself than he would have had he made the primary season about issues rather than personalities. Besides being a conservative seeking progressive ends, another irony of his campaign was that even while looking to the future, Obama was motivated by a conscious effort to redeem his and the nation's past. The same was true of his campaign against the Republican candidate for president, John McCain. However, the worst economic and financial crisis facing the nation since the Great Depression of the 1930s overshadowed all other issues.

The Philadelphia Speech

Even as he addressed the crowd that had gathered in Des Moines to celebrate the night of his victory in the Iowa caucuses, Obama tied his message of hope to his unique experience as the biracial child of parents from entirely different backgrounds. "Hope," he said, "is what led me here today—with a father from Kenya; a mother from Kansas; and a story that could only happen in the United States of America." Throughout the rest of the campaign he returned repeatedly to his life story.[1]

Following Iowa, all signs pointed to a decisive victory for Obama in New Hampshire. In the five days before the primary in the Granite State, he campaigned throughout the state, drawing overflow crowds wherever he went. Polls gave him a sizable lead over Clinton and John Edwards. Outwardly,

Clinton tried, with a shrug and a smile, to play down the importance of her third-place finish in Iowa, but inwardly she was demoralized. Her campaign organization was rife with backstabbing and blame-calling for what might be the end of the campaign before it had even gotten started.[2]

What went undetected by most observers was a growing wave of sympathy for Clinton, who remained widely admired among women for her efforts throughout her career on behalf of children and women's causes and for being the first female candidate with a real chance to win the nation's highest office. Voters were also annoyed by a dismissive comment Obama made about Clinton during a debate with her four days after his victory in Iowa. In response to Clinton's remark that she found Obama "very likeable," he said he found Clinton "likeable enough." Voters were turned off by his flippancy. They also began to wonder whether he was experienced enough to be president.[3]

What swung the election finally in Clinton's favor was her tearing up while responding to an inquiry about how she remained so positive on the campaign trail. Instead of reacting negatively to her moistened eyes, voters reacted positively to the humanizing of a candidate widely perceived as being cold and aloof. Her response to the question—"I couldn't do it if I just didn't passionately believe it was the right thing to do"—resonated with the voters. When the votes were counted, Clinton won over Obama gaining 39.1 percent of the vote to his 36.5 percent. Easily overlooked was the fact that while the New York senator narrowly defeated her Illinois rival, both candidates received the same number of delegates to the national convention in July. Eleven days after New Hampshire, Clinton won the popular vote in the Nevada caucuses, but Obama actually received one more elected delegate than Clinton.[4]

Attracting more national attention than the Nevada caucuses was the South Carolina primary on January 26 with its large Black population and more elected delegate seats at stake than Nevada. By winning a major victory over Clinton in South Carolina, Obama made clear that Black voters, convinced after Iowa that he could win the presidency, were prepared to come out in record numbers to vote for him.[5]

Former president Bill Clinton, whom the African American author Toni Morrison had once referred to as the "first Black president," took it personally that a freshman senator with only two years of national political experience might defeat his more experienced wife. Acting as a surrogate for Hillary during much of the campaign, Bill Clinton even challenged Obama's record of opposition to the Iraq war, pointing to his support of funding for the conflict. What struck many of those covering the primary was the bitterness of his remarks against his opponent. After Obama won the South Carolina primary, gaining 55 percent of the vote to Clinton's 27 percent and Edwards's 16 percent, he set off a firestorm of criticism by suggesting that Obama won because of his race.[6]

Making matters worse for Senator Clinton, Senator Ted Kennedy of Massachusetts, and Caroline Kennedy, the daughter of President John F. Kennedy, joined with Obama at one of his rallies to announce that they were backing him. Other members of the Kennedy family appeared on stage with the Illinois senator as did the highly influential celebrity and successful businesswoman, Oprah Winfrey, who had already thrown her support behind Obama in Iowa, and the Democratic presidential nominee in 2004, John Kerry, who had already been campaigning for him in South Carolina.[7]

Following South Carolina, the primary season settled into a long, drawn out and often heated contest between Obama and Clinton. On February 5 came Super Tuesday during which twenty-two states from across the country and the territory of American Samoa held their primaries or caucuses. At stake were 1,681 pledged delegates. At his rallies Obama drew crowds of as many as fifteen thousand. When all the votes were counted, he won a narrow victory over Clinton, carrying thirteen states to her nine states and the territory of Samoa and gaining 847 pledged delegates to her 834.[8]

Obama won decisively in Illinois and did his best in the caucus and in more rural states of the West, Midwest, and South, while Clinton did her best in the Northeast and the Southwest with their large and loyal Hispanic votes. Even in the states that he lost to Clinton, he was able to pick up large blocks of pledged delegates.[9]

In the two weeks following Super Tuesday, eight more states, the District of Columbia, Americans living abroad, and the Virgin Islands held primaries and caucuses. By sweeping to victory in all these contests and winning big in Virginia, Maryland, Wisconsin, and in the caucus state of Washington, the Illinois senator developed a small but insurmountable lead over Clinton in total delegates. Not only did he win pledged delegates, he also gained pledges from an increasing number of superdelegates, many of whom had earlier supported Clinton.[10]

As early as the end of February, David Plouffe, his cautious campaign manager, even telephoned him to tell him that he would probably be his party's presidential nominee. His response was more one of solemnity than exhilaration. "After we hung up," the former president later recalled, "I sat alone, trying to take the measure of my emotions. There was pride, I suppose. . . . Mostly, though, I felt a certain stillness, without elation or relief, sobered by the thought that the responsibilities of governance were no longer a distant possibility."[11]

While Plouffe's detailed strategic plan accounted in part for Obama's campaign success, it was not the only reason for his success. In the three weeks before Super Tuesday, the candidate engaged in a series of bus tours and town halls throughout the caucus and rural states without ceding the large industrial states that the Clinton campaign had targeted. For a politician who did not enjoy retail politics and was known for the brilliance of his oratory, Obama proved most effective in town hall meetings, where he seemed to take inspiration from the back-and-forth that took place.[12]

No matter the type of the gathering, the Illinois senator inspired his audiences with the force of his personality, his vision of change, and the redemptive value of his biography. He also motivated them with his talk about collective redemption, not only for Black people but for white people. Unlike previous Black candidates for president, such as Jesse Jackson, who ran in 1984 and 1988 on behalf of a "rainbow coalition" of minority groups, and Al Sharpton, who ran in 2004 as the candidate of civil rights, Obama was not a product of the civil rights movement and did not run on behalf of any minority group, including Black Americans.[13]

Yet by presenting himself as a transformational president and as potentially the first African American president, Obama offered the nation a way for it to redeem itself. Former governor L. Douglas Wilder of Virginia, the nation's first elected Black governor, sensed this early in Obama's campaign. After having several conversations with him in the late summer of 2007, he remarked, "One thing we discussed is that there are no such things as 'Black issues.' Health and education are not Black issues. Improvement of job opportunities is not a Black issue." In an interview for *Politico* about the same time, Wilder commented about Obama. "He's not race-less, but the skin color is of no moment. I don't think he would be an easy target for the Republicans." A white Obama supporter also understood the message he was trying to deliver in his campaign. In a question and answer session during a forum with Neal Conan of NPR, he remarked about Obama, "you know, he's not a Black candidate, and he's not a white candidate. . . . He's all of us. . . . And his unique history is going to allow him to inspire that next phase in the healing of this country's racist past."[14]

Although Obama tried to avoid racial issues in his bid to be president, they took center stage on March 13 when ABC televised portions of a sermon that his pastor, Reverend Jeremy Wright, delivered after 9/11 in which he fulminated about the "chickens coming home to roost . . . in response to America's own acts of terrorism." "For killing innocent people," he also ranted, "God damn America."[15]

Wright's comments threw Obama's campaign into crisis mode. His relationship with Wright went back nearly twenty years. He was his religious adviser and had baptized his two children and himself. He had also presided at his wedding to Michelle. Obama had titled his book, *Audacity of Hope*, after the name of one of Wright's earlier sermons. Because of this close relationship and the widespread outrage at his pastor's remarks, they threatened to destroy his chances of getting the Democratic nomination.[16]

The playing of Wright's sermon also came at a low point in his campaign. In another attempt to defeat Clinton for the nomination, the Illinois senator campaigned hard and poured millions of dollars into the upcoming primaries in Ohio and Texas, both of which Clinton needed to win to stay in the race. To make this happen, her campaign went all out in its efforts to defeat Obama in these states.[17]

In one of their debates, Clinton even raised questions about her opponent's character and judgment because of his association with Bill Ayers, a founding member of the militant Underground Weathermen, who in the 1970s bombed the Pentagon and the United States Capitol. To avoid prosecution Ayers fled the country, but gave himself up in 1980. Because of the government's mishandling of his case, the charges against him were dropped, and he went on to become a distinguished professor at the University of Illinois in Chicago.[18]

Obama had known Ayers since the time he hosted a gathering for the first-time candidate during his campaign for state senator. They also served together for three years on the board of directors of the Woods Foundation, the grant-giving organization that had supported Obama's work as a community organizer in the 1980s. Although most news organizations concluded that his relationship with Ayers was not close, Clinton's questions about his judgment were effective. So was an ad about the same time that suggested she was more prepared to be president than he was if a crisis developed.[19]

On March 4 Obama lost handily to Clinton in Ohio and more narrowly in Texas. He also lost by a sweeping margin in Rhode Island. Even though he won by a solid margin in Vermont, and the next week won in Wyoming and Mississippi, political observers began to wonder whether Clinton might yet win the Democratic nomination. "She's like a fucking vampire," Plouffe complained. "You can't kill her off." Flying back from San Antonio to Chicago, Michelle was glum and hardly spoke a word. Even Obama grew exasperated. "Her tenacity was admirable, but my sympathies extended only so far," he later recounted.[20]

Complicating matters still more for him was his involvement with the convicted real estate developer, Tony Rezko. Although Rezko had a reputation as a shady political insider and dealmaker, he had a relationship with Obama going back to at least 1991 when he offered the new graduate of Harvard Law School a job with his firm. While he was never part of his inner circle of friends, he kept in touch with the senator and raised about $150,000 for his campaigns over the years.[21]

In 2005, Obama purchased a home in the Hyde Park area of Chicago and Rezko's wife bought an adjacent house and lot. Seven months later he bought a piece of the Rezko land in order to enlarge his yard. Although he paid fair market value for both pieces of property and there was no evidence that he had done anything wrong, when news broke about the land deals between Obama and Rezko, he was accused in the media of a surprising lack of judgment. Some even charged him with unethical behavior for continuing to take campaign contributions from Rezko even after he became a target of an FBI investigation. The candidate admitted bad judgment in buying land from Rezko, calling his action "boneheaded," and he donated to charity money Rezko had personally given to his senatorial campaign, but the incident raised new questions about his ethics and his judgment, which he tried to answer by meeting with the editorial staffs of the *Chicago Tribune* and *Chicago Sun-Times*.[22]

Exhausted from being on the campaign trail, frustrated by the results from Ohio and Texas, and faced with putting out a fire over his ties to Rezko, Obama realized he had to respond immediately to Reverend Wright's inflammatory remarks about white racism. "I vehemently disagree and strongly condemn the statements that have been the subject of this controversy," he wrote in a blog for the HuffingtonPost. "I categorically denounce any statement that disparages our great country or serves to divide us from our allies." In other comments, he termed Wright's words "incendiary."[23]

Obama realized this was not enough. Despite having tried to avoid racial issues during the campaign, he understood that, in the heat of a presidential race, they were bound to come up. Before the broadcasting of Wright's post-9/11 sermon, he had informed his advisers, some of whom already suspected the Clinton campaign of race baiting, that he wanted to deliver a speech on racial issues. In the wake of the outrage against Wright, he felt he had to make the speech as soon as possible.[24]

He wrote most of his remarks himself, spending three nights after full days of campaigning, to write them. The speech resurrected his campaign. Understanding its importance, his advisers chose the National Constitution Center in Philadelphia as its venue. Before a small audience in a talk that was broadcast nationally, he dealt directly with Wright's comments, stating that they "were not only wrong but divisive, divisive at a time when we need unity; racially charged at a time when we need to come together to solve a set of monumental problems." [25]

He could not disown Wright, Obama remarked. "Imperfect as he may be, he has been like family to me," he added, just as he could not disown his grandmother who raised and loved him but who "once confessed her fear of Black men who passed by her on the street, and who on more than one occasion has uttered racial or ethnic stereotypes that made me cringe." At the same time, he tried to place Wright's sermon within the broader context of race relations going back to the founding fathers and to the nation's failure to fulfill its commitment in the Constitution to form "a more perfect union." That would not be achieved, the candidate noted, until the nation moved beyond "its original sin of slavery" and the racial divide that followed in the wake of its extinction nearly a century and a half earlier. While much racial progress had taken place, much remained to be done. [26]

When Wright delivered his sermon, he was expressing the pent-up anger and emotions of the largely Black congregation to whom he spoke, Obama continued. "For the men and women of Reverend Wright's generation, the memories of humiliation and doubt and fear have not gone away; nor has the anger and the bitterness of those years. . . . And occasionally it found voice in the church on Sunday morning, in the pulpit and in the pews." "The profound mistake of Reverend Wright's sermons was not that he spoke about racism in our society. [It was] that he spoke as if our society was static: as if no progress has been made; as if this country [was] still irrevocably bound to a tragic past." [27]

Not only was context important for understanding the anger Wright expressed, Obama added, it was as important for appreciating the white outrage at his remarks. Both were part of the same racial divide that was the legacy of the nation's original sin. Both were equally justified. Why, white workers wondered, should they have to pay the price in terms of lost jobs and low wages, for previous discrimination in which they did not participate? Why should they be denied the opportunity of their parents to work hard, raise families, and give their children the hope of an even better life than they enjoyed? "In an era of stagnant wages and global competition, opportunity comes to be seen as a zero sum game, in which your dreams come at my expense." [28]

As justified as Black and white grievances were, they were also counterproductive. To make race an issue "would be making the same mistake that the Reverend Wright made . . . to simplify and stereotype and amplify the negative to the point that it distorts reality.". The "real culprits of the middle class squeeze," Obama argued, were "a corporate culture rife with inside dealings, questionable accounting practices, and short-term greed; a Washington dominated by lobbyists and special interests; economic policies that favor the few over the many."[29]

Because of his unusual American story as the son of a Black man from Kenya and a white woman from Kansas, Obama maintained he was in a unique position to bridge the divide that has separated the nation and move it finally toward the more perfect union envisioned by the founding fathers. That is why he was running for president. His story did not make him "the most conventional candidate," he said. "But it [was] a story that has seared into my genetic makeup the idea that this nation is more than the sum of its parts—that out of many, we are truly one."[30]

By electing him president of the United States, the nation would be electing a candidate who did not represent any special group or interest and who was not tied down by the past but looked to the future. It would be electing a president who would be able to finally end the nation's racial stalemate and move it on the path toward a more perfect union. For Blacks this meant binding "our particular grievances—for better health care, and better schools, and better jobs—to the larger aspirations of all Americans." For white Americans it meant "acknowledging that what ails the African American community does not just exist in the minds of Black people; that the legacy of discrimination—and current incidents of discrimination, while less overt than in the past—are real and must be addressed."[31]

Redeeming the nation's past by electing him as president, was the subtle subtext of Obama's Philadelphia speech and of his entire campaign. A number of Republicans and even some independents criticized the speech as a failed attempt on his part to move beyond his relationship with the Reverend Wright. Some African Americans complained again that he was compromising his Blackness to appeal to whites. In his comments, Obama made the point—which, he acknowledged, was "quintessential conservative"—that while Blacks had legitimate grievances, they also needed to engage in self-help. That meant, he said, "taking full responsibility for our own lives—by demanding more from our fathers, and spending more time with our children, and reading to them, and teaching them that while they may face challenges and discrimination in their own lives, they must . . . always believe that they can write their own destiny."[32]

Many Black leaders found Obama's advocacy of a traditional, middle-class road to success demeaning to Blacks. "He seems to want it both ways, Peter Bell, the Black chairman of the Minneapolis Metropolitan Council, said of the candidate. "He wants to be both above race and yet heal the racial wounds of the country, and he wants to do that as someone other than a Black man." Jesse Jackson thought that he was "talking down to Black people."[33]

In contrast to these Black leaders, most commentators praised the speech. A number of them even compared it to Kennedy's famous address in Houston in 1960 before a group of Southern Baptist ministers in which he tackled head on all doubts about his Catholicism. Kennedy's chief speech-writer and close adviser, Ted Sorensen, called Obama's remarks "historic." The well-known biographer and president of the Aspen Institute, Walter Isaacson, added that Obama "wrestled with the most important issue we have faced throughout our history, and he did it in a way that wasn't politi-cally calculating, but was intensely personal as well as insightful." Even the presumptive Republican nominee for president, John McCain, called it an "excellent speech" remarking that "it was good for all of America to have heard it."[34]

The Presumptive Democratic Nominee

In the nearly three months still remaining in the primary season, Obama continued to suffer setbacks. The most serious one was in Pennsylvania on April 22 where he lost by a margin of 54.6 percent for Clinton to 45.4 percent for Obama. A comment he made earlier that Pennsylvania voters were tied to their Bibles and guns hurt him badly in the middle and western parts of the state where religion and hunting were part of those regions' culture. He later called that his "biggest mistake of the campaign."[35]

Less than a week after the Pennsylvania primary, the Obama campaign was rocked again by more of Reverend Wright's remarks, this time at the National Press Club in Washington. Despite the hornets' nest stirred by the clip of his fiery statements after 9/11 and Obama's public denunciation of them, Wright had remained quiet. But he harbored deep resentment at how he was being treated in the media. He felt his remarks had been taken out of context. Notwithstanding Obama's statement to the contrary, he also believed his parishioner and longtime friend had disowned him. "You've not only dissed me," he said referring to Obama, "you have urinated on my tra-dition. . . . You've urinated on my parents, my grandparents, and our whole faith tradition."[36]

In a question and answer session following his speech to the National Press Club, Wright lashed out at his critics and became increasingly combat-ive. He seemed to identify himself with the racist leader of the Nation of Islam, Louis Farrakhan, who, he said, "did not put me in chains . . . did not put me in slavery, and . . . did not make me this color." He even conjured up a conspiracy theory that the HIV virus was invented as a weapon to be used against people of color. For Obama, Wright had crossed one bridge too far. Speaking the next day in Winston-Salem, North Carolina, he rejected his remarks and disowned him completely.[37]

Despite these bumps on the road, in a come-from-behind victory, the Illinois senator won decisively in North Carolina on May 6 and lost the Indiana primary by only 1 percent. All told, he picked up 101 delegates to Clinton's 86, leading to Tim Russert's declaration of Obama as the presumptive Democratic nominee for president.[38]

One remaining problem that continued to weigh on the campaign was the outcome of primaries that had been held in Florida and Michigan in January. Contrary to rules established by the Democratic National Committee (DNC), the two states held their primaries in January in anticipation of playing a more prominent role in the final outcome of the primary season. As a result, the DNC announced it would not recognize their primaries and urged the candidates not to campaign there. It also asked them to remove their names from the ballot in Michigan before they were printed. All of them agreed to the DNC's request about not campaigning, but in contrast to the other candidates, Clinton and Chris Dodd refused to remove their names from the ballot in Michigan. The result was that Clinton gained 222 pledged delegates from Florida and Michigan to Obama's 189 and claimed "a tremendous victory" after the Florida primary.[39]

Had these delegates been figured into the pledged superdelegate count, Clinton maintained she would have been solidly ahead of Obama when South Carolina held its primary, and the whole momentum of the campaign would have changed in her favor. Obama responded that had he campaigned in Florida and not had his name removed from the Michigan ballot, the outcome of the two primaries would have been different.[40]

In the final month of the primary season, Clinton picked up more pledged delegates (305) than Obama (261). The additional delegates Clinton gained, however, did not matter. The delegates and superdelegates he picked up were enough for all the major media outlets and party leaders to declare him the presumptive Democratic nominee for president.[41]

Still, the issue of the pledged delegates from Florida and Michigan stayed unresolved, and the Obama campaign worried that a failure to come to an agreement over the problem could lead to a floor fight at the convention. Despite a cordial meeting between the two candidates at the home of California senator Dianne Feinstein, Obama and his advisers were taken aback that Clinton's aides asked him to help pay off the $23 million debt Clinton had borrowed during the campaign ($11 million of which she had lent herself).[42]

Because Obama thought Clinton's request would backfire on him, he turned it down. Assured of the nomination, however, his campaign advisers became more flexible about the final delegate count. On May 31, they agreed to a ruling that gave sixty-nine delegates pledged in Michigan to Clinton and fifty-nine to Obama. A week later, Clinton ceded the nomination to Obama, who was able finally to turn his full attention and resources to defeating John McCain. By staking his campaign on a single speech in Philadelphia three months earlier on a topic he had tried to avoid, he had turned a potential disaster into the major turning point in his march toward the Democratic presidential nomination.[43]

Just as he did at the end of February, when Plouffe had told him that he was most likely going to be the Democratic presidential nominee, Obama responded more with reflection than elation, and even with uncertainty, now that he was about to win the nomination. What had brought him to the cusp of victory? To whom did he owe the most gratitude? What lay ahead in the campaign against the presumed Republican nominee, John McCain? And, if he were to be elected president, what would be his priorities as the leader of the world's most powerful nation? Besides his campaign staff, especially Axelrod and Plouffe, he singled out the role in the campaign of Michelle, "who had put up with my absences, held down the home front, and overridden her reticence about politics to become effective and fearless on the campaign."[44]

As for his priorities as the Democratic nominee and then as president should he prevail in November, he seemed to place greater stress on domestic matters than on foreign policy. "I had asked something hard of the American people—to place their faith in a young and untested newcomer," he later recounted, "not just a Black man" but one with a strange name and unconventional background. "Despite all that, they'd given me a chance . . . they'd heard my call for something different [and] that for all our differences, we remained bound as one people. . . . I promised myself I would not let them down."[45]

As Obama thought about his coming campaign against McCain, he made a momentous decision. Despite promises to the contrary, he became the first major presidential nominee to turn down public financing ($84.1 million in 2008) in favor of raising unlimited funds for his campaign. Claiming that he still supported "a robust system of public financing of elections," he justified his decision on the grounds that the existing system of public financing, first employed in the 1976 presidential campaign between Jimmy Carter and

Gerald Ford, was "broken," and that his opponents had "become masters at gaming" the system.[46]

Actually, the candidate made his decision on the pragmatic grounds that he needed more than $84 million to defeat McCain, whom he considered "the most worthy" and decent of the Republican candidates for his party's nomination, and that the Democratic candidate's campaign had developed an election apparatus able to raise far more money than his opponent. As early as April, Plouffe had begun planning and budgeting for the fall campaign against McCain. He decided to expand the campaign beyond the traditionally few so-called battleground states, like Ohio and Florida, that had determined the outcome of earlier elections. "From an electoral perspective," he later wrote, "nothing was more important to us strategically than having a wide playing field." To carry out this strategy, he settled on a budget figure of around $450 million with $350 million being raised by the campaign and the rest coming from the Democratic National Committee (DNC). This was far larger than the maximum the campaign would have received had it chosen to rely on public financing.[47]

Although Plouffe wanted to reject public in favor of private fund-raising, the campaign staff realized the problems that uncoupling the campaign from public funding would create. In the first place, Obama would have to devote much of the remaining months before the election to fund-raising, something he hated doing. Second, he had always been openly supportive of public financing. In February 2007, he had pledged to accept public financing if he won the Democratic nomination for president. Third, the decision to reject public financing would result in a strong backlash not only from Republicans but from Democrats who were against private financing on principle and would regard raising funds privately a betrayal of the very moral grounds on which he based his campaign. For them, "change we can believe in" would become little more than another hollow political sound bite by one more gifted, but otherwise traditional, politician.[48]

Obama understood all the concerns raised by his staff, but in a short video, which he sent out to his supporters on February 20, 2008, he offered what he called a new system of campaign financing controlled by the "American People." He was not rejecting public financing, he maintained, but seeking to amend it in such a way that it was no longer controlled by lobbyists and corporate interests.[49]

By rejecting funds from interest groups during the primaries and soliciting small donations of less than $200, Obama's campaign raised over $200 million and increased the base of Obama voters. Were he to accept public financing in the national election, that option would not be available to him. He would have to rely, instead, on outside groups to fund the campaign. Worse, he would have no control over them since the law prohibited his staffers and him from discussing campaign strategy with any outside political action committee (PAC) or interest group. "Instead of forcing us to rely on millions from Washington lobbyists and special interest PACS, you've fueled this campaign with donations of $5, $10, $20, whatever you can afford," Obama told his supporters. "We've won the Democratic nomination by relying on ordinary people coming together."[50]

In one short video Obama turned the argument in favor of public funding on its head and offered a new paradigm of campaign financing. "You've already changed the way campaigns are funded because you know that's the only way we can truly change how Washington works," he told his supporters. "I'm asking you to try to do something that's never been done before. Declare our independence from a broken system, and run the type of campaign that reflects the grassroots values that have already changed our politics and brought us this far."[51]

As Obama had anticipated, he was attacked from both the right and left for rejecting public financing. But by doing so while portraying himself as a forward-looking reformer, he emerged largely unscathed from his decision over private financing. In June his campaign raised over $54 million compared to about $23 million a month earlier.[52]

Because he opted out of private funding, the Illinois senator had to devote extensive time traveling to fund-raising events throughout the country. During this time, however, his campaign operation became a money-making machine, perfecting its ground game, harnessing it to the internet, and raising approximately $400 million by June. After Clinton ceded the nomination to him, his campaign picked up its pace even more by tapping into a whole new pool of Clinton donors. At the same time, it became the most efficient operation in the nation's history for identifying voters and volunteers and making sure the one got the other to the polls. "Technology was core to our campaign from Day One," Plouffe later explained, "and it only grew in importance as the primary went on. We started out with fewer than ten thousand e-mail addresses, and by June 3, 2008, our list had grown to over 5 million. A huge portion of that group . . . had either volunteered or contributed."[53]

Yet Obama still remained a puzzle to many Americans. Despite sixteen months of campaigning, thousands of rallies and town halls, and twenty-six presidential debates, polls showed that as many as 13 percent of the voters in the primaries cast ballots against him because they thought he was a Muslim. A chain email had already gone viral complaining that he was hiding his radical Islamic background.[54]

From the beginning of his campaign, Obama realized that he could not ignore the issue of his faith, which also came out during the Wright controversy. Was he a Christian? How deep was his faith? Why was he baptized so late in his life? What attracted him to join Reverend Wright's church? These were some of the questions raised during the campaign. Although he never addressed them in a single televised speech as he did in his Philadelphia address on race in March, he talked about them at length throughout the campaign. He peppered his comments with biblical references and gave several speeches devoted entirely to issues of faith and religion.[55]

As the senator made clear throughout the campaign and in his campaign biographies, *Dreams from My Father* (1995) and *The Audacity of Hope* (2006), he was raised in a secular household. His father was an atheist, and his mother and grandparents were only nominal Christians. His mother was also highly skeptical of organized religion. In her view "it too often dressed up close-mindedness in the garb of piety, cruelty and oppression in the cloak of righteousness," he wrote in *Audacity*.[56]

Yet Obama also regarded his mother as "the most spiritually awakened . . . person" he had ever known. Although rejecting organized religion, she exposed him to a number of religious faiths from the Bible to the teachings of Buddhism, Hinduism, and the Quran, as well as to Greek, Norse, and African mythology. Like "the anthropologist that she would become," he remarked, she looked at religion as a "phenomenon to be treated with a suitable respect, but with a suitable detachment as well." Similarly, she believed that religion was a way "that man attempted to control the unknowable and understand the deeper truths about our lives."[57]

Obama shared his mother's skepticism about organized religion. Like her, he was not so much religious as he was spiritual. Until he became a community organizer in Chicago and saw the power of the Black church in the community where he worked, he had not attended church on a regular basis or given much thought to his own religious beliefs. Issues of race were always of more concern to him than issues of religion. He was not even baptized until 1988 just as he was about to leave Chicago to attend Harvard Law School.[58]

Despite his being baptized at the age of twenty-seven, Obama and Michelle never became regular churchgoers. Even as a community organizer, however, he was profoundly influenced by the centrality of the Black church to the clientele he served. In a city still new to him, he found in the church the sense of community and belonging which he had sought since graduating Columbia University. From a practical standpoint, he learned the power of church pastors and ministers to mobilize their congregations behind political causes and candidates they supported.[59]

When he attended church services, he was able to cite verse as well as the other congregants. Even so, he realized he could not be part of the community until he fully embraced its values and beliefs. This did not happen easily or naturally for him. He described his acceptance of religion as "a journey" he had to travel. "The Christians with whom I worked recognized themselves in me," he later wrote. "But they sensed that a part of me remained removed, detached. . . . I came to realize that without . . . an unequivocal commitment to a particular community of faith, I would be consigned at some level to always remain apart." He would be free to enjoy the wonders of the world like his mother, but he would be alone at the same time.[60]

Beyond the practical reasons why Obama decided to become baptized, he also held the Black church in high esteem because it was grounded in the historic struggle against slavery and injustice, and because it served the everyday needs of its constituents from day care to providing meals and clothes for the poor. As he explained, the Black church "rarely had the luxury of separating individual from collective salvation. . . . It understood in an intimate way the biblical call to feed the hungry and clothe the naked and challenge powers and principalities. In the history of these struggles, I was able to see faith as more than just a comfort to the weary or a hedge against death; rather, it was an active, palpable agent in the world."[61]

Black clergymen typically delivered sermons linking the Bible to remedying social injustice. One of these pastors was Jeremiah Wright, who turned the Trinity United Church of Christ into the largest Black church in Chicago with a membership of 8,500 that included some of the wealthiest and most powerful Blacks in the city as well as parishioners of modest and lesser means. Albeit fiery and sometimes intemperate, he was one of the nation's most learned and respected Black ministers, holding two master's degrees and a doctorate in ministry. Taking Obama under his wing, he spent hours with him, talking about the historic role of the Black church in resisting social injustice and government-sanctioned acts against people of color. He also talked about the power of faith in giving believers a sense of redemption, renewal, and wonder. Obama rejected the more hot-tempered views of his pastor, but he came to agree with him about the wondrous power of faith.[62]

By also acknowledging that the very definition of faith meant acceptance of a set of beliefs about the core of human existence without basing it on any sense of objective or scientific truth, Obama was able to accept the teachings of religion in a way that his mother was not. Religious faith did not mean that one could not share his mother's doubts about organized religion, for faith was not doctrinaire. Faith, he argued, bonded people and gave them a sense of community. Religious doctrinism separated them.[63]

Obama espoused ideas similar to those of the social gospel at the end of the nineteenth and early twentieth centuries, which applied the teachings of the Bible to rectifying such social problems as poverty, education, poor nutrition, alcoholism, and crime. "I came to see my faith as being both a personal commitment to Christ and a commitment to my community," he stated in a speech in July. He could pray in church all he wanted, he continued, but he "wouldn't be fulfilling God's will unless [he] went out and did the Lord's work." Much to the annoyance of many of those who supported him but also believed in the total separation of church and state, he even advocated a place in the public square for religious believers. He also pledged as president to reform the Bush administration's centralized Office of Faith-Based and Community Initiatives with a more decentralized Council for Faith-Based and Neighborhood Partnerships.[64]

President-Elect Obama

In the five months between the time Obama became the presumptive Democratic nominee for president in June and the time he was elected president in November, he continued to stress the importance of building a consensus among secular liberals and religious conservatives. This was part of a larger mosaic he envisioned for the United States, which went beyond partisanship, political party, economic status, religious belief, race, or gender. [65]

His proposal to continue Bush's program of providing federal aid to faith-based initiatives was part of that vision, but it was also an indication of his growing confidence and boldness as a candidate as all the early polls showed him being slightly ahead of his presumptive Republican opponent, Senator John McCain of Arizona. A hero of the Vietnam War with a reputation for honesty and straight talk, McCain was also a maverick who was not well liked by much of the conservative base of his party even though he voted solidly along party lines on such matters as abortion, a strong military, states' rights, and tax cuts. His life story, while compelling, was well known and not as captivating as Obama's story. When speaking, he also lacked his eloquence. Because of the growing opposition of Americans to the Iraq War, which McCain supported and Obama opposed, and President Bush's unpopularity, the forthcoming election in November was shaping up to be a "wave election" for Democrats.[66]

Obama's campaign also seemed to be doing everything right. He mended relations with both Bill and Hillary Clinton. Regarded throughout the primaries as leaning politically left, he moved more to the center. He accepted the right of individuals to own handguns, moved away from total opposition to offshore drilling, and even voted for legislation permitting wiretapping for national security purposes. He also continued to outpace McCain in the amount of money he raised and the number of campaign offices he opened in targeted states like Iowa, Colorado, Florida, Virginia, New Mexico, and Nevada.[67]

As part of an effort to bolster his foreign policy bona fides, Obama traveled in July to Iraq, Afghanistan, Israel, and Europe. "I knew that if I was to earn Americans' trust on this front, I needed to speak from the most informed position possible, especially about the nation's role in Iraq and Afghanistan," he recalled. In Kabul, he met with President Hamid Karzai, whose comments about his country being on the brink of a modern, tolerant, and sufficient nation, he might have believed, he added, "were it not for reports of rampant corruption and mismanagement in his government." In Iraq he met with President Nuri al-Maliki, who seemed to endorse a proposal he made during the campaign to withdraw American troops from Iraq within sixteen months. He was also briefed by General David Petraeus, in charge of American forces, who opposed his withdrawal plan, and he found ample opportunity to be photographed eating and mingling with the troops on the ground. In Israel he was seen praying at the Wailing Wall. In Europe he was treated by its leaders almost like a head of state. In Berlin he addressed a crowd of around two hundred thousand cheering spectators. As a final reassurance to American voters about his competency to lead foreign policy, he chose as his vice presidential running mate the chairman of the Senate Foreign Relations Committee, Delaware senator Joe Biden.[68]

Realizing Obama's celebrity status worldwide and responding to growing commentary about the "inevitability" of his victory in November, the McCain campaign turned his celebrity status against him by implying that he was little different from other "celebrities" like Kim Kardashian and Paris Hilton. Like them, McCain spokesmen suggested, Obama owed his fame to the media coverage he received rather than to any major achievement he could point to other than getting himself elected to office. In contrast, McCain was a highly decorated veteran of the Vietnam War, who had served in the US Senate since 1987 and was the ranking member of the powerful Armed Services Committee.[69]

The point of the media campaign was clear. Would voters prefer an inexperienced and unaccomplished "celebrity" as president or a genuine war hero who stayed in captivity rather than leave his fellow prisoners and was serving his third term as one of the most powerful members of the US Senate? Did they want a self-consumed star with a possible messianic complex rather than a proven leader who, after being tortured in captivity, has devoted his entire life to public service? The strategy seemed to work, as charges from right-wing conspiracy theorists that Obama was a foreign-born, drug-dealing Muslim seeking to subvert the nation's democratic institutions also began to gain traction. As the late summer blitz against him continued, his lead in the polls fell.[70]

In August, the Democratic Convention in Denver went off flawlessly. Chosen by acclamation as the Democrats' nominee for president after Hillary Clinton cut short a first ballot roll call vote, Obama delivered his acceptance speech in a packed outdoor stadium, Invesco Field. Even before he began to speak, the crowd of eighty-four thousand, which had begun lining up eight hours before he spoke, was chanting, "Yes we can."[71]

In delivering his speech, the newly chosen Democratic candidate decided to make it "more prose than poetry." He wanted "a hard-hitting critique of Republican policies" and the steps he intended to "take as president—all without being too long, too dry, or too partisan." Although not as memorable oratorically as some of his earlier addresses, his forty-two-minute speech was still able to keep the gathering on its feet. Remarking that the American "promise that has always set this country apart" had been threatened by eight years of the Bush administration, he declared that the country could not tolerate the continuation of Bush's policies under a McCain administration. He also attacked McCain for voting 90 percent of the time with the Bush administration and for advocating policies, which, he said, were predicated on "that old, discredited Republican philosophy—give more to those with the most and hope that prosperity trickles down to everyone else." Instead, he pledged that his administration would strive to achieve the American promise, which, he stated, was "that through hard work and sacrifice, each of us can pursue our individual dreams but still come together to ensure that the next generation can pursue their dreams as well."[72]

The significance of Obama's speech was its emphasis on hard work and sacrifice. In talking about providing new educational opportunities for young Americans, for example, he promised to expand preschool programs, recruit more teachers, and pay them higher salaries. In contrast to proposals for free college education by more liberal members of his party, however, he emphasized parental responsibility for a child's early education and promised "affordable college education" only to those who committed themselves to serving their community or country. He also called for eliminating capital gains taxes on "small businesses and startups that will create the high-wage, high tech jobs of the future." Government, he said, "should ensure opportunity . . . for every American who's willing to work." An economy is strong, he added, "if it honors the dignity of work."[73]

As Obama neared the end of his speech, which also called for the development of renewable energy sources like wind and solar power, criticized McCain for voting in favor of the Iraq war, and described his plan for withdrawing American troops from Iraq, he invoked the words of Martin Luther King. "America, we cannot turn back," he said. "At this moment, in this election, we must pledge once more to march into the future." Following the speech, which was seen by an estimated thirty-eight million people, believed to be the most-watched convention address ever, his poll numbers rose once again.[74]

In a significant way, however, the convention played into the hands of McCain. The Democratic candidate arrived on a stage whose entrance looked like the columns of a classic Greek temple. He exited alongside Biden and their families before a raucous, banner-waving crowd as red, white, and blue fireworks lit the sky. Together the two images reinforced the Republican portrayal of the Democratic nominee as a celebrity with a godlike complex appealing to the raw emotions of an adoring audience.[75]

More important in changing the dynamic of the election was the Arizona senator's announcement, less than twelve hours after Obama gave his acceptance speech, of the little-known but controversial governor of Alaska, Sarah Palin, to be his vice presidential running mate. In selecting a forty-four-year-old Christian conservative, who described herself as a "hockey mom" and who had been governor of Alaska for only two years, McCain was gambling that her relative lack of experience in higher political office would be offset by the novelty of his selection and her personal appeal. Highly popular in her state, she was young, attractive, highly competitive (she had earned the nickname of "Sarah Barracuda" in high school), and known in Alaska for successfully challenging her own party's corrupt leadership and the state's powerful oil industry.[76]

At the Republican nominating convention, held in St. Paul, Minnesota, from September 1 through September 4, Palin delivered an acceptance speech, which eclipsed Obama's address two weeks earlier. Step-by-step, Palin appealed to the base of the Republican Party, spending much of the first part of her speech introducing her family, including a son who was about to be deployed to Iraq and her five-month-old Down syndrome boy whom she chose to bring to birth rather than have him aborted. Appealing to the pro-life and family values of the large evangelical Christian base of the party, she told a compelling story. "No family ever seems typical, and that's how it us with us," she remarked. "Our family has the same ups and downs as any other, the same challenges and the same joys. . . . And children with special needs inspire a very, very special love."[77]

Immediately after her speech, the media pointed to Palin as a rising star within the Republican Party, whom McCain had plucked from obscurity. Even liberal commentators compared her to Obama in terms of her charisma and ability to deliver a stirring speech. "She did everything, she had to do, and more," wrote Mark Halperin of *Time Magazine*, who had earlier raised doubts about her selection. "The Alaska Governor was poised, stirring, charming, confident, snarky, cozy, well-rehearsed, biting, utterly fearless, unflappable, and self-assured." "Conservatives have found their Obama," NBC political director Chuck Todd, remarked, while MSNBC's Chris Matthews called Palin "a torpedo aimed directly at the ship." Even Obama, who found her speech "incoherent" and lacking in knowledge, recognized her power as a performer.[78]

McCain's acceptance speech the next night was well crafted and delivered. Its highlight came toward its end when McCain told the story of how, during the Vietnam War, a privileged and self-centered son of a naval admiral, learned, through the adversity of being shot down, imprisoned, tortured, and saved only by the heroism of his colleagues, to place his love of country and sense of duty above all else. "I was never the same again," he remarked referring to his years of imprisonment in Vietnam. "I wasn't my own man anymore; I was my country's."[79]

In the speech, McCain was respectful of Obama, whom, he said, he admired for winning the Democratic nomination and with whom he had more in common than their differences. The Republican candidate even made many of the same pleas for change in America as Obama did, emphasizing the same values of rewarding hard work and risk-taking. "We believe in the values of families, neighborhoods . . . communities [and] personal responsibility," he added.[80] The difference between Obama and McCain, however, was that Obama's calls for change rang real while McCain's did not. In contrast to his Republican opponent, his theme of change embraced changes in public policy, such as major health reform and policies to reshape the economy, especially in the areas of energy consumption and environmental protection. By also stressing such core Republican values as hard work, personal responsibility, and tax relief for small businesses, Obama also reached out beyond the liberal base of his party to include conservative Republicans and independents of all political stripes, just as he did in his earlier speeches on race and religion.[81]

In contrast to Obama, McCain said little in his speech that deviated from traditional Republican orthodoxy. Instead of proposing a government offering the nation a bright future by helping Americans of all backgrounds who were trying to help themselves, the only change McCain seemed to offer was to turn the clock backward toward a darker past. "And let me just offer an advance warning to the old big-spending, do-nothing, me-first, country-second crowd," he said. "Change is coming."[82]

Following McCain's speech, some liberal commentators like Frank Rich of the *New York Times* noted how old the Arizona senator looked and how pedestrian were his proposals for change, calling his speech "largely a repetitive slew of stump-speech lines and worn G.O.P. orthodoxy." For the most part, though, McCain's speech was well received. Even Rich acknowledged that in his remarks the Republican candidate "reminded us of what we once liked about the guy; his aspirations to bipartisanship, his heroic service in Vietnam, his twinkle."[83]

By all measurements, including favorability rankings and press coverage, the real star of the two conventions turned out to be neither McCain nor even Obama, but Palin, who helped give McCain a bigger convention bounce than Obama received after the Democratic convention. For the first time in months, McCain jumped into a lead over his Democratic opponent as more Republicans and independents showed up at campaign offices to volunteer their services and more money was raised over the internet.[84]

Unfortunately for McCain, his bounce was short-lived. Even before the convention, reporters had begun to question Palin's qualifications and the hasty manner in which she had been selected. The *Christian Broadcasting Network* reported that Palin's husband, Todd Palin, had been arrested on a DUI charge in 1986. Beyond these issues, the fact that she had been named as McCain's running mate renewed discussion of social issues like abortion and religion that both sides had tried to avoid.[85]

As the investigators probed deeper into Palin's background, the reporting on her turned decidedly negative and public opinion began to turn against her. In October, an investigation by the Alaskan legislature determined that Palin had abused her powers by pressuring subordinates to try to get her former brother-in-law, a state trooper, fired because of a bitter divorce and custody battle with her sister. About the same time, news stories broke about how Sarah Palin had spent over $150,000 of campaign funds on her personal wardrobe. "It looks like nobody with a political antenna was working on this," said Ed Collins who had run President Ronald Reagan's reelection campaign in 1984. "It just undercuts Palin's whole image as a hockey mom."[86]

What was most damaging to Palin and the McCain campaign was a series of interviews for later viewing that Palin held with CBS broadcaster, Katie Couric, on September 24 and 25. More than any other event they exposed how ill-informed Palin was about current affairs and raised doubts about her qualifications to serve in the White House. In her response to a number of questions that should not have been hard to answer for someone who was a heartbeat away from the Oval Office, Palin gave answers that were convoluted and even incoherent. When queried, for example, about what newspapers and magazines she read, she responded, "I read most of them, again with a great appreciation for the press, for the media . . . Um all of them, any of them that have been in front of me all of these years."[87]

Criticism of the Couric interview was harsh. "Dreadful" was how Rich Lowry of the conservative *National Review* described Palin's performance. Jack Cafferty of CNN reminded his viewers that if McCain won the election, Palin would be "only one heartbeat away" from being president "and if that doesn't scare the hell out of you it should." The comedian Tina Fey mocked Palin in a widely hailed impersonation of the governor that drew millions of voters to the popular television show, *Saturday Night Live*.[88]

Throughout the remainder of the campaign, Palin retained the loyalty of the more conservative wing of the Republican Party, especially its large evangelical Christian base, a fact that deeply troubled Obama, given what he considered her total lack of qualifications to be president. Most Americans also liked her personally. But she became an increasing drag on McCain's chances to win in November. A Gallup poll taken after her one debate with her opponent, Joe Biden, on September 26 showed that while 55 percent of all voters still had a favorable opinion of her as a person, only 40 percent believed she was qualified to serve as president.[89]

As the campaign continued into October, doubts about Palin's qualifications to serve in the Oval Office grew more pronounced. Even young evangelicals grew unsure about Palin, more concerned about health care than her attacks on Obama and also objecting to the divisions they feared she was causing among Americans. In a *New York Times/CBS News* poll conducted near the end of the campaign, 59 percent of voters surveyed said Palin was not qualified to be vice president, up 9 percent since the beginning of October. Nearly a third of those polled said the vice presidential selection would be a major factor in deciding how they voted.[90]

In its final weeks, the campaign became nasty. McCain's supporters accused the media of being biased in favor of Obama. Palin brought up his troubled relationships with Jeremiah Wright, Tony Rezko, and Bill Ayers. She even accused the Democratic candidate of "palling around with terrorists," and remarked that Obama was "not the man who sees America the way you and I do." At McCain-Palin rallies Obama became the target of racial epithets as insistent shouts rang out of "Terrorist," "Kill Him," and "Off with His

Head." Right-wing conspiracy theorists raised doubts about whether he was even born in the United States and whether he had attended Harvard Law School.[91]

A scandal involving charges of voter fraud on the part of the Association of Community Organizations for Reform (ACORN) also followed the Democratic candidate through the last weeks of the campaign. A longtime target of conservatives, ACORN was eventually forced to close down because of videos showing some of its employees (subsequently fired) turned in registration forms for people who did not exist or lived outside the appropriate geographic area. Over the years, Obama had dealings with the organization, including the payment by Project Vote, which he had directed after moving to Chicago, of over $830,000 to an affiliate of ACORN for a voter registration drive aimed at minorities. As a result, Republican strategists accused him of having an "intimate relationship" with an agency engaged in voter fraud, forcing the Democratic candidate to make a statement in which he "strongly condemn[ed] voter registration fraud or any other breach of election law by any party or group."[92]

Even though the charges against Obama took their toll and most polls still showed a close race between him and McCain, there were numerous signs that the election was moving toward an Obama victory. Not only was Palin's selection as McCain's running mate hurting the Republican ticket, the Obama campaign was having success in tying the Republican candidate closely to Bush, whose popularity stood in the low twenties.[93]

A growing number of leading conservatives were also either throwing their support behind the Democrat or not endorsing McCain. "He has within him the possibility to change the direction and tone of American foreign policy, which needs changing," wrote Peggy Noonan of the *Wall Street Journal* about the Illinois senator. "His rise will serve as a practical rebuke to the past five years, which needs rebuking; his victory would provide a fresh start in a nation in which a fresh start would come as a national relief." Other conservative spokesmen who favored or endorsed him included the columnists George Will, Charles Krauthammer, and Andrew Sullivan, and the former secretary of state, Colin Powell, who called Obama a "transformational figure."[94]

What made the final difference in the election, however, was the banking and financial crisis that began in the middle of September but grew worse over the next six weeks. The reasons for the crisis are complicated, but the immediate cause was the collapse of a housing bubble that had begun several years earlier and grew worse because of easy credit, insufficient regulation, and the insertion into financial markets of creative, but complex, types of securities that were hard to understand even on Wall Street. These securities, known as derivatives, hid the severity of the crisis until the bankruptcy on September 15 of the Wall Street brokerage firm Lehman Brothers, the largest bankruptcy in the nation's history. In danger of going under next was the American International Group (AIG), a major insurance firm. It was saved only by Treasury Secretary Henry Paulson's decision to infuse $182 billion of federal funds into the firm.[95]

At first, the Democratic candidate was unaware of the dimension of the economic crisis about to hit the country. Like many Americans, he was able, after being elected to the US Senate, to sell the condo he and Michelle had purchased in 1993 for a tidy profit. Then he began to notice that many other condos in Chicago were being left unoccupied and unsold. A wealthy friend and Wall Street bond trader warned him that these "were just the start."[96]

He was made fully aware of the pending financial crisis, however, by Robert Wolf, the chairman and chief operating officer of the American division of UBS, one of the world's largest investment banks. A liberal Democrat, Wolf, who had been huddling in New York with Paulson and other bankers and policy makers, warned the candidate of a possible panic ahead. Already concerned that his campaign was being too reactive to the Republican charges being made against him, Obama decided to go on the offensive by calling for greater federal regulation of the financial markets. "I wanted people to understand that there was a precedent for bold government action. FDR had saved capitalism from itself."[97]

For the last few weeks of the campaign, when the economy was tanking, McCain fumbled the ball, leaving it to Obama to pick it up and carry it to an election night victory. Reaction of the two candidates to the downward spiraling of the economy could not have been more different. Throughout his career on Capitol Hill, McCain's interests and experience had always been in the areas of defense and foreign policy, not finance or banking. On these issues, he followed the lead of conservative colleagues in supporting free markets and deregulation. That is why his initial response to the crisis following the collapse of Lehman Brothers was his statement that "the fundamentals" of the economy were "strong."[98]

Although McCain issued a different statement the next day recognizing the gravity of the crisis facing the country, he continued to stumble. Intending to look strong and decisive, he seemed confused in his response to President Bush's proposed "Troubled Asset Relief Program" (TARP) intended to bail out the country's banks by allowing the government to buy up to $700 billion of their illiquid assets. He declared that he was suspending his campaign and would not participate in the first official debate in order to devote his entire time to the crisis. He asked Obama to do the same. He also asked President George Bush to call a meeting at the White House to include his Democratic opponent, himself, and the leaders of both political parties in the House and Senate. The Republican candidate, however, offered no proposals of his own or even articulated a governing philosophy.[99]

At the White House meeting, McCain remained largely silent, while Obama led much of the discussion that followed. Although he had also not displayed much interest in financial matters, he engaged in what amounted to a tutorial on macroeconomics after Wolf warned him of the impending crisis. He talked regularly with former top government officials in the Clinton administration, FED chairman Ben Bernanke, and even with Paulson as well as the Democratic leadership of the House and Senate. He opened the discussion at the White House by calling for greater federal financial oversight and flexibility as well as caps on executive compensation and retirement packages for top business executives, two proposals that the majority of the public favored. "I think just about everyone has agreed on these," he stated, and then jabbed at House Republicans by commenting, "I understand there are some who may not be as far along as the rest of us."[100]

Leaks from the meeting portrayed Obama as the stronger and more informed of the two candidates. Without McCain's leadership, Republicans also continued to wrangle among themselves over TARP, which failed in the House. Although many political insiders regarded McCain's announcement that he would not participate in the first official debate "a master stroke," the Democratic candidate felt otherwise. "Not only did I think that the two of us posturing in Washington would lessen rather than improve the chances of getting TARP passed, but I felt that the financial crisis made it that much more important for the debate to take place," he later commented. By stating that he would not suspend his campaign and intended to participate in the first nationally televised debate regardless of whether McCain showed up, Obama also reinforced his growing image as the more ready of the two candidates to seize the mantle of leadership. Under these circumstances McCain had no choice but to resume his campaign and participate in the first debate. In it and two other presidential debates that followed, both candidates came off well. But because McCain failed to gain any traction against Obama, they amounted to victories for the Democratic candidate.[101]

On October 13, Obama gave a major speech in which he set forth a series of long- and short-term measures to deal with the nation's economic crisis. These included tax cuts for most workers, health-care reforms, and measures to make higher education affordable for anyone attending college. He also reached out to Republicans by again emphasizing job creation and embracing tax cuts for small business. As he had throughout the campaign, he stressed hope for the future, not despair about the past. "Together, we cannot fail," he concluded. "Together, we can renew an economy that rewards work and rebuilds the middle class. . . . Together, we can change this country and change the world." [102]

Polls taken on November 4 as election day neared showed that the Iraq War and the handling of terrorism remained McCain's greatest strengths but that 51 percent of voters considered the economy the most important issue and that Obama was winning these voters by a margin of 62 to 35 percent. The same polls also showed that, by a wide margin, the same voters considered him the stronger leader of the two candidates and, by a smaller margin, the more honest and trustworthy and the one more likely to stand up to lobbyists and special interests. A composite of all the major polls made by *Real Clear Politics* on the eve of the election had Obama winning the election by 52.9 percent to McCain's 45.6 percent.[103]

Actual results on election day came close to these figures. He won 69 million votes (or 53.9 percent of the 128 million votes cast) to McCain's 59 million votes (or 46.1 percent of the total ballots). More impressive was the fact that he won over two-thirds of the electoral college (365 votes to McCain's 173). As forecast, his strength was in the Northeast, the Midwest, and the West Coast. McCain was strongest in the South, Southwest, Great Plains, and Rocky Mountain states. Except for Missouri, which he lost by less than 1 percent, Obama took most of the tossup states, again by margins of 1 percent or less, including North Carolina, Ohio, and Florida. He even won Indiana, a traditional Republican state.[104]

As it became apparent to Obama that he was about to be elected President of the United States, he was once more taken aback by the enormity of the task that lay before him. "I was contending with the likelihood that . . . it would be impossible to meet the outsized expectations now attached to me," he later wrote. "Every headline, every story, every expose" he read was "another problem for [him] to solve." He was confident of his ability to solve these problems. At the same time, he realized that he would need the help of a "cooperative Congress, willing allies, and an informed mobilized citizenry." He could not be "a solitary savior." These were the thoughts he retained even as he welcomed the news that he had been elected the nation's forty-fourth president.[105]

In postelection analyses, numerous reasons were given for Obama's victory over McCain including the large voter turnout, the size of the youth, women, and minority votes, the choice of Palin as McCain's running mate, the weakness of McCain and the strength of Obama as candidates, anti-Bush sentiment, and the onslaught of the financial crisis. While all of these explanations were valid, Obama also won the election for more fundamental reasons. As Adam Nagourney of the *New York Times* wrote on the eve of the election, the 2008 campaign represented a "sea change for politics." "To a considerable extent, Republicans and Democrats say this is a result of the way that the Obama campaign sought to understand and harness the Internet (and other forms of so-called new media) to organize supporters and to reach voters. . . . Even more crucial," Nagourney concluded, "has been Mr. Obama's success in using the Internet to build a huge network of contributors that permitted him to raise enough money. . . [to] compete in traditionally Republican states."[106]

Throughout the campaign Obama had also given hope to Americans by hammering away at his message of change and a brighter future ahead. While he offered social programs for bringing about these changes that appealed to the liberal base of the Democratic Party, he made a concerted effort to attract Republican voters by emphasizing work, personal responsibility, and tax cuts for small businesses that created jobs. For Obama, this was not just a campaign tactic. He believed deeply that Americans in need of help had to be given help. As much as possible, however, they also had to take responsibility for improving their own lives and, especially, those of their children. This was a position he would retain throughout his presidency.

CHAPTER 5

Landmark Achievement

The Affordable Care Act

Celebrations around the world greeted the news that Barack Obama had been elected the nation's forty-fourth president. In Chicago, an estimated 240,000 people poured into Grant Park, the scene of bloody rioting during the 1968 Democratic presidential convention, to watch the election results and then to cheer and hail the president-elect and his family. Jesse Jackson Sr. shed tears as he heard the news that Obama had become the nation's first Black president. Crowds large and small also gathered in cities and towns from San Francisco, Boston, and New York to Selma, Alabama; Gainesville, Florida; and Jackson, Mississippi. In each of these places, they watched together on television or on large monitors set up on the streets as the forty-seven-year-old senator from Illinois took to the stage with his family to deliver his first speech as president-elect. "It's the answer told by lines that stretched around schools and churches" to vote, they heard him say about his election. "It's the answer spoken by young and old, rich and poor, Democrat and Republican, Black, white, Hispanic, Asian, Native American, gay, straight, disabled, and not disabled," he added.[1]

Obama's call for unity and hope that transcended all the fault lines of a heterogeneous and politically divided nation resonated powerfully with broad swaths of Americans who sought an alternative to what they regarded as an administration that had falsely led the United States into war in Iraq in 2002, revealed racial blinders in responding to the catastrophic damage in New Orleans as a result of Hurricane Katrina in August 2005, and shared responsibility for a looming financial disaster in 2008.

The immediate issues facing Obama as president-elect were filling his cabinet and other high-level positions within his administration and developing his response to the rapidly deteriorating economy. Despite the vetting effort conducted by his transition team, several of his appointments to cabinet and other high-level positions were forced to withdraw their names; these failures of the vetting process left even some of his supporters wondering about his competence to be president. Notwithstanding his largely successful efforts to prevent a depression and his achievement in saving the nation's auto industry from collapse, his response to the economic crisis was also attacked from both the political right and the political left.

Once he took office, the new president sought to carry out the promise he had made throughout the campaign to provide affordable health care for every American. Aside from preventing a full-scale depression, this became his highest domestic priority. It is also became his single greatest domestic achievement.

Throughout the turmoil of his first two years in office Obama remained determined to get his proposals through Congress, both houses of which were controlled by Democrats. What was significant about this time was how he stayed true to his character and to the message he had been advocating throughout his political career. Unmoved by the attacks against him and his administration, he remained cool, dispassionate, and thoughtful. Already political commentators and others were referring to him as a pragmatic progressive. More than that, however, he remained committed to being a president healing the political wounds of the recent past by tying together liberal proposals with core conservative beliefs.

The Transition

Although Obama's inauguration was still eleven weeks away and Bush was still making important decisions about the financial crisis and the war in Iraq, the president-elect acted as if he had already taken office. If this rankled the president, he did not show it. Throughout the transition, he remained gracious, kept his successor fully informed, and welcomed his input. Obama was grateful for the courteous manner in which the Bush White House treated him. "Only once did he say something that surprised me," he later recounted about his first meeting at the White House with the outgoing president. "'The good news, Barack, is that by the time you take office we'll have taken care of the really rough stuff for you,'" Bush remarked. His comment did not comport with Obama's view of an economy worsening day by day. "For the moment, I was at a loss for words," he recalled. Finally, he merely congratulated Bush on the passage of TARP. "I saw no point in saying more," he thought to himself.[2]

Just three days after being elected and only one day after his first press conference as president-elect, Obama held the first of what became eleven weekly transition addresses to the nation in which he acted very much as if he were already speaking from the Oval Office. "We must recognize that we only have one President at a time," he said. "[Nevertheless], I want to ensure that we hit the ground running on January 20th because we don't have a moment to lose. . . . First, we need a rescue plan for the middle class that invests in immediate efforts to create jobs and provides relief to families that are watching their paychecks shrink and their life savings disappear." In his second transition address a week later, he went even further. "We must act right now. . . . If Congress does not pass an immediate plan that gives the economy the boost it needs, I will make it my first order of business as President."[3]

The progressive agenda the president laid out appealed to the liberal wing of the Democratic Party, but it had the opposite effect on conservative forces within the Republican Party. Even among independents and moderates in both parties, there was skepticism among those who wanted change but were uncertain about what kind of change beyond replacing Bush with someone else. Seeking to establish bridges between these different groups as well as reasserting his own centrist political views, Obama incorporated conservative principles into his progressive platform. Carrying out his agenda, he said, "will require not just new policies but a new spirit of service and sacrifice, where each of us resolves to pitch in and work harder and look after not only ourselves, but each other."[4]

Outgoing treasury secretary Henry ("Hank") Paulson, a strong believer in the free market, was against doing anything to prop up the existing financial structure. He and the president of the Federal Reserve Bank of New York, Timothy Geithner, concluded, nevertheless, that the big banks and investment houses were simply "too big to fail"; that if they collapsed, they would take down with them the nation's whole credit structure. The collapse of Wall Street would lead to the collapse of Main Street. Together they would set off a vicious chain reaction. Credit would freeze up. Local merchants and small manufacturers would not be able to borrow to replenish stocks and meet payrolls. The number of layoffs would grow, businesses would collapse, and stocks would decline in value. As large pension funds and individual IRAs dropped in value, retirees would face a drastic decrease in their incomes, and those intending to retire soon would have to rethink their retirement plans. Because of foreign investments in American bonds issued by these financial institutions, the crisis in the United States would spread worldwide.[5]

These were the views Obama adopted. To prevent an economic catastrophe from happening, Paulson persuaded a reluctant White House to bail out the banks through passage in October 2008 of the Troubled Assets Relief Program (TARP), which allowed the Treasury to inject up to $700 billion (divided into two "tranches" or draws) into the nation's banking system by purchasing its most troubled assets. Instinctively, the president-elect was against bailouts of this kind. He blamed the crisis on the excesses of the banking system, including the banks' willingness to make subprime loans and then to package and sell them as top rated, safe securities. Most of his advisers during the campaign, such as former treasury secretary and chairman of the Federal Reserve Bank, Paul Volker, University of Chicago professor Austan Goolsbee, and former labor secretary, Robert Reich, wanted to nationalize or break up the nation's biggest banks and financial institutions.[6]

As Obama met with Paulson and other administration officials, however, he became persuaded by their argument that allowing the existing banking structure to collapse would be economically catastrophic. As president-elect, he also grew increasingly influenced by a group of advisers from the Clinton administration, including former treasury secretary Robert Rubin, the president of the Federal Reserve Board of New York (FRBNY) Timothy Geithner, the former head of the Congressional Budget Office (CBO) Peter Orszag, and another former treasury secretary, Larry Summers. While they acknowledged the need for long-term reforms, including stress tests and larger capital requirements, they joined Paulson in emphasizing the need to save the existing banking structure through the infusion of public capital.[7]

The Democratic candidate for president forecast his plans for dealing with the financial crisis if elected to the White House in a speech he gave in the Senate on October 1 just before it approved the legislation establishing TARP. Like all Americans, he said, he was appalled that the lack of regulation of the nation's largest banks allowed the crisis to develop. It was an outrage, he added, "to every American who works hard, pays their taxes, [and] is doing their best every day to make a better life for themselves and their families." "There will be time to punish those who set this fire," he continued. But this was not the time.[8]

He acknowledged that TARP was not perfect and promised legislation that would protect the interests of taxpayers and homeowners, including a pledge that every dollar spent on saving the banks would be paid back either by future bank profits or a fee imposed on financial institutions. Then he went even further. "As soon as we pass this rescue plan," he stated, he and his colleagues had "to move aggressively with the same sense of urgency to rescue families on Main Street who are struggling to pay their bills and keep their jobs." Among the measures they needed to pass were a large stimulus package that would save one million public jobs and rebuild the nation's infrastructure. Congress also had to extend expiring unemployment benefits, give the middle class a reduction in taxes, and help homeowners stay in their homes. The government needed to tighten the regulations of the banking structure. First, however, the Senate needed to approve TARP "to prevent the possibility of a crisis turning into a catastrophe."[9]

Once President Bush signed TARP into law on October 3, Obama emphasized the other side of his proposal for preventing another depression in the United States. He even made a number of new or expanded proposals, including a new American jobs tax credit, an additional tax incentive through the following year to encourage new small business investment, elimination of all capital gains taxes on investments in small businesses and start-up companies, and an emergency fund to lend money directly to small businesses to meet payrolls or to buy inventory. "Congress should pass this emergency rescue plan as soon as possible," he remarked in a speech on October 13.[10]

Soon after the election on November 5, the president-elect announced his new economic team. In putting the team together he "decided to favor experience over fresh talent." The team included Geithner as treasury secretary, Orszag as director of the Office of Management, and Christina Romer, a highly respected economics professor at the University of California, Berkeley, as chair of the Council of Economic Advisers (CEA). Volker was named to a lesser position as chairman of the Economic Recovery Advisory Board and Goolsbee as a member of the CEA.[11]

Some progressives were disappointed by these appointments, especially those of Summers and Geithner. A brilliant economist who had served as president of Harvard University before being dismissed because of sexist remarks about women's ability in math and science, Summers was known for his arrogant and dismissive demeanor. In contrast, Geithner, who was the protégé of Robert Rubin and Summers, and spent most of his career in the treasury department before being appointed in 2003 as director of the FRBNY, was withdrawn and reticent. Both played instrumental roles in fashioning TARP.[12]

Progressives who voted for Obama but were opposed to TARP resented the fact that he seemed to be adopting the very course that Bush and Paulson had proposed and gotten through Congress with the president-elect's help. He ran in the primaries and general election as an agent of change. He portrayed both Hillary Clinton and John McCain as representing the status quo. Instead of change, he seemed to be advocating "more of the same"; instead of the break from the previous administration he promised, he appeared to be embracing its policies.[13]

These progressives were not wrong in their criticisms of the president-elect. What they failed to understand, though, was that he was never a pure ideologue. Throughout his career he came to embrace a set of core values, essential to which were the importance of community, the need for inclusion, and the uniting force of faith. He also combined a belief in such conservative values as the importance of individual responsibility, hard work, and a free market with a core progressive belief in the need of an active government to work toward a more perfect society. His ideal was that of thriving, vibrant, middle-class America.[14]

Ever since he was a community organizer in Chicago in the 1980s, Obama had grown skeptical of pure ideologues. Instead, he learned to incorporate into his own thinking, without accepting fully, the ideas of such ideologues as the advocate of community organizing, Saul Alinsky, who believed that entrenched power at the top could be toppled by organization at the bottom. Alinsky was correct, he believed, in emphasizing the importance of organizing locally to achieve a political agenda. The future president learned from his own experience in trying to organize residents of the Altgeld community in Chicago's South Side how difficult it was to organize at the bottom when faced with entrenched opposition even from those seeking similar goals (in this case, local pastors and preachers). Successful political organization, he determined, required a more nuanced and pragmatic approach than Alinsky seemed to suggest.[15]

The president-elect might still have looked more widely for his cabinet and staff had the economy been different. Deeply concerned about the crisis facing the nation, he felt he could not take chances with the appointments he made. "As steward of the economy, he would need a seasoned team prepared from day one to grapple with a financial crisis that was spiraling out of control," David Axelrod, whom he appointed as a senior adviser in the White House, later explained.[16]

Most progressives, including even those who would later become some of his harshest critics, were at first willing to go along with his new economic team. After Paulson announced that most of the $350 billion in TARP funds would be funneled to a few selected financial institutions like AIG in order to keep them from failing instead of buying out the toxic assets of smaller institutions so that they could lift the virtual freeze in lending, progressive Democrats began to speak out more forcefully against TARP. They were also incensed by the fact that only about $1 billion of TARP funds was set aside to help homeowners with subprime loans renegotiate their loans with lenders to prevent a massive wave of foreclosures.[17]

Even more disturbing to many of these same progressives was the size of the stimulus package that the incoming administration put together ($787 billion), which was far lower than what they believed was necessary. As Obama prepared to take the oath of office on January 20, the economy seemed to have collapsed. Eight million workers had lost their jobs. Unemployment had risen from 5 to 7.6 percent. The economy had contracted by 8 percent. Trillions of dollars had been lost in the stock market. Average housing prices had dropped by more than 30 percent. Estimates of the amount needed to stop the nation's economic slide and turn these figures around ranged as high as $1.2 trillion, a figure put forth by Obama's own CEA chairman, Christina Romer. He turned down the chairman's recommendation. He was persuaded by others in his administration, including Summers and Emanuel, that Congress would never pass any measure above the mid- to upper-$700 billion range, especially given the huge bailouts needed to rescue the nation's financial and banking industries. "There's no fucking way," Emanuel remarked.[18]

As many as two million people, the largest turnout for a presidential inauguration, flooded into the streets of Washington, DC, and the National Mall from the steps of the Capitol to beyond the Washington Monument. The president-elect played little role in putting together the details of his inauguration. Instead he vacationed in Hawaii, going through Toot's belongings, swimming in the ocean, enjoying time together with his half sister Maya and her family, and playing basketball with some of his old teammates from high school. He tried to pretend he was not surrounded by the new security attached to him after being elected president, including Navy Seals, and a Coast Guard cutter in the distance when he swam.[19]

Mostly, though, he thought about what was yet to come. He mixed self-confidence with uncertainty about the future. He knew that politics were not just going to be tough, they were going to be brutal. He also worried about the impact of his role as the nation's leader on his family. He was aware that Michelle's greatest concern remained that their daughters, Malia and Sasha, be able to enjoy a normal childhood. While he was more confident than she that they would be able to do so, he shared some of her worries. He was pleased, therefore, when Michelle's mother, Marian Robinson, whom he described as following a doctrine "of no fuss and no drama," agreed to live with them in order to help raise the children and be there for Michelle when he was away from the White House.[20]

The day before the inauguration, he and his family were inspired by a concert at the National Mall adjacent to the Lincoln Memorial of leading figures in the musical world. Young and old filled the two-mile Mall and sang and danced along with the music believing that a new period in American history was about to begin.[21]

Instead, Obama's speech the next day turned out to be a combination of remarks that Franklin D. Roosevelt and Ronald Reagan might have made. His theme was conquering the challenges of the present by returning to the principles of the past. "On this day," he remarked, "we gather because we have chosen hope over fear, unity of purpose over conflict and discord." At the same time, he added that the nation's problems were "parallel and proportional to the . . . unnecessary and excessive growth of government" and that only by committing to the same virtues of individual responsibility, entrepreneurship, and hard work that had sustained the nation since its establishment could America's recovery be achieved. "Our nation," he emphasized, "has never been one of short cuts or settling for less. . . . Rather, it has been the risk-takers, the doers, the maker of things—some celebrated but more often men and women obscure in their labor, who have carried us up the long, rugged path toward prosperity and freedom."[22]

His twenty-minute speech was well received nationally. Most commentators acknowledged that there were no memorable phrases in his address, such as John F. Kennedy's 1960 remark, "Ask not what the country can do for you but what you can do for the country." A few journalists went even further, saying it lacked the soaring language and inspirational tone of Obama's best speeches, such as his keynote address at the Democratic Party Convention in 2004 or his Philadelphia speech on race in the National Constitution Center in 2008. Some conservative commentators expressed anger at the lack of respect they claimed he showed for Bush, who, he suggested, had jettisoned American ideals in order to pursue security.[23]

The consensus, however, was that the speech was well delivered and motivating. "Just as he reshaped the Democratic Party to win its nomination, and the American electorate to defeat John McCain," the *New York Times* editorialized, "Mr. Obama said he intended to reshape government so it will truly serve its citizens." "It was a moment of hope," the *Washington Post* added, "because Mr. Obama sought to combine a sober acknowledgment of the perils the nation faces . . . with an unflappable assurance that they can be overcome."[24]

The First Hundred Days

Besides his economic team, Obama moved quickly after being elected president to fill other cabinet and high-level positions, a task made easier by the fact that he had begun to put together a transition team well before the election. As his chief of staff, the president-elect named Congressman Rahm Emanuel of Chicago, a close friend, who, at the time of his appointment, was serving as chairman of the Democratic caucus, but had earlier served as an assistant to the president for political affairs during the Bill Clinton administration. He was known for his hard-charging personality and frequent use of expletives. Obama later described him as "hugely ambitious, and manically driven," who was "smarter than most of his colleagues in Congress and not known for hiding it." According to the incoming president, when he asked the congressman to be his chief of staff, he responded, "No fucking way," but then relented.[25]

As his secretary of commerce, Obama named Governor Bill Richardson (D-NM), who had a long record of cabinet and sub-cabinet-level positions. In January, Richardson announced that he was withdrawing his name from further consideration after a grand jury began looking into charges that his administration had exchanged contracts in return for political donations. The next month Nancy Killefer, the president's choice for the newly established position of chief White House performance officer, and former senate majority leader Tom Daschle, one of his mentors, whom he had appointed to head the Department of Health and Human Service (HHS), also announced that they were removing their names from further consideration because of issues having to do with payment of back taxes.[26]

The withdrawal of two cabinet nominees raised issues about Obama's vetting process and forced him to make a public statement admitting his mistake. "I'm here on television saying I screwed up," he told Brian Williams of NBC's *Nightly News*. Raising even more questions about his ability to lead the nation was his response after he took office to the financial and banking crisis that seemed to get worse each day as the number of housing foreclosures, unemployed, and personal bankruptcies continued to rise. Most experts agreed on what contributed to the severity of the financial crisis, such as the housing bubble, easy credit, exotic financial instruments, and lack of regulation of the banking industry. They disagreed on what sparked the flames threatening to consume the entire economy.[27]

Liberals and progressives who had gone along with Obama's appointment of economic advisers, most of whom seemed to represent the tired economics of the Clinton administration, and supported a bank bailout, began to speak out against his rescue plan. He was also attacked by the Republican opposition on Capitol Hill. Although Democrats controlled both houses of Congress as well as the White House, in the Senate Republican minority leader Mitch McConnell made clear that he would do everything in his power, including not supporting a single measure the president proposed, to make his a failed presidency.[28]

Despite the criticisms that began to be logged at the new president from both the left and the right, he remained cool and steady as he moved quickly to direct the nation through the shoals of increasingly troubled waters. He issued a series of executive orders, the most important of which were the closing of Guantanamo Bay, which held the most dangerous members of the militant terrorist group known as Al-Qaeda, and prohibiting the use of torture against captured combatants in the Middle East. On January 24, he gave his first presidential weekly speech. Two days later he followed it up with an interview on the Arabic television station, Al Arabiya, and on February 9, he gave his first prime time press conference. Meanwhile, he ordered the first drone strikes of his presidency against terrorist leaders in the mountains of west Pakistan, and signed into law his first piece of legislation, the Lilly Ledbetter Fair Pay Act, which provided equal pay for equal work regardless of sex, race, or age. In signing the law, he thought about Toot, who never received the same salary as her male counterparts at the bank where she worked. "The legislation I was signing," the former president later recounted, "wouldn't reverse centuries of discrimination. But it was something. That's why I ran I told myself."[29]

In his weekly address and press conference, the president emphasized the same themes he had stated in his inaugural address. Both times he stressed the importance of getting his stimulus package through Congress. "We begin this year and this Administration in the midst of an unprecedented crisis that calls for unprecedented action," he began his weekly address. "What we have to do right now is to deliver for the American people," he added at his press conference. That is why he proposed his stimulus package, which could create between three and four million jobs over the next several years. He was aware of the skepticism about the size and scale of his stimulus package. In response to such concerns, he promised complete transparency in deciding where and how stimulus funds were spent. "But if we act now and act boldly," he concluded, "if we start rewarding hard work and responsibility once more" and become less partisan, "we will emerge from this trying time even stronger and more prosperous than we were before."[30]

One thing that stood out in the new president's remarks was his decision to subordinate efforts he had been making at reaching across party lines to passing his stimulus package. Since being elected president, he had met with both the House and Senate Republican caucuses, retained Robert Gates as secretary of defense, and nominated two other Republicans to his cabinet: Congressman Ray LaHood (IL) as secretary of transportation, and Senator Judd Gregg (NH) as secretary of commerce (a nomination that Gregg ultimately turned down). He even met with conservative columnists at the home of one of the most widely read and respected of these journalists, George Will. But he felt burned by Republicans who lined up solidly against his stimulus package. "I can't afford to see Congress play the usual political games," he remarked at his press conference. "Doing nothing—that's not an option from my perspective."[31]

Another aspect of Obama's press conference, which would become more apparent throughout his presidency and ultimately harm him, was his seeming inability to give short, direct answers to the questions he was asked. His well-known skills as an orator failed to translate into his dealings with the media. He was both too resolute and commanding, and too professorial and pedantic in his answers. As one journalist put it, "his answers were an oddly unexciting combination of familiar talking and wonky dissertations."[32]

Instead of reporters raising their hands and shouting to be heard as in prior presidential news conferences, Obama also prepared a list ahead of time of the journalists he called on for questions. The ones they asked were wide-ranging and included topics on foreign policy, the president's plans for the future, and his reaction to the use of steroids by professional athletes. In the one-hour conference, however, he took only thirteen questions and permitted only one follow-up. Rather than being the transparent president he promised, he seemed more of a gatekeeper, guarding against probing inquiries, and creating a gulf between himself and the reporters in charge of covering him.[33]

Peter Baker of the *New York Times* described the message the president conveyed in his press conference as "gloomy rather than inspirational." As in his campaign for president, he proved more effective in small gatherings. Both before and after his meeting with reporters, he held a series of town meetings and similar gatherings where he promoted his stimulus package and sought once again to inspire the nation with his promise of change. Wherever he went, he was met by cheering crowds often chanting "Obama, Obama." Poll numbers indicated that twice as many Americans supported Obama on the economy as they did congressional Republicans.[34]

Still the sands below Obama were shifting. The voices that began to speak out against him grew louder after he decided to extend the bailout to include the American automotive industry, recommended a stimulus package smaller than what they believed was necessary, and made clear that his first priority would not be jobs for unemployed Americans but the passage of an affordable care act.[35]

Almost as threatening to the nation's economy as its faltering financial structure was the imminent collapse of two of the nation's largest automobile manufacturers, General Motors (GM) and Chrysler, both of which were on the verge of bankruptcy. Although industry experts differed over how this happened, few disputed the fact it was the result of a number of issues, ranging from global competition, rising oil prices, the inability of consumers to take out loans, and changing consumer tastes, to listless executive leadership and too many brands, dealerships, and cars. Industry experts disagreed largely on the apportionment of blame.[36]

The collapse of these two industrial giants could mean the loss of millions of jobs in auto plants spread throughout Michigan, Ohio, and Indiana as well as job losses among their suppliers and the local economies of towns and cities dependent on them. To prevent this disaster from happening, President-Elect Obama persuaded a reluctant Bush administration to provide $17.4 billion in TARP money to keep GM and Chrysler afloat until he took office. As president, he decided to provide the two companies with a total of $80.7 billion in TARP funds, in return for the government assuming a controlling interest in GM, forcing out its CEO, Rick Wagoner, and replacing him with a group of Wall Street investment bankers led by Steven Rattner, who was soon referred to as the "czar" of the auto industry. To encourage car sales, he adopted other provisions, most notably a measure providing a subsidy to consumers who traded their gas guzzling "clunkers" for new, more fuel-efficient models.[37]

Commentators who had opposed the use of TARP funds to save the nation's largest financial institutions argued that they should be allowed to fail without further government action. They were disturbed that TARP funds were once again being used to save two more "too-big-to-fail" firms, GM and Chrysler. The administration did this first by forcing both GM and Chrysler into bankruptcy. Then it effectively nationalized GM by using TARP money to buy a controlling interest in the newly restructured firm while compelling Chrysler to be bought out by the Italian company Fiat. Many critics also objected to the administration firing Wagoner rather than leaving the decision up to GM's board of directors, as was customary.[38]

The head of the United Steelworkers, Leo Gerard, also spoke out against the lack of labor voices around the president, while the leader of the United Auto Workers (UAW), Ron Gettelfinger, protested against the concessions plant workers were forced to make, including agreeing to a two-tier system in which newer workers received drastically reduced hourly wages. Even leading Democrats from the auto-producing states, such as Representative Sandy M. Levin and his brother, Senator Carl Levin, both from Michigan, spoke out against the nationalization of GM and Chrysler, and the cutbacks being forced on them in terms of models, plant closings, and dealerships.[39]

Opinion polls also showed strong public opposition to the auto bailout. A CNN/Opinion Research Corporation Poll conducted in April found that 76 percent of respondents preferred letting GM and Chrysler go into bankruptcy rather than giving them more federal assistance. In an NBC/*Wall Street Journal* survey conducted in June, 53 percent of those polled disapproved of the government providing loans and financial assistance to Chrysler and GM, while only 28 percent approved. Other polls showed similar results.[40]

Despite the widespread opposition to the auto bailout Obama remained resolute in his decision to save GM and Chrysler. Reflecting as a former president about the lost jobs he could not save as a community organizer in Chicago's South Side, he recalled how, as president, he thought about the jobs he could save across Michigan, Indiana, and Ohio by the bailout. According to him, his "mind wander[ed] back to [his] earliest days as an organizer in Chicago, when [he'd] meet with laid-off steelworkers in cold union halls, or church basements to discuss their community concerns."[41]

Obama's determination paid dividends. The bailout lasted from December 2008 to December 2014, when the Treasury Department sold its last shares of GM's assets for a total of $70.5 billion, or a net loss of $10.2 billion. Despite the cost to the Treasury, GM and Chrysler emerged as profitable companies producing higher quality cars with better fuel efficiency, safety, and affordability than before the bailout. As a result of the changes demanded by the president, model lines were cut back, plants and dealerships were closed, and jobs were lost. Almost every economist who studied the automobile industry agreed that, absent the changes demanded by the White House, the losses in each of these categories would have been far greater than they were.[42]

In his first one hundred days in office (a benchmark used by political analysts to measure an administration's legislative success against the significant legislative accomplishments of the first one hundred days of Franklin D. Roosevelt's administration), the president had successfully pushed for legislation providing legal protection for women seeking equal pay, got Congress to pass on February 17, 2009, a $787 billion stimulus bill to promote short- and long-term economic growth (the American Recovery and Reinvestment Act or ARRA), and helped save the US automobile industry. He also helped expand health insurance for children, and, at the end of May, he nominated Sonia Sotomayor to be the first Hispanic Supreme Court justice.[43]

Passage of the Affordable Care Act

His greatest accomplishment, however, was passage in March 2010 of the Affordable Care Act (ACA), a complex piece of legislation of 2,400 pages covering virtually every aspect of health care. Its major purposes were to make health-care insurance available to every American not already covered by insurance while containing the rapidly rising costs of health delivery. Since Roosevelt's administration in the 1930s, opponents of national heath insurance had been able to fend off these efforts for universal coverage by pinning on them the label of "socialized medicine"—a system, these opponents claimed, by which the blunt force of government would be imposed upon the people without their consent.[44]

Obama was sensitive to the need to reform the nation's health system. Although the majority of Americans were already covered by health insurance (mainly through their employers, or, for those over sixty-five, by Medicare and Medicaid), over forty-six million other Americans lacked any form of health insurance, mainly because they could not afford it. Insurance companies could also deny coverage to those with preexisting conditions and apply lifelong limits on the dollar amount of health-care coverage. The total cost of health care in the United States ran between two and three times the equivalent care in other industrial countries without any evidence of a higher quality of health-care delivery. The lack of adequate health coverage was the single greatest cause of personal bankruptcy.[45]

Until Obama ran for president, he had not made the need for a comprehensive plan of national health insurance a high priority. As the media began to pay increasing attention to the problems of the nation's health system and the hardships individuals and families encountered because of the lack of health coverage, he began to focus more of his attention on developing a program of national health care.

In the spring of 2007, the candidate issued a position paper, "Barack Obama's Plan for a Healthy America," which promised to lower health-care costs while "ensuring affordable, high-quality health care for all." Included in the plan were provisions for subsidizing the insurance premiums of middle-class Americans who could not afford to pay for them and a set of provisions for modernizing the nation's health-care system. Among them were $10 billion to replace the nation's antiquated system of keeping most medical records on paper with electronic record keeping and for reimbursing physicians based on the quality of the care they provided rather than on the present system of fee-for-service.[46]

On May 29, Obama unveiled his plan in a major speech at the University of Iowa. He began by recounting the story of a small-business owner in an Iowa town who, after seventeen years, was free of cancer, but who found himself and his family on the verge of bankruptcy because of high monthly premiums. "This is not who we are," the candidate declared. "We are not a country that rewards hard work and perseverance with bankruptcies and fore-closures." Even large corporations like GM and Ford were becoming uncompetitive because they were paying far more to cover their employees than their competitors operating in countries with national health insurance.[47]

To deal with this problem, Obama outlined his plan for universal health care predicated on one first proposed by the conservative American Heritage Foundation (AHF) in 1989 as an alternative to single-payer health care. It later became the basis of Massachusetts' recently enacted statewide system of health care signed into law in 2006 by Republican governor Mitt Romney. On one crucial matter, Obama's plan was even more conservative than the AHF proposal or the Massachusetts legislation. Unlike them, his plan did not include the individual mandate, which required every American to have health-care coverage or face a penalty. He opposed the mandate believing it would be intrusive, unenforceable, and unnecessary since most individuals, young and old, would want the security provided by insurance coverage.[48]

Reminding his audience at the University of Iowa of the resistance to Medicare fifty years earlier by special interests and those fearful of big government, the president told the gathering that he expected similar resistance to his own health-care program. Just as reformers of the 1960s were able to overcome this resistance, he predicted the same would happen with health reform. "Never forget that we have it within our power to shape history in this country," he concluded. "It is not in our character to sit idly by as victims of fate or circumstance. The time has come for affordable, universal health care in America."[49]

His unveiling of his health plan marked a crucial step for him. Until he offered his plan, he was often criticized for being too inexperienced to be a serious candidate for his party's presidential nomination. The thoroughness and specificity of his plan began to deflect some of those criticisms. Because polls showed that voters ranked health care among their top concerns, it also put him in good stead with many of these voters, who may not have earlier taken his candidacy seriously.

During the primary debates, health-care reform became a major issue between Obama and Clinton. The two rivals agreed on the urgency of health reform legislation and even of the specifics of a measure, such as subsidies for middle-class families earning above the poverty level, and the so-called public option, a government-run health-care plan to compete with the private market. They disagreed, however, over whether a program of universal health care should include an individual mandate. In contrast to Obama's plan, Clinton insisted that a program of national health insurance had to include a mandate requiring most individuals to have minimally essential health insurance, just as car owners were required to purchase liability insurance. Otherwise, she maintained, those who were young and not in need of care would opt out of the insurance market, driving up the costs of health coverage for the nation's aging and sicker population that insurance carriers would still be required to cover.[50]

Next to dealing with the economic crisis facing the nation, health-care reform remained Obama's highest priority after taking office. "My interest in healthcare went beyond policy or politics," he later recalled. "Each time I met a parent struggling to come up with the money to get treatment for a sick child, I thought back to the night Michelle and I had to take a three-month-old Sasha to the emergency room for what turned out to be viral meningitis." He also thought about the costs his mother faced because of her terminal cancer. "Passing a health care bill wouldn't bring my mom back. . . . But it would save *somebody's* mom out there."[51]

For the president, expanding the nation's health system to include all Americans was more than a moral imperative: pragmatic considerations were also involved. In return for his endorsement during the primaries, he had promised Senator Ted Kennedy of Massachusetts, who was dying from inoperable brain cancer, to make it a central goal of his administration. Its achievement would also fulfill the needs and goals of a varied group of constituencies. The most obvious of these were the uninsured. They included not only the poor, but the middle class, such as small business owners, independent contractors, those with preexisting conditions, the underinsured, and those employed by businesses not offering health coverage. Through cost containment measures, Obama also sought to end the spiraling cost of health care, which was increasing at about twice the rate of inflation and threatened to hold back the nation's economic recovery.[52]

The president realized the many obstacles he would have to overcome before achieving what his predecessors had failed to accomplish. Even within his own administration he encountered strong resistance, including from his chief of staff, Rahm Emanuel. Along with other staff members, Emanuel argued that the new president's first priority should be creating jobs for the growing number of unemployed Americans through rebuilding the nation's crumbling infrastructure, which was not only needed but was also politically less risky than attempting to overhaul the nation's health system.[53]

Outside his administration, the president knew he would encounter formidable opposition from the groups vested in the existing health system—from insurance providers and pharmaceutical companies to the doctors and hospitals on the front line of health delivery. Fearing that he might propose, in lieu of the private market, a government-run health-care plan being promoted by more left-wing members of the Democratic Party, the insurance industry launched an extensive campaign against the so-called public option. Afraid that he would press for price controls on prescription drugs, the pharmaceutical companies prepared a multimillion-dollar ad campaign against the idea.[54]

In addition to opposition from within the health industry, Obama was aware that the nation's polarized political environment and escalating budget deficits also stood in the way of enacting health reform. Similarly, he knew he would encounter strong resistance from conservatives ideologically opposed to big government and from those who were satisfied with their existing health insurance. Finally, he was sensitive to the fact that in 1993 the Democratic-controlled House of Representatives had rejected reform legislation prepared by Hillary Clinton. This was, in part, because of an effective ad campaign against the act. Mostly, though, it was because of the measure's complexity and lawmakers' resentment of the fact that they had played no part in developing the legislation.[55]

The president decided, nevertheless, that the goal of making health care available to every American was too important to be replaced with less ambitious objectives, especially since the Democrats controlled the House by a comfortable margin and had the sixty votes in the Senate needed to defeat any filibustering attempt by the Republicans against health care. On February 24, 2009, he presented the outlines of his health-care proposal in his first address to Congress. The country, he said, could not afford to put health-care reform on hold. "The cost of health care has weighed down our economy and conscience long enough. So let there be no doubt, health-care reform cannot wait. It must not wait and it will not wait another year," the president concluded.[56]

On March 5, he called together representatives from the medical, hospital, pharmaceutical, and insurance companies for a well-publicized White House forum on health care. Ailing Senator Kennedy also made a surprise appearance. "The purpose of this forum," Obama stated, "is . . . to determine how we lower costs for everyone, improve quality for everyone, and expand coverage to all Americans. And our goal will be to enact comprehensive health care by the end of the year."[57]

Providing quality health care for every American, Obama warned again, was not only the right thing to do, it was necessary to save the nation's economy. "At the fiscal summit that we held here last week, the one thing that everyone agreed was the greatest threat to America's fiscal health . . . is the skyrocketing cost of health care. . . . That's why we cannot delay this discussion any longer." "That's why today's forum is so important—because health care reform is no longer just a moral imperative, it's a fiscal imperative."[58]

Instead of confronting the major interest groups within the existing health system, as had been Clinton's approach to health reform, the president (and congressional leaders) decided upon a strategy of neutralizing stakeholder opposition by working with them in developing a plan. All sectors of the health industry would have to make financial concessions, he remarked. As part of that process, he proposed a $634 million health-care reserve fund that would be paid in part by targeted cuts in payments to insurance and drug companies, doctors, hospitals, and other providers, and he vowed to fight attempts to water down the package. He made clear, however, that his purpose was not to replace the existing health system with a new one but to work within the system. He also stressed how his initiative offered health-care providers the opportunity to tap into a huge new market of individuals and families who had not been able to buy insurance or who, in the case of younger Americans, did not think they needed it.[59]

The administration's strategy of working within the health-care industry paid off. In May, the insurance companies agreed to allow greater government regulation of the industry as long as it did not include the creation of a public option. Through their representatives, other health-care sectors, like drug makers and hospitals, also gave their conditional support for more regulation of health care.[60]

In another effort to avoid the mistakes of past administrations, Obama emphasized that while he would work hard to reform health care, he would leave it to Congress to develop the plan. His roles would be advocate, lobbyist, and consultant to the lawmakers as they worked through the complexities of developing a legislative package. He would also be there to put out any brush fires that might develop along the way. Through the first six months of the struggle to gain approval of what became the Affordable Care Act (ACA), he stuck closely to this hands-off approach. In July, House Speaker Nancy Pelosi and the chairpersons of the Committees on House Ways and Means, Energy and Commerce, and Education and Labor revealed their plan for overhauling the nation's health-care system.[61]

Over the spring and summer, however, opposition to health-care reform began to harden as efforts continued on the part of the Democratic left to include in the legislation the public option. On Capitol Hill Republicans, and some Democrats, who were against the whole concept of comprehensive health insurance, spoke out against health-care reform as did Republicans who believed they were not being consulted in the legislative process. The opposition was strong enough to prevent approval of the health-care bill past the August deadline the president had set for passing the legislation.[62]

To keep up public pressure for a sweeping reform measure, the White House got the governors of several states to hold health-care forums where Obama made video appearances. The Democratic National Committee (DNC) also helped arrange house parties, rallies, and other events throughout the country and conducted an eleven-city campaign-style bus tour with a colorful bus featuring the slogan, "Health Insurance Reform Now: Let's Get It Done." As a way of striking at the home base of Obama's Republican opponent, John McCain, the bus tour began with a rally at a labor hall in Phoenix.[63]

Opposition to the legislation, even among Democrats, remained strong enough that in September, the president decided to deliver a major speech on health care before a joint session of Congress. In his address, he warned once again of the economic necessity of health-care reform and of the responsibility of government to make health care available to every American. The ACA was based on a "belief that in this country, hard work and responsibility should be rewarded by some measure of security and fair play," he said. "Put simply, our health-care problem is our deficit problem. Nothing even comes close."[64]

So poisoned was the atmosphere on Capitol Hill that when Obama said his plan would not pay for health care for illegal immigrants, Republican congressman Joe Wilson of South Carolina shouted "you lie." Not until November 7 did the House narrowly pass (219 to 212) the ACA. Only one Republican supported the measure, while thirty-four Democrats joined the rest of the Republicans in voting against it. Despite an intense lobbying effort by the insurance industry against the public option, it was included in the measure.[65]

In the Senate, the hurdles to passage of health reform legislation remained even more difficult than in the House. In September, reform legislation finally came to the floor from the Senate Finance Committee, headed by Max Baucus, a conservative Democrat from Montana. In order to prevent a Republican filibuster of the bill, Democrats needed the vote of every one of the sixty Democratic senators in the upper chamber. The problem was that even though the bill was less expansive and less expensive than the House bill, a few of them still had reservations about the measure. Two days before the Senate was to vote on the measure, the insurance industry complicated matters even more by releasing a report claiming health-care premiums would increase sharply under the bill.[66]

In order to win the votes of swaying Democrats, the White House and the Democratic leadership began making deals. "Politically and emotionally," Obama later wrote, "I would've found it a lot more satisfying to just go after the drug and insurance companies and see if we could beat them into submission. . . . But as a practical matter, it was hard to argue with Baucus's more conciliatory approach." Without the agreements, he would not get the sixty votes needed for passage of the ACA.[67]

Accordingly, the administration and leadership agreed not to support the public option if it were brought up on the floor, which pleased Senator Joe Lieberman (CT) and other conservative senators. To win the vote of Senator Evan Bayh (IN) they lowered proposed taxes on medical device makers. For Senator Mary Landrieu's (LA) vote, the administration agreed to extra Medicaid funds to correct accounting problems having to do with Hurricane Katrina.[68]

The deal for which the White House was most criticized by lawmakers and journalists was with Senator Ben Nelson, a conservative Democrat of Nebraska, who had made clear that he was going to vote against the measure unless the administration agreed to exempt his state from a provision of the bill requiring all states to pay 10 percent of the costs of an expanded Medicaid program. In what became known as "the Cornhusker Kickback," the White House caved in to Nelson's demand. Unlike the other states, where the 10 percent requirement would be phased in over a number of years, Nebraska would have the cost of its Medicaid expansion fully funded from Washington. With this and other concessions agreed to by the White House, the Senate, in a rare Christmas Eve session, passed the health-care measure on December 24 by a vote of 60 to 39.[69]

Under normal circumstances, the House and Senate would then have resolved their differences in conference committee before sending the health-care measure to President Obama for his signature. In August 2009, however,

Senator Kennedy died, and in a special election to fill his seat, Republican state senator Scott Brown, promising that he would vote against the ACA, defeated the Democratic candidate, Attorney General Martha Coakley, in this normally safe Democratic state. Since the Democrats now lacked the sixty votes necessary to defeat a Republican filibuster, it appeared to most political observers that Obama's gamble in making health care his highest domestic priority had failed.[70]

At first, the president was stunned by Scott's victory in Massachusetts. "I know that at the time, all of us felt we'd committed a colossal blunder" in making passage of the ACA the White House's highest priority, he later recounted. But after the initial shock wore off, he began a concerted effort to sell the public on the ACA. "The president said to us that he would do anything, he would call anyone, meet with anyone. He will speak anywhere. He will do whatever it takes to make the case," recalls White House Communications Director Dan Pfeiffer. In response to Republican complaints that they had been left in the dark in the development of a health-care measure and that the whole legislative process lacked transparency, the president held a summit at Blair House at the end of February, attended by leading Democrats and Republicans and carried nationally on television, to try to iron out their differences on health-care reform.[71]

Instead of resolving these differences, the forum highlighted them. When Democrats tried to make the case that the two parties were closer than they thought, Republicans countered that the gap between the two parties was too vast. Republican senator Jon Kyl (AZ) summed up the fundamental difference between the two sides: "Does Washington know best about the coverage people should have, or should people have the choice themselves." Concluding the summit, Obama observed, "Politically speaking, there may not be any reason for Republicans to want to do anything. But I thought it was worthwhile to make the effort."[72]

While the president was reaching out to the public and to Republicans, House Speaker Pelosi, a gifted politician and tactician, who was as fully committed to comprehensive reform as Obama, worked her skills on her caucus. Her strategy was to get the caucus to vote for the Senate bill without changes. The measure could then be amended in a way that would satisfy most House concerns through a budget process known as reconciliation, which allowed for no legislative debate and required only a majority vote. Only in this way, Pelosi told the Democrats, could a health reform measure win final approval on Capitol Hill.[73]

One amendment Obama made clear he would oppose was inclusion of the public option, which, he decided, would never be approved by those who feared a government takeover of the nation's health system. This was enough to keep a number of Democrats from voting for the bill, but on March 21, the House passed the Senate measure by the barest possible majority (219 to 212) with thirty-four Democrats and all Republicans voting against it. At a White House ceremony in the Oval Office two days later, the president signed the ACA into law. "What had happened . . . wasn't just Barack Obama talking to the American people about health care," explained Nancy-Ann DeParle, the president's Health Reform Director. "It was also the Democratic House and Senate becoming a team, as opposed to the House versus the Senate, which is basically what it had been for the last year."[74]

Throughout the legislative process, Pelosi had resented the pressure Obama had placed on her. She was angry with the White House for not having consulted more with the House leadership. Her relationship with Senate Majority Leader Harry Reid of Nevada was also strained. Pelosi objected to what she regarded as Reid's arrogant disregard of the House and of her unique problems in trying to maintain unity among her caucus of 257 disparate Democrats.[75]

That said, Pelosi and Obama had found a way to pass a landmark piece of legislation establishing a national health insurance framework. The measure promised to make affordable health care available to all Americans while also improving the quality and reducing the costs of the nation's health-care system. While the ACA touched on virtually every facet of the nation's health-care system, its most immediate benefits for most Americans included subsidies for the uninsured so that they could buy insurance in competitive state exchanges (or a federal exchange for those living in states without exchanges). Insurers would also have to cover all Americans regardless of preconditions and without caps on the amount of their coverage. In addition, the measure provided funds to expand state-run Medicaid programs for the states' most indigent populations and extended family coverage to include young adults under the age of 26. To offset the costs of expanded coverage, all Americans would be required to have health coverage (the individual mandate) or pay a fine that could amount by 2017 to 2.5 percent of their taxable income.[76]

What is almost as significant as the ACA itself was how conservative it was, having been built on the conservative principles of the American Heritage Foundation and implemented in Massachusetts by a Republican governor. Instead of seeking to replace the privately structured health system in the United States, the president sought to reform it. Instead of launching a broadside against the health industry, he sought to work with it. Throughout the struggle over reform, Obama also acted pragmatically even as he sought to combine conservative principles with progressive values. At first he rejected the individual mandate. While he initially supported a public option, he withdrew his backing for it when he realized the strong opposition against it. While he believed in the moral imperative of health-care reform, he also emphasized its economic necessity as a way of dealing with the fiscal crisis he faced when he took office.

Finally, the president's image of Americans who deserved health-care coverage was one of an aspiring or hardworking middle class, many of whom were small businesspeople or entrepreneurs, trying to live the American dream but stricken with medical hardships and unable to afford insurance. His vision of health reform was consistent with his overall political philosophy predicated as it was on a combination of pragmatism, on the one hand, and progressivism and conservatism, on the other.

CHAPTER 6

Quest for a Common Purpose

Although the Obama administration managed to pass the Affordable Care Act (ACA) resulting in the largest expansion of health insurance in the nation's history, the legislation became the single most unpopular measure of his administration. Instead of being widely hailed in the country as a historic achievement standing alongside Social Security and Medicare and Medicaid as one of the four most important pieces of social welfare legislation in the nation's history, the ACA met a frosty reception by the American public. It also became the target of repeated attacks by Republicans and conservative groups throughout the country who were determined to repeal what they derisively called "Obamacare."[1]

Obama's $787 billion stimulus package, the American Recovery and Reinvestment Act of 2009 (ARRA), also received a harsh public reception. Although the legislation achieved much of what it set out to accomplish, it, too, became a target of outrage both from the political left, who felt the measure was not as large or as effective as it should have been, and from the political right, who highlighted it as an example of wasteful government intrusion into the economy and of an inefficient and bloated federal bureaucracy. Part of the problem was poor communication and messaging on the part of the White House. More important was widespread concern about the activism of the Obama presidency.

Instead of making any midcourse changes, the president remained committed to the fundamental policies he had outlined both before and after he became president. Rather than bowing to ideological appeals, he explained to the people of the United States that what he offered them was reform based on deeply held American values rather than drastic change.

Obama's foreign policy was an extension of his domestic policy. Still promoting a multicultural, multiethnic, and multiracial world, he advocated a world order that restrained authoritarianism, brought democratic accountability to global capitalism, tackled the ever-present danger of nuclear proliferation, and confronted other transnational challenges, such as climate change. Unfortunately for the president, the American people did not buy his message. Instead, many of them joined into a political movement known as the Tea Party. In the 2010 off-year elections, the movement helped to inflict huge losses on the Democrats.

The Tea Party

Fearing what they regarded as a massive expansion of the federal government, groups of conservatives bonded together in associations to defeat liberal officeholders. Although the groups were loosely organized, ranged in degree of their conservatism, and lacked any central leadership, they built upon a political base going back at least to the election of Ronald Reagan in 1980.[2]

In 1984, David Koch and his brother, Charles G. Koch, two conservative billionaires, established *Citizens for a Sound Economy* (CSE), a political group committed to "less government, lower taxes, and less regulations." In February 2009, an arm of CSE, *FreedomWorks*, organized a protest against President Barack Obama, who was holding a town hall on his stimulus bill. Less than a dozen people showed up at the protest, where they decried government waste and "Obama's socialism." The next week, one hundred people in Seattle protested against the "pork" in the stimulus package. On February 19, 2009, CNBC's news editor, Rick Santelli, called on his viewers to come to Chicago in July for a "Tea Party" to protest the government's mortgage lending policies. This was the origin of what became the Tea Party movement. Later, Obama referred to Santelli's remarks as "bull shit." "It was hard for me not to dismiss the whole thing for what it was: a mildly entertaining shtick intended not to inform but to fill airtime, sell adds, and make the viewers [of his show] feel like they were real insiders."[3]

Encouraged by such conservative commentators and organizations as the right-wing conspiracy theorist, Glenn Beck, and Oath Keepers, a new player in a resurgent militia movement, Tea Party protestors organized into groups that included not only militia types but libertarians, anti-immigration advocates, and those who argued for the abolition of the Federal Reserve, which they considered a plaything of big banks. In their view, President Obama and his predecessors sought to undermine the Constitution and free enterprise for the benefit of an elitist, international, cabal.[4]

There was also a significant element of racism among the promoters of the Tea Party, such as when Beck famously stated that the president had "a deep-seated hatred for white people [and] the white culture" or when Richard Butler, the leader of the Aryan Nations, preached white separatism from his compound in Idaho, and his followers showed up at Tea Party gatherings. At these events, attended by mostly Caucasians, crude depictions were shown of Obama as an African witch doctor and signs labeled him a terrorist. Civil rights leaders worried about the coincidence of the nation's first Black president and the return of racist rhetoric and violence.[5]

Often led by political neophytes, much of the Tea Party support came from those who were badly affected by the recession, including many who had lost their jobs, had their homes foreclosed, or witnessed the depletion of their retirement funds. Influenced by Beck and other conspiratorialists, they accepted as gospel exposes on the Federal Reserve, and read the work of George Orwell and Ayn Rand, both of whom wrote about the dangers of omniscient government. A popular T-shirt at Tea Party rallies read "Proud Right-Wing Extremists."[6]

At first, Obama responded to the Tea Party movement by ignoring it, not only because David Axelrod made clear to him that white voters responded "poorly to lectures about race," but because he did not believe "as a matter of principle" that "a president should ever publicly whine about criticisms from voters." To the contrary, he soon made clear that he shared the concerns of the protesters on such matters as budget deficits and the extension of government authority in a free market economy. In an interview on NBC's *Today* show, he remarked that while the movement was "still a loose amalgam of forces," including those "who weren't sure" whether he was born in the United States or was a socialist, there was a "broader circle around that core group of people who [were] legitimately concerned about the deficit," and who were "legitimately concerned that the federal government may be taking on too much." "And so," he concluded, "I wouldn't paint in broad brush and say that, you know, everybody who's involved or have gone to a tea party rally or a meeting are somehow on the fringe. Some of them, I think, have some mainstream legitimate concerns."[7]

At the same time, the president went on the attack. He welcomed journalists to the White House, made television appearances on late nighttime shows, and held a series of town meetings in which he defended his policies and condemned the Tea Party movement.[8] Their extremist beliefs in internal conspiracies and international cabals and the overt racism of some of them put the movement beyond the pale, he stated. At a White House dinner in May 2010, he added that there was a "subterranean agenda" in the anti-Obama movement that was racial. There was nothing he could do about that except to be as effective and empathetic a president as he could be. He was the president of all Americans, not just Black ones, he emphasized. His agenda was not a Black agenda but an agenda for all Americans.[9]

The president's rejection of extremism of any kind cost the Democrats heavily in public opinion polls and revealed the racism of many of those participating in Tea Party rallies. One poll in January found that while 96 percent of African Americans still approved of the president's job performance, the percent among whites had dropped from 62 percent the previous April to 44 percent at the beginning of the new year. Another poll in the spring found that 48 percent of voters believed that Tea Party members were closer to their views than the president. Even independents preferred the Tea Party over Obama by 50 to 38 percent.[10]

Making matters worse for the president was the fact the economy continued to hemorrhage jobs. Obama's message that it would take time for the economy to turn around failed to resonate with the voters. Democrats appeared to an increasing number of Americans as members of a party whose constituency differed only to the degree they wanted to expand government power. The worst purveyor of bloated government was the president.[11]

Even those who had backed the president in 2008 began to question his policies. In a town hall meeting in September 2010, just two months before the congressional elections, he confronted a barrage of questions from these disillusioned backers. "I've been told that I voted for a man who was going to change things in a meaningful way for the middle class," one African American woman, remarked, "and I'm waiting sir, I'm waiting."[12]

Part of Obama's problem could be explained by the numbers, as the figures of those unemployed continued to mount and remained high. In January 2009 the unemployment rate was 7.8 percent. In January 2010, it stood at 9.8 percent. Although this was down from 10 percent in October 2009, it was still considerably higher than when Obama took office.[13]

The president insisted that his stimulus package was already beginning to turn the economy around and was actually growing jobs, such as by giving states and local communities the funds to retain and hire teachers, police officers, and other public workers. He also argued that without the package, more Americans would have been unemployed and the nation would have gone from recession into a depression similar to the Great Depression of 1932.[14]

By saving the big banks and the major auto companies and by gaining legislative approval of the largest stimulus package and the most far-reaching overhaul of the nation's health system in the nation's history, however, the president became the perfect foil of the antiestablishment protestors, who accused him of being a would-be despot. What he advocated was not an agenda for all Americans, they maintained, but one for the corporate world or, just the opposite, a socialist agenda that threatened the nation's core belief in free enterprise.[15]

In reality, Obama continued to advocate a form of marketplace consumerism. In the same town hall meeting in September carried by CNBC, the president repeated much of what he had been saying throughout the first eighteen months of his presidency, telling his critics he favored free enterprise and free markets. He was in favor of limits on the role of government and on government spending. "We've always had a healthy skepticism about government, and I think that is a good thing," he said. "I think there's also a noble tradition . . . of saying that government should pay its way."[16]

Turning to the Tea Party, the president remarked once again that while he understood many of the movement's grievances, protesters running for office were obligated to identify what cuts in government spending they would make. "I think it's important for you to say, 'I'm willing to cut veteran's benefits, or I'm willing to cut Medicare or Social Security benefits, or I'm willing to see these taxes go up. What you can't do . . . is saying [sic] we're going to control government spending."[17]

Unfortunately for Obama, he was unsuccessful in moving hearts and changing minds. One poll after another showed double digit gaps between those intending to vote Republican and those planning to vote Democratic. Much of the excitement prior to the 2010 elections came from the Tea Party movement's efforts to get the Republican candidates they had backed in the primaries elected to Congress. Sensing what was happening in the country, the White House blamed the media for what it considered its over-coverage of the Tea Party protestors.[18]

Foreign Policy

Clearly the president was troubled by the development of the Tea Party movement, but he was also concerned about the US standing in the world and what he considered the misguided foreign policy of the Bush administration. Following the terrorist attacks of September 11, 2001 (9/11), Bush declared a war on terrorism and announced that "either you're with us or you're with the terrorists." His policy of militant unilateralism and the fact that the United States was widely blamed for the worldwide economic recession led to a wave of anti-American sentiment even among America's closest allies.[19]

In place of Bush's foreign policy, the newly sworn-in president called in his inaugural address for multilateral cooperation and mutual understanding. He sought to fulfill a promise he made during the campaign "to build bridges across the globe." The dilemma he faced was that he inherited from Bush an unpopular six-year-old war in Iraq and another eight-year-old one in Afghanistan. The imperatives of being a wartime president led him to adopt policies similar to those of the Bush administration.[20]

In April, Obama made the first of three trips overseas in 2009 that took him to Europe, the Middle East, and the Far East. In each of his visits, the president made clear to foreign leaders that he sought to change the direction of American foreign policy as he promised in his inaugural address. In his first trip, the president traveled to London for the second meeting of the G20 nations and then to Strasbourg, on the French-German border, to attend a NATO summit meeting. Afterward he traveled to the Czech Republic, where he met with the country's prime minister, Vaclar Klaus, and delivered a major address in historic Hradcany Square in Prague. This was followed by stops in Turkey, where he conferred with its prime minister, Recep Tayyip Erdogan, and Iraq, where he held talks with its president, Jalal Talabani, and its prime minister, Nouri al-Maliki.

When Obama went to Europe, there were 161,000 American troops in Iraq and another 38,000 in Afghanistan. A few weeks before he left office, Bush ordered 12,000 more troops to Afghanistan to provide security for elections scheduled to be held later in 2009. Convinced the war in Iraq was a terrible mistake, Obama had drawn up a plan during the campaign to withdraw American combat forces from Iraq within eighteen months after he took office. While in Iraq he presented the plan to General David Petraeus, the commander of American forces in Iraq, who had carried out a successful military surge against Sunni insurgents in the western province of Al Anbar, where some of the most difficult fighting of the war had taken place.[21]

Afghanistan was an entirely different matter for Obama. In the mountainous regions of southwest Afghanistan and northeast Pakistan, the Taliban and Al-Qaeda operated freely, and the leader of Al-Qaeda responsible for 9/11, Osama bin Laden, was believed to be hiding. What concerned the president was not just the stability of the Afghan government and the terrorist threat Al-Qaeda posed throughout the world, but the instability of Pakistan. His worst nightmare was one in which the Taliban succeeded in overthrowing the Islamabad government, thereby gaining access to the country's nuclear arsenal. He was determined not to allow this to happen.[22]

During the campaign, the Democratic candidate had promised to remedy what he considered the inadequate resourcing of the war in Afghanistan during the Bush administration by sending additional troops to the country. Shortly after taking office, he ordered a two-month review of America's Afghan policy. In the interim, the president approved an additional 17,000 combat forces to the 12,000 that Bush had committed to the Afghan conflict.[23]

The administration was divided over the issue of what policy to pursue in Afghanistan. Vice President Joe Biden, whom the president sent to Pakistan and Afghanistan shortly before he assumed office, argued that the United States should withdraw from what he believed was a hopeless quagmire in which a volatile and untrustworthy leader, Hamid Karzai, was unable to control the country outside the capital. Instead, he favored a policy of counterterrorism involving strikes by drones (unmanned aerial vehicles used by the military to target and kill enemy combatants) and combat missions against Taliban and Al-Qaeda leaders. In contrast, Defense Secretary Bob Gates and Secretary of State Hillary Clinton favored a more robust policy of counterinsurgency involving winning the support of the Afghan and Pakistani people by assuring their safety and security through a larger NATO presence in Afghanistan.[24]

Listening to both sides, the president agreed with his two secretaries. After the review was completed in March, he set out a new strategy for Afghanistan aimed at strengthening the government in Kabul and eradicating the Taliban and Al-Qaeda elements in their mountainous strongholds by adding 4,000 trainers for Afghan security forces to the 17,000 combat forces he had already approved for a total almost twice the size of Bush's commitment. He also doubled the number of drone attacks Bush had ordered against Al-Qaeda targets on Pakistan's side of the border with Afghanistan. "I want the American people to understand that we have a clear and focused goal: to disrupt, dismantle, and defeat al Qaeda in Pakistan and Afghanistan," he said in a televised speech on March 27. He looked to his NATO allies, who had sent their own forces to Afghanistan after 9/11, to increase their commitments.[25]

The tension between what the president regarded as his responsibilities as a wartime president and his liberal values was palpable. At the meeting in London, the president sought to reach a final agreement with the G20 nations that would coordinate their economic recovery while getting them to work together to assist the world's poorest nations. At Strasbourg's town hall, he tried to reassure US allies that he hoped to "renew" Washington's partnership with them. "America is changing," he said, "but it cannot be America alone that changes. We are confronting the greatest economic crisis since World War II. The only way to confront this unprecedented crisis is through unprecedented coordination."[26]

In his speech at Hradcany Square in Prague, the president emphasized the need to prevent nuclear proliferation and warned specifically of the danger of nuclear weapons falling into the hands of terrorist groups. Over the years he had come to believe that the spread of nuclear weapons posed the greatest threat to national and world security. He could not understand why world leaders did not take the issue more seriously. One way to harness the threat, he told the massive crowd assembled in the square, was to "build a new framework for civil nuclear cooperation."[27]

In Turkey, a majority-Muslim nation, tensions ran high with the Ankara government because of what Turkish leaders believed was anti-Muslim sentiment in Washington. In a speech to the Turkish parliament, Obama stressed the point that his administration respected all religious faiths and that he regarded Turkey as an indispensable partner in fighting the war against terrorism. He also expressed his support for Turkey becoming a member of the European Union. Then he went a step further. "I also want to make clear that America's relationship with the Muslim community, the Muslim world, cannot and will not, just be based upon opposition to terrorism," he said. "We seek broader engagement based on mutual interest and mutual respect."[28]

Obama's efforts to replace Bush's unilateralism with multilateralism had mixed results. In London, the G20 leaders agreed to commit $1.1 trillion in additional loans and guarantees to bail out troubled countries. While a significant achievement, it fell short of the more direct and larger stimulus measures the president wanted. France and Germany also resisted his pressure to boost their economies with big, coordinated stimulus packages, proposing instead tighter regulation of financial markets. France was also reluctant to reduce its nuclear program. An internal memo leaked to the press said his speech in Prague was mainly aimed at "improving America's image."[29]

Overshadowing the president's European trip was the war in Afghanistan. At the same town hall meeting in Strasbourg in which he offered a new partnership with Europe, he made clear that he expected NATO members to step up their commitments in Afghanistan. "I think it is important for Europe to understand," he told them, "that even though I'm now President and George Bush is no longer President, al Qaeda is still a threat, and that we cannot pretend somehow that because Barack Hussein Obama got elected as President, suddenly everything is going to be okay."[30]

Obama was, in other words, accelerating, not rejecting, Bush's policy toward Afghanistan even as he rejected his predecessor's militant unilateralism. He wanted Afghanistan to be NATO's main mission. Faced with mounting casualties in a seemingly intractable war and an economic recession and widespread opposition to the war at home, NATO members were reluctant to make that commitment They were willing to make Afghanistan a strategic goal of NATO, but not its main mission. They also agreed to increase the size of their forces in Afghanistan, but not to the level Obama wanted. Instead of combat roles, they also expected to employ their additional ground troops in noncombatant functions such as advising and training Afghan troops.[31]

While abroad, Obama made clear in his meetings with foreign leaders that his highest priorities remained the domestic economy and getting his legislative agenda through Congress. Returning home, he concentrated on these matters, saying so little publicly about the war that some journalists commented on his commitment to the conflict. Yet he never put building new bridges abroad or confronting the wars in Iraq and Afghanistan on the back burner. To the contrary, he went forward with his plan to withdraw most American combat forces from Iraq.[32]

An essential question continued to trouble the president. As he asked one of his advisers: "If this doesn't work then what?" He was especially worried about developments in Pakistan, where Taliban fighters attacked Pakistani outposts within an hour's drive of Islamabad, virtually paralyzing the Pakistani government. When asked by his friend and former colleague in the Senate, Dick Durbin, how things were going, he responded that he had to deal with a lot of issues at once, but that the one thing that kept him "awake at night [was] Pakistan." He grew impatient at the news that the additional troops he had approved for Afghanistan would not arrive in the country for at least six months.[33]

In June, the president traveled to the Middle East where he met King Abdullah of Saudi Arabia before going on to Egypt where he delivered a highly billed address, "A New Beginning," before a crowd of three thousand at Cairo University. He decided to make the speech as a way of letting the Muslim world know that he wanted to make a clean break from the Bush administration policy in the Middle East. He also told one of his speechwriters, Ben Rhodes, that he wanted the speech's focus to be "less about outlining new policies and more geared toward helping the two sides understand each other." He chose Cairo to deliver the speech because it was historically and geographically at the center of the Arab world. In preparing his message, he consulted with Islamic religious leaders, other experts on Islamic history and culture, and Islamic business leaders in the United States. He also sought out Jews and people of other faiths and experts from academia.[34]

As in all his speeches, Obama spent much time thinking about what he wanted to say. He wrote many of its key sentences and paragraphs himself. Because he regarded his speech as his most important statement on foreign policy since assuming office and wanted to attract worldwide interest in what he was about to say, he had his administration leak key portions of his message to the press. In it, he committed the United States to a policy responsive to regional needs and aspirations. In language almost identical to what he said in his inaugural address and in his first interview with Al Arabiya a week later, he remarked that he had come "to Cairo to seek a new beginning between the United States and Muslims around the world, one based on mutual interest and mutual respect."[35]

In his fifty-five-minute address, the longest he delivered since becoming president, he made flattering remarks about Islam's contribution to civilization, stretching from algebra to poetry. He also acknowledged US complicity in overthrowing the democratically elected government in Iran in 1953. At the same time, he criticized Iran's ambition to be a nuclear power at a time when he considered nuclear proliferation to be one of the greatest threats to world peace and envisioned a nuclear-free future. He sought a new dialogue with Iran, he said, and acknowledged that, like any other nation, Iran should have the right to peaceful nuclear power. First, though, Tehran needed to comply with its responsibilities under the Nuclear Non-Proliferation Treaty, which gave the nuclear watchdog the right to conduct snap inspections of its nuclear facilities. Iran had signed the agreement in 2003 as a way of disproving US claims that it had a secret bomb program.[36]

The longest part of Obama's speech was a candid assessment of the Israeli-Palestinian conflict. He defended passionately the Jewish right to a homeland, blamed the Palestinians for their acts of violence against Israel, and condemned Muslim anti-Semitism and Holocaust denial. In the same paragraphs, he also called for a Palestinian state and criticized Israeli settlements on the West Bank, which, he said, "violates previous agreements and undermines efforts to achieve peace" between Israel and the Arab world. "Progress in the daily lives of the Palestinian people," he said, "must be a critical part of a road to peace."[37]

During his address, the president addressed a host of other issues ranging from women's rights and human rights to religious freedom and economic opportunity, all of which he supported. "No system of government," he acknowledged, "can or should be imposed by any other." But he had "an unyielding belief" that all people yearned for such things as freedom of expression, confidence in the rule of law and the equal administration of justice, and the freedom to live as one chooses. "These are not just American ideas," he concluded, "they are human rights. And that is why we will support them everywhere."[38]

His speech was carried live on state-run television. Most of those who commented on it welcomed it. Daoud Kuttab, a Palestinian journalist and critic of the president, wrote that he "clearly won over the hearts and minds of many people, who have so far rejected America, by being empathetic—warm but honest." As Arab and Israeli leaders and commentators in the United States pointed out, however, Obama spoke in platitudes and generalities rather than offering specific recommendations that might have persuaded the Arab world that he had really turned a new leaf in US-Arab relations.[39]

One issue the president mentioned in his address that commentators largely ignored was his ongoing concern about Pakistani instability and the danger of nuclear weapons falling into the hands of terrorists. He would, he said, "gladly bring every single one of our troops home [from Afghanistan] if we could be confident that there were not violent extremists in Afghanistan and now Pakistan determined to kill as many Americans as they can. But that is not yet the case." As he all but acknowledged, there was simply no detailed strategy for keeping the Pakistani government intact.[40]

Over the summer and fall, Obama was pressed by his military commanders to increase the number of American ground forces in Afghanistan by another 40,000 troops. The president was skeptical about the need for such a large deployment, especially on the heels of the additional 30,000 troops he had already committed. He and his advisers had read a number of books on the Vietnam War, which described how little White House scrutiny there had been of military requests for additional troops to fight the war. Not enough attention had been paid during the conflict to such basic questions as how the additional troops would be used, where they would be deployed, for how long, or even what constituted victory in Vietnam. Obama was determined not to repeat the mistakes of the past. He also believed, correctly, that his commanders were trying to box him into supporting a longer and more sustained conflict than he intended.[41]

Weary of the military, the president ordered in September a three-month review of war strategy, including a province-by-province assessment of Taliban strength, the effectiveness of the local leadership, and a determination of how quickly American forces could leave certain provinces. Obama participated actively in the review. By all accounts, he was a tough interrogator of the military asking them thoughtful, detailed, and specific questions. In

October, he told the Joint Chiefs of Staff that he did not intend to make an open-ended commitment in Afghanistan.[42]

At the beginning of October, the president received notice from the Norwegian Nobel Committee that it was awarding him the Nobel Peace Prize for 2009. In announcing the award, the committee said it had selected the president for the prize because "of his extraordinary efforts to strengthen international diplomacy and cooperation between people." The panel's decision surprised the world. Many journalists asked how the panel could give the award to a president who had been in office for only six weeks when nominations for the award were closed and who had accomplished so little in enhancing world peace compared to other persons whose names had been floated as deserving of the prize.[43]

No one was more surprised than Obama when he learned he was receiving the world's most prestigious award. "To be honest, I do not feel that I deserve to be in the company of so many of the transformative figures who've been honored by this prize," he remarked in a brief statement to the press corps in the White House Rose Garden. He went on to say that he would accept the prize as a "call to action." Walking back to the Oval Office, he later recalled thinking to himself, about "the widening gap between the expectations and the realities of my presidency. . . . October would become the deadliest month for U.S. Troops in Afghanistan. . . . And rather than ushering in a new era of peace, I was facing the prospect of committing more soldiers to war."[44]

In November, the president made the third of his trips abroad, this time to the Far East. In Japan, he delivered a major address on Asia's relationship with the United States. Then he went to Singapore to attend the Asian-Pacific Economic Cooperation (APEC) economic summit. On the third, and most important, leg of his trip, he traveled to China, where he met with Chinese president Hu Jintao, and premier Wen Jiaboa, in an effort to bridge major differences between their two countries and to seek China's assistance in persuading Iran and North Korea to give up their efforts at developing nuclear weapons. The president ended his eight-day trip with a ceremonial visit to Seoul, where he met with South Korean president Lee Myung-bak.[45]

In his speech in Japan, the president sought to revitalize US-Japanese relations, which had been strained for some time because of the US military presence in Okinawa and became even more tense as a result of an impending decision to build a new airstrip for the US Marines stationed there. Speaking in Tokyo, the president tried to frame US-Japanese relations within the broader context of Washington's relations with all Asian-Pacific nations. While Washington's ties to the region begin with Japan, he said, "it doesn't end here." Although the United States may have started as a group of ports and cities along the Atlantic Ocean, "for generations we have also been a nation of the Pacific. Asia and the United States are not separated by this great ocean: we are bound by it." Obama also tried to show that he was more in line with Asian interests than his predecessors, even calling himself "America's first Pacific President" because of his upbringing in Hawaii and Indonesia.[46]

In traveling to Singapore, he emphasized the point that the United States' interests in Asia extended beyond the traditional American focus on North East Asia. Despite a population of six hundred million, some of the world's most thriving economies, and its location on the strategic crossroads between China and India, Southeast Asia had been largely overlooked by the Bush administration. He wanted to change that. Earlier he had sent Secretary of State Clinton to Indonesia where she acceded to the ASEAN (Association of Southeast Asian Nations) Treaty of Amity and Cooperation, and he also appointed the first US ambassador to ASEAN.[47]

One issue of major concern to Obama that he took up in Singapore was climate change: his belief that the use of carbon-based fuels, specifically coal and oil, were destroying the climate in ways already visible in global warming and major changes in weather patterns. In his speech following his election as president, he vowed that his would be the administration "when the rise of oceans began to slow and our planet began to heal." As president, he made dealing with global warming one of his administration's goals. He sought to replace fossil fuels with climate-friendly energy sources like solar panels and wind turbines, which were becoming increasingly competitive with oil and coal.[48]

On the day after arriving in Singapore, Obama attended a breakfast meeting on climate change that attempted to lower expectations for a global summit in Copenhagen the following month. Talks ahead of the summit had not gone well enough to anticipate any major breakthrough, Danish prime minister Lars Lorke Rasmussen told those at the breakfast. Afterward, the president and other leaders announced that a binding climate-change agreement could not be negotiated in time for the Copenhagen meeting. Nevertheless, he continued to press the issue of cooperation on climate change.[49]

At the ASEAN summit, Obama was greeted with a flurry of complaints about US trade policies. Mexican president Felipe Calderon was the bluntest in his remarks, accusing the United States of moving "in the opposite sense of free trade." The president tried to allay these fears, stating that the United States would "engage" in a free-trade Trans-Pacific Partnership, but without a full trade policy, this failed to diminish the concerns of the ASEAN members.[50]

From Singapore, Obama traveled to Beijing for talks with President Hu and Premier Wang. The administration had been preparing for months for the president's visit to China, the most important leg of his trip to Asia. It even delayed a scheduled visit in late October from the Dalai Lama, the spiritual leader of Tibet, which Beijing had forcibly incorporated as part of China, knowing that such a meeting would provoke the Chinese government. It also deferred a decision on arms sales to Taiwan.[51]

In contrast to previous administrations, which pushed China to follow the Western model of governance, the president sought to strike a more conciliatory policy toward China that recognized its status as one of the world's leading powers and the largest foreign lender to the United States. Instead of prodding China, he sought to reassure it. His aim was to align the government more closely to the United States on matters ranging from currency reform to encouraging Iran and North Korea to give up their nuclear weapons programs.[52]

Obama spent three days in China. Following six hours of meetings with President Hu and two state dinners, he held a town hall meeting in Shanghai, visited historic landmarks, and issued a joint statement with the Chinese leader. Afterward, he left for Seoul for a brief visit before returning to Washington. As critics later pointed out, the Chinese tightly controlled every aspect of the president's visit. The administration wanted, for example, an audience of 1,500 at the town hall meeting, but the Chinese restricted it to 500, and they handpicked the audience.[53]

The Chinese also resisted most of the administration's wish list for the visit. These included support for tougher sanctions against Iran and North Korea if they failed to curb their nuclear programs, revising China's policy of currency manipulation, and reaching agreement on climate change. Instead, the Chinese managed to shift public discussion from the global risks posed by China's currency policy to the dangers of loose monetary policy and protectionist tendencies in the United States. In the news conference that followed the end of his talks with Obama, President Hu did not allow any questions and candidly acknowledged that Beijing and Washington "have differences." As one critic described the president's visit to China, "Lots of talk, little action—just the way the Chinese like it."[54]

What most of these critics ignored was that his purpose in visiting China was not to pressure the Chinese on issues that divided their two countries, but to place them within the broader context of replacing confrontation with cooperation. Past American leaders had usually insisted in advance on some concrete development from their visits abroad. This was not Obama's intention. As Richard C. Bush of the Brookings Institution pointed out, it was "not useful to assess President Obama's trip according to goals he didn't set for himself. . . . Among other things, he set to affirm that the United States remains a Pacific Power. . . . The major goal . . . was to make the case for multilateral cooperation regarding the pressing challenges of the global economy, climate change, proliferation, and Afghanistan-Pakistan." In these limited respects, he succeeded. President Hu even agreed to visit the United States and to resume US-Chinese military-to-military exchanges that had been suspended since Bush's notification to Congress of arms sales to Taiwan.[55]

A month after returning to the United States, the president delivered yet another major address, this time at the at the US Military Academy. He spoke after reading the review he had ordered on increased troop levels to Afghanistan. Unlike his often lengthy and didactic responses to questions in press conferences and in other speeches, his thirty-three-minute address was characterized by clarity, precision, and conciseness. "I want to speak to you tonight about our efforts in Afghanistan," he told his audience of 4,200 cadets. Point by point he then laid out the case for why the United States and its NATO partners had combat forces in Afghanistan. He also explained why he was ordering an additional 30,000 troops in what he hoped would be a rapidly executed surge that would end eighteen months later when they would begin to be withdrawn.[56]

"The people and governments of both Afghanistan and Pakistan are endangered," Obama warned. "And the stakes are even higher within a nuclear-armed Pakistan, because we know that al Qaeda and other extremists seek nuclear weapons, and we have every reason to believe that they would use them." Although he was committing an additional 30,000 forces to Afghanistan, he reiterated the need for the NATO allies to step up their own commitments. He wanted them to provide an additional 10,000 troops, bringing the total number of forces in the country to well over 100,000. "For what's at stake is not simply a test of NATO's credibility," he argued, "what's at stake is the security of our allies, and the common security of the world."[57]

He also made clear, as he told the generals earlier, that he did not intend to make an open-ended commitment to Afghanistan. After eighteen months he expected to leave the fate of the country to the Afghans themselves. "The days of providing [the Karzai government] a blank check are over," he commented. In an overly optimistic assessment, he predicted that by July 2011, the date when the withdrawal was supposed to begin, the momentum of the Taliban would be reversed and it would even be possible for the Afghan government to open negotiations with those Taliban who abandoned violence and respected the human rights of their fellow citizens.[58]

Obama anticipated that his decision to send additional troops to Afghanistan and to set an end date for the withdrawal of these forces would be criticized by Republicans objecting to any end date, and by Democrats opposed to additional troops for another unwinnable war like Vietnam. Unlike Vietnam, he reminded the cadets "the American people were viciously attacked from Afghanistan, and remain a target for those same extremists, who are plotting along its border." To continue the war without adding additional forces, "would simply maintain a status quo in which we muddle through, and permit a slow deterioration of conditions" on the ground. To not set a time frame for withdrawal "would commit us to a nation building project of up to a decade." As president, he added, "I refuse to set goals that go beyond our responsibility, our means, or our interests."[59]

In ending his speech, Obama tried to tie together his foreign and domestic policies by addressing what he considered the overarching problem confronting the country as he neared the end of his first year in office: the breakdown of the national unity that existed at the time of 9/11 and the growing partisanship in Washington in recent years. "This vast and diverse citizenry will not agree on every issue—nor should we," he remarked. "But I also know that we, as a country, cannot sustain our leadership nor navigate the momentous challenges of our time if we allow ourselves to be split asunder by the same rancor and cynicism and partisanship that has in recent times poisoned our national discourse." With "every fabric" of his being, he concluded, he believed Americans could "still come together behind a common purpose."[60]

As he had done in the past, Obama later recounted the solemnity of his surroundings in delivering his address and the self-doubt he felt, but hid so well at the time, about his ability to achieve the goals he set forth in his speech, especially given his realization that young men and women would die as a result of the decision he was announcing. "As I entered the stage to the band playing the ceremonial ruffles and flourishes, the cadets stood in unison and applauded; and looking out at their faces," he commented, "I felt my heart swell with an almost paternal pride. I just prayed that I and the others who commanded them were worthy of their trust."[61]

For the most part, the president's speech was well received. It was even singled out as his most important address since taking office. Even Republican skeptics, including McCain, who served on both the powerful Senate Armed Services and Foreign Relations Committees, his running mate, Sarah Palin, and the chairman of the Republican National Committee, Michael Steele, welcomed the fact that the president was now sending enough troops

to Afghanistan to defeat the Taliban and Al-Qaeda. As the president anticipated, however, other Republicans criticized his speech for setting an end
date for withdrawing American forces from Afghanistan, while some Democrats, including House Speaker Nancy Pelosi, took issue with his decision to
commit more troops to the Afghan conflict.[62]

Other points Obama stressed were the unity of the United States and the
NATO alliance after 9/11, the distraction of the Iraq War from the real threat
in Afghanistan, and the rifts at home and "between America and much of the
world" as a result of the decision to go into Iraq. That was the past, he continued. Now combat forces in Iraq were being withdrawn, and the United
States found itself in a better position to carry out the war where the real
danger to America's national security rested. The additional troops he was
recommending for Afghanistan would be deployed in opium-rich Helmand
Province and nearby Kandahar Province, the Taliban heartland in the country's southern region next to Pakistan.[63]

A week after his address at West Point, Obama flew to Norway to accept
the Nobel Peace Prize. He had spent the night before writing a draft of his
speech before handing it to his chief speechwriter, Jon Favreau, and his deputy national security adviser in charge of communications, Ben Rhodes, to
turn it into final form. According to Rhodes, he looked tired and annoyed.
"I had to stay up all night writing this," he told his speech writers, handing them seven pages from a yellow legal pad he had filled with his neat
but small handwriting. The only other time he had written an address from
scratch was his 2008 address on race in Philadelphia during his campaign for
the Democratic nomination. Favreau, Rhodes, and Obama spent the entire
overnight flight to Oslo and the morning of his address revising and polish-
ing his remarks.[64]

In his address, the new Nobel Laureate sought to reconcile what seemed
irreconcilable—accepting the peace prize at the same time he was escalating the war in Afghanistan. Developing the theme of a "just war," he relied
on the reflections of one of his favorite thinkers, the theologian, Reinhold
Niebuhr. During World War II and the Cold War, Niebuhr tried to justify the
principles of Christianity with the imperatives of national security by engaging in what he referred to as "morally hazardous action," such as the use of
military force to confront evil in the world. In an interview with Obama during the presidential campaign, the columnist David Brooks asked the future
president what he took away from Niebuhr. Obama responded, "I take away
the compelling idea that there's serious evil in the world, and hardship and
pain. And we should be humble and modest in our belief we can eliminate
those things. But we shouldn't use that as excuse for cynicism and inaction."[65]

Obama echoed these thoughts in his acceptance speech. Acknowledging the controversy that the prize committee had stirred by awarding him the peace prize, he addressed directly "the most profound issue" surrounding his receipt of this prize, the fact that he was commander-in-chief of the military in the midst of two wars. How, he asked, could he accept the peace prize while being in the midst of two wars, one of which he was ending but the other of which he was expanding?[66]

The president's response was to talk about "just wars," which emerged as codes of law that were established "to regulate the destructive power of war." Although the concept of a "just war" was rarely observed as the "capacity of human beings to kill one another proved inexhaustible," it remained his responsibility to protect the national interest (in this respect by defeating Al-Qaeda and the Taliban) without engaging in limitless war. "So yes," he remarked in his address, "the instruments of war do have a role to play in preserving the peace. And yet this truth must co-exist with another: that no matter how justified, war promises human tragedy. The soldier's courage and sacrifice is full of glory. . . . But war itself is never glorious. . . . War is at some level . . . an expression of human folly."[67]

The president also justified force on humanitarian grounds. Inaction in the face of evil, he continued, "tears at our conscience and can lead to more costly intervention later. That is why all responsible nations must embrace the role that militaries with a clear mandate can play to keep the peace."[68]

The real issue for Obama, then, was not engaging in war when it was justified, but on how "to build a just and lasting peace." One way was through the use of meaningful sanctions against nations that break rules and laws. Another was to protect human rights. "If human rights are not protected, peace is a hollow promise," he remarked. This did not mean "an endless campaign to impose our values on the world" because such principles as the right of citizens to worship as they please or assemble without fear, or choose their own leaders were predicated on the inherent rights and dignity of every individual. "So even as we respect the unique culture and traditions of different countries," the president continued, "America will always be a voice for those aspirations that are universal."[69]

The final way to bring about the type of world he advocated was to assure economic security and opportunity for every inhabitant of the globe. "For true peace is not just freedom from fear, but freedom from want." Besides adequate nourishment for even the world's poorest inhabitants, it included the same goals he sought to achieve at home—guaranteed health care, better educational opportunities for children, and alternatives to fossil fuels.[70]

Everything Obama advocated was predicated on the need for nations to come together, whether that involved the use of military force or economic sanctions, preventing nuclear proliferation or confronting climate change. "America's commitment to global security will never waver," the president remarked. "But in a world in which threats are more diffuse and mission more complex America cannot act alone. America alone cannot secure the peace."[71]

Obama then argued that no Holy War, such as that being waged by Al-Qaeda and the Taliban in the name of God, can be a "just war" as he claimed the war being fought in Afghanistan by the United States and its allies was a "just war," because no Holy War could ever be a "just war." "For if you truly believe that you are carrying out divine will, then there is no need for restraint—no need to spare the pregnant mother, or the medic, or the Red Cross worker, or even a person of one's own faith." In fact, a cardinal principle of all the major religions was "that we do onto others as we would have them do unto us."[72]

In accepting the peace prize, the president was arguing the ethics of war against terrorism, while mapping out the road to world peace. "As Dr. [Martin Luther] King said at this occasion so many years ago," the president concluded, "'I refuse to accept despair as the final response to the ambiguities of history.' . . . Let us reach for the world that ought to be—that spark of the divine that still stirs within each of our souls."[73]

Like many of his speeches at this time, his address received a mixed response in the United States and abroad. Antiwar activists criticized the president for increasing troop levels in Afghanistan, but other commentators pointed out how, instead of using traditional arguments to defend what the president called "just wars," he had taken a much more difficult and subtler path. Fred Kaplan of the *Daily Beast* remarked that the president "outline[d] nothing less than a vision of moral realism for the conduct of war and peace in the modern era—as clear and complex statement on the subject as any American president has delivered in nearly a half-century." Even former house speaker, Newt Gingrich, one of Obama's harshest critics, credited the president for taking a realistic view of war and peace. One thing most commentators agreed upon was that, in his speech, he was reintroducing into the dialogue about the ethics of war the views expressed by Niebuhr, which had been so influential during the Cold War.[74]

The 2010 Midterm Elections

Little that the president said or did, including passage of the ACA two months later, worked to his advantage in the midterm elections. Before the elections, he had traveled throughout the country in support of Democratic candidates. Everywhere he went, he later recounted, the crowds seemed "energized, filling up basketball auditoriums and public parks, chanting 'Yes we can' and 'Fired up! Ready to go.'" "But," as he also remembered, "even without looking at the polls, I could sense a change in the atmosphere on the campaign trail; an air of doubt hovering over each rally, a forced, almost desperate quality to the cheers and laughter." On election day, Axelrod predicted that the Democrats would lose thirty congressional seats or more.[75]

He underestimated the size of the party's defeat. In November the Democrats were shellacked at the polls. Republicans gained control of the House, capturing 63 formerly Democratic seats, the largest number of turnovers since 1948. Although Democrats were able to retain control of the Senate, Republicans picked up 6 seats narrowing the Democratic hold in the upper chamber to 4 seats (51 to 47 with 2 independents caucusing with the Democrats). On the state level, Republicans gained 680 legislative seats and won a net 5 gubernatorial seats, including Ohio, Michigan, Wisconsin, and Pennsylvania, all important to the reapportionment and redistricting of House seats following the 2010 census. They also won the governorship in Maine for the first time in decades, won the gubernatorial race in New Mexico, regained the governorships in Iowa, Kansas, and Tennessee, and held key governorships in Nevada, Georgia, Texas, and Florida.[76]

There were a few bright spots for the Democrats who won Senate races in Colorado, West Virginia, and Nevada, where Majority Leader Harry Reid beat off a tough challenge from a Tea Party favorite, Sharry Angle. In California, Barbara Boxer defeated her Republican challenger, Carly Fiorina, while Jerry Brown reclaimed the governorship by defeating his Republican opponent, Meg Whitman. Brown replaced Republican governor Arnold Schwarzenegger, "the Governator," who had held the post for eight years.[77]

Despite these Democratic victories, there was no denying that Republicans had pummeled the Democrats. "Election Day proved to be an even bigger 'wave election' than anyone anticipated," said the former chairman of the Republican National Committee, Ed Gillespie. Political analysts attributed much of the oversize Republican victory to the Tea Party movement. In interviews with local and national media, many of these newly elected lawmakers, at least forty of whom had gotten help from the Tea Party, made clear that they were not looking simply to blend in with other legislators.[78]

Still shocked by the size of the Democratic defeat, the president held a lengthy news conference the day after the election in which he took much of the blame for the magnitude of the Democratic defeat. "I think there is no doubt that people's number one concern is the economy," he stated. "People are frustrated—they're deeply frustrated—with the pace of our economic recovery and the opportunities that they hope for their children and grandchildren. They want jobs to come back faster, they want paychecks to go further." And for not making enough progress in these regards, "I've got to take direct responsibility."[79]

At the same time, the president pointed to the success his stimulus package was already having on the economy and defended other initiatives his administration had undertaken in such areas as clean energy and education. "I don't think there's anybody in America who thinks that we've got an energy policy that works the way it needs to. . . . I think everybody in this country thinks that we've got to make sure our kids are equipped in terms of their education, their science background, their math backgrounds, to compete in this new global economy."[80]

Following the president's remarks, reporters asked him hard questions. Several reporters pointed out that in defending his administration, he did not seem to reflect on or second-guess the policy decisions his administration had made. Was this true? Another reporter asked whether he was willing to concede that the election results were not just an expression of frustration about the economy but a "fundamental rejection" of his agenda? "If you're not reflecting on your policy agenda," Sandra Guthrie of NBC wondered, "is it possible voters can conclude you're still not getting it?"[81]

Obama responded to these questions by reiterating that he was "doing a whole lot of reflecting" and that there were areas where his administration "was going to have to do a better job." One exception was health-care reform. When asked about Republican opposition to the ACA and whether it might be repealed as a result of the previous day's election, he made clear that he considered the measure off-the-table for discussion. "I know that there's some Republican candidates who won last night who feel very strongly about it," he remarked. "As I said before, though, I think we'd be misreading the election if we thought that the American people want to see us for the next two years relitigate arguments that we had over the last two years."[82]

The point the president emphasized throughout the press conference was that the actions he took during his first twenty months in office were a response to an emergency situation. The decisions he made with respect to the bank and auto bailouts were not reflective of his core values or his agenda for the nation, which, he stated once more, was his belief in a free market economy as the best engine to expand and strengthen the nation's middle class. "My core responsibility is making sure that we've got an economy that's growing, a middle class that feels secure, that jobs are being created," he stressed.[83]

One point hardly touched upon during the press conference was the messaging of Obama's legislative initiatives during his time in office. Most media experts agreed that the president allowed himself to be overexposed—too many TV appearances, interviews, and town meetings. His problem extended beyond overexposure, however. The Tea Party simply out-messaged him. Because Obama's domestic programs were complex and came with enormous price tags, they were difficult to explain and justify to the American people, and, unlike former president Bill Clinton, he lacked the ability to do so in ways his audience could easily understand. He was also reluctant to boast about his accomplishments. He did not allow himself to get credit for what he achieved. Instead, his explanations lacked self-congratulations and were too often long and complicated. The Tea Party message, in contrast, was simple and direct; cut back the size of government and lower taxes.[84]

Although the 2010 election was fought mostly over domestic issues, differences among Democrats over expanding the war in Afghanistan made disaster at the polls all the more likely. Even leading members of the party and international allies criticized the president over the lack of progress, including whether it was even possible to work with President Karzai because of his erratic behavior and corrupt regime. Although the president thought progress was being made in Afghanistan, American casualties in that mountainous country gnawed at Obama as he grappled with the issue of whether their sacrifice was worth it. "Each time, I met with wounded soldiers at Walter Reed and Bethesda," he remembered about his visit to these two hospitals, "I was reminded of the awful cost of such incremental progress. Whereas my earlier visits had taken roughly an hour, I was more often spending at least twice that time, as the hospital appeared to be filled almost to capacity."[85]

In the election campaign, the president also failed in his effort to bring his domestic and foreign policy together in a winning message for 2010. In March, Obama visited Afghanistan, where he met with President Karzai and then visited American forces in nearby Bagram Air Field. In his meeting with Karzai, the president told the Afghan leader that the corruption taking place within his government had to stop. He also made clear that there was a timeline for the withdrawal of American troops from the country and that it was up to the Afghans to provide for their own security. Three months later, he fired the commander of American forces in Afghanistan, Stanley

McChrystal, after he and his staff made critical remarks about senior administration officials, culminating in an article in *Rolling Stone* harshly critical of the administration's Afghan policy. The article was based on access McChrystal, whose relationship with Obama had always been strained, gave to the article's author, Michael Hastings. The president's ongoing problems with Karzai and his firing of McChrystal crystallized for many Americans the failure of Obama's Afghan policy rather than any success on his part.[86]

CHAPTER 7

The Comeback President

Having humiliated President Barack Obama in the 2010 elections, the Republicans turned immediately to winning back the White House in 2012. Senate Minority Leader Mitch McConnell even vowed to defeat any legislation the administration initiated. Their strategy seemed to work. Throughout this period the president's poll numbers hovered below 50 percent. Yet, in 2012 he was elected to a second term.[1]

Despite the polls, Obama remained steadfastly committed to the same principles that guided the first two years of his presidency. Facing the reality of Republican control of the House and the dilution of Democratic control of the Senate, he began to call increasingly for civility and legislative compromise on Capitol Hill. His hope for a racially, ethnically, and socially diverse society had always been predicated on building a consensus even among opposing groups, but after 2010 he gave new emphasis to finding common ground with Republicans. Remaining the same was his ideal of a middle-class society predicated on free enterprise principles and marketplace consumerism.

The Lame-Duck Congress

As Obama began his third year as president in 2011, he faced a more difficult situation than when he first took office in 2009. Gone was the hope he elicited when he won the 2008 election. Gone was also Democratic control of both houses of Congress. Not only was the House now run by Republicans and the Democratic majority in the Senate reduced to just six seats, which, by invoking the sixty-vote cloture rule, made it possible for the Republicans to keep the Democrats from passing legislation, most of the newly elected members of the House and the Senate were indebted to the Tea Party for their election. Former Democrats and moderate Republicans were replaced by a new group of congress members determined to repeal the Affordable Care Act (ACA), make major cutbacks in the budget at the expense of entitlements programs, and work to defeat the president in 2012.[2]

Before the 112th Congress convened in January, the outgoing Democratic-controlled Congress met for a lame-duck session, which the president used to push through legislation providing additional stimulus to the economy. He also won repeal of a policy known as "Don't Ask Don't Tell" (DADT), established during the Clinton administration, which prohibited gay members of the military from acknowledging their sexual orientation, and he gained passage of a new START agreement (Strategic Arms Reduction Treaty) with Russia requiring both superpowers to make further reductions in their nuclear arsenals.

He was able to pass the stimulus package only by working closely with the incoming reduced leadership. The measure maintained the Bush cuts and reduced the 6.2 percent Social Security payroll tax by 2 percent for one year, letting average workers making $50,000 a year increase their take-home pay by approximately $1,000. It also added ninety-nine weeks of jobless benefits to unemployed workers, and extended tuition tax credits, the child tax credit, and the earned income tax benefit. In exchange for these Republican concessions, Obama agreed to Republican demands to include in the extension of the estate taxes the wealthiest 2 percent of taxpayers, despite his previous promises to the contrary. The legislation he approved also reduced for two years estate taxes from 50 to 35 percent while increasing the exemption on these estates from $1 million to $5 million. Finally, it adjusted upward the amount of income a taxpayer could earn before being subject to the alternative minimum tax and allowed businesses to write off the entire costs, instead of 50 percent, of certain equipment purchases. Since no provisions were included in the measure to pay for it, the cost of what amounted to a second stimulus package around the size of the first package in 2009, was added to the national debt.[3]

Immediately Republicans attacked the massive bill for adding to the debt, while Democrats on the left complained that, contrary to his long-standing promises, Obama skewed the tax cuts too much to the nation's wealthiest citizens. The president did not help his cause when he called liberal opponents of the measure "sanctimonious."[4]

Most commentators agreed, though, that the measure represented a significant victory for the president. "At a moment of political weakness," Dan Baltz of the *Washington Post* wrote, "the tax package provided [Obama] the vehicle to quickly reassert that part of his political personality at a time when he needed the public to take a fresh look at him." David Axelrod, the president's senior adviser, and others close to Obama denied this was the case. "His attitude is we've got goals to move this economy forward, strengthen the middle class, deal with our long-term competitive challenges, and we shouldn't be dogmatic about how we achieve them." Axelrod then added that Obama's basic view was not "'Go out and find me some *centrist* positions to signify some sort of change in positioning.' That's not what he is doing." In addition to the stimulus package, the president sought to pass legislation he had tabled during his first two years in office including repealing DADT and approving the new START agreement.[5]

Before President Clinton's administration, official policy had been not to allow homosexuals to serve in the military. At the time Clinton became president, most commanders continued to oppose having gays in the military on the basis that they would destroy the esprit de corps and teamwork essential on the battlefield. They also viewed gays as potential security risks. As a compromise between the military's exclusionary policy and the increasingly influential gay community who wanted inclusion of gay people in all walks of life, Clinton implemented DADT, which the gay community found offensive because it said that gays could serve in the military and die for the country only if they kept their sexual orientation private. [6]

Having felt it necessary to delay repeal of DADT because of more pressing needs, Obama had faced growing anger within the gay community ever since he chose Rick Warren, a megachurch pastor, best-selling author, and an outspoken opponent of gay marriage, to deliver the invocation at his inauguration as president. Since the implementation of DADT, almost fourteen thousand gay service members had been discharged from the service because of their sexual preferences. Several cases of service members able to speak Arabic, who had come out in the media, highlighted what seemed like the absurdity of the DADT policy.[7]

Even during the campaign Obama had championed gay rights, including repeal of DADT, which he considered within the context of a litany of civil rights measures he strongly supported, including the Lilly Ledbetter Fair Pay Act of 2009 (his first major piece of legislation as president) and the Matthew Shephard and James Byrd Jr. Hate Crimes Prevention Act of 2009, named after two young men who had been brutally tortured and murdered in 1998, the former because he was gay and the latter because he was Black. He also looked at repeal of DADT from the perspective of his own goal of a more inclusive society. "Who do we consider a true member of the American family, deserving of the same rights, respects, and concern that we expect of ourselves?" he asked himself. "I believed in defining that family broadly—it included gay people as well as straight," he answered, "and it included immigrant families that had put down roots and raised kids here. . . . How could I believe otherwise, when some of the same arguments for their exclusion had so often been used to exclude those who looked like me?"[8]

Finally, Obama wanted to hold onto the waning support of the gay community, who were disappointed that, in a speech in October at a dinner of the Human Rights Campaign, a gay activist group, Obama had promised to repeal DADT, but had provided no timeline or specifics.[9]

For all these reasons, the president was determined to repeal DADT before the Republicans, many of whose incoming members had campaigned against gay rights, took control of the House. In his first State of the Union address in January 2010, he called explicitly for repeal of DADT. At the same time, Obama understood that there remained strong opposition in the military to allowing gays to serve openly and that without the support of Secretary of Defense Bob Gates and the Joint Chiefs of Staff, the policy would run into insurmountable roadblocks.[10]

Aware of Obama's views on DADT, both Gates and the chairman of the Joint Chiefs of Staff, Admiral Michael Mullen, decided to support its repeal. In February 2010, they testified to this effect before the Senate Armed Services Committee, but they insisted upon six months to win over the support of military commanders and to draw up plans for fully integrating gays into the services. Despite ongoing opposition from some gay activists, who continued to believe Obama was not moving fast enough, and from influential lawmakers like Ike Skelton of Missouri, the chairman of the House Armed Services Committee, and John McCain of Arizona, the senior Republican on the Senate Armed Services Committee, both of whom strongly opposed allowing gays to serve in the military, the president agreed to a study, and established the Comprehensive Review Working Group to evaluate how it might be done.[11]

Over the spring and summer he continued to defend his policy of moving steadily but cautiously toward repealing DADT. Working in favor of lifting the ban immediately were cases making their way through the judiciary challenging the constitutionality of DADT. In a case originally brought in 2004 by Log Cabin Republicans (a group of gay Republicans) a federal judge in

October ordered the military to stop administering DADT. The message of the court was clear. Unless the Pentagon took immediate steps toward integrating gays into the military, the courts would make them do it.[12]

Because the president believed more time was needed before the military services completed their plan for open service, his administration asked for a stay on the implementation of the judge's ruling. Even though this decision continued to turn gay activists against the president, trying to achieve change through consensus rather than confrontation remained his approach to repeal, which, he continued to maintain, was his ultimate goal. It had, however, "to be done in a way that is orderly." Finally, at the end of November the Pentagon issued its plan for integrating the services, concluding, as Obama expected, that open service posed no serious risks.[13]

There remained high-level resistance to repeal of the ban on gays in the military, and McCain carried out his threat of filibustering against the repeal provision that the administration had included in the defense authorization act. At this point, the White House moved into action, getting House Speaker Pelosi and Senate Majority Leader Reid to introduce identical standalone repeal measures on their sides of Capitol Hill and using the internet to urge millions of Obama's supporters to pressure Republicans to support the legislation. On December 15, the House passed the measure by a vote of 250 to 175. After holding two days of hearings during which Gates and Mullen testified in favor of immediate repeal, Reid brought an identical bill to the Senate floor on December 18. Having secured enough Republican votes to defeat another filibuster effort, he then moved for a final vote on the standalone measure, which the Senate approved by a vote of 65 to 31. On December 22, the president signed the bill into law. It was a major achievement for him in the waning hours of the lame-duck Congress.[14]

On that same day, Obama achieved another significant victory when the Senate ratified the New START Treaty with Russia that the president had signed in April with Russian president Dmitry Medvedev, exactly one year after he had made a major speech in Prague's historic Hradcany Square calling for nuclear disarmament. The agreement replaced the original START Treaty, signed by Presidents George H. W. Bush and Mikhail Gorbachev in 1991. It called for reducing the number of deployed strategic nuclear warheads to 1,550 (about a third lower than existing arsenals) and cutting in half the number of launchers (missiles and bombers) to a ceiling below 700. It also included provisions for inspection and verification of these stockpiles.[15]

In signing the agreement, the president remarked that it was part of his commitment to "resetting" relations between Russia and the United States, which had "drifted" over the past several years. It was also meant to have worldwide significance and to be a warning to Tehran that it faced strong economic sanctions if it flouted the Nuclear Non-Proliferation Treaty (NPT), which Iran had earlier signed. "Nuclear weapons are not simply an issue for the United States and Russia," he emphasized. "A nuclear weapon in the hands of a terrorist is a danger to people everywhere." By continuing to violate the terms of NPT, Tehran risked creating an arms race in the Middle East, which the world would not tolerate. By signing the agreement, Obama was also telling the world that he was serious about working toward a nuclear-free world.[16]

Once the New START agreement with Russia was signed, the president still faced the difficult task of getting the needed two-thirds of the Senate to ratify the pact. That meant he had to have the support of at least nine Republicans along with the unanimous backing of the Democratic caucus to win approval. He did not have those votes. Realizing that the agreement stood little chance of being approved in the incoming Senate, he decided to add ratification of New START to the already crowded agenda of the lame-duck Congress. After meeting again with President Medvedev during an economic summit in Seoul in November, he reiterated his pledge to push the treaty through Congress.[17]

Shortly after returning to Washington, Obama held a meeting at the White House of both Republican and Democratic leaders to emphasize the importance of ratifying the New START Treaty. "There is no higher national security priority for the lame duck session of Congress," he told them. "The stakes for American national security are clear, and they are high. . . . We cannot afford to gamble on our ability to verify Russia's strategic nuclear materials, or in maintaining a strong sanctions regime against Iran."[18]

In the weeks remaining before the 111th Congress ended, the president had Pentagon generals and arms control advocates join forces in lobbying for the New START agreement. He also enlisted the support of high-ranking Republicans, including five former secretaries of state and former president George H. W. Bush, who argued the treaty was essential for the nation's security.[19]

On December 18, the day after the Senate voted to repeal "Don't Ask Don't Tell," the White House instructed Reid to file for a cloture vote ending debate on the ratification legislation. After winning the vote on cloture, thirteen Republicans defied their leaders by joining the entire Democratic caucus in voting for the New START agreement. The final tally on December 22 was 71 to 26.[20]

Several other measures that Obama had hoped the lame-duck Congress would approve never made it through the legislative process. The most notable of these was an agreement to provide a pathway to citizenship (the Dream Act) to those persons who had been brought by their parents to the United States when they were younger than eighteen, many of whom had no recollection of having lived elsewhere.[21]

As a number of commentators wrote, however, ratification of the New START Treaty was another major victory for the president—in several respects his most significant of the lame-duck Congress. In deciding to add ratification of the agreement to his agenda for the lame-duck session, Obama took an enormous risk. Not only did he need seven more Republican votes in addition to the two required for passage of his other agenda items, something several journalists thought he could never achieve in the last days of the 111th Congress, especially since several Democrats had their own doubts about the treaty, its defeat would have been a major setback for the administration's entire foreign policy. It would have damaged Obama's standing in the world, harmed the chances of resetting Washington's relationship with Moscow, raised the possibility of another nuclear arms race, and made it more difficult for the president to negotiate other treaties. "It's one of those things in life where failing to get it would be more important than actually what you get with it," remarked George Perkovich, a scholar on nuclear nonproliferation at the Carnegie Endowment for International Peace.[22]

More positively, while the New START Treaty still left Russia and the United States with enough nuclear warheads and delivery systems to blow up the world several times over, its reductions paved the way for further negotiations with Russia on nuclear weapons and the other issues that strained relations between the two countries. It also gave the president new confidence about his ability to work with the Republicans in the new Congress and erased many of the doubts that other world leaders were having about his abilities as leader of the free world. Finally, it stood as a warning to Iran that Washington and Moscow would work together in implementing increased economic sanctions against Tehran unless it curbed its ambition to become another nuclear power. Once more Obama was able to achieve his goal by a combination of active lobbying and a willingness to compromise on such issues as agreeing to adding additional funds for modernizing the military's existing nuclear stockpiles and to an amendment excluding missile defense systems from the treaty, language to which Russia would still have to agree before it could ratify the treaty.[23]

The president regarded his failure to win approval of the Dream Act "a bitter pillow to swallow." That disappointment notwithstanding, he later commented pridefully on how much he had achieved during the lame-duck Congress and the renewed confidence it had given him to lead the nation in the coming years. We had "managed to pull off the most significant lame-duck session in modern history," he recounted. Together the House and Senate had clocked forty-eight days in session and passed ninety-nine laws. Axelrod reported a rise in consumer confidence and in his approval ratings. "It was as if, for the span of a month and a half democracy was normal again. . . . What more might we have accomplished, I wondered, and how much further along would the economic recovery be, had this sort of atmosphere prevailed from the start of my term."[24]

The Recalcitrant 112th Congress

Any hope the president might have entertained that the accomplishments of the lame-duck Congress would carry over into the newly elected 112th Congress were quickly shattered. This was apparent during the debate on Capitol Hill over tax cuts and extending the federal debt. Cutting the debt, which increased during Obama's first two years in office by an unprecedented $2.80 trillion dollars compared to $3.293 trillion during Bush's two terms, had been a key issue for the Tea Party during the 2010 midterm elections. [25]

It was also a concern for the White House, which in early 2010 had appointed a bipartisan commission led by Erskine Bowles, a former chief of staff during the Clinton administration, and Alan Simpson, a former senator from Wyoming, to make recommendations for cutting the budget. Even though its final, controversial, report failed to receive the votes needed to make it out of the commission, it received widespread attention in the media, and its findings of $4 trillion in spending cuts and tax increases over twenty years, became the basis for much of the discussion that followed on Capitol Hill.[26]

Although much of the increase in the debt was a result of an unpaid prescription drug program enacted during the Bush administration, the bank bailout, the economic stimulus act, lower tax receipts as a result of the recession, and the cost of the wars in Iraq and Afghanistan, Republicans blamed it on the administration's alleged wasteful spending. They sought to cut the debt by making major cuts in the very entitlement programs Obama promised to protect. He was determined not to let this happen. Instead, he favored eliminating tax cuts for the wealthiest taxpayers passed during Bush's presidency while maintaining them for lower- and middle-class taxpayers. He also wanted to keep the tax credits for lower- and middle-class wage earners approved during his administration.[27]

On April 11, the president delivered a major speech at George Washington University on fiscal policy and the debt crisis. Since the very establishment of the country, he began his remarks, Americans have put their "faith in free markets and free enterprise as the engine of America's wealth and prosperity." We are "rugged individualists" with a "healthy skepticism of too much government." At the same time, Americans believed in the need for government to "do together what we cannot do for ourselves. . . . And so we contribute to programs like Medicare and Social Security" and other programs like unemployment insurance and Medicaid.[28]

The federal government also provided unemployment for those who have lost jobs through no fault of their own, and Medicaid for senior citizens in nursing homes, poor children, and those with disabilities. These are commitments that needed to be retained, Obama emphasized. Not only was the US a better nation because of them, "we would not be a great country without" them. In paying for them, wealthier individuals should bear a greater share of the tax burden than the middle class or those less fortunate, "not because we begrudge those who've done well—we rightly celebrate their success, [but because of] our belief that those who have benefited the most from our way of life can afford to give back a little bit more."[29]

Obama recognized he needed to practice fiscal restraint and rein in the federal debt, but he made clear he would not do this at the expense of the economic recovery taking place or "the investments we need to grow, create jobs, and help us with the future." His dilemma was how to cut spending while protecting programs like Medicare, Medicaid, and Social Security, providing for essential services like national defense, and looking to the future with investments in such areas as education and medical research.[30]

The president's response to this fundamental question was to reject the budget released by House Budget Committee chairman Paul Ryan of Wisconsin, who was sitting in the audience. The Ryan proposal called for drastic cuts in vital services with the goal of achieving $4 trillion in cuts over ten years. Not knowing that Ryan was present for his speech, Obama attacked his plan repeatedly and harshly. Pursuing this path, he said, "would lead to a fundamentally different America than the one we've known certainly in my lifetime." It painted a very pessimistic view of crumbling roads and collapsing bridges and of bright young Americans unable to go to college because we "can't afford to send them. . . . It's a vision that says Americans can't afford to keep the promise we've made to care for our seniors. . . . It's a vision that says up to 50 million Americans have to lose their health insurance in order for us to reduce the deficit," while at the same time affording "more than $1 trillion in new tax breaks for the wealthy."[31]

Instead, Obama proposed reducing the deficit by $4 trillion over twelve years. His approach, he said, was based on the recommendations of the Bowles-Simpson commission and the $1 trillion in reductions he had included in his 2012 budget as a result of planned troop withdrawals from Afghanistan and Iraq. In deciding on budget cuts, every program would be put on the table, including programs "he care[d] deeply about." They would also have to include significant reductions in defense spending. What the president would not do was sacrifice core investments for future growth. "We will invest in medical research. We will invest in clean energy technology. We will invest in new roads and airports and broadband access. . . . We will do what we need to compete, and we will win the future."[32]

A heated debate followed the speech on Capitol Hill during which the president was attacked even by moderate commentators for embarrassing Ryan, and by conservative Tea Party Republicans who tied major budget cuts in entitlement programs to raising the debt ceiling (the amount the Treasury was allowed to borrow in order to pay the nation's bills). The possibility that the government might be forced to default on the debt sent havoc into the financial markets, resulting in a stock market trending downward but with major daily swings in stock prices. Even Minority Leader McConnell became irritated by what he considered the antics of such conservative members of the Senate as Jim DeMint of South Carolina, whom he later accused of "hijacking" the Tea Party movement by raising funds "from well-intentioned conservatives," ostensibly to further conservative causes, but in fact to attack more moderate, but "the most electable Republicans."[33]

The debate over the deficit and debt ceiling began to extend beyond economic issues. As the former president later recounted, because of the Tea Party and individuals like the real estate developer and television personality Donald Trump, who at one time supported Obama but now began the birther movement accusing him of not having been born in the United States, he was even accused of being a Muslim socialist and a Manchurian candidate, who had been groomed from childhood to be at the highest levels of government. At first the president paid no attention to Trump, whom he "found it hard to take . . . too seriously," and the radical fringe of the Republican Party, but as the fringe grew into a major movement, he became concerned about the nation's future, and he placed much of the blame for what was happening on the media, especially Fox News but including also such respected news outlets as ABC, NBC, and CNN.[34]

On several occasions in July the White House seemed to arrive at a far-reaching agreement (the so-called grand bargain) with the new Speaker of the House, John Boehner of Ohio, and Minority Leader McConnell in which both sides agreed to a major overhaul of the tax code and significant budget cuts in return for Republicans consenting to raise the debt ceiling. But while Obama and Boehner had developed a measure of trust for each other, McConnell disliked the president, whom he accused of lecturing to him and never really listening to Republican concerns over spending. When it became clear that enough conservatives, including House Majority Leader Eric Cantor of Virginia, who aspired to Boehner's position, intended to vote with enough Democrats, unhappy because they felt the measure gave too much away to the Republicans, the negotiations broke down. Instead of blaming the budget stalemate on these recalcitrant legislators, Boehner and McConnell claimed the president had not acted in good faith in negotiating with them, maintaining that as the negotiators drew closer to an agreement, Obama kept moving the goal posts insisting that Republicans increase tax revenues.[35]

The unraveling of the "grand bargain" only underscored for Obama and the Republican leadership the urgency of finding common ground in resolving the debt ceiling crisis before the government would have to default on its debts, estimated by the Treasury Department to happen on August 2. Already a new round of negotiations was underway between White House officials and the Boehner staff to reach an agreement short of a comprehensive one, but with a solution for the debt crisis that would extend through 2012, a concession Obama insisted upon in order to prevent Tea Party members in the House from using the debt ceiling as a bargaining chip in future negotiations over budget cuts.[36]

On July 25, the president addressed the nation on the dangers of default. On the nation's current course, he warned, the growing debt could do serious damage to the economy. Businesses would be less likely to hire workers in a country unable to balance its books. Interest rates would rise, and the nation would not have enough money to make job-creating investments in areas like education and infrastructure, or pay for vital programs like Medicare and Medicaid. The nation's AAA credit rating would be downgraded.[37]

Obama called again for an approach for solving the debt based on the recommendations of the Bowles-Simpson Commission, which involved increased taxes on the wealthiest taxpayers as well as cuts in entitlement programs. He rejected the latest Republican proposal, unveiled just a few hours earlier by Speaker Boehner, that provided for only a six-month extension of the debt ceiling. He closed his remarks by urging his audience to pressure their representatives in Washington to compromise on the debt ceiling. "History," he said, "is scattered with the stories of those who held fast to rigid ideologies and refused to listen to those who disagreed."[38]

Following his address, lawmakers' telephone lines were jammed with callers urging them to reach an agreement before August 2. The websites of key lawmakers, including Boehner, crashed as their constituencies weighed in on the debate over the debt ceiling. Boehner told unhappy conservatives in his caucus to "get your ass in line" on an agreement. Several more days followed of bickering among Republicans, and the defeat on Capitol Hill of two competing Republican and Democratic measures before the president was able to announce that an agreement had been reached over the deficit between the White House and the House and Senate leadership.[39]

The measure approved by both House and Senate leaders provided for a complicated two-stage process in resolving the debt crisis that required the administration to come up with at least $1.2 trillion in budget cuts over ten years in exchange for increasing the debt ceiling by more than $2 trillion, which would last through the 2012 election. Anything less than $1.2 trillion in deficit reductions would trigger automatic across-the-board spending cuts (known as "sequestering") split between defense and nondefense spending. On August 1, both the House and the Senate agreed to the deal, although enough House Republicans voted against the measure that it required a bloc of Democrats to join with Republicans in passing the legislation. The next day, Obama signed the legislation into law, just a few hours before the deadline set by the Treasury Department for preventing a default.[40]

In his remarks announcing the deal, the president made clear that it was not the agreement he preferred, pointing out that it cut domestic spending as a percentage of the gross domestic product (GDP) to the lowest level since the Eisenhower administration. It was a level, however, that still allowed the administration "to make job-creating investments like education and research." He urged Congress to take "bipartisan, common-sense steps" after the August recess to bolster job creation and encourage economic growth, including keeping the Bush taxes for middle-class families while allowing cuts for the wealthy to expire.[41]

In fact, the compromise was more a temporary patch than a permanent agreement for resolving the deficit and debt ceiling crisis. It pleased hardly anyone and, according to most commentators, it weakened Obama looking to the 2012 elections. Pressured by the Tea Party, Republican leaders warned that they would not appoint anyone to the special committee who might consider raising taxes, while the president's announcement that "everything [was] on the table" infuriated left-leaning Democrats. They were angry that the White House did not pressure Republicans enough to include revenue increases, such as by closing loopholes for oil companies and removing tax deductions that benefited the wealthy. Democratic leaders threatened a hard line against cuts to Social Security and Medicare benefits. Worried about future crises over the debt ceiling and concerned that the US economy was stalling, business leaders issued dire warnings about the worldwide impact of the American economy. The major rating services, such as Standard and Poor's, lowered their ratings on Treasury bills from AAA to AA+, causing an increase in interest rates. Investors in the stock market went on a selling spree. Major indexes dropped by as much as 4 percent after Obama announced the agreement.[42]

As for the president, the whole experience of reaching an agreement on the debt ceiling, beginning with the breakdown of the "grand bargain," altered the way he looked at Washington. According to David Plouffe, the bargain's collapse was a "searing experience," whose lesson was to forget negotiations and rely on the bully pulpit. "You're never going to convince them by sitting around the table and talk about what's good for the nation," John Podesta said. "You had to demonstrate that there's political pain if you don't produce an acceptable outcome." This did not mean that the president gave up on seeking common ground with Republicans. It did mean that he intended to appeal more to the public than he had in the past and negotiate from a position of strength rather than weakness.[43]

Almost overshadowing the struggle in the nation's capital over the budget and debt ceiling were developments in Middle East and North Africa where, in what was known as "the Arab Spring," democratic change seemed on the march as local demonstrations, larger protest movements, and militant uprisings against autocratic leaders, spread throughout the region. Beginning in Tunisia, anti-government actions blanketed the entire area as far away as Yemen in the southernmost part of the Arabian peninsula. In three of the most important nations in the area, Egypt, Libya, and Syria, the uprisings led to the overthrow of Egyptian president Hosni Mubarak and civil wars against Libyan leader, Muammar al-Qaddafi, and Syrian president Bashar al-Assad. Unfortunately for the protestors—and much to the disappointment of the White House—most of these experiments in democracy had limited success or failed entirely. The one exception was Tunisia where the Arab Spring began and where a democratically elected government was established.[44]

Throughout the uprisings in the Middle East, Obama was excoriated by both the political left and the political right, either for not giving, or giving too much, support to the protestors or the leaders in power. In fact, the president carried out a circumspect policy, basic to which was avoiding increased American involvement in the region in the manner of his predecessor, George Bush. In part this was because he believed in the efficacy of the grassroots movement taking place there, which, he was persuaded, would bring about reform without heavy-handed tactics on his part. In part, this was because he wanted to decrease America's footprint in the region.[45]

Of increasingly more concern to the president than developments in the Middle East was making sure that nuclear weapons were kept out of the hands of terrorist organizations, such as Al-Qaeda, which continued to operate in the mountainous region of southwest Afghanistan and northeast Pakistan, and of rogue states such as Iran and North Korea. His eyes also turned increasingly to China, which was already an economic and military behemoth that threatened American and allied interests in the South Asian Sea.[46]

The Arab Spring did not come as a complete surprise to the president. As early as the previous August, he had considered the possibility of democratic change in the Middle East and instructed his national security staff to prepare strategies for supporting political reform when autocracy was challenged in the region. He was surprised, however, by the scope of the uprisings that swept the region in late 2010 and early 2011. He was deeply concerned about how responsive the repressive regimes might be to the demands for change. He was especially worried about Mubarak, who had ruled Egypt with an iron fist since 1981.[47]

To avoid becoming bogged down in the Middle East, he responded to the Arab Spring by encouraging and nudging change in the region, but never openly promoting liberal democratic regimes in the manner of his predecessor George Bush. As much as he would have liked to see democratic institutions established throughout the region, he acted more as a pragmatic realist than as a political idealist. He responded to the uprisings and demands for democratic reform on a country-by-country basis, sometimes more forcibly in the name of reform than in other countries, such as Bahrain, where he supported the ruling monarch even as he thwarted reform.[48]

The largest crowds of the Arab Spring were in Cairo where, just a few months earlier, Obama had delivered a speech at Cairo University in which he promised to replace President Bush's policy of unilateralism with one more respectful of the history and culture of the Arab world. Beginning at the end of January and lasting eighteen days, hundreds of thousands of Egyptians poured into its Tahrir Square, the site of a number of earlier demonstrations calling for the overthrow of the Mubarak regime. The protests quickly spread throughout Egypt, including its second largest city, Alexandria.

As the protests grew larger, Mubarak, who, at age 82, had an irregular heartbeat and was widely reported to be seriously ill, agreed to cede all power to the vice president, but in a speech to the nation shortly thereafter, he announced that he intended to remain in power until his term ended. He also tried to cut off the protestors' access to the social media. In response, the demonstrations grew increasingly violent and remained so until Vice President Suleiman announced that Mubarak had resigned and transferred all his powers to the military, which quickly proceeded to dissolve the parliament, suspend the Egyptian Constitution, appoint a new prime minister, and promise democratic elections for the election of a new president.[49]

When those elections were held, the Muslim Brotherhood, led by the newly elected president, Mohamed Morsi, took control of the government. As Morsi attempted to turn Egypt, a largely secular nation, into an Islamic state, the military took control of the government once more, suspending the constitution of 2012, arresting Morsi, appointing an interim president and then naming General Abdel Fattah el-Sisi as Egypt's new leader.[50]

Throughout this period Obama applied increasing pressure on Mubarak to resign. He did so, despite being urged by hardliners within his administration, including even Secretary of State Hillary Clinton, and by Saudi Arabia and Israel to halt his support of the protestors, and by critics who believed that he was not being forceful enough in getting the Egyptian leader to leave office. "It's tempting and it would be easy, to go out day after day with cathartic statements that make us feel good," explained Benjamin J. Rhodes, Obama's deputy national security director. "But ultimately, what's most important is achieving outcomes that are consistent with our values, because if we don't, those statements will be long-forgotten."[51]

As soon as Mubarak left office, the president made a speech congratulating the Egyptian people on their historic revolution. "The word *Tahrir*," he remarked, "means liberation. . . . And forevermore it will remind us of the Egyptian people—of what they did, of the things that they stood for, and how they changed their country, and in doing so changed the world." [52]

Less than a week later, he had to contend with a revolution in Libya against the dictatorial regime of Muammar al-Qaddafi. For forty-two years, the Libyan people had lived under a leader who, at times, seemed mentally unbalanced. Swept up by the fervor of the Arab Spring, the revolution quickly evolved into a civil war in which anti-Qaddafi forces took control of much of the eastern part of the country, including cities and towns along the Mediterranean and, battled pro-Qaddafi forces in Benghazi, Libya's second largest city.[53]

Unlike Western Europe, the US economy was not heavily dependent on Libya's oil. In contrast to its European allies, Washington did not have a vital stake in restoring stability to Libya. For that reason, many "realists" within the administration, including Defense Secretary Gates and National Security Adviser Tom Donilon, believed the United States should stay out of the Libyan struggle. Obama felt otherwise. He was under pressure from the allies and the more humanitarian-inclined members of the administration, including UN Ambassador Susan Rice, Samantha Power, a member of the NSC in charge of human rights issues, and, later, Secretary Clinton to intervene in the war. Like them, he was concerned by Qaddafi's statements that he was going to employ his considerable military power to put down the insurgency in Libya's eastern provinces and annihilate Benghazi.[54]

Although the president did not believe the United States should be the world's policeman in preventing genocidal acts, especially when the national interest was not involved, he also felt there were instances when intervention might have been justified, such as during the genocidal war in Rwanda in 1994 where, in 100 days, 800,000 people were killed. He was deeply impressed by Power's study of past genocides in the twentieth century, including the failure of the Clinton administration to respond in Rwanda. In a statement the White House issued on January 9, 2009, to mark the fifteenth anniversary of the genocide, he stated: "The memory of these events also deepens our commitment to act when faced with genocide and to work with partners around the world to prevent future atrocities."[55]

To prevent a humanitarian disaster and because Obama was assured the support of the Arab League and America's European allies (Germany being a notable exception), and also because he believed a failure to support the anti-Qaddafi forces economically and militarily might discourage democratic forces in other Arab countries, he felt he had to intervene in Libya despite his concern about the legality of doing so. He froze Qaddafi's assets, imposed an arms embargo, and established a no-fly zone over Libya. More important, he committed America's air and sea forces, *but not ground forces*, against Qaddafi's forces threatening the rebels.[56]

Intended at first to keep Qaddafi from attacking his own people, the strikes from the air and from allied warships offshore turned into an all-out assault on Libya's military. After the operation stopped Qaddafi on the outskirts of Benghazi, Obama continued to approve strikes in support of the insurgents. Frustrated that it was not being consulted about the intervention, the House rejected a bill authorizing the effort, but it did not cut funding for it. With the help they were receiving, including logistical and support troops on the ground, the insurgents launched a counterattack against Qaddafi, forcing him to flee Tripoli and go underground. In October, he was captured in his hometown of Sirte and executed.[57]

Throughout the American involvement in Libya, Obama portrayed his decision to intervene as a limited, humane action on his part to prevent the destruction of a city the size of Charlotte, North Carolina. Although he hoped to topple Qaddafi from power through nonmilitary means, he emphasized he was not seeking regime change. "Broadening our mission to include regime change would be a mistake," he told the American people at the end of March. "If we tried to overthrow Qaddafi our coalition would splinter" and we could repeat the mistake we made when sending US armed forces into Iraq. His administration "intervened to stop a massacre," he concluded, and we will work "with other nations to hasten the day when Qaddafi leaves power."[58]

If the president's explanation for US intervention in Libya seemed contradictory—not seeking regime change, but yet working to get Qaddafi to relinquish power—it appeared to work when the longtime Libyan tyrant fled into hiding. Unfortunately, the outcome remained a splintered nation with two different capitals, one in Benghazi and the other in Tripoli, and its exports of oil to Europe much lower than at the start of the war. In Libya, "the Arab Spring" turned into "the Arab Winter."

Taking place about the same time as the civil war in Libya was another war in Syria against the regime of Bashar al-Assad, a seemingly mild-mannered British-trained ophthalmologist, who had taken power in 2000 following the death of his father, Hafez al-Assad, a cunning and brutal dictator. Although many experts on Syria anticipated the son would be more open to political reform than his father, he proved just as ruthless.[59]

What set off the Syrian civil war was the death of a thirteen-year-old boy after attending a peaceful protest in April. When images of his body, which had been mutilated and burned, were released by someone filming his father pulling the covers off his dead son, they went viral. Demonstrations became violent, and Assad intensified the torture and killing of his opponents. By the summer, a full-scale civil war was underway in the country.[60]

In contrast to the war in Libya, the White House did not come to the military assistance of the insurgents in Syria. As bad as Assad was, Obama felt the alternative to the Syrian dictator could be even worse, especially since there was not any organized opposition as in Libya but rather a divided group of political rivals, exiles, and armed militias. The White House was not under pressure from its allies to intervene. Unlike in Libya, a bombing campaign would also involve the killing of massive numbers of innocent civilians living in crowded neighborhoods throughout Syria. Russia, which had economic and strategic interests in Syria, might react strongly against any NATO interference in Syria. Assad had the backing of a well-disciplined and trained military with a strong and loyal officer corps. It would take far more than a war fought largely from the air and sea to topple him. The president was determined not to have a repeat of Iraq and Afghanistan.[61]

Both for strategic and humanitarian reasons, the administration felt it could not entirely ignore the plight of the Syrian people. Immediately, it supplied a token amount of $12 million to the anti-Assad forces for satellite-communications equipment and night-vision goggles. For the next two years, however, it struggled over whether to arm the so-called moderate rebels even as critics like former vice president Dick Cheney attacked the Oval Office for wobbling and equivocating.[62]

Another issue confronting the president as the Arab Spring unfolded was how to respond to terrorist attacks against US interests in the Middle East and elsewhere. Terrorism had become a major worldwide problem going back to the 1970s when, in the United States, such diverse groups as the Weather Underground, the Symbionese Liberation Army, the Black Panthers, and the Jewish Defense League committed various acts of terrorism. Other terrorist incidents included airline hijackings and airline bombings at the rate of one a month.[63]

For all of Obama's attacks on the Bush administration for its conduct of the war against global terrorism, he differed little from Bush in terms of the vigor he applied to hunting down terrorists. Even during the campaign, he accompanied his appeals to principle with the implacable toughness of someone determined to wipe out terrorism. As president, he was faced with the question of whether he could order the killings of known terrorists wherever they were found while staying true to American values and the rule of law. He believed he could. While he ended the practice of torture, he expanded greatly the use of drones, including the killing of an American citizen, Anwar al Awlaki, a leader in the Yemeni affiliate of Al-Qaeda.[64]

The killing of Awlaki in 2011 was only the most controversial of numerous drone attacks the president ordered against terrorist leaders. Almost from the time he took office, he and his advisers were impressed by the ruthless precision of drones. He had an issue, however, about their legality. As a Harvard-trained lawyer who taught constitutional law at the University of Chicago, he was always deeply concerned about the legality of the actions he took as president. That was one reason why he surrounded himself with some of the country's most talented legal minds.[65]

During the 2008 campaign, Obama questioned what he regarded as illegal acts Bush committed in the name of national security, such as when he used warrantless searches to identify terrorists and intercept their communications. What bothered him was not only that Bush violated someone's civil liberties, but that he acted outside the law. At the beginning of his administration, he also told a group of civil libertarians that he wanted to limit the scope of presidential action in the fight against terrorism, reflecting another of his concerns about the expansion of executive power under Bush.[66]

Still, the question for him remained whether it was possible to fight a war against terrorism within the rule of law. What convinced him that it was legal was the advice of the lawyers in his administration and the nearly successful attempt by a terrorist, Farouk Abdulmutallab, to set off a bomb on a large Airbus filled with passengers while nearing the end of a flight from Amsterdam to Detroit. The president was determined not to allow another 9/11 incident to happen. He was also deeply annoyed by the outcry following the arrest of Abdulmutallab over whether and when he should have been read his Miranda rights. The near miss of a mass murderer flying over the United States and the outcry over his rights had profound implications for his legal position.[67]

Having decided it was legal to use drones in the war against terrorism, Obama greatly expanded drone attacks against suspected terrorist leaders. But his greatest achievement in this respect was the killing on May 2, 2011, of the leader of Al-Qaeda and the mastermind of 9/11, Osama bin Laden, by Navy SEALs. Bin Laden had evaded capture since he had slipped away from his mountain headquarters in Tora Bora during a failed siege eight years earlier. The hunt for him had gone cold, and President Bush had declared that his capture was not important.[68]

Obama thought otherwise. Reflective of his determination to eliminate all terrorist leaders, he entered office bent on hunting down the worst terrorist of all. By giving up on the hunt for bin Laden and his band of terrorists, the former president later reflected, and "instead defining the threat as an open-ended, all encompassing 'War on Terror,' we'd fallen into what I believed was a strategic trap—one that elevated al-Qaeda's prestige, rationalized the Iraq invasion, alienated much of the Muslim world, and warped almost a decade of US foreign policy."[69]

After a meeting of his national security advisers in May 2009, he pulled aside his newly appointed CIA director Leon Panetta, his deputy national security adviser Tom Donilon, his chief of staff Rahm Emanuel, and his director of the National Counterterrorism Center Mike Leiter and directed them to find bin Laden. "Here's the deal," he told his four advisers. "I want this hunt for Osama bin Laden [and his second-in-command of Al-Qaeda, Ayman al-Zawahiri] to come to the front of the line. I worry that the trail has gone cold. . . . I want regular reports on this to me, and I want them starting in 30 days."[70]

In an operation known by the code word, "Geronimo," the name given to bin Laden, the SEALS shot to death the leader of Al-Qaeda following a helicopter attack on his compound in Abbottabad, Pakistan. The president did not inform Islamabad of the attack because Pakistan had not been fully cooperative with the United States in fighting the Taliban. In the global war to defeat terrorism, he believed nations had responsibilities as well as rights.[71]

The president approved the raid knowing there might be someone else, perhaps an Afghan warlord, living in the compound. His security team was never able to say with certainty that bin Laden was the one who could be seen taking daily walks around the gardens in the compound. The most optimistic assessments placed the probability that person was bin Laden as high as 95 percent. The Counterterrorism Center's assessment was 40 percent. Obama placed the level of certainty at 50 percent. Nevertheless, he decided to go forward with the raid. "One of the things you learn as president is you're always dealing with probabilities," he later told a journalist writing about "Geronimo." "No issue comes to my desk that is perfectly solvable. . . . That's true of most of the decisions I make during the course of the day."[72]

Once the president determined that bin Laden was most likely living in the compound, he had to decide the best way to kill him. He considered several alternatives, including bombing the compound or using armed drones. He decided to employ the SEALS because it was the only way bin Laden's death could be confirmed. By using the counterterrorist team, the US could also retrieve valuable intelligence believed to be within the compound. The issue of violating Pakistani sovereignty was raised but immediately dismissed.[73]

Using Black Hawk helicopters designed to evade radar detection, the mission succeeded brilliantly, but it had the unanticipated consequence of further destabilizing the Pakistani government. The White House anticipated the raid would embarrass Islamabad. It did more than that. It underscored just how dangerous the situation in Pakistan was. Left unanswered after the raid was how the most wanted person in the world could hide out in a compound, outside the gates of a military academy, and close to the capital of an important American partner without a deep support structure?[74]

Obama announced bin Laden's death late on May 2 in a nine-minute address to the nation from the East Wing of the White House. Just a few hours earlier, he had attended the White House Correspondents' Dinner. As was customary at this annual black-tie affair, he bantered with the audience, including directing a few humorous remarks at Donald Trump. The real estate developer and television personality grimaced at his roasting by the president, clearly not liking what he heard. Throughout the evening the president gave no hint of the top-secret military operation that had killed bin Laden. He was waiting for final confirmation that he was dead and had been given a proper Muslim funeral before his body was dropped into the

Arabian sea. Earlier he had joined others involved in the planning of the raid to watch grainy transmissions of the operation in a small office across from the top-secret Situation Room.[75]

News that bin Laden had been killed spread quickly throughout the country. Everywhere celebrations took place spontaneously. In big cities and small towns people took to the streets or celebrated in small gatherings the death of a man who had hit the homeland in a way never done before, taking down the Twin Towers in New York City, striking at the Pentagon, and threatening the Capitol or the White House before a group of passengers in an airplane in western Pennsylvania took control of the plane and crashed it into an open field.[76]

Total deaths caused by bin Laden and the other terrorists involved in 9/11 neared three thousand. For almost a decade the Al-Qaeda leader had gone missing and had been nearly forgotten in the media. The celebrations that took place after Obama's announcement became celebrations of the president as well. A crowd in front of the White House chanted "Obama got Osama! Obama got Osama!"[77]

Despite the "catharsis" that he later described Americans feeling at the death of bin Laden, the former president later remembered wondering if it took the killing of a terrorist like him to recreate such feelings of national unity. The question "nagged" on him, he recalled. For all his pride and joy in successfully carrying out a such a dangerous and risky mission, he did not feel the same sense of "exuberance" he felt when the Affordable Care Act was passed. "I found myself imagining what America might look like if we could rally so that our government brought the same level of expertise and determination to reducing poverty or curbing greenhouse gases or making sure every family had access to decent day care," he said.[78]

Obama's Reelection Campaign of 2012

Bin Laden's killing had an immediate effect on the president's chances for reelection in 2012. On April 11, a month before the raid on Abbottabad, he announced that he was seeking a second term. His announcement took place at a time when he was dealing not only with the Arab Spring, but with his struggle on Capitol Hill over budget cuts and the debt ceiling. Despite his achievements in his first two years in office, including his accomplishments during the lame-duck session of Congress, he was an unpopular leader whose administration seemed in disarray and who appeared incapable of leading.[79]

Obama realized the difficulty he faced in seeking a second term. Speaking to his supporters, he noted the skepticism even within their ranks. "I know that a lot of you who were involved in the campaign earlier, over the last two years you've probably felt some frustration. . . . But I want everybody here to remember everything we've accomplished over the last two years, and the record of accomplishment in making a difference for ordinary people."[80]

To prepare for the campaign, the president shook up his White House staff. After his 2010 beating in the elections, he replaced Rahm Emanuel as his chief of staff with William Daley, the brother of Mayor Richard Daley and secretary of commerce during the Clinton administration. He also accepted the resignations of two of his most loyal aides, Senior Adviser David Axelrod, who was probably more responsible for his political career than anyone else, and Press Secretary Robert Gibbs, who had been with him since his 2004 campaign for the US Senate. He concluded that Emanuel was too abrasive, Axelrod was burned out, and Gibbs was needlessly contentious with the press. All three men had planned to resign for their own reasons, but Obama hastened their departures. He replaced Axelrod, who returned to Chicago to reprise his role as chief strategist for the campaign, with David Plouffe, who had managed his 2008 campaign, and Gibbs with Jay Carney, the top spokesman for Vice President Biden.[81]

In strategy sessions for the campaign, he made clear he would cooperate with the Republicans when he could and confront them when he could not. He would be the adult in the room above the political frays that angered the American public and motivated the Tea Party. Unfortunately for him, Trump, who was by then already considering running for president in 2012, claimed that the president was holding office illegally because he was born in Kenya. Even though the evidence of his birth in Hawaii was overwhelming, including a short form of his birth certificate, the accusation that he was an illegal president resonated with a fringe element of the population who, for several reasons, including the fact that he was Black, was determined to oust him from office in 2012.[82]

Not until Obama was able to display a long version of his birth certificate, which Hawaii did not normally provide in place of a short form as proof of birth, did the so-called birther movement begin to dissipate. Even then, charges continued to circulate over some right-wing media that Obama was a Kenyan who shared the anti-colonial and anti-western views of the Kenyan people, including his father, grandfather, and other family still living in Kenya. One effect of the birther movement was to deflect his campaign away from the message it was trying to send about the president's accomplishments during his first two years in office. Another was to raise new questions about his political beliefs and whether his presidency was legitimate.[83]

Obama was also frustrated by the distraction the birther movement caused from his efforts on Capitol Hill, where he sought to work with Congress on a number of issues, ranging from the budget and debt ceiling to jobs, infrastructure, and education. In a short speech carried by all the networks in which he announced the release of the long form of his birth certificate, he made clear his frustration. "We live in a serious time right now," he said, "and we have the potential to deal with the issues that we confront in a way that will make our kids and our grandkids and our great grandkids proud. . . . But we're going to have to get serious to do it."[84]

Although a number of Republicans decided to run for their party's nomination for president, Governor Mitt Romney of Massachusetts, who was able to win his office in an overwhelmingly Democratic state, emerged as the likely Republican nominee. Handsome and from a political family, the son of the former governor of Michigan, Romney made hundreds of millions of dollars as a founding partner in the investment firm, Bain Capital, and then almost single-handedly saved the beleaguered Salt Lake City Olympic games in 2002. As governor of the Bay State from 2003 to 2007, he passed what became a model for the Affordable Care Act. By the end of his term, he was openly running for president.[85]

Romney still faced a number of opponents, including Governor Rick Perry (TX), former speaker of the house Newt Gingrich (GA), and former senator Rick Santorum (PA), and a number of other lesser-known candidates. But by April 2012, he had a commanding lead over all of them. Good organization and fund-raising, and the tradition within the party of selecting the next in line for the nomination, accounted for much of his lead. (Romney had come in second in 2008 to John McCain.) The fact that he had moved more to the political right during the primary campaign, even disowning his health-care act, which, he said, would only work on a state level, accounted for most of the rest.[86]

As the campaign continued, it became clear that whoever won the Republican nomination would be running on a conservative platform. That nominee would try to reject the many accomplishments of the Obama administration, including the ACA. In response, the president, who faced primary opposition in a few states like Louisiana and Arkansas, where his nationally unknown opponent received 42 percent of the votes, decided to confront the Republican Party and rouse Democrats by doing what he did best: speaking directly to the American people. On December 6, 2011, he traveled to Osawatomie Kansas, the site of President Teddy Roosevelt's famous "New Nationalism" speech of 1910, where he delivered a major speech on the economy. In no other address did the president state more clearly his vision of a middle-class nation predicated on free enterprise that rewarded creativity and entrepreneurship, but provided for government regulation to prevent the power of money from becoming too great, much as Teddy Roosevelt had envisioned in his speech at Osawatomie, almost a century earlier.[87]

Attacking Republicans now in office for their corporate greed and lack of concern for those struggling to reach or remain in the middle class, Obama spoke out against the accumulation of wealth into the hands of a smaller percent of the population and the power of money that followed. "Long before the recession [of 2008] hit," he remarked, "hard work stopped paying off for many people. . . . Fewer and fewer of the folks who contributed to the success of our economy actually benefited from that success."[88]

The president stressed that he was not against the free enterprise system. Nor did he oppose the accumulation of wealth. Quite the opposite. He believed free enterprise remained foundational to a new middle class built on entrepreneurship and hard work and that successful entrepreneurs should be rewarded handsomely. Unfortunately, Republicans had abandoned the principles enunciated by Teddy Roosevelt a century earlier. Through deregulation, regulators who "looked the other way or didn't have the authority to look at all," and changes in the tax laws favorable to large corporations and the wealthiest Americans, these Republicans allowed massive accumulations of wealth and power in the hands of a few.[89]

The solution for Obama was to return to the principles of the New Nationalism enunciated by Roosevelt. Free enterprise should be allowed to flourish, but it should be regulated in a way that avoided excesses of wealth. Just as "there was in Teddy Roosevelt's time, there is a certain crowd in Washington," the president declared, "who for the last few decades, have said, let's respond to this economic challenge with the same old tune. 'The market will take care of everything.'" The theory has never worked. "We simply cannot return to this brand of 'you're on your own' economics if we're serious about rebuilding the middle class in this country."[90]

The choice for the voters in 2012 was clear. They could continue along the lines that stacked the deck for the wealthy. Or they could keep competition fair while ensuring the government had sufficient funds to protect the vulnerable and invest in research and education. What did this mean "for restoring middle-class security in today's economy?" Obama asked. "Well, it starts by making sure that everyone in America gets a fair shot at success. . . . The race we want to win is a race to the top—the race for good jobs that pay well and offer middle-class security."[91]

In the months that followed, the president pressed this theme of assuring opportunity for a new middle class. Government should not be the instrument of the wealthy. But neither should it promote dependency or be an obstacle to free enterprise and the entrepreneurial spirit that built the middle class. Its role, instead, should be limited. In his State of the Union address on January 24, 2012, he remarked: "I'm a Democrat. But I believe what Republican Abraham Lincoln believed: that government should do for people only what they cannot do better by themselves, and no more."[92]

His message was still one of hope. "As long as we are joined in common purpose, as long as we maintain our common resolve, our journey moves forward, and our future is hopeful," he concluded in his State of the Union. But the hope the president offered in 2012 was more qualified than what he offered in 2008, with more emphasis on individual responsibility.[93]

Despite the obstacles that Obama faced in getting reelected, he always held a lead in opinion polls against Romney. Some of those who voted for him in 2008 may have been disappointed at his seeming inability to deal with an economy in which unemployment remained high and wages were stagnant. Others may have been concerned that he appeared as a weak leader who could not even control his own staff, Progressives within his party may even have accused him of adopting the slogan "too big to fail" in dealing with the banking and financial structure they held responsible for the recession of 2008–2010.[94]

The voters appeared willing, however, to give the president another opportunity to fulfill his promises of 2008. They appreciated his accomplishments as president, and they blamed Congress far more than they blamed him for the nation's political and economic stagnation. They liked him personally and were impressed by his family life—by the fact that he set aside time whenever he was in the White House to have dinner with his family and to attend Malia's and Sasha's school activities.[95]

In contrast to 2008, when Michelle Obama appeared at times a liability to her husband, she proved in 2012 to be an important asset in the campaign, just as she had become a popular First Lady as a result of her efforts on behalf of reducing child obesity and providing for military families. At the Democratic convention in Charlotte in September, which nominated Obama for a second term, she made a rousing speech that even conservative columnists acknowledged was a great success, tying her story and Barack's to the American dream of parents' being able, through hard work and initiative, to give their children a better life than their own.[96]

The same voters were less impressed by Romney and his wife, Ann. The former governor seemed more a wealthy businessman than a politician, a candidate who appeared out-of-touch with the needs of most voters and whose views on issues seemed to change as the political winds changed. The fact that Romney was a Mormon also raised questions among some Christians as to whether the Mormon Church was a sect rather than a Christian church. As for Ann, she was a sympathetic figure who had been diagnosed with multiple sclerosis in 1998, and she delivered a well-received speech at the Republican nominating convention in August, in which she tried to humanize her husband. She seemed, however, to lack the poise, vibrancy, and common touch of the more experienced First Lady.[97]

The president's campaign operated on all cylinders, while Romney's backfired time and again, sometimes for reasons beyond his control. At the Republican convention in Tampa during the week of August 27, a hurricane forced the cancellation of the first day of speeches. Governor Chris Christie (NJ) gave a keynote address that was more one about him than about the presumptive Republican candidate. The most memorable moment of the gathering was not any of its major speeches, but the surprise address by the actor, Clint Eastwood, in which he tried to inject humor into his presentation by talking to an empty chair, allegedly representing Obama. Although well received in the convention hall, he was ridiculed in the media. Ann Romney was embarrassed by the whole incident, and both she and her husband were distressed that Eastwood's presence on stage took the spotlight away from him.[98]

As his running mate, Romney chose Representative Paul Ryan, the fiscally conservative head of the Budget Committee, who proposed to replace the popular Medicare program with individual grants to eligible retirees. Ryan's acceptance speech, in which he attacked the Obama administration for not living up to its promises of 2008, was panned in the press for falsely describing the president's role in the shutdown of a GM plant in Ryan's hometown of Janesville, Wisconsin. Romney's own acceptance speech succeeded in humanizing the Republican. As a result of the convention, he even got a small bump in the opinion polls.[99]

In contrast to the Republican convention, the Democratic gathering, held the following week in Charlotte, went off with only a few hitches. One high-powered speaker after another went onstage to praise the accomplishments of the Obama administration. There were no "Eastwood-like" events to take the spotlight away from the president. An opening night tribute to deceased Senator Ted Kennedy showed the former senator endorsing Obama for president four years earlier and sparring effectively with Romney, who sought his Senate seat in 1994. The video threw the packed convention hall into near frenzy.[100]

On the third night of the convention, former president Bill Clinton delivered an electrifying speech that once more kept the delegates on their feet applauding and cheering for almost the entire forty-eight-minute speech in which he nominated the president for reelection and mocked the Republicans for refusing to work with him. They "hate" him, he said. Even though the former president spoke beyond the two hours allotted by the networks for live coverage of the convention, they kept him on the air. After the speech, Obama came on stage to embrace his former rival. It was a stunning close to end a successful day.[101]

The next day Vice President Biden was chosen by acclamation to be the president's running mate a second time. Then the president was nominated for a second term unanimously. (The few delegates won by Obama's opponents had been disqualified due to lack of a delegate slate.) In his acceptance speech later that night before a crowd of twenty thousand, the president continued with the theme that while he had accomplished much during his first term, the country's business remained undone. He proposed a "harder" path to a "better place." "I won't pretend the path I'm offering is quick or easy; I never have," he said. "You didn't elect me to tell you what you wanted to hear. You elected me to tell you the truth. And the truth is, it will take more than a few years for us to solve challenges that have built up over decades." Like the convention as a whole, the president's comments were well received. In contrast to the small bump in the polls following the Republican convention, the Democratic bump was significant.[102]

A week after the Democratic gathering a video was leaked to the liberal magazine, *Mother Jones*, showing Romney speaking to a group of wealthy Republican donors at a fund-raiser in Boca Raton, Florida. In his remarks, Romney could be heard saying that in the campaign (and presumably in his administration if elected president) he could ignore the 47 percent of voters who did not pay any taxes (clearly meaning federal taxes) and would never vote for him. These are people, he added, "who are dependent upon government, who believe they are victims, who believe government has a responsibility to care for them, who believe that they are entitled to health-care, to food, to housing, to you-name it. . . . And they will vote for this president no matter what."[103]

As critics of the video pointed out almost immediately, while the 47 percent figure was technically correct, it included many low-wage workers and workers with families, who, after exemptions, did not owe the government anything. It also included retirees and the elderly who paid taxes while they were gainfully employed but who no longer had a taxable income high enough on which to pay taxes. The largest percentages of those not paying taxes also lived in states that normally voted Republican.[104]

After the election, Romney acknowledged in an interview that his "47 percent" comments "did real damage to my campaign." Most commentators agreed. What was so damaging was that because everything he said was documented on video, there was no way he could walk back his remarks, such as by claiming they were taken out of context or that he had been misquoted.[105]

Also going for Obama in the campaign was the brilliantly conceived technical infrastructure that his campaign developed in his headquarters in Chicago. Most political analysts attributed a good part of the president's success in 2008 to the sophisticated technology his team, led by David Plouffe, had put in place that year, which allowed the campaign to identify likely Obama voters and use that information to bring them. The infrastructure put in place in 2012 was more sophisticated than even that, making it possible for the campaign to identify and solicit undecided voters and to allow the field offices to share information in ways not possible in 2008.[106]

The campaign that followed turned out be one of the more negative in recent years. Both sides ran endless ads attacking the other for the negativity of the campaign. The president warned that, if elected, Romney would turn the clock backward eliminating the gains for the middle class achieved since the end of World War II. In contrast, he promised to advance the efforts to bring more Americans into the middle class begun during this first administration. The Republican nominee countered by accusing what he called an "incompetent" administration led by a weak president of failing to deliver on any of the promises he had made four years earlier.[107]

The worst day of the campaign for Obama occurred on October 2, when the president and his opponent held the first of three debates in Denver. The president did not expend the time he should have in preparing for it. His advisers instructed him not to be combative with Romney, advice which they later regretted. During the debate, in which both candidates claimed their policies would improve the lives of the middle class, they seemed to talk past each other and to ignore the moderator, Jim Lehrer of PBS.[108]

On stage, Romney, who regarded the debate as his last chance to save his struggling campaign and had prepared extensively for it, appeared more presidential than the president. He was confident and knowledgeable as he presented himself as the true champion of the middle class. In contrast, the president, who regarded debates disdainfully for their lack of substance, appeared arrogant, pedantic, and detached. He often digressed in answering questions, looked down at his lectern, and fumbled with his notes. The consensus after the debate was that Romney had bested Obama by a considerable margin.[109]

In the two remaining debates, the president turned things around for the rest of the campaign. Believing that his reelection was on the line, he prepared meticulously for his second meeting with Romney. He was much more relaxed than in the first debate, much less professorial, quick on his feet, and frequently displaying the big smile and wit for which he had become well known. [110]

Near the end of the debate a spectator asked him how he could claim to be defending the country when, on September 11, four Americans, including the ambassador to Libya, Chris Stevens, were killed in Benghazi by rioters who overran the American compound. He said he could only explain the steps he had taken to defend the embassy. Romney then miscalculated, accusing the president of never using the term "terrorist" in describing the attack when, as the president pointed out, he had used the term in the Rose Garden the day after the attack. The Republican candidate also failed to show why he and not Obama should be in charge of the nation. He could not escape the "47 percent" comments he made a month earlier as his opponent pounded his credibility and conservative views, denounced his budget proposals as a "sketchy deal," and accused him of not telling the truth to the American people.[111]

In the third debate, which was devoted to foreign policy, Romney was out of his depth as he embraced what had become the standard Republican line: accusing Obama of failing to give the military the support they needed to defend the country and calling for an increase of $2 trillion for the Pentagon. When he argued that, ship-for-ship, the "Navy was smaller now than at any time since 1917," the president reminded him that the navy was no longer the battleship navy of 1917 but a highly sophisticated fleet, including submarines, employing the latest technology and capable of launching highly accurate missiles against targets hundreds of miles away. He also pointed to numerous contradictions Romney seemed to make in talking about his foreign policy and remarked that his opponent appeared "to want to import the foreign policies of the 1980s, just like the social policies of the 1950s and the economic policies of the 1950s." A poll taken by CBS after the debate had the president winning it by thirty points. [112]

In the last days of the campaign, Romney attempted to portray himself as a moderate and agent of change. His crowds grew in size, convincing him that the polls showing the president holding on to a narrow lead were wrong and that when the votes were counted, he would be the next president of the United States. Even Karl Rove—often regarded at the time as the best strategist in the Republican Party and credited by many with George Bush's two victories in 2000 and 2004—believed Romney would win.[113]

In the last month of the campaign, Obama campaigned round-the-clock, portraying himself as the candidate of change fighting the forces of reaction and status quo. Instead of a president content to live in a self-made bubble, he appeared to be a leader using his last reserves of energy to protect the achievements of his first administration and wanting another term to complete his agenda. Even as he campaigned, a number of developments broke in his favor. Former chairman of the Joint Chiefs of Staff and secretary of state during the Bush administration, Colin Powell, announced he was endorsing him for reelection. Another Republican, Governor Chris Christie of New Jersey, commended the president for his quick response to Hurricane Sandy, which ravaged the Northeast during the last week of the campaign.[114]

When the votes were counted on November 4, the president defeated Romney by a margin of 51 percent to 47.5 percent. He received 65.9 million votes to his Republican opponent's 60.9 million. He won the electoral college by a landslide, gaining 332 electoral college votes to Romney's 206. Even Ohio, which Romney regarded as key to his victory, went to Obama.[115]

The president won because the voters were inclined to give him a second chance and because Romney could never shake the image of a wealthy businessman favoring the wealthy and indifferent to the needs of almost half the nation's population. His campaign was also outplayed by the smartest strategists in the business, the best organization on the ground, and the most technologically sophisticated campaign in the nation's history.[116]

The president's victory was not as stunning as his election in 2008. Although his margin of victory was about the same as four years earlier, overall voter turnout, especially among Blacks, was down, and he lost two states that he had won in 2008, North Carolina and Indiana. After he was declared the winner by the major television networks, the crowds welcoming his reelection were fewer and smaller. Missing was the confidence that his reelection would bring about the fundamental change he had promised four years earlier.[117]

The Republicans also held on to the House and nearly recaptured the Senate, meaning that government was now divided as it had never been before in the twenty-first century. Not only was the executive branch controlled by the Democrats and the House controlled by Republicans, the Supreme Court was evenly divided between four liberals and four conservatives. A ninth justice, Arthur Kennedy, generally voted with the conservatives, but in key cases, like upholding the landmark decision *Roe versus Wade*, or affirming the constitutional right of same-sex couples to marry, he voted with the liberals.[118]

All that said, Obama was "the comeback president," just as former President Clinton had been able to term himself as the "comeback kid" after turning his campaign around in 1992. Often written off as a one-term president following his stunning rejection in the 2010 congressional elections, he maintained his coolness. At a rally that followed his victory, he even seemed more animated and happier than he had been four years earlier when he realized the weight of the presidency had just fallen onto his shoulders. Having been in office for four years, he was more confident about his ability to serve another four years, although he continued to be concerned about what he sensed were growing national political divisions and the undermining of any sense of national unity.[119]

Throughout the two years between his repudiation in 2010 and his reelection in 2012, Obama held steadfastly to his vision of an inclusive middle-class nation predicated on free enterprise, entrepreneurship, and individual responsibility. As president, he sought to achieve that goal by offering opportunities to even the most disadvantaged Americans, whether through tax cuts and credits, or health reform, or increased support for public education. But the burden of achieving success was on individuals willing to make the most of the opportunities before them by their own hard work and initiative. This was the vision he retained and the message he carried into his second term as president.

In foreign policy, Obama's priority was dealing with the Arab Spring of 2010–2012. In his response in the Middle East, he was guided by two principles: (1) stay out as much as possible; and (2) when intervention was required, international consensus was necessary before the United States would intervene. Even then, the response had to be limited and the US should act only as part of a coalition. As in his domestic policy, he believed in responsibility—individual responsibility at home and national responsibility abroad. He encouraged and assisted nations to succeed, but ultimately the burden of success rested with them. This was true in Egypt, Libya, and Syria. These nations did not succeed as the president hoped. And for that, he opened himself to criticism by those who argued that he should have done more or that he should have done less to assist them. Still this was the message he carried into his second term.

CHAPTER 8

Dysfunctional Government

Although Barack Obama became the "comeback president" in 2012 by being the first president since Ronald Reagan to be reelected with more than 50 percent of the vote, his victory did not translate into a new chapter in his relations with Congress. Government remained dysfunctional as right-wing Republicans tightened their grip on both houses of Congress. Despite their opposition, Obama was able to win several legislative victories on Capitol Hill, but they caused a further poisoning of the relationship between Democrats and Republicans that forced, in one instance, a two-week government shutdown. As a result, by the midterm elections of 2014, voters had lost faith in either of the two major parties to govern.[1]

Another problem the president had to deal with even before his second term began was a series of tragic developments at home and abroad. Throughout his meteoric rise from his election to the Illinois state senate in 1996 to his reelection in 2012, good fortune had followed his political career. After he was returned to office, that changed when events, mostly beyond his control, shocked the nation and the world and forced him to reshape his agenda for the next two years. At home he had to deal with the killing in December of twenty children, ages six and seven, and six adults, at Sandy Hook Elementary School in Newtown Connecticut and, a few months later, with the setting off of two bombs among spectators watching the Boston

Marathon. Abroad, he had to respond to the takeover of much of Iraq and part of Syria by the small, radical Sunni Islamic terrorist group known as ISIS (the Islamic State of Iraq and Syria) or ISIL (the Islamic State of the Levant) and the use of chemical weapons by the Syrian leader, Bashar al-Assad, in the civil war against his regime.

In both cases, Obama responded with executive actions. He did so only when he became convinced that he could not work with Capitol Hill. The agenda he presented to the 113th Congress was much the same as the one on which he campaigned against his Republican opponent, Mitt Romney, in 2012. As in his first administration, his purpose was to expand and strengthen the nation's middle class through a program of progressive reforms, fundamental to which were a core set of conservative principles.

Legislation, Division, and Domestic Terrorism

At the top of the president's legislative list was eliminating the tax break approved during the Bush administration on earned income over $250,000; this meant that most Americans and small businesses would keep the Bush tax cut, while much of it would be eliminated for the wealthiest 2 percent of Americans. Having won reelection by a comfortable margin and aware of the political cost to the Republicans if they allowed the Bush tax cuts to expire for all Americans, he adopted a hard bargaining position with the Republican leadership over extending the tax cuts to the richest Americans.[2]

While he was not able to get Republicans to agree to eliminate the tax cuts on household incomes over $250,000, he was able to reach an agreement eliminating the cuts for incomes over $450,000. Although progressive Democrats criticized him for giving away too much to the Republicans, by eliminating the Bush tax cuts for the wealthiest Americans, he put the issue to rest before his second term began. He also won other concessions from the Republicans including increases in estate and capital gains taxes, renewal of tax credits for childcare, college tuition, and the working poor, and extension of unemployment benefits for two million jobless Americans. After the House passed the legislation, the president put down a marker for the next fiscal year. "The one thing that I think, hopefully, the next year will focus on," he commented, "is seeing if we can put a package like this together with a little bit less drama, a little less brinkmanship, and not scare the heck out of folks quite as much."[3]

At his press conference the day after his reelection, he proposed comprehensive immigration reform. It had not been a high priority during his first administration, but he made reform of the nation's complex and controversial immigration system one of his highest priorities during the 113th Congress. In particular, he sought to put into law the DREAM Act, which he had instituted by an executive order (DACA) and which provided a path to citizenship for the children of illegal immigrants who had been brought into the United States by their parents and either had a record of military service or were seeking a college education.[4]

The president also sought a comprehensive budget deal, something he also carried over from his first administration. He addressed the nation's mounting debt through new sources of revenues other than closing loopholes and deductions, and budget cuts that preserved the nation's social network and allowed investments in research, education, and infrastructure. He hoped to work with the Republicans, but he reminded them at his press conference that he had nothing to lose since he would never again run for office and warned that if there was no cooperation, he was prepared to act on his own. "I've got a mandate to help middle-class families and families that are working hard to try to get into the middle class," he remarked. The American people want compromise, and they want action. "But they want to make sure that middle-class folks aren't bearing the entire burden and sacrifice when it comes to some of these big challenges. . . . And that's going to be my guiding principle during these negotiations."[5]

Republican leaders responded to Obama's remarks quickly. A few days after the press conference, Susan Rice, the US ambassador to the United Nations and a candidate to replace departing Secretary of State Hillary Clinton, said on a Sunday news show that the recent Benghazi attack appeared to have developed spontaneously from public demonstrations spreading throughout the Middle East over a video disparaging the prophet Muhammed. The comments came from talking points approved by the White House before evidence mounted that the attack was planned and carried out by members of Al-Qaeda. Republican Senators Lindsay Graham (SC) and John McCain (AZ), who said earlier that they wanted to have Watergate-style hearings on the Benghazi attack, remarked that Rice was unqualified to head the State Department because of her allegedly misleading account. The response of the Republicans to Rice's statement infuriated the president and signaled their obstructionist intentions when the 113th Congress began in January.[6]

Before the new House and Senate convened, the nation was rocked by the mass killings at the Sandy Hook Elementary School. A mass shooting at a movie theater in Aurora, Colorado, five months earlier had left twelve people killed and seventy others injured. It had the highest number of casualties at the time and led to calls for new gun control measures, including more extensive background checks of purchasers of guns and the prohibition of assault weapons. But the powerful National Rifle Association (NRA) helped defeat these efforts at gun control, just as they had defeated earlier proposals following the shootings at Columbine High School in nearby Columbine, Colorado, in 1999, which left twelve students and one teacher dead, and at Virginia Tech in 2007, which left thirty-two dead.[7]

Because of the age and innocence of the children killed at Sandy Hook and the fact that the shootings occurred so soon after those in Aurora, news of what took place at the presumably safe town of twenty-seven thousand, about seventy-five miles by car from New York City, shocked the nation as no earlier act of domestic terrorism had done.

President Obama was so upset by the news of Sandy Hook that he told his deputy director of speechwriting, Cody Keenan, that he did not know if he would "be able to get through this." In short remarks he made to the nation after learning of the shootings, he found himself having to stop several times to collect his emotions. "We've endured too many of these tragedies in the past few years," he said. "And each time I learn the news I react not as a President, but as anybody else would—as a parent. And that was especially true today. I know there's not a parent in America who doesn't feel the same overwhelming grief that I do."[8]

Four days later, the president spoke again at a prayer vigil for victims of the Sandy Hook shootings. Once more, he had difficulty controlling his emotions. "You must know that whatever measure of comfort we can provide, we will provide," he told the families of the victims. "Newtown you are not alone."[9]

When Congress reconvened on January 3, there was a widespread sense that the House and the Senate would finally adopt meaningful gun control legislation. The president had already decided to use his political capital to do something about guns. He assigned Vice President Biden, Attorney General Eric Holder, and Secretary of Homeland Security Janet Napolitano the task of coming up with gun safety proposals that he could submit to Congress.[10]

In his second inaugural address on January 20 and in his State of the Union address on February 13, which White House Press Secretary Jay Carney characterized as "two acts of the same play," he made clear his commitment to gun control, including requiring stronger background checks for purchasers of guns and prohibiting the sale of assault weapons. While his emphasis in both speeches was Washington's responsibility to give every American the opportunity to enter the middle class, he closed both of them by turning to the shootings in Newtown and elsewhere. "Our journey is not complete," he said in his inaugural, "until all our children, from the streets of Detroit to the hills of Appalachia, to the quiet lanes of Newtown, know that they are cared for and cherished and always safe from harm."[11]

Unfortunately for the White House, passage of gun control measures still proved too hard. On April 17, a bipartisan measure offered by Senators Joe Manchin (D-WV) and Pat Toomey (R-PA) that would have required expanded background checks for private sales of guns and gun show sales and banned the sale of some military-type semiautomatic weapons was defeated in the Democratic-controlled Senate by a vote of 54 to 46 with four Democrats from conservative states joining with Republicans to prevent the Senate from getting the sixty votes needed for approval. One by one other gun control measures also went down to defeat by even larger margins.[12]

The failure to pass gun control legislation was a resounding defeat for Obama, who had delivered major addresses on the need for gun control legislation in Colorado and Connecticut two weeks earlier and had made final appeals to Republicans to vote with the majority in favor of what he argued were modest first steps to prevent massacres like the one at Newtown.

As if to underscore the president's message, on April 15, just two days before the Senate votes on gun legislation, two powerful bombs exploded killing three spectators and wounding 260 others at the finish line of the Boston Marathon. One of the two brothers responsible for the bombings was killed in a shootout with police, while the other was apprehended in a Boston suburb later that night. The bombings reverberated beyond Boston. Officials in New York and Washington stepped up security in important locations throughout the two cities. The Secret Service shut down Pennsylvania Avenue near the White House.[13]

That the Senate could still block legislation that might prevent future acts of domestic terrorism, especially when parents of the victims of the Newtown shooting had come to Washington to lobby the senators and were seated in the Senate gallery watching the votes on gun control, infuriated the usually unflappable president. As David Plouffe explained: "When gun control failed, that was a very personal issue for the president. He had gotten close to many of the victims' families." "This is a pretty shameful day for Washington," the president stated shortly after the Senate vote at a media event outside the Oval Office. He was accompanied by Gabby Gifford, the congresswoman who had been nearly killed at an earlier shooting outside a Tucson supermarket, and parents of the Sandy Hook victims, one of whom introduced him. Most of the senators who voted against the gun control legislation, the president remarked, "could not offer any good reason why we wouldn't want to make it harder for criminals and those with severe mental illnesses to buy a gun. . . . It came down to politics. . . . They worried that the gun lobby would spend a lot of money and paint them as anti–Second Amendment."[14]

Despair at the White House

Even before the Senate's failure to pass gun control legislation, friends of Obama and Michelle began to notice subtle changes in their personalities. While Michelle grew more comfortable in her role as First Lady, she felt more isolated than in the past. She regretted that she could not see her beloved cherry blossoms along the Tidal Basin in the spring without having to wear a hat and sunglasses. She stopped taking girls into a mentorship program she started because she worried that other teenagers would feel left out. At the same time, she and her staff began to consider ways she could take advantage of her popularity and take on other causes beyond child obesity and caring for military families.[15]

Obama also became more comfortable in his role as president, and more accustomed to some of the rituals of his office he had previously disdained, such as the annual pardoning of a turkey during the Thanksgiving holiday. Yet he had also become more cynical about Washington and more bloody-minded when it came to confronting the Republicans.[16]

In the winter and spring of 2013, the White House was rocked by a series of disclosures, including one by the Justice Department that it had taken possession of the records of AP reporters as part of an investigation into leaks of national security information and another that the Internal Revenue Service (IRS) was targeting conservative nonprofit groups seeking tax-exempt status. The first revelation seemed to belie Obama's frequent statements on the importance of a free and independent media, while the second appeared to prove that the IRS had become a political arm of the White House. The disclosures led to calls by conservative groups for the resignation of Attorney General Eric Holder and eventually forced the resignation of Lois Lerner, director of the IRS Exempt Organization Division. Only after congressional scrutiny into IRS activity did the agency approve dozens of conservative groups for tax-exempt status, a sharp break from the previous two years when only a handful of such applications had been approved.[17]

Coming on top of the administration's failure to gain gun control legislation, these scandals left Obama exasperated about his ability to shape events. Privately, he spoke about "going Bulworth," a movie about a senator running for president who risked everything by saying publicly what he felt like saying regardless of the political consequences. He bristled at a column by Maureen Dowd of the *New York Times*, who wrote that while he had "searing moments" of connecting with the American public, he had not learned how to govern. Blaming the president for not getting Congress to approve gun control legislation, Dowd compared him unfavorably to the Michael Douglas character in the film *The American President*. At the annual White House Correspondents' Dinner in April, which Douglas was attending, Obama turned to the actor and commented sarcastically, "Michael, what's your secret, man." He was determined to free himself of what he regarded as hypocritical power-seeking legislators, greedy money-making lobbyists, and even a shallow and sensational press, all of whom seemed to put their own self-interest ahead of the public good.[18]

In May, the president traveled to Mexico to discuss immigration, energy, and security matters with President Enrique Peña Nieto followed by a courtesy call to Costa Rica, where he met briefly with President Laura Chinchilla. In June he went overseas, visiting Belfast, Berlin, and Cape Town. In each of these places, he spoke to groups of young people. In each, he reminded them of the hardships that their forefathers had to bear—the first to end a bloody civil war between Catholics and Protestants in Northern Ireland, the second, to tear down the wall that divided Germany, and the third to end apartheid in South Africa—before they could have the freedom and prosperity they now enjoyed. A common theme in these addresses was that just as young people needed to be aware of the past sacrifices earlier generations made in their behalf, they needed to realize that authoritarianism, sectarianism, racial injustice, poverty, and terrorism were still widespread and that they had to carry on the struggle begun by their parents and grandparents. Speaking from the east side of the Brandenburg Gate that once divided East from West Berlin, he told his audience that what he wanted was "peace with justice." "Peace with justice," he went on to say, meant "free enterprise that unleashes the talents and creativity that reside in each of us," the elimination of intolerance that "breeds injustice," assurances that "our wives and daughters [have] the same opportunities as our husbands and sons," "a world without nuclear weapons," and the fulfillment of our moral obligations, including taking "a profound interest in the impoverished corners of the world."[19]

The president's most important visit, however, had occurred two months earlier, in March, when he made a fifty-hour trip to Israel, his first since taking office. His visit there left him doubting his role as a world leader. While in the Jewish state, he met with President Shimon Peres and Prime Minister Benjamin Netanyahu and held a press conference before traveling to Ramallah in the West Bank where he held a joint news conference with Palestinian Authority president Mahmoud Abbas and later that day delivered a speech before a large group of Israeli students at a convention center in

Jerusalem. He concluded his trip by briefly visiting Jordan where he held talks in Amman with its leader, King Abdullah II.[20]

His visit was more symbolic than policy-driven, but it had two main purposes. The first was to repair the president's frayed relations with Netanyahu and the Israeli people as a result of a series of diplomatic slights on his part, including his failure to meet with the Israeli leader during his visit to the United States in 2010, and a statement he had made in Cairo in 2009 to the effect that the establishment of Israel was a result of the Holocaust. In an effort to take back that comment, he laid a wreath at the grave of Theodore Herzl, widely considered the father of the modern Zionist movement. Later, he went to the Yad Vashem Holocaust Memorial, where he remarked that Israel did not exist because of the Holocaust: Israel's existence assured the Holocaust would never happen again.[21]

Israelis were also concerned about Syria's development of chemical weapons that might be used against them and about the administration's ongoing blunder, in their view, of not doing more to prevent Iran from developing nuclear weapons, something they considered an existential threat to their survival. In response, Obama tried to reassure Israel (and King Abdullah) that he would not tolerate Syria's use of chemical weapons or allow Iran to develop a nuclear weapons capacity.[22]

His other purpose in going to Israel was to rekindle the stalled effort to bring about an Israeli-Palestinian agreement based on a separate state for the Palestinian people on the West Bank and in the Gaza Strip; this meant ending Jewish settlements on the West Bank. In his meetings with Israeli leaders and in his talks with President Abbas and King Abdullah II, with whom he also discussed Abdullah's concern about the flow of Syrian refugees into Jordan as a result of the ongoing civil war in Syria, he raised the issue of a two-state solution to the Israeli-Palestinian conflict. In his address to one thousand Israeli students in Jerusalem, and a worldwide television audience of millions just before leaving for home, the president made a forceful case for a separate Palestinian state. Afterward, he told the students that peace was possible. "I'm not saying it's guaranteed. . . . But it is possible."[23]

Israel's response to the president's visit was favorable. Calling Obama's address in Jerusalem "a corker of a speech," D. L. of the *Economist* blog *Pomegranate* reported that the president "scored with the Israeli public." Referencing his Jerusalem speech, Robert Taite of the *Telegraph* added: "With soaring rhetoric, he resembled the Barack Obama that a majority of the American public and much of the world beyond once loved—and had almost forgotten." Even Prime Minister Netanyahu proved surprisingly courteous to the president. In the joint news conference he and Peres had with Obama after he arrived at Ben Gurion Airport, the prime minister expressed solidarity with Washington and remarked about a Mideast peace that his government sought a two-state solution to the Israeli-Palestinian conflict. [24]

Yet little resulted from Obama's visit to Israel. As David Remnick of the *New Yorker* pointed out, "for anyone looking for a real diplomatic initiative, this trip was . . . a real disappointment. Obama was all embrace: no pressure, no initiative, no insistence." Outside Israel, the US remained as unpopular as ever. The Palestinians were deeply disappointed that during a press conference with Abbas, the president failed to repeat a previous demand for an end to further Israeli settlements on the West Bank. They were also disturbed that he failed to make any mention of a long-standing Palestinian insistence that, before agreeing to any peace settlement, Israel had to agree to the establishment of East Jerusalem as the capital of Palestine and to the right of return of Palestinian refugees to the new state of Palestine.[25]

Obama's troubles in the Middle East were not limited to his failure to resolve the Israeli-Palestinian problem. He also came under increasing criticism, even from his own supporters, for his use of drones in the Middle East. Almost from the time he took office, his advisers were fascinated by President Bush's effective use of drones in killing many of the Al-Qaeda leaders in the badlands of Afghanistan and Pakistan. The president had doubts about Bush's delegation of power in ordering drone attacks. As a former law professor, he was also concerned about the legality of detaining captured terrorists indefinitely and using drones to kill terrorist leaders. He drew sophisticated distinctions between what was legally permissible (targeting specific terrorist leaders) and what was not (torturing terrorists or being indiscriminate in using drone strikes). For that reason, he was deeply troubled by the use of drones to attack meetings of senior leaders instead of surgical attacks against single individuals. He was also rattled by growing criticism of the drone program on Capitol Hill and from civil and human rights groups. He increased the role of the White House in managing drone attacks, and he insisted on a complete review by the intelligence services of the reasons justifying a drone attack on a terrorist target, including any collateral damage it might cause nontargeted civilians.[26]

On May 23, 2013, Obama delivered a major address on US drone and counterterrorist policy at the National Defense University. Point by point, he outlined his reasons for employing targeted drone attacks on individual terrorist leaders. He also remarked on the expansion of Al-Qaeda from the mountains of Afghanistan and Pakistan, where, he claimed, its leadership had been largely decimated, to Yemen and Somalia. Together, the two countries controlled the entrance to the Gulf of Aden, a vital waterway for Persian Gulf oil.[27]

The United States was "at a crossroads," in the war against terrorism, the president said. "We must define the nature and scope of this struggle or else it will define us." Despite Obama's ending the war in Iraq and making Afghanistan more responsible for its own defense, and despite the killing of Osama bin Laden and most of his top lieutenants, terrorists remained a threat to the United States in the Arabian Peninsula as well as in countries like Libya and Syria and in the United States itself. "We have to take these threats seriously," the president continued, "and do all that we can to confront them."[28]

Because these threats were scattered and unified only by a common extremist belief that the United States and the West posed a threat to Islam, the war against terrorism could not rely "on military and law enforcement alone." Instead, the US had to define its effort, "not as a boundless 'global war on terror,' but rather as a series of persistent, targeted efforts to dismantle specific networks of violent extremists that threaten America." He wanted a strategy that was "proportionate and smart." His administration's preference was to detain and prosecute terrorists. He had already signed a set of guidelines meant to rein in the indiscriminate use of drones, including working with other countries to capture known terrorists. This was not always possible. In these cases the use of drones was justified, recognizing the need for a complete review of the planned attacks he had described earlier. "We were attacked on 9/11," the president stated. "Under domestic law and international law, the United States is at war with al Qaeda, the Taliban, and their associate forces. . . . So this is a just war—a war waged proportionately, in last resort, and in self-defense."[29]

Obama's address was widely criticized by foreign policy experts who took him to task for lacking specifics in his speech and by civil libertarians and the progressive wing of his party, who maintained that the indiscriminate use of drones violated international law and laid the foundation for the expansion of drone attacks. The administration appears "to be broadening the potential target threat," said Christopher Swift, an expert on international law. "I don't think anyone should feel reassured by anything that President Obama said about the use of lethal force," added Zeke Johnson of Amnesty International.[30]

As spring gave way to the summer and fall, problems mounted for the White House. Even more controversial than the president's decision to use drones against terrorist targets was his opting out of a statement he made in August 2012 that he would not allow Syrian president Bashar al-Assad to use chemical weapons in the ongoing civil war in Syria, remarking that "a red line for us is [when] we start seeing a whole bunch of chemical weapons moving around or being utilized" and adding, "that would change my calculations significantly."[31]

The president later denied he ever made such a unilateral statement, remarking that it was the world, not he alone, who drew the "red line." He was being sincere in his denial. In a speech before the Veterans of Foreign Wars (VFW) a month earlier, he remarked with respect to Syria, "we will continue to make it clear to [President] Assad and those around him that the world is watching, and that they will be held accountable by *the international community and the United States* (my italics), should they make the tragic mistake of using those weapons."[32]

Furthermore, when he made his unilateral "red line" statement he was responding at length to a reporter's question at the end of a thirty-minute press conference. Unlike his earlier, prepared remarks at the VFW convention, his comments were delivered off-the-cuff, and he may not have expected them to be taken as literally as remarks that normally went through a long, interagency, vetting process.[33]

Regardless, when in August 2013, Assad actually used sarin gas—a nerve agent that paralyzes the lungs causing death from suffocation—against a rebel-held suburb of Damascus killing fourteen hundred men, women, and children, the president failed to respond militarily against the Syrian leader even though he ordered the Pentagon to prepare to attack. "Our finger was on the trigger," General Martin Dempsey, Chairman of the Joint Chiefs of Staff, later commented.[34]

Despite his orders to the Pentagon, the president began to have second thoughts about a military response. Having withdrawn troops from Iraq, aware that the overthrow of Qaddafi in Libya had resulted in an ongoing civil war, and seeking to exit from Afghanistan, he became reluctant to make any long-term military engagement in Syria. During his visit to Germany in June, German chancellor Angela Merkel, whom Obama greatly admired, cautioned against a unilateral military strike, preferring he go to the UN for its approval of an attack.[35]

Seeking a way out of the dilemma he had created for himself and aware that Congress was also weary of further military commitments abroad, Obama decided to ask its authorization for an air strike. He described his request as seeking strong political support for a decisive military action against Syria, even though he acknowledged that he had the right to strike Syria without congressional approval. "He had all the rhetoric of action," David Ignatius of the *Washington Post* later stated. "But in truth, [the administration] was stepping back from the imminent attack that it was heading toward . . . and at the last minute, the president blinked."[36]

The president was still faced with the issue of what to do when, as seemed likely, Congress failed to approve the authorization legislation he requested. Under those circumstances, he might still have to launch some kind of military response against Syria. Otherwise, he would look like a toothless tiger, and there would be little to stop Assad from continuing to use chemical weapons against his enemies, opening the way for Iran or another country in the Middle East to do the same against their enemies.[37]

Fortunately for Obama, he was saved from military action by President Vladimir Putin of Russia. At a gathering of the G20 in St. Petersburg in September, Obama and Putin held an unscheduled meeting. The Soviet leader asked the president if a decision by Syria to turn over its stockpiles of chemical weapons to an international group would be a way of avoiding military action. Answering the question cautiously, the president suggested they have their top diplomats discuss the matter. Shortly thereafter, Secretary of State John Kerry, who had replaced Hillary Clinton following her decision to resign after Obama completed his first term, was asked whether there was anything Assad could do to avoid an attack. Certainly, Kerry responded. He could acknowledge that he had chemical weapons and then give them up peacefully.[38]

A few days later, the secretary of state received a call from his Russian counterpart, Sergei Lavrov, asking about Kerry's "initiative." Undoubtedly under Russian pressure, the Syrians acknowledged the next day that they had chemical arms and agreed to sign the Chemical Weapons Convention banning such weapons. Not only were they pledging to come clean, they committed to getting rid of their chemical weapons altogether. At least for the moment, the Russians appeared to have saved Obama for resorting to the military action.[39]

On September 9, the president began a media blitz in which he gave interviews to six television networks. The next day, he elaborated on what he said in these interviews delivering a tough-sounding address to the nation in which he emphasized Assad's use of chemical weapons against his own people and suggested strongly that his administration was on the precipice of taking military action against the Syrian government with or without congressional approval. In response to comments that a US response would amount to little more than a "pinprick," the president said: "Let me make something clear, the United States military does not do pin-pricks. . . . If we fail to act, the Assad regime will see no reason to stop using chemical weapons. . . . Even a limited strike will send a message to Assad that no other nation can deliver."[40]

About halfway through his speech, his rhetoric changed. It might not be necessary, he continued, to take any military action against the Assad government. He asked for a postponement of a vote in Congress supporting military intervention while Secretary of State Kerry met with his Russian counterpart in Moscow to work out the details of the Russian proposal to put Syria's chemical weapons under international control. "It's too early to tell whether this offer will succeed," the president stated. "But this initiative has the potential to remove the threat of chemical weapons without the use of force, particularly because Russia is one of Assad's strongest allies."[41]

Eventually, an agreement was reached with Syria, which began in October, to destroy its chemical weapons under the supervision of an international body committed to destroying such weapons (although Syria continued to develop its chemical weapons stockpile and to use them against the rebels in its ongoing civil war). As a result, the immediate crisis caused by the president's "red line" statement in 2012 ended.[42]

Yet the whole incident caused Obama serious damage both from the right and the left, and from military hawks and military doves, who accused him of fecklessness in drawing a red line and then backing down from it just as it seemed he was about to intervene militarily in Syria. The hawkish former ambassador to the UN, John Bolton, referred to the line as an unforced error that put America in a red-line box. If the president allowed the "red line" to be crossed without retaliation, Bolton said, his inaction will provide "further proof to Iran, North Korea and other adversaries, whether states or terrorists, that he is not a force to be reckoned with." Barry Pavel, a former defense policy adviser to Obama who had moved to the Atlantic Council, commented, "I am not convinced [the 'red line' statement] was thought through. I am worried about the broader damage to U.S. credibility, if we make a statement and then come back with lawyerly language to get around it." Journalists and commentators even called the "red line" statement the worst foreign policy blunder of the Obama administration.[43]

Obama Battles Congress

By the spring of 2013, the despair already evident at the beginning of the year was beginning to envelop the entire White House. Obama's problems were not limited to developments abroad. Most of his attention was, in fact, taken up by domestic matters as he continued to speak out about the need to implement change at home in order to expand the nation's middle class. As in earlier comments, he emphasized both government's responsibility to provide opportunity for change but also the importance of self-help and individual responsibility. Speaking in February at a charter school in the Hyde Park section of Chicago, not far from the South Side where Michelle grew up and where he worked as a community organizer, the president spoke about how he wished he had had a father to help raise him. "Don't get me wrong," he said, "as the son of a single mom, who gave everything she had to raise me with the help of my grandparents, I turned out okay. . . . But I wish I had had a father who was around and involved. . . . Unconditional love for your child—that makes a difference."[44]

In February the president was able to claim a victory on Capitol Hill when, after a long legislative battle, Congress voted to reauthorize the *Violence against Women Act* (VAWA) of 1994. Renewed in 2000 and 2005, the original measure provided funding for the investigation and prosecution of violent crimes against women, imposed mandatory restitution on those convicted, and established an Office on Violence against Women in the Department of Justice. In 2011, when the measure was scheduled to be reauthorized a third time, conservative Republicans objected to a new provision extending the measure's protections to LGBT Americans, Native Americans, and undocumented immigrant victims of violence. Because of their objections, efforts to renew VAWA stalled in the 112th Congress.[45]

Beginning with the Ledbetter Act of 2009, Obama had supported policies important to women. Two months after taking office, he established the White House Council on Women and Girls to develop and coordinate priorities across government agencies. In his State of the Union address in 2013, he urged Congress to renew the VAWA. "We know our economy is stronger when our wives, our mothers, our daughters can live their lives free from discrimination in the workplace, and free from the fear of domestic violence," he said.[46]

In February, the Senate passed overwhelmingly the measure that was similar to last year's bill except that it excluded visas for immigrant victims of violence. "This important step shows what we can do when we come together across party lines to take up a just cause," the president remarked following the Senate vote. In the House, Speaker John Boehner still confronted significant opposition to the measure including from his own majority leader, Eric Cantor. Even though a majority of Republicans opposed the legislation, a smaller group of moderate Republicans supported it. In February, Boehner agreed to bring the legislation up for a vote. On February 28, 87 Republicans joined all the Democrats to pass the measure by a vote of 286 to 138.[47]

A week later, Obama held a signing ceremony during which he spoke about the White House's commitment to enlarging the scope of the VAWA to include Native American women, who had been victimized by their often unemployed and drunken companions. But what the president emphasized as much as the achievements of the measure, was the bipartisan support it garnered. "And this victory shows that when the American people make their voices heard, Washington listens."[48]

His overtures to the Republicans fell on deaf ears. Overshadowing his success in getting renewal of the VAWA for another five years was his failure to get Congress to stop the mandatory sequestering of spending as provided in the Budget Control Act of 2011 (BCA). According to the legislation, mandatory sequestering was to begin in 2013 unless the Joint Select Committee on Deficit Reduction, a congressional committee established by the measure, was able to reduce the federal deficit by $1.2 trillion through any combination of revenue enhancements and budget reductions. The cuts were to be evenly divided between defense and domestic spending. Although sequestering was supposed to have begun after December 31, the deal reached by the president and the House Speaker delayed it until March 1, 2013.[49]

Because Democrats and Republicans failed to resolve their difference over the budget, sequestering took effect on March 1. At a press conference following its implementation, Obama made clear his position on sequestering. While he recognized the need to cut the federal deficit and agreed to the sequestering provision of the BCA, he opposed its mandatory feature and strongly objected to the budget reductions Republicans demanded. Instead, he proposed a combination of cuts even for such entitlement programs as Medicare and Social Security, which were exempted from sequestering, and additional tax enhancements, including additional taxes for the nation's super-rich.[50]

Above all, he was determined to protect the rising middle class from the ravages of sequestering. Even though not everyone will feel the pain of budget cuts immediately, the president stated, the pain will be real for the middle class. "Communities near military bases will take a serious blow. Hundreds of thousands of Americans who serve their country—Border Patrol agents, FBI agents, civilians who work at the Pentagon—all will suffer significant pay cuts and furloughs. This will have a ripple effect throughout the economy "cost[ing] about 750,000 jobs at a time when we should be growing more quickly."[51]

In both the House and the Senate, Republicans made various proposals to deal with the budget deficit, but they rallied around the proposal by House Budget Committee chairman Paul Ryan (WI), who had been Mitt Romney's running mate in 2012. Long a proponent of major budget cuts to deal with the federal deficit, Ryan called for maintaining the cuts mandated by the sequestering provision of the BCA. In addition, he proposed repealing

Obamacare, replacing Medicare with partially subsidized private insurance, and making significant cuts to Medicaid.[52]

On April 10, Obama submitted to Congress his budget plan for fiscal 2014. As the *Washington Post* reported, his purpose was to find an end to the debt standoff. The ten-year budget request provided for $300 billion in new spending on jobs and public works. In an effort to reach a budget agreement with Republicans, the president also called for trimming Social Security benefits by changing the way cost-of-living adjustments (COLAs) were calculated, reducing Medicare benefits, and increasing Medicare premiums for couples making more than $170,000 a year.[53]

Over the next six months, the White House and Congress remained deadlocked over the budget for fiscal 2014. Significantly, the issues of sequestering and reducing the budget deficit took a back seat to the demands, especially among those who had Tea Party affiliations, to revoke the ACA. Efforts to repeal were fought more along ideological than fiscal lines. Encouraged by Senators Mike Lee (R-KS) and Ted Cruz (R-TX), both of whom had been elected to the Senate with the strong backing of the Tea Party, the Republican-controlled House adopted a series of resolutions for funding fiscal 2014 but with language that called for defunding the ACA. In August Majority Leader Cantor sent a memo to House Republicans stating that his caucus would "continue at full throttle" its opposition to the administration's agenda when Congress returned from its summer recess.[54]

On September 20, 2013, the House approved a Continuing Resolution (CR) that kept the government funded for the first eleven weeks of fiscal 2014. The measure also defunded Obamacare. The president made it clear that he would veto any legislation that did so. In what seemed like a giant game of ping-pong, the Senate and House then went back and forth, the Senate rejecting the House's efforts to defund Obamacare and the House proceeding once more to restore the defunding provisions. Even though the House and Senate remained in session late into the night of September 30, they were unable to solve the budgetary impasse. On October 1, the government was shut down.[55]

Obama did not escape unscathed from the battle over defunding the ACA and the shutdown of the government. Even some of his supporters wondered whether he could have done more to keep it open. The rollout of the ACA on the very day the government was being shut down was also a disaster. The contractors who had been hired to build and launch a website with little government oversight were not up to the job. They were not prepared for the complexity of connecting in one easily usable website the various government agencies involved in establishing an insurance marketplace. The website they developed was also not ready for the high volume of traffic that tried to access the portal. Technical problems made logging in and signing up for the insurance marketplace nearly impossible. Error messages plagued the system. Although fourteen sites established by states and the District of Columbia performed better, they did not always work smoothly. Hawaii's marketplace did not fully open until October 15.[56]

Critics of the president used the failures of the rollout to criticize the ACA for being ill conceived, poorly developed, and hastily instituted. They accused the president of lying to the American people when he said that if they were happy with their present policies, they could keep them; in reality, there were thousands of policies that did not meet the minimum standards for coverage required by the ACA and had to be replaced by more expensive policies. They also complained that the effect of Obamacare was to have the middle class pay the expense of providing health care for the forty million Americans not already having insurance (mostly minorities) through higher premiums for their insurance.[57]

Speaking in the Rose Garden the day after the shutdown, the president blamed it on the Republicans. "They've shut down the government over an ideological crusade to deny affordable health insurance to millions of Americans," he remarked. "In other words, they demanded ransom just for doing their job." He was willing to reopen negotiations, he said. "But as long as I am president, I will not give in to reckless demands by some in the Republican Party to deny affordable health insurance to millions of hardworking Americans."[58]

For the next two weeks, the government remained closed. Most government employees and contractors were furloughed and went unpaid, causing severe hardship to the thousands of workers, especially those in unskilled and low-skilled jobs, who lived from paycheck to paycheck. Callers jammed the phone lines of their senators and representatives demanding that they reopen the government. As Boehner feared, public opinion turned decidedly against the Republicans, who were blamed for causing the shutdown.[59]

At a lengthy press conference one week into the shutdown, Obama reaffirmed his willingness to negotiate with the Republicans on a CR that would reopen the government. He even broke with the more progressive wing of his party by accepting sequestering and current levels of funding as part of any compromise agreement with the Republicans. Acknowledging that sequestering would hurt some of the programs he most cherished, like Head Start, he took the pragmatic position that, by not being willing to compromise, he would be hurting these programs even more, adding thousands more families to those already not able to enroll their children in Head Start because of the lack of funding. He made clear, however, that he would not budge from his position of vetoing any measure that included defunding his landmark achievement. "We're not going to pay a ransom for America paying its bills," he said. [60]

Looking ahead to January when the debt ceiling needed to be raised, and borrowing from former president Bill Clinton's playbook in explaining complex issues through easily understood examples, he also spoke of the dangers of not raising the ceiling. "Imagine in your private life, if you decided that I'm not going to pay my mortgage for a month or two. First of all, you're not saving money by not paying your mortgage. You're just a deadbeat. And you can anticipate that will hurt your credit, which means that in addition to the debt collectors calling, you're going to have trouble borrowing in the future."[61]

After the Treasury Department warned that it could run out of money to pay national obligations, the Republicans threw in the towel. On October 16, the Senate voted overwhelmingly, 81 to 18, to approve a measure worked out by Democratic and Republican leaders to continue funding of the government through January 15 and to raise the debt ceiling through February 7 without defunding the ACA. There were also some minor changes to the health law to make certain that those who received federal subsidies to buy health insurance were eligible to receive them. The major difference between this resolution and earlier CRs, however, was that this time a majority of Republicans voted with the Democrats to pass it. Among those who voted against the resolution were Senators Lee and Cruz, the libertarian Ron Paul (R-Ky), and Marco Rubio (R-FL) who was weighing running for president in 2016.[62]

With the Senate having approved the funding measure, it went to the House. This time the legislative logjam broke. Aware of how damaging the government shutdown was to Republicans, moderate House members split with the conservatives by voting for the Senate resolution. Speaker Boehner, a moderate himself who always felt uncomfortable aligning himself with the Tea Party wing of his party, realized that his caucus had boxed itself into an increasingly unpopular position at a time when the nation faced the possibility of defaulting on its debts. He concluded that he had no option other than to agree to a CR without the offending provision.[63]

Accordingly, on October 17, the day after the Senate sent its CR to the House, it passed the legislation by a vote of 285 to 144. Eighty-seven Republicans joined a unanimous Democratic caucus in approving the legislation, one day before the Treasury Department said it would run out of money. In passing the measure, not a single member of the Republican leadership spoke out in support of the bill. Majority Leader Cantor broke again with the Speaker by voting against it, as did most Republicans. Afterward, Cruz claimed that, by showing Americans the harm the ACA was causing consumers, employers, and the American economy, the fight to defund the measure had been worthwhile.[64]

Most Republicans knew better. Representative Charlie Dent (R-PA), a moderate Republican, said Congress should have passed legislation funding the government without strings attached weeks ago. "For the party, this is a moment of self-evaluation," added Senator Graham. "We are going to assess how we got here. If we continue down this path, we are really going to hurt the Republican Party long-term." "We fought the good fight," said Speaker Boehner. "We just didn't win."[65]

Speaking shortly after signing the legislation reopening government, the president praised Congress, but urged it not to allow a repeat performance of what he called a "self-inflicted crisis that set our economy back." As he almost always did, he also held out the prospect of a bright future for the country, *provided* it did not default on its debt. Looking to February, when the nation would again be unable to pay its obligations unless Congress raised the debt ceiling and aware that conservative legislators were once again preparing to tie defunding of the ACA to raising the ceiling, he made clear that America's economic standing in the world was tied to defeating this effort. "Now the good news is that we'll bounce back from this," he said. "We are the indispensable nation that the rest of the world looks to as the safest and most reliable place to invest."[66]

Obama laid out his priorities for the next fiscal year, which included closing tax loopholes in order to fund education, infrastructure, and research. In addition, he sought passage of a farm bill and an immigration reform measure, both of which had already passed the Senate. The farm bill, he maintained, would give "rural communities opportunities to grow and the long-term certainty that they deserve," while the immigration reform bill would include the nation's "biggest commitment to border security" in its history, but also a path to citizenship for illegal immigrants.[67]

On each of these measures and others, the president said what he had always said: that he would seek to find common ground with the Republicans. Under no condition, however, would he allow the ACA to be held hostage to a congressional agreement on the debt ceiling. Having been burned by shutting down the government over the defunding of the ACA, the Republican leadership on Capitol Hill was in no mood to risk another shutdown by tying conditions to a bill raising the debt ceiling. Although a majority of Republicans still opposed raising the ceiling without conditions, Boehner stunned his caucus when he dropped a condition that would have provided for cuts to retirement pensions approved in December, allowing instead a vote on a clean debt ceiling measure. He was then able to get enough moderate and retiring Republicans to vote with the 193 Democrats to approve the legislation by the narrow margin of 221 to 201, the first such measure since 2009 that was not attached to other legislation.[68]

Although Cruz was able to delay final approval of the measure in the Senate by filibustering against it, enough Republicans joined with Democrats, including Minority Leader McConnell and Minority Whip John Cornyn, to have the sixty votes needed to invoke cloture ending debate. The Senate then approved the clean resolution sent over from the House by a vote of 55 to 43, which Obama quickly signed into law.[69]

With passage of the clean resolution allowing the government to pay its bills, Obama had won another legislative victory over Republicans in Washington. Throughout the struggle over funding the government through fiscal 2014, the president had not wavered in his determination not to allow the ACA to be used as a pawn by the Republicans. And he had won.

The president had done so, however, at the cost of further alienating Republicans. In the House, Speaker Boehner came under withering criticism from Tea Party Republicans and conservative lobbying groups for his decision to allow a vote on a clean debt ceiling measure. In a nearly impossible situation already because of the strength of these Republicans, Boehner's position as Speaker was weakened even more, and for that he blamed Obama. "He won't even sit down and discuss these issues," the Speaker remarked as the vote on raising the debt ceiling was about to be taken. "He's the one driving up the debt and the question [his caucus is] asking is, why should I deal with his debt limit."[70]

Through the Congressional Elections of 2014

As the president began the second year of his second term, his chances of getting any of his legislative priorities through the House were bleak. On January 28, he delivered his fifth State of the Union address. Like his earlier addresses before Congress, it contained a list of these priorities, including immigration reform, an increase in the minimum wage, addressing climate change by shuttering carbon-emitting coal-fired plants, and proposals to address the growing problem of inadequate retirement savings for those who needed help the most. Pointing to the economic strides his administration had made since he took office, the president remarked that more work still needed to be done. What he was offering was "a set of concrete, practical proposals to speed up growth, strengthen the middle class, and build new ladders of opportunity into the middle class."[71]

Two features of this State of the Union made it different from his earlier ones. First was the stern warning he gave to the lawmakers that he was prepared to take action on his own if Congress failed to act first. "Let's make this a year of action," he stated. As an example of what he was prepared to do was his announcement that he was issuing an executive order increasing the minimum wage for future federal contracts from $7.50 to $10.10 an hour. He was also taking other measures to lower the burden of student loans in higher education, to reduce unemployment, to create new ways for working Americans without retirement plans to start their own plans, and to try, with or "without Congress," to stop gun-related tragedies like the one in Sandy Hook. "I am eager to work with all of you" he told the legislators in his sixty-five-minute speech. "But America does not stand still—and neither will I."[72]

In his address, Obama also tried to position his administration as a champion of those left behind after a contentious year on Capitol Hill that left the president with approval ratings hovering around 50 percent. Breaking from the past, he offered no sweeping programs of reforms of the nation's health system, its industrial structure, and its banking system. Instead, he proposed incremental changes. Although he made clear his determination to act unilaterally if necessary, he reiterated his desire to work with the Republicans in achieving his goals.[73]

Distrustful of the president and having their own conservative agenda, the Republicans rejected his proposals. To respond to his State of the Union message, they chose Cathy McMorris Rodgers (R-WA), an ardent conservative, and vocal opponent of same-sex marriage and abortion. Ignoring Obama's own emphasis throughout his presidency on free markets and a thriving middle class, she spoke of a "more hopeful Republican vision" that "champions free markets and trusts people to make their own decisions." The stalemate between the White House and Congress that had begun after Obama's reelection thus continued largely unabated through November.[74]

Overseas, problems continued to mount for the White House. Through March and into the summer, Obama had to respond to the Russian seizure of Crimea from Ukraine and to the threat Moscow posed to the independence of Ukraine, which was ethnically divided. A narrow peninsula in southern Ukraine surrounded by the Black Sea and the Sea of Azov, Crimea had historically been part of Russia. In 1954, Moscow transferred the territory to Ukraine, which had been a republic within the former Soviet Union until 1991, when it became an independent nation. After Putin became president of Russia in 2012, he decided he wanted the Crimea—with its large gas and oil reserves and strategic location—back. He seized the territory by force and then annexed it after a disputed plebiscite voted overwhelmingly in favor of reannexation. The Russian military also moved troops along the Crimea-Ukrainian border that threatened southern and eastern Ukraine.[75]

For a time, it seemed the entire Ukraine, led by Viktor Yanukovych, a corrupt and pro-Russian politician, might fall under Russian control. After Yanukovych backed away from an agreement that would have had Ukraine affiliate with the European Union (EU), demonstrators took to the streets forcing Yanukovych to flee to Russia. In May they elected a pro-Western candidate, Petro Poroshenko, president of Ukraine. But Russian troops continued to engage Ukrainian forces in Russian-speaking areas of eastern Ukraine.[76]

In response, Obama joined the United States' Western allies in imposing sanctions on sixteen Russian officials and wealthy businessmen with close ties to Putin. In numerous calls he had with the Soviet leader, often playing scrabble while he waited for Putin to join the conversation, the US president raised the possibility of more sweeping measures against core parts of the Russian economy, including its oil and natural gas sectors. In addition, he sent Vice President Biden to reassure Poland and the Baltic states, Estonia, Latvia, and Lithuania, that he would uphold its collective security commitment to them as members of NATO. "Going forward, we can calibrate our response based on whether Russia chooses to escalate or to deescalate the situation," he said in a statement on the White House South Lawn on March 20, 2014.[77]

On July 17, insurgent forces loyal to Russia in eastern Ukraine shot down Malaysia Airlines Flight 17, a civilian jet passing overhead, using an antiaircraft battery supplied to them by Moscow, killing all 298 passengers and crew aboard including 80 children. Although there is no evidence Putin had advance knowledge of the insurgents' plan, the incident had a major affect on Obama's relations with the Soviet leader. For most of his administration, the American president had hoped to improve relations with Putin. The shooting down of the Malaysian flight with a weapon supplied by the Russians ended any remaining hope of that happening. Even so, Obama refused to contemplate opening up a new military front in a part of the world he still did not consider crucial to America's national interest. He remained reluctant even to send military equipment to Ukraine.[78]

More threatening to American interests than developments in the Ukraine was the rise of ISIS (ISIL). In the spring and summer of 2014, ISIS was able to spread its power from its small base in Syria into large parts of Iraq and Syria, and capture the major cities of Fallujah and Mosul in western Iraq. Thirty thousand Iraqi forces equipped with the latest American weapons laid down their arms and were either captured, killed, or fled the scene rather than engage one thousand members of ISIS being transported on the back of pickup trucks mounted with machine guns and light artillery and waving the black flag of the self-proclaimed ISIS caliphate. Through its terrorist tactics, including its threats to export these tactics to Europe and the United States, ISIS sent tremors of fear throughout the West unlike any since 9/11.[79]

As Ben Rhodes described the situation within the administration, "for a couple of days, a sense of crisis enveloped the White House." Obama was incensed about what was taking place in Iraq. He could not understand the apparent breakdown in American intelligence about ISIS and the abject failure of the Iraqi military, which he described as "folding like a cheap tent," to stand up to the outmanned and out-armed terrorist organization. He made his displeasure clear to his entire national security team, including his director of national intelligence, Jim Clapper, who was already under fire for embarrassing leaks by Edward Snowden, a whistleblower and former National Security Agency (NSA) contractor, showing that the NSA was spying on some of America's closest allies, including German chancellor Merkel, who was infuriated by the revelation. "We didn't get a warning that the Iraqis were going to melt away," the president complained. "I'm not happy with the information I'm getting." "I'm aggravated," he added.[80]

After the fall of Fallujah, pressure mounted on the president to launch some kind of major military response against ISIS. It grew even stronger following the public beheadings of two American journalists, James Foley and Steven Sotloff, as they kneeled on the ground with their hands tied behind their backs. The world was shocked by the videos that ISIS sent to the media of Foley's and Sotloff's beheadings.[81]

Having withdrawn American troops from Iraq and intending to do the same for most American forces in Afghanistan, the president still refused to be drawn back into another major military commitment in Iraq. Displaying an anger he rarely showed in remarks about the Iraq War, he denounced the beheading of Foley as "appalling." Promising to be "relentless" and to see that "justice is done" in protecting Americans abroad, he launched fourteen new airstrikes against ISIS, destroying ISIS Humvees and other military equipment and weapons.[82]

He made clear in a statement the day after Foley was beheaded, however, that he considered it up to the people of the Middle East, not the United States, "to extract this cancer so that it does not spread." His only concession was to commit a small force to Baghdad to help train Iraqi forces. He blamed much of the rise of ISIS on Iraq's Shiite leader, Nuri Kamal al-Maliki, who refused to share power with Iraq's Sunni minority. His hope was that once al-Maliki was replaced as leader in the next election, a more pro-Sunni government would help undermine support for ISIS and a better trained Iraqi military would overwhelm ISIS forces on the battlefield.[83]

On the day after Foley's beheading, the Pentagon acknowledged that a month earlier, on July 4, it had tried to rescue a group of fourteen hostages being held by ISIS in Syria, including Foley and Sotloff and a third hostage, Kayla Mueller, a human rights activist who was beheaded later that year. The mission failed when it was discovered that the hostages had been moved to another site.[84]

From both the right and the left, the president was attacked for his response to Foley's and Sotloff's beheadings and then for the Pentagon's belated revelations of the failed rescue attempt. Critics took the president to task for allowing ISIS to become a worldwide threat and then for not taking more vigorous military action against the terrorist organization. His national security team was criticized, even by some of those who worked on a rescue mission, for delays in bringing an operational plan to the president. Other critics were troubled by the administration's long-standing policy of not negotiating with terrorist organizations for the release of hostages. They were angry that the president launched the rescue mission without consulting with the families of the hostages and without trying to negotiate with ISIS for their release.[85]

The White House tried to defend itself. Although Obama acknowledged that his administration "probably missed [the hostages] by a day or two," he said it was wrong "to say that the United States government hasn't done everything we could." He also made clear that while he should have done a better job of consulting with the families of the hostages, he remained committed to the long-held American policy of not bargaining with terrorists for the release of hostages. "We will do everything we can, short of providing an incentive for future Americans to be caught," he said in an interview. Senior administration officials also denied there was any delay in approving the hostage rescue effort once the rescue plan reached the White House. "For us, the clock starts when they tell us that they have an operation that they want the president to review and approve. . . . It can't happen any faster than that," Susan Rice commented. [86]

Altogether, the events of the first six months of 2014—indeed, of the last year when criticism of the "Red Line" statement is taken into account— left leading figures within the White House exhausted and the administration reeling. Clapper was prepared to resign or be fired from his job, and Rhodes considered resigning. The problems and criticisms he faced also took their toll on the president. He felt trapped in the White House. His hair was grayer, his face more lined. "President Obama's hair is definitely grayer these days, and no doubt trying to manage foreign policy in a world of increasing disorder accounts for at least half of those gray hairs. (The Tea Party can claim the other)," commented Thomas Friedman of the *New York Times*.[87]

Obama tried to shrug off the attacks directed at him. For a few weeks, he fantasized with Rhodes about creating a dome under which he could place ISIS and the Russian special forces in eastern Ukraine. "Put 'em in the terror zone," he said, but the criticisms continued. Despite his administration's best efforts to defend itself, he was losing the battle of public opinion going into the 2014 congressional elections. Even some of the administration's own supporters began to question Obama's capacity to lead.[88]

Doubts about the president's leadership, were reflected in the midterm elections. On November 4, 2014, the Democratic Party suffered a humiliating defeat at the polls. In the House, Republicans gained thirteen seats, giving them the largest majority since the Great Depression. Even more striking, they won nine Senate seats—the largest change of seats since 1980—giving them control of the Senate for the first time since 2006. On the state and local levels, Republicans did equally well, winning twenty-four of the thirty-six governorships being decided that year for a net gain of two and flipping ten legislative chambers.[89]

Republicans touted their victory as a rejection of the president and his policies. "This race wasn't about me or my opponent," said Mitch McConnell (R-KY) who was easily reelected to the Senate and was slated to be its new majority leader. "It was about a government people no longer trusted." Most analysts agreed with McConnell. Beginning with Obama's reelection in 2012, when his approval rating hovered slightly above 50 percent, it had begun to drop steadily, reaching a low of around 40 percent a year later and never rising much above that level through 2014.[90]

Throughout the campaign, Republicans had kept the president on the defensive. They focused on the alleged failures of the administration, including the slow economic recovery from the 2008 recession and the still high unemployment rate at around 6 percent. They also continued to criticize Obamacare, especially its individual mandate and the high deductibles and copayments that policy holders had to pay. So, too, with respect to the White House's foreign policy, they continued to argue that it was irresolute, and they held the administration responsible for the rise of ISIS.[91]

"I hear you, I hear you," Obama commented at a news conference the day after the elections. He also spoke with Speaker Boehner and congratulated McConnell, who, after the election, promised to work with the administration over the next two years, on becoming the next Senate majority leader. The president looked forward to working with him "to deliver for the

American people," he said at his news conference. He also looked forward in two days to hosting the entire Republican and Democratic leadership at the White House "to chart a new course forward." He refused, however, to interpret the election as a personal rebuke of his leadership. "Obviously, Republicans had a good night," he remarked. "And they deserve credit for running good campaigns. Beyond that, I'll leave it to all of you and the professional pundits to pick through yesterday's results."[92]

Rather than appearing contrite about the huge losses the Democrats—many of whom had tried to run away from him during the campaign—had suffered, Obama remained defiant, interpreting the elections as a repudiation, not of himself, but of an ineffectual Congress. He had good reason to feel this way. The turnout for the election was the lowest since 1942 with just 36.4 percent of the electorate voting. The exit polls showed that more voters (79 percent) disapproved of Congress's performance than the president's. They suggested that in 2014 the voters were not so much repudiating Obama and the Democrats as they were the whole governing system in Washington.[93]

As a result, the president took an even harder stand than before in his determination to defy Congress and to take executive action when he felt it necessary. "My presidency is entering the fourth quarter; interesting stuff happens in the fourth quarter," he commented in the Oval Office a few days after the election. "This elicited . . . a sense that perhaps we were going to spend the last two years of the presidency doing big things, unencumbered by the caution and exhaustion that had crept in at points over the last few years," Ben Rhodes later wrote.[94]

Chapter 9

A Second Recovery

Despite a second major humiliation at the ballot box, Obama made another major comeback as president, and his rating improved dramatically in the polls. One reason for this was his ability to effect change through executive action. By the end of 2015, his popularity as measured by the polls was above 50 percent, laying the ground for restoring diplomatic relations with Cuba and signing bilateral and multilateral agreements to reduce carbon emissions.

Beyond his overtures to Cuba and confronting the problem of global warming, Obama undertook a number of other new initiatives. These included an unsuccessful effort at comprehensive immigration reform and an agreement with Iran to stop its development of weapons-grade uranium and plutonium. Because of a number of incidents involving police shootings of Black youth, Obama also placed new emphasis on the issue of race relations, a matter he had largely ignored through his first six years as president.

By the end of 2015, Obama was displaying a new confidence, including about his legacy as president, believing that the odds-on-favorite to win the Democratic nomination, Hillary Clinton, would confirm as his legacy a middle-class society crossing all cultural, racial, and ethnic lines.

Election Aftermath

Even in the two months between the end of the midterm elections and the delivery of his State of the Union address, Obama proceeded boldly with his plans for the future, acting all the while as if he had a won a referendum from the voters in the midterms rather than being rejected by them.

On November 29, 2014, the president delivered a televised address in which he described the steps his administration was already taking to fix what he described as a shattered immigration system, including expanding the Deferred Action for Childhood Arrivals Program (DACA). "For more than 200 years, our tradition of welcoming immigrants from around the world has given us an advantage over other nations," he stated. "But today, our immigration system is broken—and everybody knows it." For this, the president blamed the Republican-controlled House, which failed to consider the bipartisan legislation the Senate had passed in the previous Congress. The measure provided for a major overhaul of the immigration system, including providing a path to citizenship for illegal immigrants. "Had the House of Representatives allowed that kind of a bill as a simple yes-or-no vote," the president remarked, "it would have passed with support of both parties, and today it would be the law."[1]

The president's own policies toward illegal immigrants were mixed. At the same time he established the DACA program, he deported more immigrants (estimated around 2.5 million) than any of his predecessors. Part of the reason for this large number had to do with changes on how deportees were counted. The president's supporters claimed the increase in deportations was a way for the president to show his Republican critics that he understood their concerns and was determined to limit illegal immigration. His position also had to do with his commitment to respect the law by insisting that those seeking entrance into the United States follow proper legal procedures.[2]

Another reason for Obama's crackdown on illegal immigration was his determination to wrest control of immigration enforcement from state and local officials, who, as in the case of Sheriff Joe Arpaio of Maricopa County, Arizona, engaged in racial profiling and treated illegal immigrants cruelly. In response to passage of an anti-immigration law, which criminalized the failure to carry immigration documents, the president directed Attorney General Eric Holder to challenge the constitutionality of the law.[3]

In his November speech, he outlined his administration's efforts regarding immigration. It was providing additional resources for border security and the speedy return of those who crossed the border illegally. At the same time, it was instituting measures to make it easier for skilled immigrants, graduate students, and entrepreneurs to remain in the country. It was also doing something for the millions of undocumented immigrants already in the country.[4]

"I want to say more about this third issue because it generates the most passion and controversy," the president continued. "Even as we are a nation of immigrants, we're also a nation of laws. . . . That's why, over the past six years, deportation of criminals are up 80 percent." He intended to continue focusing on deporting those illegals with criminal records. For illegal immigrants who had lived in the country for five years and maintained productive lives, he offered them assurances they would not be deported.[5]

Obama's most notable action had to do with DACA, which, it will be recalled, extended deportation relief and employment authorization to those young immigrants who entered the country before their sixteenth birthday and went on to graduate high school or serve in the US military. The cutoff date for entering the country had been June 2007 and those eligible for the program had to be under thirty-one. Under these criteria an estimated 600,000 immigrants had been granted DACA status. Through executive action, the president changed the cutoff date to January 1, 2010, and eliminated the age requirement, thereby making an estimated 290,000 additional undocumented immigrants eligible for the DACA program. In addition, he extended deferred action and employment authorization to illegal immigrants with children who were US citizens or living lawfully in the country, and he eliminated the mandatory fingerprinting program.[6]

His changes in policy, he stressed, did not grant undocumented immigrants citizenship or even the right to stay permanently in the country. He was not granting amnesty. "What I'm describing," the president continued, "is accountability—a common sense, middle ground approach: If you meet the criteria, you come out of the shadows and get right with the law." He was acting within the law. His actions were similar to those taken by every president for the last fifty years. "And to those members of Congress who question my authority to make our immigration system work better or question the wisdom of me acting where Congress has failed, I have one answer," he told the members of the House and Senate. "Pass a bill."[7]

On December 17, less than a month later, the president delivered another major address in which he revealed that his administration was in the process of negotiating the restoration of relations with Cuba. He made this announcement despite long-standing opposition to resuming relations from Congress and the influential Cuban community living in and around the city of Miami.[8]

As far back as 2008, Obama made clear that he wanted to establish a dialogue with the Cuban people with whom relations had been broken since 1959. When asked during the Democratic presidential debates in July whether he would be willing to meet without preconditions with a number of US adversaries, including Cuba, the Democratic candidate responded that he would. "And the reason is this," he explained, "that the notion that somehow not talking to countries is somehow punishment to them . . . is ridiculous."[9]

After Obama became president in 2009, he lifted restrictions on Cuban Americans wanting to travel to Cuba and to send remittances to their families still living there. He also began eighteen months of secret talks with the Cuban government. At the funeral of Nelson Mandela in December 2013, he shook hands with Cuba's leader, Raoul Castro. With the assistance of Pope Francis and after a telephone call between the president and Castro, the negotiations concluded in a prisoner swap. Among the Americans released was Alan Gross, a subcontractor working for the United States Agency for International Development (AID), who had been in prison for five years accused of being a spy.[10]

During his call with Obama, Castro described at length Cuba's grievances with the United States. When Ben Rhodes, who was listening to the conversation, sent a note to the president telling him he could cut the Cuban leader off, Obama shook his head. "It's been a long time since they've talked to a U.S. president," he told Rhodes. "He's got a lot to say."[11]

With the release of Gross, he instructed Secretary of State John Kerry to begin discussion with Cuba and to open an embassy in Havana. He also asked Kerry to review Cuba's designation as a "State Sponsor of Terrorism." In announcing his actions, Obama told the nation he intended "to create more opportunities for the American and Cuban people. . . . Neither the American nor Cuban people are well served by a rigid policy that is rooted in events that took place before most of us were born," he added.[12]

The president realized that Cuba continued to oppress its people, but he hoped his liberalization of commerce and communication with Cuba might over time lead to a liberalization of its society. He was also aware that, given its history, its foreign policy would often be sharply at odds with the United States, but, in his view, it made no sense to restore relations with Communist China and Vietnam, against which the United States fought at the cost of fifty-eight thousand American servicemen dead, and not establish relations with Cuba.[13]

Once again, Obama's announcement that he was taking steps toward restoring relations with Cuba angered Republicans, who would take control of both houses of Congress in January. They warned that they would never lift the fifty-four-year-old trade embargo on the country.[14]

Nuclear Weapons Agreement with Iran (February 2015–July 2015)

On January 20, 2015, the president delivered his sixth State of the Union address to Congress. "Middle-class economics works. Expanding opportunity works," he began his remarks. "Tonight, after a breakthrough year for America, our economy is growing and creating jobs at the fastest pace since 1999," he continued. What he emphasized in his address, though, were not the economic gains achieved during his administration, but what he believed still needed to be done to achieve the type of society he envisioned in his keynote address at the 2004 Democratic convention when he spoke of a United States of America" rather than a nation of blue states and red states. "At this moment . . . we have risen from recession freer to write our own future than any other nation on Earth. It's now up to us to choose who we want to be over the next 15 years and for decades to come," he said.[15]

His one-hour address was optimistic, ambitious, and delivered with humor and defiance. "The improving economy is the backdrop for the speech, and context for the economic debate over the next two years," his senior adviser, Dan Pfeiffer, stated. When the president remarked that he had run his last campaign, Republicans broke out in cheers. Smiling, Obama responded by saying he knew he had run his last campaign because he had won both of them.[16]

Undeterred by Republican control of both houses of Congress, Obama laid out one of his most ambitious agendas as president. He made no mention of the midterm elections, offered no concessions about his leadership, and offered no compromises on issues important to the Republicans like tax cuts. Rather than proposals to rein in government, he asked for new government spending to create "a 21st century infrastructure." The money would also be used to train workers better, assure free community colleges, establish a system of national high-speed internet service, guarantee sick days, and provide childcare and paid parental leave for those with newborns and young children. "Today we're the only advanced country on earth that doesn't guarantee paid sick leave or paid maternity leave to our workers," he remarked. "Fifteen years into this century, we have picked ourselves up, dusted off, and begun again the work of remaking America. . . . Let's begin this new chapter together."[17]

Obama proposed such an ambitious set of goals not because he believed Congress would approve any of it. but because he wanted to make clear what he wanted as his legacy. The irony of the midterm elections was that its results emboldened him to be more defiant of a Congress he knew would defy him. As a lame-duck president, he was prepared to take even bolder executive action than in the past.[18]

As he anticipated, the Republican response to his State of the Union address was quick and almost entirely negative. Senator Lamar Alexander (R-TN), widely regarded as a moderate Republican, remarked that the president's speech was replete with "things Congress wouldn't ever do."[19]

Alexander's prediction was borne out. On April 2, the president announced that his administration had reached a preliminary agreement with Iran by which Tehran would stop the development of a nuclear weapon in return for lifting economic sanctions against Iran. Since taking office, his administration had made clear that he considered nuclear proliferation one of the most dangerous threats to world peace. Despite a protocol Iran had signed in 2003 giving the UN International Atomic Energy Agency (IAEA) the right to conduct snap inspections of its nuclear facilities, it secretly continued developing weapons-grade uranium and plutonium. The president was committed to stopping Tehran from developing a nuclear weapon. In response to Iran's violation of the 2003 agreement, the White House imposed increasingly harsher sanctions against the country.[20]

In his speech Obama delivered at Cairo University in June 2009, he stated that he wanted to open a new dialogue with Iran and even acknowledged its right to have peaceful nuclear power, but he made clear that Tehran had to stop producing and stockpiling weapons-grade nuclear material. Two developments that year delayed progress toward any negotiations with Iran and led, instead, to the imposition of additional sanctions against Tehran. First, Iran's president, Mahmoud Ahmadinejad, cracked down harshly on dissidents who had taken to the streets in opposition to the government. Second, the US revealed the existence of a secret, underground Iranian nuclear facility.[21]

By the spring of 2013, the way seemed open once again to try diplomacy. That year a more moderate government, led by Hassan Rouhani, who had campaigned on a platform of seeking improved relations with the West and tying progress on the nuclear issue to the lifting of sanctions, was elected to power. Sensing the opportunity to turn a new page in the United States' relations with Iran, the president sent a letter to Rouhani proposing talks on the nuclear issue. Within weeks, he received a response in which the Iranian president made clear he wanted to start the negotiating process.[22]

Almost two years of negotiations followed. Just deciding on a place to hold the talks (Oman) and on an agenda for the discussions took months. A routine followed where the negotiating team, led by career diplomats, would get Obama's input before traveling back to Muscat (Oman's capital) in one of their many trips between Washington and Muscat. "Obama would probe what elements of their nuclear program the Iranians would put on the table, delving into arcane details of nuclear infrastructure and sanctions policy," wrote Rhodes, who sat in those meetings.[23]

After a few weeks, the American negotiators settled on a framework for an interim agreement in which Iran would freeze its nuclear weapons program in return for limited relief from sanctions. Once Washington got the support of its partners for the framework, the administration discussed whether Obama should meet Rouhani, who would be attending the opening of the UN General Assembly in September. When Iran indicated it would be interested in a meeting, Obama decided to see Rouhani, but when the time came for the meeting, the Iranian leader failed to show.[24]

Despite his no-show, the president made a last stab at contacting Rouhani. In a fifteen-minute conversation, the two leaders agreed on the urgency of reaching agreement on Iran's nuclear program. Later that fall, American negotiators, led by Secretary of State Kerry, held a series of meetings in Geneva and Lausanne, Switzerland, with their Iranian counterparts to finalize an interim agreement.[25]

The meetings were contentious as the Iranian negotiators hammered the US for its history of helping overthrow its legitimately elected government in 1953, opposing the Iranian Revolution of 1979, and supporting Israel. Still Obama was able to announce on April 2, 2015, that an agreement had been reached. "Iran will face strict limitations on its program," the president stated, "and Iran has also agreed to the most robust and intrusive inspections and transparency regime ever negotiated for any nuclear program in history."[26]

As he expected, his announcement of a preliminary agreement with Iran resulted in a strong backlash from Republicans and the powerful Israeli lobby in the United States. Two months earlier, House Speaker John Boehner had departed from protocol by inviting, without any input from the administration, Israeli prime minister Netanyahu to address a joint session of Congress. In his speech Netanyahu emphasized his disappointment with the White House for reaching an agreement on Iran's nuclear weapons program with a regime, which, he said, "pose[d] a grave threat, not only to Israel, but also the peace of the entire world." Afterward, forty-seven Republican senators wrote a letter to Iran's supreme leader, Ali Hosseini, warning him against reaching an agreement with the White House not endorsed by them.[27]

Once the White House announced the accord in April, Republicans and the Israeli lobby stepped up their attacks on the deal. The president, nevertheless, called the preliminary agreement a "once in a lifetime opportunity" to limit the spread of nuclear weapons while reassuring critics that he still kept all options open if Iran violated the accord. As a way of providing assurances to skeptics, he met in the Oval Office with Thomas Friedman of the *New York Times* to discuss at length the draft deal.[28]

To win the support of those doubters who accused him of giving away too much to the Tehran government, Obama emphasized once more his determination not to allow, under any circumstances, the development of an Iranian nuclear weapon, which, he acknowledged, posed an unacceptable threat to Israel. "If anybody messes with Israel, America will be there," he told Friedman. He was distressed by what he regarded as false suggestions, even from Prime Minister Netanyahu, that he was anti-Israel. "Look, Israel is a robust, rowdy democracy," he told the *New York Times* journalist. "We share so much. We share blood, family. . . . And part of what has always made the US-Israeli relationship so special is that it has transcended party, and I think that has to be preserved." But I must be able "to disagree with a policy . . . without being viewed as . . . opposing Israel."[29]

Another matter that Friedman raised with the president was what he regarded as a common denominator in his remarks on Iran. Was there such a thing, he asked Obama, as an "Obama Doctrine?" The president said there was and described it as a willingness to take "calculated risks" predicated on the principle that America's "overwhelming power" should give it the confidence to venture in new directions, like restoring relations with Cuba and reaching an agreement with Iran, which, he acknowledged, was "a complicated country." "The activities that they engage in, the rhetoric, both anti-American, anti-Semitic, anti-Israel, is deeply disturbing." But, he added, "there is a practical streak to the Iranian regime. I think they are concerned about self-preservation." Iran had a defense budget of $30 billion compared to the US defense budget, which was closer to $600 billion. "Iran understands that they cannot fight us, he responded in answering most directly Friedman's earlier question about an Obama Doctrine. "The doctrine is: We will engage, but we preserve all our abilities."[30]

One other matter that the president made clear to Friedman was his insistence on entering into binding agreements with foreign powers without congressional approval. Referring to the preemptive letter Republican senators had already written to Iran's supreme leader warning him against signing the agreement, he added, "I felt the letter that was sent was inappropriate."[31]

On July 15, after three more months of difficult negotiations, Obama announced a "comprehensive long-term deal [with Iran] that will prevent it from obtaining a nuclear weapon." Among the more noteworthy provisions of the accord were the stipulations for Iran to shut down the core of one of its nuclear facilities so that it would no longer be able to produce weapons-grade plutonium and to ship its spent fuel out of the country. Additionally Iran agreed to stop production for at least the next fifteen years of any heavy water reactors used in the production of nuclear weapons and to remove by two-thirds the number of centrifuges needed to produce weapons-grade uranium. Finally, the deal gave IAEA inspectors access to Iran's entire nuclear supply chain to keep it from covertly developing a nuclear weapon at some secret facility.[32]

In return for Iran's stoppage of its nuclear weapons program, the sanctions put in place because of the program would be phased out as Tehran completed the steps outlined in the agreement. In the final phase, the freeze on $100 billion of Iran's assets being held around the world would be lifted. "This deal meets every single one of the bottom lines that we established when we achieved a framework earlier this spring," the president remarked in announcing the accord. He also vowed to veto any Republican attempt to undermine the agreement.[33]

The next day Obama held a press conference in which he reiterated the points he had made in his announcement of the deal. In response to questions from reporters, he emphasized that the only alternatives to the nuclear weapons agreement were either no deal in which case Iran could continue to develop a nuclear weapon, setting off a nuclear arms race in the Middle East, or some kind of military response, which could lead to a regional conflagration. He directed many of his remarks to congressional Republicans, the Israeli lobby in Washington, and Israeli prime minister Netanyahu, all of whom expressed their strong opposition to the deal with Iran and were lobbying hard against the agreement. "I'm hearing a lot of talking points being repeated about 'this is a bad deal'—'this is a historically bad deal,'" the president commented. "What I haven't heard is, what's your preferred alternative?"[34]

Because the administration failed to submit the agreement to Congress within thirty days after it was signed, the period for reviewing—and lobbying against—the deal was extended to sixty days. In response to the lobbying effort, the administration launched its own intense effort on behalf of the agreement. The president became the chief lobbyist, inviting the entire Democratic caucus on Capitol Hill to the White House, holding interviews and making speeches on behalf of the agreement, and even going on the popular *Daily Show* as a way of reaching a younger audience.[35]

As August gave way to September, the White House's lobbying effort began to pay off. European diplomats lobbied on behalf of the agreement. Former ambassadors to Israel and retired national security officials wrote letters in support of the accord. Dozens of retired Israeli generals and a former head of Israel's highly respected clandestine service, Mossad, turned against Netanyahu. Public opinion polls indicated that a majority of American Jews favored the agreement.[36]

When the vote was taken in the Senate, Democrats were able to prevent Republican efforts to block the agreement from going into effect. (A formal treaty required an unattainable two-thirds vote.) Although the Senate and House leadership vowed to fight on, even threatening to bring a lawsuit against Obama over the Iran deal, the president had won his greatest foreign policy victory since taking office six years earlier. "This vote is a victory for diplomacy, for American national security, and for the safety and security of the world," the president remarked in a statement he issued after a vote he termed "an historic step forward."[37]

The Trans-Pacific Partnership

The signing of the nuclear agreement with Iran did not lead to any significant change in Washington's overall relations with the Tehran government, but it prevented another possible war, this time between Israel and Iran that could have sucked the United States deeper into Middle East policy and politics. From Syria to Ukraine, Yemen to Iran, the president was bent on avoiding getting involved in another quagmire. Reaching an agreement with Iran on its nuclear weapons program also allowed Obama to reorient US foreign policy away from the Middle East and toward Southeast Asia, where, he thought, China posed a major threat to US global interests.[38]

Ever since taking office, Obama tried to accommodate China. In 2009, the president traveled to Beijing where he sought to replace the previous confrontational relationship between his country and the ancient kingdom with one of cooperation. While making clear to the Chinese that the United States remained a Pacific power, he acknowledged that China had become one of the most important economic players in the world and was entitled to have a far bigger voice in the global economy than it had in the past. He also understood the economic dependency on the Chinese of North Korea, which in 2009 had conducted a successful underground nuclear test. He hoped China might use its economic influence to constrain the erratic behavior of its leader, Kim Jong-un, and place limits on its nuclear ambitions.[39]

This did not happen. Instead, China turned coral reefs in the South and East China Seas into islands eight hundred miles from the mainland and claimed as its territory what had been international waters. It also tested a new Stealth jet fighter and hacked into the computers of such large American corporations as Google and Boeing. It even threatened to depress the American economy by selling some of its holdings of American debt if US budget deficits continued to worsen.[40]

In response Obama embarked on a two-track course. He kept the door open to better relations with China, but in the summer of 2010, at a conference of the Association of Southeast Asian Nations (ASEAN) in Vietnam, to which Secretary of State Hillary Clinton had been invited, the secretary persuaded these countries to speak out against China's policy in the South China Sea. The president made clear to Chinese president Jinping Xi that China's effort to seize or build on lands occupied by a US ally could escalate into a US-China conflict. The administration also invested in new military technologies and increased spending on cyber defense and offense. Most important, it developed a strategy of increasing the US's military presence in Southeast Asia starting with a small base in Australia, and reaching a multi-lateral trade agreement with Southeast Asian countries as an alternative to China's own regional economic ambitions.[41]

The concept of such an agreement went back to 2005 when four countries with trans-Pacific interests—New Zealand, Brunei, Chile, and Singapore—signed the Trans-Pacific Strategic Economic Partnership (TPSEP). Beginning in 2008, additional countries, including the United States, participated in talks to expand the partnership. Obama expressed a deep interest in having the US become part of the union, which, he hoped, would establish "a high standard, enforceable, meaningful trade agreement" that would be "incredibly powerful for American companies who . . . have often been locked out of those markets." It would also benefit American workers by allowing America to compete on a more level playing field. "I view smart trade agreements as a vital part of middle-class economics," he later added.[42]

The president also believed an expanded Pacific agreement would have important strategic value. It would make clear to doubters America's commitment to the nations bordering on the South and East China Seas and its staying power. It would also create a strategic wedge against China's increasing influence in the region.[43]

In early November 2011, Obama visited a number of Pacific Rim nations before becoming the first American president to attend a meeting of the ASEAN countries on the island of Bali. On his way across the Pacific, he stopped in Honolulu where he announced, along with the leaders of eight other trans-Pacific countries, the broad outlines of what became the Trans-Pacific Partnership (TPP). He also called together some of his closest advisers to express his frustration at how he was being characterized in Washington as distant and detached. "Few things irritate me more," he said mimicking those who described him this way. " 'He's aloof, he doesn't have friends.' " They could not be more wrong, he continued. "I'm almost always around people. I just have a different group of friends than people who've been running for office since they were twenty-two."[44]

In Bali, the president and leaders of the other ASEAN nations once again challenged China's claims to the resource-rich South Asian Sea. Obama rattled Chinese premier Wen Jiabo by announcing that he was stationing twenty-five hundred Marines in Australia and had gained backing for a regional free-trade bloc. He also revealed that he was considering restoring diplomatic relations with Myanmar (Burma), a Chinese ally. In response, the Chinese claimed the United States was trying to destabilize the region and said that conflicting territorial disputes should be settled by bilateral negotiations.[45]

The president remained undeterred. The next year he visited Myanmar on his way to the 2012 meeting of the ASEAN countries in Cambodia. Even though the country of fifty-three million had been shut off from the rest of the world by a xenophobic military junta that had ruled it for nearly fifty years, the situation in Myanmar had begun to change by the time Obama took office. The military adopted a new constitution paving the way for a civilian-led government and freed from more than twenty years of house arrest the Nobel Laureate and leader of the democratic movement in Myanmar, Aung San Suu Kyi. By visiting Myanmar, meeting with Aung San Suu Kyi, and delivering a speech at the University of Yangon in Rangoon, in which he stated that the US was "a Pacific nation" whose future was "bound to those nations and peoples to our West," the president was reasserting the United States' position as a Pacific power and warning the Beijing government not to interfere with the transition taking place in the country.[46]

At the ASEAN meeting in Phnom Penh and in the three years of negotiations that followed, the administration worked out the difficult details of a final TPP agreement, which ranged from the complex issues of copyright law to labor conditions and tariffs among the twelve signatory nations. The negotiations were complicated by the fact that due to the government shutdown at home, the president had to cancel his planned trip to Asia in October 2013. China's president Xi Jinping also offered economic incentives to the ASEAN countries, including establishing a $50 billion Chinese infrastructure bank, as a way of drawing them into its orbit.[47]

Despite the obstacles along the way, twelve Pacific Rim countries agreed to the TPP in February 2016. Even many Asian critics of TPP feared China's expansionary ambitions in Southeast Asia and, despite being wary of Washington's commitment to the region, understood that only the United States had the economic and military power to contain the Chinese threat. In addition, they were so anxious to gain greater access to American markets that they made numerous concessions to the US in the negotiations.[48]

The signatories to the TPP represented roughly 40 percent of the world's economic output. The agreement was designed so that it could eventually create a new single trading bloc akin to the European Union (EU). In order for it to go into effect, at least six of the original twelve negotiating countries accounting for at least 85 percent of their combined GDP had to ratify the agreement within two years of its signing. Since the US had by far the largest GDP, this meant it needed Senate consent. Because of opposition to the agreement, even Democrats, who feared that the free trade nature of TPP would cost American jobs, and complaints about the domination of the large corporate interests in determining America's negotiating positions, ratification of the agreement in an election year seemed unlikely. Even one of the architects of the agreement, former secretary Clinton, disavowed it because of the flack she was getting from her chief opponent for the Democratic presidential nomination, Senator Bernie Sanders (VT), a strong opponent of all free trade agreements.[49]

Despite the opposition, Obama sought TPP's speedy ratification. He hoped to avoid having the agreement drawn into the politics of a presidential election year. Even when it became apparent in August that the Senate would not ratify the agreement before the 2016 presidential elections, Obama remained determined to have it passed by the end of the year. If the Senate failed to ratify the TPP before the elections, he said he would bring it up again during the lame-duck session that followed. "We are part of a global economy," he added. "We are not reversing that."[50]

In retrospect, the president never had a chance of getting the Senate to ratify the agreement. The opposition was simply too great. Fearful of losing more jobs to Asia, key labor leaders, who had been among his strongest supporters, spoke out against the agreement. Partisanship also played its role. Once the party of free trade, Republicans, led by Paul Ryan (R-WI) who had replaced John Boehner as House Speaker in September 2015, and Senate Majority Leader McConnell, condemned the agreement as a sellout of American interests. The fact that the final terms seemed to favor large corporate interests even led to accusations that the president had always been a tool of corporate America.[51]

Most of the foreign policy officials and advisers in the administration agreed that the president regarded TPP as a way to expand American trade into Southeast Asia and to create an economic bloc that would contain Chinese expansion into the region. As Defense Secretary Ash Carter later wrote, it was part of a "rebalance in American foreign policy." It was driven by Obama's "conviction that the United States had dissipated too much of its strength in the Middle East." Just as in the case of the ACA, the president allowed corporate interests to have their way in the negotiations so that they would not obstruct completion of the final agreement.[52]

Global Warming and Climate Change

One of the problems the president took up with the Chinese in the last years of his administration was the twin issues of global warming and climate change resulting from carbon emissions. As a new US senator in 2007, Obama introduced legislation mandating reductions in emissions from the burning of fossil fuels. As a new president in 2009, he made a commitment to reduce greenhouse emissions by 17 percent below 2005 levels by 2020. He also committed $90 billion of the Troubled Asset Relief Program (TARP) to promote renewable energy sources. By the end of his first administration, electricity generated from wind, solar, and geothermal sources had more than doubled.[53]

In late December 2009, the president traveled to Copenhagen, Denmark, in an effort to get most of the world's developed and less-developed nations to reach an agreement that would mitigate the effects of climate change already being felt throughout the world. He decided to go to the meeting despite having recently returned from Oslo, Norway, where he had accepted the Nobel Peace Prize. During the conference, Secretary of State Clinton announced that the US was prepared to lead a collective effort by developed countries to provide $100 billion annually by 2020 to help the poorest and least prepared nations respond to climate change.[54]

Getting representatives from virtually every nation in the world to reach a binding accord proved impossible. China, rapidly becoming the largest emitter of greenhouse gases, led a group of other developing nations in opposing stringent emission controls. Other countries complained during the negotiations about corporate favoritism, the lack of funding to help developing countries combat the effects of climate change, and the lack of transparency. As a result, signatories to the final agreement pledged to curb carbon emissions by modest amounts through 2020, but without providing any enforcing mechanisms.[55]

On Capitol Hill, a number of senators, including the chairman of the Senate Foreign Relations Committee, Richard Lugar (R-IN), and Lisa Murkowski (R-AK), praised the administration for what it had accomplished at Copenhagen. Most environmental groups, however, blamed the White House for what was widely regarded as a failed summit. They were especially critical of the speech Obama gave at the conference. He offered the poor and developing countries nothing to help them reduce emissions other than the $100 billion global fund Clinton had already promised them. "We have charted our course, we have made our commitments, and we will do what we say," he told the delegates at the Copenhagen summit.[56]

Limiting carbon emissions meant cutting back on the use of fossil fuels, such as coal and oil. There was no broad base of support to reduce the use of coal to produce electricity or oil to heat homes and fuel vehicles. To the contrary, even those who regarded global warming and climate change as important issues, thought of them as long-term problems rather than ones requiring immediate structural changes. Others regarded them as developments that occurred periodically over millions of years rather than being man-made, the argument fostered by the powerful oil and coal lobby.

The key congressional battle between environmentalists and the fossil fuel industry after Obama took office was over legislation allowing the Environmental Protection Agency (EPA) to set a limit on carbon emissions each year and, then, in an auction system known as "cap-and-trade," permit firms to buy or sell the rights to these emissions. Instead of the government regulating limits on carbon emissions for each industry, the proposal would allow the marketplace to determine which industries owned the right to these emissions. In the president's view, cap-and-trade was a conservative, market-driven, proposal for achieving a progressive policy goal.[57]

Although a number of Republicans still sought to work with Democrats on global warming and climate change when Obama took office in 2009, by 2010 that had changed. Facing Tea Party opposition in their bids for reelection in November, they came out against cap-and-trade. Because of a major leak of oil in the Gulf of Mexico in 2010, caused by an explosion on the Deep Water Horizon oil rig owned by British Petroleum (BP), resulting in the worst oil slick in the nation's history and inflicting major damage to ecosystems along the Gulf Coast from Louisiana to Florida, environmentalists lost interest in any public-private fix to global warming.[58]

Given the degree of opposition to cap-and-trade, the president decided in 2010 that he would be wasting his political capital by making global warming and climate change among his highest legislative goals. Even when he spoke to the American people about the disaster underway in the Gulf, he began his address by remarking: "As we speak, our nation faces a multitude of challenges. At home, our top priority is to recover and rebuild from a recession that has touched the lives of nearly every American."[59]

As the end of his first administration grew nearer, the president began to reconsider his position. By 2012, he had achieved most of his highest priorities at home. Having always been concerned about the damage being caused by global warming, the president now felt better able to address the issue. A report by climate scientists that 2010 had been the hottest year on record and a rash of extreme weather conditions—floods, droughts, heat waves, and cold snaps—highlighted to him the need to confront the issue. So did the BP spill and a battle between environmentalists and oil lobbyists over whether to permit the construction of a pipeline (the Keystone XL Pipeline) from the oil-producing tar sands of Alberta, Canada, to refineries in Texas.[60]

Obama joined the opposition to the pipeline. Facing an uphill fight for reelection, the president realized he needed the active support of the very environmental community he had so disappointed by his environmental record. On January 18, 2012, he issued a statement in which he rejected the application of the Canadian firm, TransCanada Corporation, for a permit to build and operate the Keystone XL pipeline. Environmentalists immediately embraced his decision. Congressional Republicans and spokespeople for the fossil fuel industry maintained that Obama's action would be harmful to the economy and the national security.[61]

After the president won reelection in 2012, he elevated the importance he attached to confronting global warming and climate change. "We, the people," he remarked in his Second Inaugural address on January 21, 2013, have an obligation to all of posterity. "We will respond to the threat of climate change, knowing that the failure to do so would betray our children and future generations." In his State of the Union address on February 12, 2013, he warned Congress that if it did not "pursue a bipartisan, market-based solution to climate change," he would take executive action "to reduce pollution, prepare our communities for the consequences of climate change, and speed the transition to more sustainable sources of energy."[62]

In June, the White House issued *The President's Climate Action Plan*, which described in detail the administration's plan for cutting carbon pollution and slowing down the effects of climate change. Predicated on his pledge to reduce by 2020 America's greenhouse emissions by 17 percent below 2005 levels, Obama offered a series of proposals ranging from cutting pollution from power plants to investing in clean energy innovation. Over the next two years, the *Action Plan* guided the administration's response to global warming and climate change. [63]

The administration's efforts culminated at the end of 2015. In November, Obama rejected the Keystone XL Pipeline once and for all, saying it was never as indispensable as both its boosters and detractors claimed. Even more important, the next month, the United States joined 194 other world powers in signing the Paris Climate Agreement. The most far-reaching undertaking ever agreed to by these powers to cut greenhouse gas emissions and avoid its worst potential, the agreement was a legally binding accord that was part of an internationally coordinated effort to tackle climate change. It was reached under intense international pressure to prevent a repeat of the Copenhagen failure six years earlier.[64]

Instead of country-specific emission targets, the agreement provided only that the signatories commit to keeping the global temperature rise for the century well below 2 degrees Celsius (preferably 1.5 percent) above preindustrial levels. Although it left it up to them on how to achieve that goal, it established a series of monitoring processes and provided for an assessment every five years of the progress being made toward their success. It also provided for greater transparency and sought to increase assistance to developing countries faced with the impact of climate change.[65]

The Paris Agreement came about only after years of multilateral and bilateral negotiations, especially between the US and China. Despite the United States' many differences with China over its restrictive trade policies and ambitions in the South China Sea, each nation shared a common interest in maintaining good relations with the other: the former as the largest importer of Chinese goods and the latter as its biggest trading partner. As the largest polluters of the environment and biggest manufacturers of alternative energy sources, including solar panels, wind-driven turbines, and electric batteries able to power automobiles, both powers also had an interest in reducing their dependence on fossil fuels.[66]

In April, Secretary Kerry traveled to Beijing where he met with his Chinese counterpart, Yang Jiechi. To Kerry's surprise, Yang was receptive to his proposal for establishing a formal working relationship on climate change. Together they launched the US-China Climate Change Working Group to reduce the growth of global emissions. Over the next several months China and the US also negotiated terms for an international agreement on climate based on the principle of "common but differentiated responsibilities and respective capabilities." Kerry's hope was that the two countries might conclude an agreement on climate change before President Obama's visit to Beijing in November 2014.[67]

The president made clear that any accord between the two countries had to include meaningful commitments by China to reduce its global emissions. Despite last-minute tensions over targets, the two sides reached an agreement that satisfied him. On November 11, 2014, as part of a trip to the Far East, Obama met with President Xi in Beijing. In a joint press conference Xi lectured him about historical grievances China still felt toward Washington and warned foreign nations not to interfere in the growing prodemocracy movement in Hong Kong. Notwithstanding his remarks, the two leaders stood together as they announced their target emissions reductions.[68]

The year of negotiations that followed between the developed and developing nations over such matters as emission targets, funding, and transparency proved difficult. In a speech at the Asia-Pacific business conference in the Philippines less than two weeks before the Paris climate summit was scheduled to meet, the president warned that there still was "a lot of work to do," but encouraged by the Chinese-American agreement, the negotiators resolved the most serious differences. To keep the Republicans from killing the agreement, they wrote it as a voluntary pact rather a treaty requiring Senate approval. For that reason a number of environmental scientists were skeptical about its importance.[69]

Congressional opponents of the Paris Agreements and every Republican running for president made the same point. In contrast, House and Senate Democrats, environmental groups, and world leaders hailed the agreement. "This is truly a historic moment," UN Secretary General Ban Ki-moon remarked. "For the first time, we have a truly universal agreement on climate change, one of the most crucial problems on earth." The overwhelming majority of environmental scientists and leaders agreed. Despite Republican opposition, over the next ten months, the administration worked out the final details preliminary to the United States' joining the Paris Agreement on September 3, 2016.[70]

As for Obama, he took full credit for the accord. "One of the reasons I ran for Office was to make sure that America does its part to protect this planet for future generations," he remarked in announcing America's entrance into the Agreement. "Over the past seven and a half years, we've transformed the United States into a global leader in the fight against climate change."[71]

Because the president signed the Paris Agreement without the approval of the Republican-controlled Senate, he continued to come under blistering attack during the last year of his administration. He was accused of asserting dictatorial powers by obliging the United States, without congressional approval, to the whims of nations like China, whose interests often conflicted with those of the United States. The same charges were made when the administration entered into the TPP in February. Congressional Republicans were also incensed by the president's empowerment of the EPA to enforce regulations on limiting carbon emissions, from increasing the gas mileage of new automobiles to requiring the construction of more heat efficient homes over the objections of the affected industries. They were also angered by his decision, as his administration neared its end, to prohibit by executive order the development of 253 million acres of public land, more than any other president.[72]

By all these actions, the president showed that he was not the dispassionate and unresponsive president that his detractors within the environmental community had once accused him of being. Instead, he proved the opposite, a leader whose actions held out the promise, for the first time, of the world coming together to deal with what environmental scientists believed was the most existential threat to global survival ever known to humankind.[73]

Racial Crisis

Beginning with the fatal shooting of Trayvon Martin Jr., a seventeen-year-old Black teenager, in Sanford, Florida, on February 26, 2012, and another fatal shooting of a Black teenager, eighteen-year-old Michael Brown of Ferguson, Missouri, on August 9, 2014, the president had to deal with issues of race relations in ways he had not since the angry outbursts of his pastor, the Reverend Jeremiah Wright, in 2008. His need to confront the issue continued through the mass murders by a white supremacist of nine Black parishioners at the Emanuel AME Church in Charleston, South Carolina, on June 17, 2015. The shock to the nation, especially within the Black community, caused by these killings tested once more the boundaries of the president's own thinking on race. They reaffirmed that while he continued to be rooted by the color of his skin, he still regarded himself as the nation's leader, who happened to be Black, rather than being defined by his Blackness.

Trayvon Martin Jr. was killed by George Zimmerman, a neighborhood watch volunteer, who claimed he had been assaulted by Martin and was acting in self-defense in compliance with Florida's "Stand Your Ground" law. Martin was returning from a convenience store where he had made some small purchases. He wore a hoodie and was new to the community. He did not carry a gun and had no juvenile record. Zimmerman was later charged with second degree murder but found not guilty.[74]

Investigators were never able to determine exactly what happened on February 26. Because the Florida law had already been criticized by Black leaders and legal justice advocates as giving license to gun owners to shoot minorities and Zimmerman's explanation of what happened did not square with the forensic evidence, his killing attracted national attention. Although Martin had been expelled several times from school and had some minor brushes with the law, he was widely portrayed in the media as a star athlete, who was trying to make a fresh start for himself. Rallies around the country called for Zimmerman's arrest and an end to racial discrimination in the criminal justice system.[75]

The president took a month before responding to Martin's killing. Acknowledging its racial element, he did so without using the term "race." "If I had a son he'd look like Treyvon," he remarked. "Obviously, this is a tragedy. . . . I think every parent in America should be able to understand why it is absolutely imperative that we investigate every aspect of this." This was the first time he talked explicitly about racism in the justice system since the arrest of Harvard professor Henry Louis Gates in July 2009.[76]

Obama did not comment immediately after Martin's killing in part because he was awaiting Attorney General Eric Holder Jr.'s decision to have the civil rights division investigate the killing. "I'm the head of the executive branch and the attorney general reports to me so I've got to be careful about my statement to make sure that we're not impairing any investigation that's taking place right now," he explained.[77]

Civil rights leaders criticized the president, nevertheless, for not addressing directly the issue of race in the criminal justice system and for his failure to call Martin's parents. "If Trayvon's mother were white, would Obama give her a call?" asked Bruce White of Syracuse University, founder of the "Your Black World" coalition. Not until the end of July, after Zimmerman had been acquitted, did Obama address the issues that concerned his Black critics. Commenting briefly after learning of the jury's decision on July 13 and more extensively at a press conference six days later, he made clear his recognition of the need for the nation to address these concerns. "There are very few African American men in this country who haven't had the experience of being followed when they were shopping in a department store," he remarked at the press conference. "That includes me." [78]

The most important of the remedies he offered, however, was racial sensitivity training on the state and local levels. On the federal level, he had little to propose other than to convene a conference of business and religious leaders, and others familiar with the racial problems young African American men encountered every day. He had doubts about convening a more general conversation on race, as some civil rights leaders were advocating. "I haven't seen that be particularly effective when politicians try to organize conversations. They end up being stilted and politicized, and folks are locked in position they already have."[79]

The president simply did not believe racial discrimination was a significant enough problem to require a lot of his attention. "I don't want us to lose sight that things are getting better," he remarked at the end of a press conference. "Each successive generation seems to be making progress in changing attitudes when it comes to race. It doesn't mean that we're in a post-racial society. [But] we're becoming a more perfect union—not a perfect union, but a more perfect union." He was sensitive to the needs of Black people but never beholden to their causes. He remained the president of all the United States who happened to be Black.[80]

His limited views on racial discrimination were tested again by the fatal shooting on August 9, 2014, of eighteen-year-old Michael Brown in Ferguson, Missouri. Brown's killing was different in several respects from Treyvon Martin's death. Even physically there were differences. In contrast to Martin, who looked and acted like the teenager and athlete he was and whom the president embraced as someone that could have been him thirty-five years earlier, Brown was tall, obese, and adult-looking. The president could never have said of him that he was like the son he never had.[81]

Martin was returning from a convenience store where he had made some small purchases when he was killed. Brown was walking away from a store where he was suspected of stealing cigarillos when he was fatally shot. In both cases, the circumstances leading to the killings were unclear, but in contrast to Zimmerman, the person who shot Brown, Darren Wilson, was a police officer. Unlike the largely middle-class city of Sanford, Ferguson, where Brown was killed, was a hard scrub, predominantly poor Black city that was part of the St. Louis metropolitan area. Its police department and municipal government were notorious for balancing the city's budget by having the police impose excessive traffic and parking tickets. In contrast to Sanford, Ferguson was a time bomb waiting to go off.

Unlike Martin Jr.'s killing, Brown's death led to four months of riots, looting, and vandalism, including the burning down of businesses. Heavily armed police from the metropolitan area and the National Guard were called into Ferguson. Tear gas filled the air. Missouri governor Jay Nixon (R) declared two states of emergency and imposed curfews on Ferguson. Attorney General Eric Holder Jr. ordered a federal investigation into the causes of the rioting and personally visited Ferguson, where he met with local leaders. The rioting did not end until the end of November. Even then, Ferguson remained on the edge, needing only the smallest incident to start more rioting.[82]

Obama's response to Brown's killing was more modulated than in the case of Martin's death. In his first comments on August 14, he announced Holder's investigation, stating that the shooting in Ferguson "deserves a fulsome review." In subsequent remarks, he spoke passionately about the long-standing problems that faced Black youths, including broken families, and inadequate schools. "In too many communities, too many young men of color are left behind and seen only as objects of fear," he remarked on

August 18. "You have young men of color in many communities who are more likely to end up in jail or in the criminal justice system than they are in a good job or in college. And part of my job . . . is to get at the root causes." The president was also highly critical of the Ferguson Police Department and of police departments throughout the country for their practice of racial profiling and the inordinate number of arrests they made of people of color as opposed to Caucasian Americans. His critics even took him to task for his criticisms of the police—one critic accusing him of an "assault on the police."[83]

As in the case of the fatal shooting of Trayvon Martin Jr., however, the president emphasized the theme of racial progress rather than racial division. While remarking upon the legitimate grievances of African Americans and other people of color, he made clear his respect for the police. Most of his criticism was also directed not at the criminal justice system but at the advocates of violence and the vandals, looters, and arsonists who followed in their wake. If they committed a crime, they needed to be prosecuted, he stated.[84]

On November 24, 2014, a St. Louis County grand jury decided not to indict Ferguson police officer Wilson for Brown's killing. On March 4, 2015, the Department of Justice (DOJ) cleared Wilson of civil rights violations in the shooting. The forensic evidence, the DOJ concluded, and changes in the testimony of witnesses who saw the shooting and claimed at first that Brown was holding his hands up when he was shot, made clear that Wilson had not violated the law.[85]

Fearing an outburst of violence in Ferguson following both announcements, Obama defended the grand jury's decision and, later, his administration's decision not to prosecute the officer, but not without first blasting the Ferguson Police Department for its discriminatory practices. "As they do their jobs in the coming days," he remarked about the department in November, "they need to work with the community, not against the community." After the Justice Department decided not to bring charges against Wilson, he went much further. "What we saw was that [the department] in conjunction with [the] municipality make traffic stops, arrests, and tickets as revenue generators as opposed to serving," he said at a town hall meeting in Columbia, South Carolina, in March. He added that the overwhelming white force was "systematically" biased, and placing minorities under its care led to an "oppressive and abusive situation."[86]

Much to the displeasure of many civil rights leaders, however, who viewed racial discrimination as a pathological societal problem requiring a major reordering of presidential priorities, Obama stressed "the enormous progress in race relations." Even in his remarks criticizing the Ferguson Police Department for its discriminatory racial practices, he added that the job of police departments and communities everywhere was to "work together to solve the problems, and not get caught up in the cynicism of 'Oh it's never going to change, everything's racist.'" Obama was not race neutral. He simply did not view politics through the prism of race.[87]

The president made his comments on the grand jury's decision not to indict Officer Wilson while he was on his way to Selma, Alabama, where he joined forty thousand marchers to celebrate the fiftieth anniversary of the historic march over the Edmund Pettus Bridge. At the front of the huge gathering that crossed the bridge, he joined hands with the leader of the march fifty years earlier, Congressman John Lewis (D-GA), who nearly died on the bridge in 1965 after a state trooper fractured his skull and left him unconscious. Afterward, the president delivered a speech, which most commentators agreed was one of the best of his political career.[88]

In elegiac terms, the president described the nation's history as a series of actions by individuals who defied convention to bring about progress. They were not just white and Black or drawn from a single socioeconomic group, he said. They were women and men, Hispanic and Asian, wealthy and poor, Protestants and Catholic, Jewish and Muslims, evangelicals and atheists, military heroes and community volunteers, entertainers and athletes. "Look at our history," he remarked at Selma. "We are the immigrants who stowed away on ships to reach these shores. . . . We're the slaves who built the White House and the economy of the South. . . . We're fresh GIs who fought to liberate a continent. . . . We are storytellers, writers, poets, artists, who abhor unfairness, and despise hypocrisy. . . . We are Jackie Robinson, enduring scorn and spiked cleats and pitches coming straight to his head, and stealing home in the World Series anyways. . . . That's what America is."[89]

Throughout his speech Obama made clear that the fight against racial discrimination was not over, and he referred repeatedly to the problems and barriers still limiting opportunities for the poor and people of color. "If Selma taught us anything," he remarked, "it's that our work is never done." What happened in Ferguson was not an isolated incident, he added.[90]

In his address, he also attacked the Supreme Court's decision invalidating that part of the Voting Rights Act of 1965 providing for federal protection of minority voting for those living in states and locations with histories of voting discrimination. The country had changed, the Court ruled, and federal supervision was no longer relevant. Disappointed by the ruling, he urged the one hundred Congress members who had come to Selma to be leaders in persuading other lawmakers "to make it their mission to restore the law this year."[91]

What the president was seeking was balance and prudence in approaching the issue of racial discrimination. Racism remained a problem that was going to exist for the foreseeable future. It demanded a meaningful response from his administration. But his mantra remained one of hope and progress rather than cynicism.

In the wake of Martin's and Brown's killing, an organizationally loose social movement, "Black Lives Matter" (BLM), spread rapidly throughout the country. Its purpose was to shine light on racial discrimination within the criminal justice system. Its adherents did not advocate violence, but they emphasized the need for a major restructuring of government and the economy and the need to police the police. Many of them were also confrontational and divisive in their tactics and language.[92]

The president recognized BLM's appeal to young Blacks throughout the country. On several occasions after Brown's killing, he met with these young activists to make clear his appreciation of their concerns. But he seemed to lecture them about the counterproductive nature of urban violence and stated that "young Blacks that commit crimes" need to be thrown in jail for the safety of poor Black communities. One young woman at a town meeting with the president said she and others "left in tears" because of his failure to respond adequately to "Black grief and pain."[93]

In contrast to his response to BLM, Obama helped organize and then devoted considerable effort to a more tightly organized movement of young Blacks, "My Brother's Keeper" (MBK). Like BLM, MBK sought to promote racial justice. In contrast to BLM, its efforts were not so much ones of protest and demands for structural change as they were to improve the educational futures of young Black and Latino boys from preschool through high school graduation. Among its initiatives were keeping track of the progress of these boys, reducing the number of minorities suspended or expelled from school, growing the number of African American boys taking gifted, honors, and Advanced Placement courses and exams, and offering more advanced math and science courses in their schools.[94]

At a White House meeting in February 2014, in which students participating in MBK were present, the president identified his own experiences as a teenager with their own. Like many of them, he remarked, he was angry that he did not have a father in the house. "I made bad choices," he continued. "I got high without always thinking about the harm that it could do. I didn't always take school as seriously as I should have." Fortunately, he had loving grandparents and a mother and "wonderful teachers and community leaders—and they'd push me to work hard and study hard and make the most of myself."[95]

Obama found the statistics on reading proficiency, suspensions and expulsions, and graduation rates of Black youths numbing. "We just assume, of course, it's going to be like that. But these statistics should break our hearts." That is why he decided to work with government officials, private philanthropies, and business leaders in expanding the scope of MBK. Announcing that the private foundations with whom he worked were prepared to add another $200 million to the $150 million they were already investing in the initiative, he described MBK as a "focused effort on boys and young men of color who are having a tough time" to make it through school and keep out of trouble with the law.[96]

The changes he envisioned as a result of MBK were not going happen quickly, he remarked. "Parents will have to parent—and turn off the television, and help with homework." But, over time, he expected to break the cycle of lost opportunity and broken lives. "And this country will be richer and stronger for it for generations to come," he concluded. In his postpresidential memoir, A Promised Land, he even stated that one of his purposes in writing the book was "to tell a more personal story that might inspire young people considering a life of public service": how the story of his life was one of "how it was only by hitching my wagon to something larger than myself that I was ultimately able to locate a community and purpose for my life."[97]

The president did not waver from this optimistic view, in which he offered hope rather than despair, even after the mass murder of nine African American parishioners at the Emanuel African Methodist Church (AME) in Charleston, South Carolina on June 17, 2015, at the hand of a twenty-one-year-old white supremist, Dylann Roof. Founded in 1817, making it the oldest Black church in South Carolina, the AME held a special place among Black South Carolinians and was often referred to as "Mother Emanuel." One of its founders, Denmark Vesey, was a former slave who was executed for attempting to organize a slave revolt in the antebellum South. In 1962, Martin Luther King had preached at the church. Its pastor at the time of the murders, and one of its victims, was Clementa Pinckney, a state senator and the youngest African American ever elected to the South Carolina legislature [98]

Despite being Caucasian, Roof had been invited into the church and sat for an hour with the parishioners in a Bible study group before he opened fire on them. Although the white supremacist fled the scene after the shootings, he was quickly captured and readily confessed to the murders, saying that he wanted "to start a race war." During the federal trial that followed, in which he was found guilty and given the death sentence, Roof refused to apologize for what he had done and did not dispute his sentence. His major concern seemed to be that he might be deemed innocent by insanity.[99]

Like most Americans, Obama was shocked that a person who had been invited into the church and welcomed by its parishioners, could suddenly slaughter them for no other reasons than they were Black, and he wanted to start a race war. That Roof chose to commit the murders in a church of significant historical importance only added to the president's state of despair. "Any death of this sort is a tragedy," he remarked on learning of the shooting. "Any shooting involving multiple victims is a tragedy. There is something particularly heartbreaking about a death happening . . . in a place of worship."[100]

Obama decided to go to Charleston to eulogize the Reverend Pickney at his funeral service, which was held on June 26 before a crowd of 5,500 at the College of Charleston. Earlier that day the Supreme Court handed the administration a major victory in a verdict upholding the constitutional right of gay couples to marry. While preparing remarks hailing the verdict as a "victory for America," the president and his senior writers were also tasked with preparing a eulogy expressing the nation's grief at the death of Pickney and the other parishioners murdered at the AME church.[101]

In considering what he wanted to say at the service, Obama decided to build his remarks around the concept of "grace." As he explained to the worshippers, he interpreted grace to mean God's gift of forgiveness to sinners that had to be earned not just given. Even so, he emphasized forgiveness in his eulogy, even for a white supremist murderer. He was inspired by the remarks of family members of the slain victims, who said he should be punished but forgave him, nevertheless, for the killings. Instead of using the shootings in Charleston to launch an attack against all white Americans and view the future in racial terms, they spoke in nonracial terms of forgiveness.[102]

As he had done in Selma and during the year since the fatal shootings of Trayvon Martin and Michael Brown, he acknowledged in his eulogy that much work still needed to be done to heal the wounds of slavery. One step would be to remove from the grounds of the state capitol the Confederate flag that had become the symbol of antebellum slavery. Removing the flag, he remarked, "would be an expression of the amazing changes that have transformed this state and this country for the better. . . . By taking down the flag, we express God's grace."[103]

In words similar to those of Martin Luther King Jr., Obama described the nation's history, from slavery through the Jim Crow laws of the late nineteenth century and the civil rights acts of the twentieth century, in terms of a moral arc that was long, but always bending toward justice. He spoke of how history "can't be a sword to justify injustice or a shield against progress. It must be a manual for how to avoid repeating the mistakes of the past."[104]

In one of the most remarkable parts of his eulogy, he paused for thirteen seconds as he neared the end of his eulogy, an unusually long pause even for skilled speakers, but a tactic commonly used by Black preachers and ministers to gain control of the moment. After the pause, he began singing the hymn "Amazing Grace." Even when he and his staff were writing the eulogy, he told them he was planning to sing. But he took the preachers, ministers, and others on the stage behind him totally by surprise. As he continued to sing, their looks of uncertainty changed to broad grins, and they began to sing along with him. Others in the audience joined them, allowing the president to end his eulogy on a note of hope and promise.[105]

Like the president's remarks at Selma, his eulogy of Pinckney was widely considered one of the great speeches of his career. Michiko Kakutani of the *New York Times* called the speech "remarkable" because he used his "gifts of language and empathy and searching intellect . . . to talk about the complexities of race and justice . . . reflecting [his] own long view of history."[106]

Obama's eulogy of Clementa Pickney capped off one of the most momentous weeks of his second administration and, indeed, of his entire presidency. About the same time as his addresses, the Supreme Court handed the administration two other major victories, in addition to upholding the right of gay people to marry, by upholding a key provision of the ACA providing subsidies for low- and-middle-income Americans and by allowing minorities to continue using a civil rights era statute in housing discrimination lawsuits. Congress also passed legislation giving the president broad authority to negotiate new trade deals.[107]

Reviewing the events of the past week, Chris Cillizza of the *Washington Post* called it "the best week of Obama's presidency," remarking that it was "filled with developments, both practical and symbolic, that will reverberate well beyond not only this week or month but his entire presidency." The conservative columnist, Peggy Noonan, added: "He's 6.5 years into a rock 'em sock 'em presidency. . . . I think he just had one of the great weeks that a modern president could have. . . . You can tell some part of him has made a turn, and he is coming out of some doldrums."[108]

In fact, the entire year was one of the most successful of Obama's presidency. During 2015 the president expanded DACA, began secret negotiations to restore diplomatic relations with Cuba, signed a nuclear weapons agreement with Iran, helped establish and commit the United States to the TPP, negotiated the Paris Agreement on climate change, and responded in an uplifting way to a series of racial crises that rocked the nation. Throughout year, Obama remained optimistic about the future and stayed true to his beliefs in interdependency, diversity, and the establishment of a middle-class society.

Much of what Obama accomplished was done by executive action and over opposition from Republicans and even activists who had supported him in the 2008 and 2012 elections. This was especially true among environmentalists and younger African Americans, who felt he had not gone far enough in responding to their demands. As the president entered the final year of his administration, however, he felt emboldened by what he had achieved in 2015 and by his rating in the polls, which had risen above 50 percent for the first time in months. With the 2016 presidential election already underway, he also felt confident his successor would be a Democrat fully prepared to carry on his legacy.

Chapter 10

The Shock of Donald J. Trump's Election

As Obama entered the last year of his presidency, he was concerned about his place in history. His vision of the United States as a middle-class society welcoming to all regardless of background remained the same as it was when he took office seven years earlier. He expected the presumptive Democratic presidential nominee, Hillary Clinton, would build on his legacy. Like most political analysts, he did not take seriously the candidacy for the Republican nomination of Donald Trump, whom he held in little regard and had already roasted at the White House Correspondents' dinner in 2011 for making false charges about his place of birth and lack of an official birth certificate.

Even after the New York billionaire won the nomination, Obama believed Trump would never be elected president. He was stung by Trump's victory in November, which he took almost as a personal insult. As he accepted the reality of a Trump presidency, he developed doubts about his legacy. As he left office on January 20, 2017, he hoped for the best but feared the worst.

Obama's Message of Hope

On January 12, the president delivered his final State of the Union address. In contrast to Republican depictions of his presidency as one of failure and incompetency, he spoke of his many achievements as president, such as the ACA, the Iran deal, his opening to Cuba, and the Paris Agreement on climate change. Acknowledging that he had failed to achieve all his priorities as president and that 68 percent of Americans still thought the country was on the wrong track, he continued to offer hope and promise about the future. "Tonight was President Obama's morning-in-America response to the malaise speech that the Republican candidates have been delivering in the last year," commented Jon Favreau, the president's former chief speech writer.[1]

Instead of presenting Congress with a long list of proposals it would never consider, Obama built his speech around four themes: (1) giving everyone a "fair shake" in the nation's new technological economy, (2) using technology "to work for us" in dealing with such challenges as climate change, (3) protecting America while leading "the world without becoming its policeman," and (4) making politics "reflect what's best in us and not the worst."[2]

Even though the president denounced the campaign's partisan politics, he intended his address to be as much an election year speech as a government document. "Last year, he spoke to Congress. This year he'll be speaking more to the American public," said Jennifer Psaki, the White House communications director. Without naming him, the president directed many of his remarks to Trump, who was now the leading candidate for the Republican nomination.[3]

His staff, who at first joined the president in ignoring Trump, remained furious that he had accused the president of hiding the fact he had been born in Kenya and that his remarks morphed into what became known as the "the birther movement" despite the president's decision in 2011 to release the document showing he had been born in Honolulu. Ben Rhodes also felt "helpless" at the Republican candidate's repeated accusations that American troops were being killed in Libya while at the same time criticizing him for not committing forces to end the civil war there.[4]

Obama was more annoyed by the media's focus on Trump the candidate rather than on his message. "I can't believe they're giving this airtime," he said with respect to the birther movement. Referring, nevertheless, to the election already underway, the president commented in his State of the Union, "there will be voices urging us to fall back into our respective tribes, to scapegoat fellow citizens who don't look like us, or pray like us, or vote like we do, or share the same background. We can't afford to go down that path." As he neared the end of his presidency, he considered his failure to mend this partisan divide one of his greatest disappointments. "A president with the gifts of Lincoln or Roosevelt might have better bridged the divide," he acknowledged.[5]

Not surprisingly, reaction to his address split along partisan lines. In a televised debate among the candidates for the Republican presidential nomination held shortly after Obama delivered his speech, they portrayed his presidency as a total failure that had diminished freedom and opportunity at home and left the nation in a weakened position around the world.[6]

Iran's seizure of two small American naval patrol boats and ten crewmen just hours before Obama delivered his message, seemed to underscore the Republican charges. The boats had wandered off course and were in Iranian territorial waters when they were captured. The seizure of the vessels and their crews became fodder for Republican attacks on the administration just when the US was supposed to unfreeze $100 billion under the provisions of the Iran Nuclear Agreement.[7]

On March 20, two months after delivering his State of the Union address, Obama traveled to Cuba to reopen the US embassy in Havana, which had been closed since 1961. "We want to make the process of normalization irreversible," said Rhodes, who had led an advance logistical group to Havana.[8]

The next day, the president was formally welcomed at the presidential palace by President Raul Castro, whom he had met in Panama in 2015. During his three-day visit, he met with Castro, spoke before a group of US and Cuban business executives, and gave a televised speech to the Cuban people followed by a meeting with a group of Cuban political dissidents. At all these events, Obama criticized the Cuban government for its violation of human rights and spoke of his efforts to open up further lines of communication with Cuba.[9]

In his talks with Castro and at a joint press conference that followed, he pointed to the progress made between Washington and Havana in the fifteen months since the decision to establish diplomatic relations between the two governments and the importance of lifting the trade embargo against Cuba, even as he criticized what he regarded as Cuba's human rights violations. The "United States will continue to speak up on behalf of democracy, including the right of the Cuban people to decide their own future," he remarked. "We'll speak out on behalf of universal human rights."[10]

When asked about the trade embargo, he said he had taken all the steps he could to ease the embargo. Now it was up to the Republican-controlled Congress to lift it completely. "Frankly, Congress is not as productive as I would like it to be," he said. Always hoping for the best, however, he thought that the large congressional delegation of forty Republicans and Democrats was an indication that there was "growing interest inside Congress for lifting the embargo." That is why he called the dialogue taking place between Washington and Cuba "so important."[11]

The president made these same points in his meeting with the US and Cuban business executives and, the next day, in his nationally broadcast address to the Cuban people. Pointing to the changes in the economic relationship between the US and Cuba, such as making more dollars available to Cuba and the resumption of commercial flights and cruises between the two countries, he acknowledged the importance of Washington lifting its trade embargo on Cuba. He also said that neither Cuba nor the United States should have anything to fear from the other country.[12]

He also spoke of "the power of entrepreneurship" to bring about prosperity even in economically poor nations like Cuba. It is about "the pride that comes from creating something new and improving the lives of those around you," he remarked. "That's the spirit of entrepreneurship. . . . Cuba's economic future—its ability to create more jobs and a growing middle class, and meet the aspiration of the Cuban people—depends on growth in the private sector."[13]

The next day, the president addressed the Cuban people from one of Havana's landmark sites, the Gran Teatro. In the audience was Cuba's leader Raul Castro, who listened intently to what he had to say. Remarking that the failed attempt to overthrow Fidel Castro, known as the Bay of Pigs Operation, occurred in the same year (1961) that he was born, he tried to separate himself from the invasion. "I know the history, but I refuse to be trapped by it," he remarked.[14]

Acknowledging once more the serious differences remaining between Cuba and the US on forms of government, foreign policy, and human rights, Obama again presented his vision of Cuba's future. "I want the Cuban people—especially the young people—to understand why I believe that you should look to the future with hope; not the false promise which insists that things are better than they really are," he said. "Hope that is rooted in the future that you can choose and that you can shape, and that you can build for your country. . . . That's where hope begins—with the ability to earn your own living, and to build something you can be proud of."[15]

Obama's three-day visit to Cuba was generally well received in Cuba and among Cuban Americans living in the United States. There remained participants in the revolution in Cuba, who stayed deeply distrustful of the United States, and exiles from Cuba, who fled the revolution and still considered Cuba a threat to all of the Americas.[16]

In contrast, younger Cuban Americans living in southern Florida and Cubans who had little memory of the Cold War, approved the restoration of diplomatic relations as a way to reunite with their families. Cubans who were poor and without a job (the majority of the population) also welcomed

Obama's vision of a more economically thriving nation with the promise even of owning one's own business.[17]

The Asian Pivot and the Partisan Divide

Even as Obama presented his message of hope and promise for a better future to the people of the United States and Cuba alike, he still had to confront the partisan divide plaguing his presidency. Following the 2014 elections, the influence of Republican right-wingers grew stronger. House Majority Leader Eric Cantor was defeated by his right-wing opponent in the Republican primaries. House Speaker John Boehner resigned from the speakership (and Congress) under pressure from his party's right wing. With the primary season already underway, Trump became the front-runner for the Republican nomination by appealing to its right-wing base. Congressional Republicans were determined not only to oppose the president's legislative agenda but to reverse his past legislative accomplishments. His decision to govern by executive order alienated them even more.[18]

Republicans also criticized Obama for what they considered an apology to Japan for President Harry Truman's decision in August 1945 to drop atomic bombs on Hiroshima and Nagasaki at a cost of 120,000 dead. The president made his remarks on May 27 during a visit to Hiroshima's Memorial Peace Park, the last leg of a trip to the Far East, where he also visited Vietnam. The official purpose of the trip was to attend the G7 economic summit in Shima City, Japan. Unofficially, it was to enhance the president's ongoing pivot toward Asia.[19]

On the flight to Hanoi, he had a long conversation with Rhodes, who had recently testified before the Republican-controlled Benghazi Committee as it prepared its report on the seizure of the American embassy in Benghazi and the deaths of Chris Stevens and three other Americans after an especially partisan hearing. Rhodes was also the subject of a controversial story in the *New York Times Magazine* by David Samuels, in which Samuels portrayed him as a cynical manipulator of the news, who, through spin, was able to gain the approval of a gullible US public for the Iran Nuclear Agreement.[20]

On the flight to Vietnam, Rhodes relayed his account to Obama of his meetings with Samuels. Although the president made clear his displeasure with some of Rhodes's comments in the *Times Magazine* story, he told his adviser not to worry too much about the piece. "No, forget about that," he said. "That's just a pimp on the ass of progress. . . . The notion that there's something wrong with storytelling—I mean that's our job. To tell a really good story about who we are."[21]

In his conversation with Rhodes, Obama began talking about a best-selling book he was reading, *Sapiens: A Brief History of Mankind*, by Yuval Noah Harari, a conversation he had to interrupt but resumed three days later as he was being helicoptered to Japan. Beginning with the "cognitive revolution" seventy thousand years ago, Harari maintained that homo sapiens went through a series of revolutions, most notably the "agricultural revolution" eleven thousand years ago and the "scientific revolution" five hundred years ago. Instead of viewing these developments as progress, he maintained they contained the seeds of humankind's destruction, arguing, for example, that the agricultural revolution has resulted in obesity and other health problems and contributed to sharp disparities in wealth. Several features of the book caught the president's attention, including the author's ability to view history as a series of stories about humankind told well. "I'm reading a good book now," he told Rhodes. "It reminds you, the ability to tell stories about who we are is what makes us different from animals. We're just chimps without it."[22]

Another matter that also caught his attention was how Harari viewed the history of humankind as one of its growing ability to kill growing numbers of other human beings to the point of being able to wipe out perhaps all life on earth with a single weapon. This made him think not only about the necessity of preventing nuclear proliferation, but of the need to eliminate war entirely.[23]

During his visit to Vietnam, the president met with three of the country's leading young entrepreneurs. In his conversation with them, he emphasized many of the points he made during his visit to Cuba, such as the fact that he was not a prisoner of the past, and the importance of looking to the future. He stressed once again the importance of entrepreneurship, this time for Vietnam, which, he said, was not only about "building businesses," it was also "about creating good jobs, and developing new products, and devising ways to serve others. [It was] the fuel for prosperity that puts rising economies on the path to success."[24]

Obama also spoke of the importance of the Trans-Pacific Partnership (TPP) to Vietnam's future. Because congressional approval of the TPP remained stalled on Capitol Hill, he tried to reassure Vietnam (and Japan) of the United States' commitment to the TPP. "And not only do all the countries who are participating stand to gain from increased trade," he remarked, "but Vietnam, in particular . . . would be one of the biggest beneficiaries."[25]

The president's most important meeting during his three-day visit to Vietnam was his private session with Nguyen Phu Trong, the general secretary of the Communist Party and the country's real power. What Trong wanted was his commitment to lift the US arms embargo on Vietnam. At a news conference on May 23, Obama announced he was rescinding the ban on sales of lethal military equipment to America's former enemy. "The decision to lift the ban," he said, was not giving Vietnam carte blanche to buy arms. The US would review future arms sales to "examine what's appropriate and what's not." Nevertheless, Vietnam welcomed his announcement as a major step toward improving relations with Washington.[26]

Human rights advocates were disappointed by the president's announcement. They wanted him to link the lifting of the ban to the release of prominent political prisoners in Vietnam and to the stoppage of police brutality against protesters. He did bring up human rights issues with Trong and in his address to the Vietnamese people on May 23, but to no avail.[27]

From Ho Chi Minh City, the president was helicoptered to Shima City just across the bay from Hiroshima. In a joint press conference, Japanese prime minister Shinzo Abe lashed out at the United States for the recent brutal rape and murder of a women by a military base worker, just the most recent of a long list of rapes and murders by American military personal going back to the occupation of the island after World War II. "I feel profound resentment against this self-centered and absolutely despicable crime," he told the president. He also emphasized the importance of the US-Japanese alliance to the global economy and to Japanese security. In response, Obama expressed regret for what had happened on Okinawa and promised to cooperate with Japan in ensuring justice according to Japanese law, but he made no commitment when it came to relinquishing the US military bases on Okinawa. Like Abe, he also spoke of the importance of the US-Japanese alliance. [28]

The next day he went to Hiroshima to visit the Memorial Peace Park, the site where the atomic bomb was dropped in August 1945. Although the drive was short, the president took a long time before deciding to visit the site. For months, Caroline Kennedy, the US ambassador to Japan, had urged him to visit the site. Secretary Kerry had gone there in April.[29]

As the first sitting American president to visit the park (former president Jimmy Carter went there in 1984), his decision to go to Hiroshima was fraught with controversy. While many Americans welcomed his decision as an opportunity to speak out against the future use of nuclear weapons, other Americans feared he would apologize for what they regarded as the justified use of the bomb against an enemy known for its brutality in the territories it occupied during the war and in the way it treated its prisoners of war. Instead of the president making an apologetic trip to Hiroshima, they thought it was more appropriate for Prime Minister Abe to go to Pearl Harbor to apologize for its unprovoked attack against the US naval base there, in which more than 2,400 Americans, including civilians, were killed.[30]

The White House made it clear before Obama went to Hiroshima that his trip was not to be interpreted as an American apology for using the atomic bomb against Japan. "He will not revisit the decision to use the atomic bomb at the end of World War II," Rhodes stated. Besides being part of the president's pivot toward Asia, the administration also thought it was time to make a statement reaffirming his commitment to the goals he announced in 2009. He also wanted to focus attention on the issue of nuclear proliferation at a time when Trump was suggesting that Japan and South Korea develop their own nuclear weapons in the face of North Korean threats.[31]

"We come to mourn the dead including over 100,000 in Japanese men, women and children; thousands of Koreans; a dozen Americans held prisoners," he said in his seventeen-minute address in the park that was broadcast throughout Japan. "We force ourselves to feel the dread of children confused by what they see."[32]

Influenced by the book he discussed with Rhodes on his flight to Vietnam and then to Shima City, he recounted in his address how, as science allowed humans to "cure disease and understand the cosmos," it also paved the way for humans to become more skillful in developing weapons of war until they had the ability to destroy themselves. One way to prevent more Hiroshimas, he remarked, was to "restrict and roll back, and ultimately eliminate the existence of nuclear weapons." Even that did not seem enough for the president. "The scientific revolution that led to the splitting of an atom requires a moral revolution, as well." What he suggested was eliminating war itself. "For we see around the world today how even the crudest rifles and barrel bombs can serve up violence on a terrible scale," he noted. "We must change our mindset about war itself."[33]

In the United States, the response to his address was mixed. Veterans' groups and other critics believed that, although the president may not have used the word "apology" in his address, he effectively apologized for a decision that did not warrant one. Indeed, he seemed to let Japan off the hook for starting the war. If war was simply the result of man's capacity for inhumanity, they asked, who should be held morally and legally responsible for causing the war? Even some proponents of nuclear disarmament wanted to know how the president could advocate nuclear nonproliferation, while at the same time wanting to modernize the US nuclear stockpile? Republican opponents of the president also pointed to the address as one more example of how the president was making America look weak in the world. [34]

Most Americas, however, welcomed the speech as appropriate for the occasion—not an apology for using nuclear weapons to end the war, but a plea that what happened at Hiroshima and Nagasaki should never happen again. Pacifist groups were especially pleased by the president's call for the end of war. "He had to do it," remarked Lester Tenney, a ninety-eight-year-old survivor of the Bataan Death March. "It was the right thing to do," he stated.[35]

Domestic Terrorism, Syria, and ISIL

Returning from Asia Obama was besieged with problems both at home and abroad. Domestically, he had to deal with renewed attacks by terrorists linked to ISIL and a series of police shootings of Black Americans that threatened to rekindle the tinderbox of racial strife. Political partisanship also reached new heights as Senate Majority Leader McConnell refused even to grant a hearing to the president's nominee for the Supreme Court, Merrick Garland, following the sudden death of Justice Antonin Scalia on February 13. Obama also found himself diverting more of his attention to the 2016 presidential election and the right-wing campaign being orchestrated by Trump against his presumptive Democratic opponent, Hillary Clinton. Abroad, the president continued to cope with the expansion of ISIL into Syria and the ongoing Syrian Civil War.

In the early morning of June 12, Omar Mateen, a twenty-nine-year-old American-born son of Afghan immigrants, opened fire at a gay nightclub in Orlando, Florida, killing fifty people and wounding fifty-three others before being killed himself by the police. His was the worst killing spree in the nation's history and the worst act of terrorism on American soil since September 11, 2001. He had been on the FBI's watch list from 2013 to 2014, but the agency was never able to charge him with a crime, and he was able to buy his weapons legally. Although he claimed his allegiance to the Islamic state in a 911 call to the police an hour before beginning his deadly rampage, no evidence was found linking Mateen to ISIL.[36]

Addressing the nation shortly after receiving news of the rampage, President Obama labeled it "an act of terror and an act of hate." Noting that the shooter had targeted a gay bar, he called his action "a sobering reminder that attacks on any American [were] an attack on all of us and the fundamental values of equality and dignity that define us as a country." He also said it was "a further reminder of how easy it is for someone to get their hand on a weapon that lets them shoot people in a school, or in a house of worship, or a movie theater, or in a nightclub."[37]

Following the Orlando attack, Trump called for the president's resignation for not using the phrase, "radical Islamists," instead of "Islamic terrorists." The Republican candidate also called for a ban on all Muslims seeking to immigrate to America. "Appreciate the congrats for being right on radical Islamic terrorism," Trump wrote. "I don't want congrats, I want toughness & vigilance. We must be smart!"[38]

Without ever referring to Trump by name, Obama responded to his attacks two days later. "What exactly would using this label accomplish?" he asked. Instead of achieving anything, "it would unfairly target all Americans of the Islamic faith [including] folks across the government . . . working really hard to protect the American people." Worse were the consequences of "this kind of rhetoric and loose talk and sloppiness. . . . We now have proposals from the presumptive Republican nominee of the United States to bar all Muslims from immigrating to America," he continued. That "suggests entire religious communities are complicit in violence." In the US there was plenty of room for individuals of all kinds regardless of race, ethnicity, gender, and sexual orientation, he concluded.[39]

The next month, when he went to Orlando to meet with the families of the victims, the president said much the same thing. "This is a country founded on basic freedoms, including freedom of religion," he remarked in response to those who would discriminate against Muslims. We also had "to end discrimination and violence against our brothers and sisters who are in the LGBT community. . . . We have to challenge the oppression of women, wherever it occurs." Speaking out once more in favor of background checks on gun purchasers, he remarked that those who opposed them should meet with the families of the Orlando victims "and explain why that makes sense."[40]

Obama was rejecting the nationalistic and discriminatory message on which Trump was basing his campaign. Instead, the president called for the type of pluralistic society he had always advocated since his years as a community organizer in the 1980s. To the president, there was no radical Islamic threat to the United States. There were only threats from terrorists who claimed to be Islamic.[41]

While the president was confronting domestic terrorism, including the Charleston church shooting a year earlier, he was also conducting military operations in Syria, where ISIL had seized vast parts of eastern and northern Syria, including its rich oil fields. A few months after the terrorist regime beheaded James Foley and another American journalist, Steven Sotloff, in widely disseminated videos in the United States, he announced that he intended to bomb ISIL targets in Syria and asked the Senate and House to authorize a program to train and arm rebels who were fighting ISIL. "We will hunt down terrorists who threaten our country, wherever they are," the president stated in a fourteen-minute address. "This is a core principle of my presidency: if you threatened America, you will find no safe haven." At the end of the month, both houses approved his request, following which he announced that he would be sending only advisers into Syria, not combat troops.[42]

The president's announcement came only a month after he said the United States did not have a "strategy yet" to bomb ISIS (used interchangeably with ISIL). At the time, he was considering military options with the NSC for destroying the terrorist group's infrastructure in Iraq and killing its leadership. He feared becoming bogged down in an expanded military commitment in the Middle East when he believed China posed "a greater threat to the national interest than ISIS."[43]

Obama realized, however, that the terrorist organization did not recognize territorial borders as it took control of large parts of northern Iraq and eastern Syria. He also understood the importance of being part of a coalition that included Arab nations. "Our military action in Iraq has to be part of a broader comprehensive strategy to protect our people and support our partners who are taking the fight to ISIL," he remarked in August. One nation he excluded as part of the coalition was Syria, where, for years, he had been trying to get rid of Bashar al-Assad. "The issue with respect to Syria is not simply a military issue," he said. "It's also a political issue."[44]

Instead of sending troops into Syria, the White House relied on air strikes against ISIL. Their purpose was to disrupt its daily operations, deny it financial resources, cause fear among its fighters, and kill its leadership. Although the United States carried out most of the airstrikes, other coalition partners launched their own operations. By December, the US and its coalition partners had carried out over 3,000 airstrikes in Syria and over 6,000 in Iraq. By the spring of 2016, the US and Russia, which was helping prop up Assad's government, were even considering joint operations to take out ISIL, including a coordinated attack against Raqqa, the self-proclaimed capital of the terrorist state.[45]

The president's decision to intensify military operations against ISIS came under widespread criticism, both from Democrats and Republicans and from home and abroad. It continued into the fall, even though ISIS was being driven out of regions where they had established their own local governments. Even Obama's supporters were concerned. From the time he announced expanded air strikes in Syria and Iraq, they were worried that the White House was leading the United States into another war in Syria in which the United States sided with the anti-Assad forces. They criticized the president for not laying out a timeline for successful completion of the war. Others were worried by what they regarded as a growing sense of militarism in America and the "hair-trigger mentality of the American people."[46]

Most critics did not think the air strikes were working. Too many of them were missing their targets. In September 2016, the White House acknowledged that one strike killed sixty-two Syrian troops and wounded one hundred more, paving the way for an ISIS offensive. Pointing to the political and social complexity of the Middle East and other places where ISIS operated, the critics also said that the strategy of air strikes and advisers on the ground was too incoherent to work. Some of them remarked that the military intervention was actually playing into the hands of ISIS by creating more terrorist groups.[47]

Phillip Gordon, the president's former Middle East adviser, argued that Obama should have bombed Assad following his use of chemical warfare against his opponents. Not getting bogged down in the Middle East was one of the determinants of Obama's foreign policy, he noted, based on a certain fatalism about his limited ability to direct the course of events in the region. Gordon mostly supported this position. But because the president took such a firm position against using chemical weapons, he felt Obama had no choice except to launch an immediate military response. "If we won't enforce accountability in the face of this heinous act," he asked in 2016, "what does it say about our resolve to stand up to others who flout fundamental international rules?"[48]

Over the summer, criticism of Obama grew even among some of his former backers. George Soros, the multibillionaire contributor to the Democratic Party, was angry that the president failed to consult with him after he won the presidency. He called him his "greatest disappointment." Obama "closed the door on me" after he was elected president, Soros complained.[49]

In early 2016 Jeffrey Goldberg of the *Atlantic* magazine, conducted a series of interviews with some of Obama's closest advisers and then with the president himself. Goldberg probed for the rationale behind the president's hardest foreign policy decisions. Obama's interviews with the writer were among the most revealing of his entire presidency. They made clear how dispirited and angry he had become by 2016 as a result of the constant harping and criticism about his leadership, even within his own administration and among his supporters and allies.[50]

In his meetings with Goldberg, Obama described himself "as a realist in believing we can't at any given moment, relieve all the world's misery." Reflecting the realist views of the theologian Reinhold Niebuhr, whom, he told the columnist David Brooks in 2007, he regarded "as one of my favorite philosophers," he described the world as "a tough, complicated, messy, mean place and full of hardship and tragedy." Underscoring Gordon's assessment of him as being something of a fatalist, he acknowledged that he came to office convinced that while he had enormous powers in foreign policy, there were also limits to the scope of executive power. [51]

The president also described himself as "very much the internationalist [and an] idealist insofar as I believe that we should be promoting values like democracy and human rights and norms and values." Reflecting his middle-class values and the importance he attached to the law (even when he was violating or raising new issues about international law by using drones or illegally crossing national borders), he singled out the "rule of law and property rights." Yet he was also convinced that the US should intervene with military force against violators of human rights only when it served the national interest. [52]

With respect to his decision not to respond to Assad's use of chemical warfare, despite violating his own "red line" threat, the president said that had he responded militarily, it would not have made much difference. "I'm very proud of this moment," he told Goldberg. "I was able to pull back from the immediate pressures and think through in my own mind what was in America's interest, not only with respect to Syria but also with respect to our democracy, was as tough a decision as I've made." [53]

That decision was the moment, he stated, when he broke from what he called derisively, "the Washington Policy playbook," which was to respond militarily whenever American interests seemed threatened. "Where America is directly threatened, the playbook works," he commented. "But the playbook can also be a trap that can lead to bad decisions. In the midst of an international challenge like Syria, you get judged harshly if you don't follow the playbook, even if there are good reasons why it does not apply." [54]

As his interviews with Goldberg continued, the president began to lash out at his critics. He showed great respect for German chancellor Angela Merkel, but he was critical of most other leaders, who, he believed, lacked the will or the wisdom to use their political capital to pursue progressive goals. He resented military leaders whose solutions for all problems was to flex America's military might and was critical of the State Department and of foreign policy think tanks in Washington. They were not as rational as he was. "What they didn't understand," he told Goldberg, was that history was "bending" in his direction. [55]

He also mused about what kind of president he wanted to replace him. That person, he said, should have an understanding of the limits of American power in the world, but recognize that the United States still had to be the world's leader. "I want a president who has the sense that you can't fix every-thing." At the same time, "if we don't set the agenda, it doesn't happen. . . . That's true whether you're talking about nuclear security, whether you're talking about saving the world financial system, whether you're talking about climate."[56]

Obama also touched on a number of other points, such as his concern that the United States avoid hubris in its foreign policy by limiting military spend-ing and sharing leadership. He was indignant that the NATO allies were not contributing the 2 percent of their GDP to their defense as they had agreed to do in 2014. He was particularly critical of Israeli prime minister Benjamin Netanyahu, who, he felt, treated him condescendingly. He also resented the power of the pro-Israeli lobby in Washington and advocated a more balanced policy with respect to the Arab-Israeli conflict. He admitted that his inter-vention in Libya was a mistake and that his administration underestimated the degree of tribalism in the country. But he also attributed much of the problem in Libya to the failure of the international coalition to live up to its responsibilities. He called its members "free riders."[57]

In sum, Obama's interviews with Goldberg revealed a disappointed and angry president, whose earlier self-doubts about his ability to lead had morphed into a self-confidence sometimes bordering on arrogance. They also made clear how well developed his views were about the US role in the world. His calibrated view of American foreign policy extended even to the demeanor he thought American presidents had to have in moments of crisis. As he told Goldberg, a misplaced word, or a frightened look, or an ill-considered hyperbolic claim, could result in panic.[58]

Police Shootings and the Garland Nomination

Obama's problems as president mounted as the summer continued. Besides domestic terrorism and the threat of ISIS, the president had to deal with the renewed threat of racial violence as a result of a series of incidents involving the suspicious shootings by police officers of Black Americans. He also faced ongoing Republican opposition to his administration, tightly controlled in the Senate by Majority Leader McConnell, who even refused to hold a hearing on Obama's nomination of Merrick Garland to replace Justice Antonin Scalia on the US Supreme Court following Scalia's death in February.

One result of the killings of Trayvon Martin in 2012 and Michael Brown in 2014 was to help turn Black Lives Matter (BLM) into a large social movement that remained active even after Martin's and Brown's deaths and the riots that followed in Ferguson, Missouri, faded in the news. BLM grew even bigger after two Black men, Alton Sterling in Baton Rouge, Louisiana, and Philando Castile in St. Paul, Minnesota, were stopped in July 2016 by the police and killed under suspicious circumstances. In Sterling's case, Officer Blane Salamoni fired six shots at Sterling after responding to a call at a convenience store. The killing was captured on the store's videotape but not released until 2017, when Salamoni, who had a record of inappropriate police conduct, was fired. No criminal charges were ever filed against him, but the Baton Rouge police chief later apologized for hiring him. In Castile's case, the incident was streamed live by his girlfriend, who was in the front seat next to him. Castile was killed by Police Officer Jeronimo Yanez after a heated exchange over a gun he owned. Yanez was charged with second degree manslaughter and endangering safety by discharging a firearm, but on the same day that Sterling was fired, he was acquitted.[59]

Although the fatal shootings sparked BLM protests throughout the country, the killing of five police officers and the wounding of eight others in Dallas on July 7 created a backlash against the BLM. The officers were killed by Micah Johnson, a Black Afghan War veteran with a troubled past. Not until the early hours of July 8 was Johnson killed by an explosive device after holding the police off for several hours in a parking garage. The heavily armed sniper, who hated white police officers, claimed to belong to the New Black Panthers, a group that advocated violence against whites and especially Jews.[60]

The killings of Sterling and Castile followed by the murders of the five police officers placed President Obama in a difficult position politically. The president condemned the first two shootings, saying they were "part of a broader pattern of racial disparities in law enforcement against people of color." In response to the slayings of the police officers, he traveled to Dallas, where, on July 12, he delivered a memorial address in which he spoke of each fatally wounded officer, most of whom left behind wives and young children. He praised them for their commitment to dangerous public service despite the stress and long hours that came with their job.[61]

Had the president concluded his address in this way, he would have delivered a forgettable memorial to five police officers killed in the line of duty. But because of the series of Black men killed by the police, the peaceful protests throughout the country, and the backlash against BLM as a result of the five slain police officers, he felt obliged to address the whole issue of the nation's racial divide the events of the last week exposed. Recognizing the seeming impossibility of healing the divide, he placed some of the responsibility for the victims of police violence on agitators against the police within the Black community.[62]

Mostly, however, he held the police responsible, but instead of delivering a despondent message, he offered, as he always did, a message of hope. "I know that Americans are struggling right now with what we've witnessed over the past few weeks," he said. "We wonder if an African American community that feels unfairly targeted by police, and police departments that feel unfairly maligned for doing their jobs, can ever understand each other's experience. . . . I'm here to insist that we are not as divided as we seem. And I know that because I know America. I know how far we've come against impossible odds."[63]

To bridge the nation's racial divides, however, he said we had "to be honest with each other and ourselves." We recognize "that the overwhelming majority of police officers do an incredibly hard and dangerous job fairly and professionally," but we "also know that centuries of racial discrimination . . . didn't just stop with the end of lawful discrimination." Racial discrimination affected entire police departments. "Whites and people of color experience the criminal justice system differently, so that if you're Black you're more likely to be pulled over or searched or arrested."[64]

One of the reasons for these inequities, the president remarked, was ingrained racial bias and often a racism that was not the result of some "bad apples," but has become institutionalized within whole police systems for entirely understandable reasons. "We ask police to do too much and we ask too little of ourselves. . . . We allow poverty to fester. . . . We refuse to fund drug treatment and mental health programs."[65]

All that said, the police had to understand the legitimate reasons for the grievances against them by BLM and other protestors. "With an open heart, police departments will acknowledge that, just like the rest of us, they are not perfect." "We need to do what we can, without putting officers' lives at risk, but do better to prevent another life like [Philando Castile's], from being lost. My faith tells me that the five slain officers "did not die in vain," he concluded. Later, he referred to himself as "Mr. Hope."[66]

Although short (about fifteen minutes) compared to his other speeches on race, Obama's remarks in Dallas were one of the most important of his presidency on racial relations. Like the others, his memorial to the five slain police officers was sympathetic in terms of appreciating the causes and aftermath of the Sterling and Castile shootings. His ultimate point, however, was the need of the police to be more aware of the racial biases that still existed in the criminal justice system. He did so, moreover, before an audience that expected a less critical view of police officers and police departments.[67]

nominee, beating her in a number of states. Not until July 12, just two weeks before she won the nomination in Philadelphia, did he endorse the former secretary of state.[74]

In a video clip from October, the president allegedly told Clinton's running mate, Senator Tim Kaine (D-VA), that he thought Trump was a "fascist." Clinton said later that she never heard the president use the term "fascist," but she did not doubt the president felt Trump had the characteristics of a fascist, and she agreed with him.[75]

In his fifty-minute address before the Democratic National Convention in Philadelphia on July 27, interrupted repeatedly with applause and chants from the floor in which the delegates shouted out, "Hillary! Hillary! Hillary!" and "Yes We Can! Yes We Can! Yes We Can!" Obama first reminded the national audience listening to him of his administration's accomplishments while he was in office. "By so many measures, our country is stronger and more prosperous than ever," he remarked. While he was not modest in taking credit for these achievements, he also attributed them to the hard work of the American people and reminded his audience of the work that still needed to be done: "more work for every American still in need of a good job or a raise, or paid leave or a decent retirement; for every child who needs a sturdier ladder out of poverty . . . for everyone who has not yet felt the progress of these past seven and a half years."[76]

Not surprisingly, most of the rest of his message was a ringing endorsement of Clinton and a harsh attack on Trump. What *was* surprising was how personal his remarks were. In both 2008 and 2012, Obama's comments were directed at his opponents' policies, not their personal characteristics. In 2008, he praised John McCain for his heroism during the Vietnam War, and in 2012 he had kind words to say about Mitt Romney's health legislation as Massachusetts' governor. But in 2016, the outgoing president did not mince words about Trump, whom he called "a self-declared savior," who has left a "trail of lawsuits, and unpaid workers, and people feeling like they got cheated." "He cozies up to Putin, praises Saddam Hussein, tells our NATO allies that stood by our side after 9 / 11 that they have to pay up if they want our protection," he continued. He just offers slogans and cheers. "Ronald Reagan called America 'a shining city on a hill.' Donald Trump calls it 'a divided crime scene' that only he can fix."[77]

The contrast between Trump and Clinton could not be sharper. Hillary "knows that this is a big, diverse country. She has seen it. . . . Hillary knows we can work through racial divides in this country. . . . Hillary knows we can insist on a lawful and orderly immigration system, while still seeing striving students and their toiling parents as loving families, not criminals or rapists. . . . It can be frustrating this business of democracy. Trust me I know it," he added. "Hillary knows, too."[78]

Michelle Obama also addressed the gathering. "When they go low, we go high," she said, clearly referring to Trump and the Republican Party that just nominated him. "We fight to give everyone a chance." "Don't let anyone ever tell you that this country isn't great, that somehow we need to make it great again," she concluded. "Because this right now is the greatest country on earth."[79]

Both the Democrats and Republicans had decided to hold their conventions in July, so as not to interference with the summer Olympics that began in Rio de Janeiro in August. Both gatherings gave their candidates a boost in the polls. The Republicans held their convention in Cleveland from July 18 to July 21, the Democrats in Philadelphia from July 25 to 28. When Trump gave his acceptance speech, it attracted a larger audience than Clinton's a week later, but for the other days, the Democrats attracted a larger audience than their rivals' gathering, and the boost of 7 to 8 percent in the polls coming out of Philadelphia for the Clinton-Kaine ticket overshadowed the temporary 3 to 4 percent gain for the ticket of Trump and his running mate, Governor Mike Pence (IN). While Trump's address was not well received by those watching it, Clinton's message drew a favorable response. The Democrats also left their convention more united than the Republicans, many of whose elected officials, including Governor John Kasich (OH), did not even attend the convention, even though his state was hosting it.[80]

By the time of the conventions, Obama's ranking in the polls had improved markedly. In one poll, 51 percent of the voters approved of his performance as president. Before the campaign was over, it rose to 58 percent. While some of his critics remained disenchanted with him, others began to write favorably. In a column that received considerable national attention, the conservative columnist for the *New York Times*, David Brooks, said that he would "miss Obama" when he left office. The president "radiates an ethos of integrity, humanity, good manners and elegance that I'm beginning to miss, and that I suspect we will all miss a bit, regardless of who replaces him," the columnist concluded while singling out Trump for lacking these same qualities.[81]

Following the convention, Obama went to Martha's Vineyard, where he vacationed each August since becoming president. At the summer White House, he combined vacation, official duties, raising money for Clinton, and strategizing for the campaign that lay ahead. His role in the campaign was to concentrate on getting Blacks, Hispanics, and young people to vote in

November. His duties as president limited how active he could be in the campaign.[82]

On September 13, the president made his first campaign appearance in Philadelphia. Before a large and rollicking crowd, he spoke for forty minutes describing Trump as "a phony champion of the working class," and a dangerous charlatan, while extolling Clinton's qualifications to be president. He seemed most energized when calling out the Republican candidate. "This is not me just going through the motions here," he said. "I really, really, really want to elect Hillary Clinton." He also ridiculed Trump for his admiration of Putin. "Could you imagine Ronald Reagan idolizing somebody like that?" he asked.[83]

A few days later, he addressed a dinner of the Black Caucus in what one commentator called "his most passionate speech EVER." "All the progress we've made is at stake in this election," the president stated. "My name might not be on the ballot, but our progress is on the ballot. Tolerance is on the ballot. Democracy is on the ballot. Justice is on the ballot. . . . I will consider it a personal insult, an insult to my legacy, if this community lets down its guard and fails to activate itself in this election," he concluded.[84]

Obama remained relentless in his attacks on Trump. When, in October, it looked like Clinton was going to win easily over her Republican opponent, and he began to complain that the presidential election was being rigged against him, the president told Trump to "stop whining." At a White House news conference, he said, "I have never seen in my lifetime, or in modern political history, any presidential candidate trying to discredit the elections and the election process before votes have ever taken place." And winding up the campaign at a huge rally for Clinton in Philadelphia on November 8, he commented, "I'm betting that America will reject a politics of resentment and a politics of blame. I'm betting that tomorrow, you will reject fear, and you will choose hope. I'm betting that the wisdom, decency, and generosity of the American people will once again win the day."[85]

Obama lost the bet when, on November 8, voters elected Trump to succeed him even though Clinton won the popular vote. The Republican candidate won by about 44,000 votes in Pennsylvania, 11,000 in Michigan, and 23,000 in Wisconsin. The difference of about 78,000 votes in those states could have changed the outcome of the election. Although the reasons for Clinton's defeat are complex, one thing is clear. Had the same number of those who voted for Obama in 2012 cast their ballots for Clinton in 2016, she would have won the electoral college as well as the popular vote. Obama's legacy would have been secure. No wonder that Michelle Obama blamed the Democratic defeat on those nonvoters in 2016.[86]

According to his national security adviser, Ben Rhodes, the president "went through stages" following the election. His immediate instinct was to try to lift the spirits of his staff who were trying to comfort each other about the totally unexpected outcome of the day before. Interrupting a senior staff meeting in the office of his chief of staff, Dennis McDonough, he told them how proud he was of what they had accomplished serving in the White House and the bright futures they had ahead of them.[87]

That afternoon, he and Vice President Biden appeared in the Rose Garden to reassure the nation that Trump's victory was part of the natural ebb and flow of politics in a democracy and that he remained optimistic about the future. He had called Trump at 3:30 a.m. to congratulate him on his victory and to make clear he would help him in the transition to a new government in any way he could, just as his predecessor, President Bush, had been gracious and helpful in his own transition to the White House. "Now, it's no secret that the president-elect and I have some pretty significant differences," he said. "But remember, eight years ago President Bush and I had some pretty significant differences. . . . And one thing you realize quickly on this job is that the presidency and the vice presidency is bigger than any of us." The president also stated that Trump's victory speech indicated that he wanted what was best for the nation. "I was heartened by that," he remarked.[88]

The president said much the same things the next day after meeting with the president-elect and at a wide-ranging press conference he held on November 14 before he left on a trip to Germany, Greece, and Peru to attend a meeting with leaders of other Pacific Rim countries. Between the election and his press conference, one of Trump's spokesmen announced that the ultranationalist, Steve Bannon, would be playing a prominent role as a senior adviser to the new president. When asked at the news conference whether, in light of the Bannon announcement, Obama still thought Trump was qualified to be president, he hedged his bet a little. "Donald Trump will be the next President," he remarked. "And it will be up to him to set up a team that he thinks will serve him well."[89]

Despite trying to portray Trump's election in the best possible light, he regarded it as a personal repudiation, which, he feared, endangered his entire legacy as president. In a postelection analysis of the election, Rhodes placed much of the responsibility for Clinton's defeat on Russian interference in the election, including the Trump campaign's collaboration with the disgraced former CIA intelligence officer, Julian Assange, who stole, and released to the public, highly classified documents before fleeing the country. Among the things the Russians did was to give Assange emails they had hacked from the Democratic National Committee (DNC) making clear that its chairman,

Representative Debbie Wasserman Schultz (FL), had showed favoritism for the Clinton campaign. In this way, the Russians hoped to sow discord among the Democratic rank-and-file.[90]

The president refused to speak out against Russian interference because he did not want to look as if he were interfering in the election on behalf of Clinton, but he was concerned enough that he confronted Putin on the issue during a G20 summit in China. He ordered the FBI to investigate Russian interference in the election. Within the White House, he also conducted a separate, high-level investigation into Russian meddling, which later issued its own report condemning the Russian activity, and recommending sanctions against Russia, including expelling thirty-five Russian officials identified as being spies and shutting down two Russian properties suspected of being involved in undermining the 2016 elections. A report of the Senate Intelligence Committee concluded in 2020, however, that Obama's response to Russian meddling in 2016 had been flawed. "Frozen by 'paralysis of analysis,'" was its major finding.[91]

Obama's trip to Europe and Peru was mostly for official business, but he also intended it to be a "farewell visit" before his presidency ended. In Berlin, he met with leaders of Germany, Britain, France, Italy, and Spain. He also made a separate trip to Greece, where he visited the Acropolis and other historic sites and met with its leader, Prime Minister Alexis Tsipras. In his meetings with the European leaders, he tried to reassure them that Washington's commitment to NATO and its European allies would remain strong, amid increasing concerns that Trump would reverse his policies on everything from security to global warming. The announcement of the president-elect's intention to appoint Bannon as a senior adviser, his comments calling climate change, "a hoax," and his appointment of Myron Ebell, a well-known climate change denier, to head his EPA transition team alarmed Europe's leaders.[92]

In an address from Athens, the president recalled that ancient Athens gave birth to the first form of democracy. Down to the present, the flames of democracy have "never died," the president continued. "As you may have noticed, the next American President and I could not be more different. We have very different points of view, but American democracy is bigger than any one person. . . . Progress follows a winding path . . . but as long we retain our faith in democracy . . . our future will be okay."[93]

In Germany, the president held a press conference with Chancellor Angela Merkel, with whom he had forged a close working relationship, including five earlier meetings with her. When asked about Russian interference in the 2016 election and whether he thought Trump would support strong sanctions against Moscow, he was more circumspect in his reply than earlier. "I don't expect that the president-elect will follow exactly our blueprint or our approach," he stated, "but my hope is that he does not simply take a realpolitik approach and suggest that if we just cut some deals with Russia, even if it hurts some people," matters will be fine. "I am encouraged by the President-elect's insistence that NATO is a commitment that does not change."[94]

In Lima, Peru, Obama met with leaders of twenty other Pacific Rim countries at the annual meeting of APEC (Asia-Pacific Economic Countries). As he had stressed in Europe, he emphasized to the APEC leaders the benefits of globalization and free trade. For him, the issue was not about choosing between protectionism and free trade, but about making "sure that the benefits of the global economy [were] shared by more people and that the negative impacts, such as economic inequalities, [were] addressed by all nations." Implicit in his message was a rejection of Trump's announced intention to reject most international agreements, including even the Paris Agreement on climate change and the TPP, which had been a cornerstone of Obama's shift from the Middle East toward South Asia, and which, he hoped, would be confirmed by the APEC meeting.[95]

The meeting proved to be a bitter disappointment for the president. He failed to get the confirmation he wanted. In truth, the TPP was probably doomed even before Trump's election. Many of the countries that agreed to the TPP were overwhelmed by the size and strength of China's economy and concluded that their best hope for economic prosperity was to strengthen their ties with China rather than to challenge it economically by tying their futures to the politics and whims of the United States. Among these states were Vietnam, Malaysia, and the Philippines whose interests in the South China Sea were being challenged by Beijing, but they also included Australia, which wanted to establish a Chinese-led trade pact that would include Asian countries from Japan to India but not the United States.[96]

Clinton's defeat in November, which many of the leaders at APEC interpreted as a repudiation of the president, made him appear as merely a figurehead, whose presence was overshadowed by those of Chinese president Xi Jinping and Russian president Vladimir Putin. Even his arrival in Lima was greeted by five thousand anti-TPP protestors, while Putin, who was widely admired in South America, was welcomed by large, cheering crowds. At the APEC meeting, the members formally rejected the TPP. Its defeat represented a major victory for China, leaving an enormous power vacuum in the Pacific, which it intended to fill.[97]

Disappointed once again, Obama returned to Washington to complete the last two months of his administration. By this time, the coalition of forces the president had put together from more than sixty countries to fight ISIS had slowly rolled back the terrorist organization, reclaiming over 30 percent of the territory it had occupied in Iraq and 30 percent it had claimed in Syria. Plans were already underway to push the remaining ISIS forces in Syria back to Raqqa and then to retake the city in what was expected to be costly house-to-house fighting. Preparations were even more advanced for retaking Mosul, Iraq's second largest city, whose occupation by ISIS posed a threat to Baghdad, 250 miles to the south.[98]

On January 10, 2017, the president delivered a "Farewell Address" to the American people. Instead of delivering it from Washington, DC, as his predecessors had done, he decided to give it to a packed audience at McCormick Place, a huge convention center on Lake Michigan, only a few miles from Grant Park, where in 2008, he had delivered his victory speech before an audience estimated at 250,000. Intending his farewell to be a major address, akin to George Washington's Farewell Address of 1796, he began to prepare the speech, most of which he wrote himself, at the beginning of January. He continued to work on it, even on the flight from the nation's capital to Chicago.[99]

Obama's valedictory combined nostalgia about his political career going back to his first job as a community organizer in his adopted city of Chicago with his hopes about the future. Many of his remarks were similar to ones he had made throughout his presidency, including the importance of early education for underprivileged children, the need for retraining workers displaced from their jobs because of new technology, and the ongoing problems of economic and racial inequality. Another point he made was how automation threatened to divide the nation, creating inequality that was the principal driver of cynicism and polarization. As he had done throughout his presidency, he emphasized the importance of a nation built on an expansive and inclusive middle class. For all "the real progress" made during his two terms in office, he said, "we know it's not enough. Our economy doesn't work as well or grow as fast when a few prosper at the expense of a growing middle class, and ladders for folks who want to get into the middle class."[100]

The heart of his address was his comments about the fragility of democracy and the need of all Americans to protect and strengthen its core principles. While mentioning President-Elect Trump by name only once at the beginning of his speech and remarking at its conclusion that he was "even more optimistic about this country than when we started," he was clearly concerned about the nation's future under Trump's leadership. "Our Founders argued, they quarreled, eventually they compromised. . . . But they knew that democracy does require a basic sense of solidarity," he emphasized.

"We weaken the ties of democracy when we allow our political dialogue to become so corrosive that people of good character aren't even willing to enter into public service: so coarse with rancor that Americans with whom we disagree are seen not just as misguided but as malevolent."[101]

On January 18, just two days before his term ended, Obama gave a final presidential press conference. Among the points he covered was his decision to pardon Chelsea Manning, a former army private who was serving a thirty-five-year sentence for leaking hundreds of thousands of military incident logs, which described the abuse of detainees and an increase in civilian deaths during the Iraq war, and his decision not to veto a UN Security Council resolution demanding an end to Israeli settlements on the West Bank.[102]

The outgoing president also took swipes at the president-elect for his stated intention to ease sanctions against Russia in exchange for cutbacks in its nuclear weapons program and his claims of "fake news." The sanctions were imposed on Russia, he said, because of its encroachments on Ukraine independence, not because of its nuclear weapons, and he defended the White House press corps with whom he had often been at odds, even taking issue with proposals being floated by the incoming administration to move the daily briefings and reporters' workspaces out of the White House and to change other White House press traditions. "I have enjoyed working with you," he said to the reporters in the press room. "Having you in this building has made this workplace better."[103]

While also acknowledging the importance of debating different points of view, he distinguished between that and positions that challenged the nation's core values, such as by challenging the free press, setting up barriers to keep people from being able to vote, and rounding up "kids who have grown up here and for all practical purposes are American kids." Reports of widespread voter fraud, he stated, were, indeed, "fake news." Finally, he made clear that while he intended to remove himself from the political arena, he was fully prepared to reenter the political fray if he thought the nation's "core values were being challenged."[104]

Obama's farewell address and final press conference were a fitting end to his entire presidency. Future historians and Obama biographers will evaluate his place among US presidents. Presidential historians have regarded only three presidents as being "great presidents": Abraham Lincoln, George Washington, and Franklin D. Roosevelt. What all three presidents had in common was that: (1) they led the country through three of its most critical times, when the nation's very future was at risk; (2) absent their unique leadership skills, the country might not have survived in its present form; and (3) as a result of their leadership, the nation emerged more united and stronger than when they first assumed office. They were both consequential and transformational.

Other presidents who received high marks for their leadership have been consequential and transformational, except during less perilous times. Much to the chagrin of President Clinton, Obama referred to Ronald Reagan as a transformational president even though he was at odds with most of his policies. Whether Obama will be regarded in that way remains to be seen, but there is little doubt he was a consequential one, taking office during a major economic crisis at home and a failing war in Iraq abroad, and ending it with rising racial tensions and an obstructionist Congress at home, climate change worldwide, and China's emergence as a superpower in Asia. How he responded to each of these issues was consequential. His election as the first African American president was also as significant as John F. Kennedy's election as the first Catholic president. Passage of the ACA changed the dialogue over health care so that the question became not whether the federal government had the obligation to provide health care for most Americans but to what extent and in what form. His support of the LGBT movement and of gay marriage was also consequential if not transformational. However historians and others may rank Obama among the nation's presidents, he will not be relegated to the ash heap of failed and inconsequential presidents.

This biography of the forty-fourth president also provides ample reason to believe that he will rank alongside Truman and Eisenhower as one who did more to improving the lives of most Americans than any other post–World War II presidents. He did so, moreover, while managing to maintain the United States as the pillar power of the world, notwithstanding mistakes he may have made, especially in terms of his misunderstanding of the Arab Spring beginning in 2010, his intervention in Libya, and his questionable response to the Syrian Civil War. He did so through a mixture of conservatism, pragmatism, and progressivism.

This alchemy was shaped by his own experience as a multiracial child who was abandoned by his father at a young age, raised as a young boy by a single parent who was often away from him, grew up in a multiethnic society, had an Indonesian stepfather and a multiethnic half sister, was educated briefly in a Muslim school, was taunted when he was living in Indonesia because of his mixed race, and was brought up as an adolescent by loving and supportive, but white, grandparents.

His education at a highly competitive private school, and his two years as a student at Occidental College also played an important role in shaping his political outlook. The same can be said about his experience at a more mixed, but much larger, Ivy League university, where he read deeply about race and political theory and came finally to identify himself as Black. His experience as community organizer in Chicago was also formative.

So were his years as a law student at Harvard Law School, where he studied constitutional law with Lawrence Tribe, one of the nation's leading authorities on the Constitution, who regarded him as one of his two best students, and his election as the first African American president of the *Harvard Law Review*, which gave him his first national exposure.

As Obama later recalled, his experience as a community organizer convinced him of the importance of local organization and participation in bringing about needed change. It also persuaded him about the need to go to a leading law school to learn the intricacies of the law and make the political connections he considered necessary to make change happen. His decision during law school to forgo a highly desirable clerkship, perhaps for a Supreme Court justice, in favor of an internship with a prominent Chicago law firm indicated that his interests were not in making money as a future partner in a leading Wall Street law firm but being politically active in Chicago. The same was true about his decision after law school to decline a position with the Chicago law firm where he had been a summer intern and where he met his future wife, Michelle Robinson, in favor of accepting a position with a smaller firm, whose specialty was defending clients involved in civil rights cases. At the same time, he taught constitutional law and a course on race theory as a lecturer at the University of Chicago Law School.

Exactly when Obama decided to seek elective political office is not clear, but by the time he decided to run for the Illinois state senate in 1995, he had made important political connections, including with retired senator Paul Simon, who was so impressed by this young and obviously talented African American that he encouraged him to run for office. Alice J. Palmer, the incumbent senator whom he sought to replace after she decided to run for Congress, endorsed him for her seat. During his campaign, he proved how determined and ruthless he could be when he declined to withdraw from the race even though Palmer, who lost her congressional bid, asked Obama to withdraw so she could run again for her seat, and then successfully challenged the number of signatures on Palmer's petitions and those of his three other Democratic opponents seeking the safe Democratic seat. As a result, he ran unopposed for the Democratic nomination, assuring his victory in November.

Even as a state senator, Obama had higher political ambitions, displaying political hubris when in 2000 he challenged the highly popular incumbent congressman, Bobby Rush, in his bid for reelection and was then thrashed at the polls. As state senator from 1996 to 2004, when he resigned after being

elected to the United States Senate, he became known for his hardball political tactics, but compiled an impressive record of political accomplishments,
especially after the Democrats gained control of the Senate following the
2000 census. The senator widened his political connections, meeting with
local political officials and community leaders as he traveled throughout the
rural, and heavily Republican, areas of southern Illinois. He also became
friends with US Senator Dick Durbin (D-IL) of Springfield, who introduced
him to many of the individuals he met on his travels.

Although much of the rest of Obama's political career came about as a
result of his own talents and skills as a campaigner, luck also played an unusually strong role in his meteoric rise from such an obscure state senator in 2000
that he could not even get a ticket to be on the Democratic convention floor
at its nominating gathering in Los Angeles, to being the keynote speaker at
the convention in Boston four year later, and then the Democratic nominee
in Denver and president-elect four years after that. Encouraged by Senator
Durbin to join him in the Senate by running in 1994, he had the way cleared
from him when, first, the incumbent, Peter Fitzgerald (R), announced that
he would not run for a second term and his predecessor, Carol Moseley
Braun (D), also said that she would not contest the race.

The state senator still faced an uphill fight in the Democratic primary
against the favorite, Dan Hynes, but Hynes was so disgraced by a sex scandal
that when the votes were counted in the primary, Obama defeated him by
more than a two-to-one margin. Another sex scandal, this time involving his
Republican opponent in the general election, Jack Ryan, who was running a
strong campaign against him, forced Ryan to withdraw his candidacy.

Unable to find any important Republican to run against the Democrat,
the Republican State Committee turned to an outsider, Alan Keyes (R-MD),
who established legal residence in Illinois only three months before the election and whose radical views on such issues as abortion, and gun control all
but assured his defeat. In 2004, Obama gained the largest statewide victory
for any candidate in Illinois history.

Luck, talent, and his considerable reputation already among party profes-
sionals as a rising Democratic star led the presumptive Democratic nominee
in 2004, Senator John Kerry, to ask him to deliver the keynote address that
vaulted him into the national political scene and led him two years later
to challenge Hillary Clinton, the favorite for the Democratic nomination in
2008. In what became a brutal seesaw campaign in which both sides resorted
to nasty accusations against the other, the first-term senator's skillful use
of technology and his decision to campaign even in the smaller, historically Republican, mountain states of the West led to his nomination as the

Democratic presidential nominee. Running as the candidate of hope against the Republican nominee, Senator John McCain (AZ), he outsmarted McCain in his response to the nation's economic recession and, according to the polls, won the three debates against him, each one by a larger margin than the one before. In November, he was elected as the nation's forty-fourth president, the news of which was greeted by outbursts of emotion throughout the nation, including the massive crowd of cheering and crying people gathered in Grant Park.

The problem that Obama faced from the time he became president-elect was that while Americans expected the incoming administration to institute a program of major progressive legislation shortly after he took office, that was never a possibility, in part because of Republican determination not to let it happen, but also because of the president himself. While his message as a candidate was one of hope and promise of change from the policies of the Bush administration, he never said it would happen during the first year of his administration or even during his term as president.

For Obama, progress was incremental, not linear. As a pragmatist as well as a progressive, he was willing to compromise in order to bring about change. Perhaps his greatest legacy as president was passage of the ACA, which was predicated on keeping the existing system of health care, including maintaining the private system of health insurance and loose regulation of the pharmaceutical industry. That measure disappointed those Americans who wanted a more significant program of national health insurance. It also angered other Americans who thought the act went too far in requiring that every American be insured or were opposed to any form of a national health program.

As an economic conservative as well as a pragmatist and a progressive, Obama sought to bring about change to the nation's failed banking system, not by allowing the nation's major banks to fail, as a number of liberal economists and spokesmen advocated, but by working closely with bank leaders to save the banks, albeit under tighter controls and regulations.

From the time Obama entered politics, he sought to reform existing institutions rather than uproot them. This was why so many of those who voted for him in 2008 and even in 2012 were disappointed by the outcome of his administration and turned in 2016, not to someone who was likely to carry on his legacy but to one who gave every sign, even as a candidate, that he was out to destroy it, but campaigning with the same message of hope Obama used in his two runs for the presidency: "Make America Great Again."

CHAPTER 11

The Postpresidency

When George Washington completed his second term as president in 1796, he returned to his residence at Mount Vernon and spent the rest of his life as a successful plantation owner and businessman. In doing so, he followed the eighteenth-century republican ideal of politically disinterested private citizens engaging briefly in public service before returning to private life. He also set a precedent for his successors.[1]

Over time, this conception of presidential power gave way to an entirely different one, in which former presidents became increasingly public figures and an "office of postpresident" (something never imagined by the founding founders) emerged, complete with generous pensions for ex-presidents and their wives, substantial office space, free postage, funds to hire a staff and maintain an office, and discretionary funds for the former presidents.

The office of postpresident also became big business. Former presidents made millions of dollars writing and promoting their memoirs and other books, going on the lecture circuit and commonly earning between $200,000 and $500,000 an appearance. Presidents Gerald Ford and Bill Clinton served on corporate boards and made millions more in the form of stock options and investments in the businesses on whose boards they served.[2]

Former presidents lent their names and joined together to raise millions of dollars for disaster relief, the most recent example being in October 2017 when all five living presidents appeared together and helped raise $31 million for hurricane relief following a series of devastating hurricanes in Texas, Florida, Puerto Rico, and the US Virgin Islands. Beginning with Jimmy Carter's postpresidency, they also established their own foundations and become involved in international philanthropy.[3]

As a former president, Barack Obama has engaged in all these activities. What has separated him from other ex-presidents has been that as President Donald Trump has destroyed most of what he intended as his legacy, launched personal attacks on him, and, most important, threatened, in his opinion, the very fabric of American society, the former president felt it increasingly necessary to assume a more active political role than other recent ex-presidents or what he intended for himself.

Obama the Private and Increasingly Public Citizen

Although Obama was concerned about his legacy and the nation's future under a Trump administration, he was happy to leave the White House after eight difficult years as president. As he made clear in his final press conference on January 17, 2017, he intended to spend the first months of his retirement reconnecting with his daughters and his wife.[4]

The former president and first lady had already signed lucrative book contracts with a major publishing house for an estimated $65 million in advances ($55 million for Barack and $10 million for Michelle), far greater than the estimated $15 million advance to Bill Clinton and a lesser amount to Hillary for their memoirs. Obama rented a new office not far from the White House and began to hire a staff. He and Michelle also purchased a nine-bedroom home in the exclusive Kalorama neighborhood of Washington, DC, also not far from the White House, so that Sasha could finish her final year at the Sidwell School, where she and Malia had attended while their father was in the White House. Malia had been accepted to Harvard University but decided to take a gap year to travel with her parents and do an internship with Hollywood producer Harvey Weinstein, working out of his New York office before he was exposed and sentenced to prison for multiple cases of sexual abuse and rape of women.[5]

According to his senior adviser and lifelong friend, Valerie Jarrett, and the White House communications director, Jennifer Psaki, the former president intended to remain politically active, working to ensure that Americans had access to affordable health care, dealing with the problem of gerrymandering, and speaking out on behalf of the Dreamers. He also planned to write his memoirs, be a mentor to the next generation of Democratic leaders, and keep open lines of communication with Trump. Most of these activities, however, would be behind-the-scenes.[6]

During the spring of 2017, he took advantage of his life as a private citizen by globe-trotting, playing golf, and engaging in such other recreational activities as sailing, water-skiing, and kite-surfing in the British Virgin Islands, where he was the guest of the British billionaire Richard Bronson. He also took long family vacations in the Tuscan countryside and river-rafting on the island of Bali. In May, he met with Prince Harry to discuss "a range of shared interest, including support for veterans, mental health, conservation, [and] empowering young people." The same month, he gave a speech for a reported $400,000 for the financial firm Cantor Fitzgerald, and secluded himself to write his memoirs on the French Polynesian atoll of Tetiaroa, once the private island of Marlon Brando, to begin writing his memoir before being joined by Michelle.[7]

A month earlier, Obama had made his first public appearance since leaving office at the University of Chicago. Reflecting on his roots as a community organizer thirty years earlier, the former president encouraged students and young activists "to take their own crack at changing the world." When he said in his keynote address in 2004 "that red states or blue states, they're the United States of America, that was [an] aspirational comment," he added, "but . . . it's one that I still believe."[8]

Having pointed in his remarks to the problem of gerrymandering, the former president asked his former attorney general, Eric Holder, to head a task force to address the issue in preparation for 2020, when states would be redrawing the boundaries of their legislative and congressional districts. A few weeks later, he and Michelle unveiled plans for the Obama Presidential Center in the Jackson Park neighborhood of the South Side. The focus of the center, Obama said, would not just be a presidential library but helping to train "the next generation of leadership, so that they can take up the torch and lead the process of change in the future."[9]

The decision to build the center in Jackson Park stirred considerable controversy from the local community, which felt the project would disrupt the neighborhood. The community also wanted more input on its construction, including pledges that a large portion of the workers hired to build the center would be from the local neighborhood. Others criticized the former president for not building it in the more impoverished and distant part of the South Side, which had suffered severely as a result of the closing of steel mills that once had provided well-paying jobs. Because of the federal regulations on operating presidential libraries, the former president had to raise private funds, estimated at $1 billion, to build the center and to provide a partial endowment for its operation.[10]

Although Obama intended to follow the precedent of former presidents to keep their conflicts with their successors private, he became increasingly irked by Trump's early acts and accusations as president, such as when he charged his predecessor with having, during the 2016 campaign, wiretapped the Trump Tower in Manhattan, the home and offices of Trump and his real estate organization. After a lengthy investigation, the Justice Department confirmed that there was no evidence to support the now president's made-up charges.[11]

Eight months into his presidency, Trump also released the private letter that the outgoing president had written him just before leaving office. It had become customary in recent years for those leaving the White House to write a letter to their successors offering their thoughts and suggestions about their experiences as president. These letters were not normally released until near the end of their terms in office. They were intended to offer their support to the new president and to be turned to during trying times.

Instead, Trump leaked Obama's letter to him. In it, the outgoing president warned his successor "to sustain the international order" and to be kind. Trump described the letter sarcastically as "long" and "complex," although he also added that he found it "thoughtful" and appreciated the time the former president took to write it. According to Jennifer Psaki, now one of Obama's staff members, the former president "was not happy," by the leak of the letter. "He thought it was cheesy."[12]

Although Obama still did not mention Trump by name, in September 2017 he criticized the president on Facebook for rescinding the Dreamers program (DACA) calling his decision "cruel." Later he warned the Republican Party that its efforts to undo the ACA would cause "real suffering." "If Republicans could put together a plan that is demonstrably better than the improvements we made to our health care system . . . I would gladly and publicly support it," he stated. The former president also campaigned successfully for two Democratic candidates for governor in the off-year elections in November, Phil Murphy (NJ) and Ralph Northam (VA). He even reported for jury duty in Chicago but was not selected to serve.[13]

Following his speech to Cantor Fitzgerald in April, the former president made at least eight more speeches in 2017, collecting more than $1 million for three speeches he delivered at separate Wall Street firms. He also visited China, India, and France, where he met with all his former counterparts, but where his main purpose was to deliver speeches to a group of business organizations for undisclosed sums of money. In 2018, he and Michelle signed a deal with Netflix to produce a set of films and series for their new production company, *Higher Grounds Productions*.[14]

Coming under growing criticism, even from his progressive allies, for profiting on his status as a former president, Obama justified his speaking engagements by stating that he needed to raise money for his center and that his speaking engagements were "true to his values" and allowed him to contribute $2 million to jobs-training programs for low-income Chicago residents. After signing his agreement with Netflix, he issued a statement in which he remarked that by dealing "with issues of race and class, democracy and civil rights, and much more, we believe each of these productions will educate, connect and inspire us all."[15]

On September 1, 2018, he delivered a eulogy at the funeral of his opponent in the 2008 presidential race, Senator John McCain. In his remarks, the former president took another indirect swipe at Trump, who had not been invited to the funeral, by denouncing self-aggrandizement in politics, remarking that McCain "understood that if we get in the habit of bending the truth to suit political expediency or party orthodoxy, our democracy will not work."[16]

When the campaign for a new Congress and a number of governorships began in earnest soon thereafter, Obama lashed out directly at Trump. In a major speech at the University of Illinois in Urbana-Champaign, the former president broke with the normal deference paid by previous presidents to incumbents by calling Trump "a threat to our democracy." "I'm here today," he said, "because this is one of those pivotal moments when every one of us . . . needs to determine just who we are, what it is that we stand for. And as a fellow citizen, not as an ex-president . . . I'm here to deliver a simple message, and that is that you need to vote because our democracy depends on it."[17]

Although the story of America has been one of progress, he continued, there has always been a "darker aspect" to America's story, a backlash against change. "It did not start with Donald Trump. He is a symptom, not the cause. He's just capitalizing on resentments that politicians have been fanning for years." He even accused his successor of bigotry and racism, recalling when Trump, a month earlier, called right-wing sympathizers at a deadly rally, which a small group of Nazis held in Charlottesville Virginia, "good people" along with the counterprotesters. "We're supposed to stand up to discrimination," the former president said. "How hard can that be, saying that Nazis are bad?"[18]

Despite Obama's attacks on Trump, his real purpose was to get his young audience to vote in November.

Thus the thrust of his remarks was familiar and threefold: (1) a plea for mutual understanding even among those of opposing political views, (2) a call for bipartisanship in the legislative process, and (3) the importance of the November elections. He rejected the view of his more progressive friends that things in the country had gotten so bad that Democrats had to "fight fire with fire." In his opinion, "the more cynical people are about government, and the angrier and more dispirited they are about the prospects for change, the more likely the powerful are able to maintain their power."[19]

The importance of bipartisanship followed from the same logic. "We believe that in order to move this country forward, to actually solve problems and make people's lives better, we need a well-functioning government," Obama continued. "We need cooperation among people of different political persuasions. And to make that work, we have to restore our faith in government. We have to bring people together, not tear them apart."[20]

Democracy worked and change was possible only if all eligible voters held to their principles and cast their ballots. As a cautionary note to young voters and others who might expect major change overnight, the former president repeated what he had said throughout his career about the incremental nature of change. "Better is good. That's the history of progress in this country," he noted. "Not perfect. Better."[21]

Following his speech at the University of Illinois, the former president and Michelle hit the campaign trail. Using different versions of the same message he just delivered in Urbana-Champaign, Barack held campaign events with Democratic candidates in California, Ohio, Illinois, and Pennsylvania, two of which (Ohio and Pennsylvania) had voted for Trump in 2016. Michelle participated in registration rallies as part of "When We All Vote," a nonpartisan group promoting voting in the 2018 election.[22]

In a record turnout in November for an off-year congressional election, the Democrats gained control of the House winning 40 seats from the Republicans. They also gained 7 governorships, 5 state legislative chambers, and 333 state legislative seats. More women and more Muslims won congressional seats than ever before. White suburbs throughout the nation that historically voted Republican cast their ballots for Democrats. The only disappointment for Democrats was that Republicans not only held onto the Senate, they gained two seats as four Democratic incumbents—Bill Nelson (FL), John Donnelly (IN), Claire McCaskill (MO), and Heidi Heitkamp (ND)—and two Republicans—Dean Heller (NV) and Martha McSally (AZ) were defeated in their bids to hold onto their seats. Although President Trump called the results of the 2018 elections "a tremendous success," most commentators regarded them a major victory for the Democrats and a resounding defeat for the president that boded ill for his chances of being reelected in 2020.[23]

Obama since the 2018 Elections

In the two years between the congressional elections of 2018 and the election of former vice president Joe Biden as president of the United States,

Barack Obama has remained active both privately and publicly. Privately he published in November his memoir, *A Promised Land* (2020). He and Michelle, whose own memoir, *Becoming*, was published in 2018 and became an instant best seller, have continued to make millions of dollars on the lecture circuit. With a fortune estimated as high as $40 million, the Obamas purchased a seven-thousand-square-foot mansion on Martha's Vineyard. The former president has also contributed an undisclosed portion of his money to the construction and endowment of the Barack Obama Presidential Center, whose architectural plans call for the construction of a multistory presidential library, and smaller structures to house the Obama Presidential Museum and the Obama Foundation.[24]

Of Obama's undertakings, none has interested him more than the Obama Foundation, which he established in 2014. Besides overseeing the establishment of the presidential center, the foundation sponsors a large array of programs. Reflecting his background as a community organizer, each of them is intended to promote local community organization and participation.[25]

Two of these programs are the Obama Foundation Scholars Program and My Brother's Keeper (MBK). The Scholars Program brings to Chicago a small group of twenty-five to forty community organizers and civic innovators from around the world. At the foundation, they take a curriculum that combines academic, skill-based, and hands-on learning. In collaboration with the University of Chicago, they have the opportunity to receive a master's degree focused on international development and policy. They are also able to participate in an initiative at Columbia University in which faculty and researchers from Columbia partner with governments, nonprofits, and other groups "to try to find solutions to real-world problems."[26]

The purpose of the program is to provide the scholars "with the tools they need to make their efforts more effective, to identify innovative solutions to complex global problems, and promote change through values-based leadership." Another is to establish close relationships among those in the program, who meet with Obama to discuss their work. While in the program, they receive a stipend and have all their expenses, including air travel, paid. Several groups of scholars have successfully completed the program and returned to their communities.[27]

As described earlier, MBK was a program based on Obama's long-held belief that education and support beginning at an early age, were foundational to the success of minority children living in impoverished conditions. As he remarked in an interview on NPR in December 2016, the "only way we live up to America's promise is if we value every single child, not just our own, and invest in every single child as if they're our own."

Moved by the killing in 2012 of Treyvon Martin, he enlisted a group of businesspeople, clergy, athletes, and celebrities, to mentor and support young minority men.[28]

By improving life's prospects for young men of color, through programs of local community activities and support, and funded in part by grants from the foundation and others from the private sector, MBK was intended to close the gaps in educational achievement and labor force participation between young men of color and young white men of the same ages.[29]

Although the former president never explicitly said so at the time he established MBK, he regarded the program as an alternative to Black Lives Matter (BLM), which, as we have seen, became a national movement following the death in 2014 of Michael Brown in Ferguson, Missouri. In a statement in October 2015 following the conclusion of a White House forum on criminal justice, the president defended BLM, remarking that the protests were giving voice to problems happening only in African American communities.[30]

While Obama appreciated the fact, however, that BLM sought to end incidents of police brutality and killings through acts of nonviolent civil disobedience, he was concerned that the movement was unprepared to sit down with elected officials and find some common ground with these officials once they were ready to meet with the activists. BLM had a "responsibility to prepare an agenda that [was] achievable," he told a group of BLM spokesmen whom he met at the White House. He also believed problems with the police were part of the larger problem of injustice in the criminal justice system, which required significant structural changes that could only take place over time. That is why he regarded MBK, with its long-term goals and gradual approach to change, a better alternative for the minority community than BLM.[31]

In May 2020, Obama issued a statement in strong support of BLM following the brutal killing by a police officer in Minneapolis, of George Floyd, while under arrest for allegedly passing a counterfeit $20 bill. Videos of the incident showed the officer kneeling on Floyd's neck for almost nine minutes, causing his death by asphyxiation. Coming in the wake of other incidents of police killings of African Americans, Floyd's death set off huge demonstrations throughout the United States and in Europe in support of BLM. "This shouldn't be 'normal' in 2020 America," the former president said in response to what happened in Minneapolis. "If we want our children to grow up in a nation that lives up to its highest ideals, we can and must do better."[32]

In an interview in November with the *Washington Post* opinion writer and MSNBC commentator, Jonathan Capehart, the former president strongly condemned the police for what he called Floyd's "killing." The interview with Capehart was part of a series of interviews he gave to promote *A Prom-ised Land*. Afterward, Capehart commented on the memoirs. On issues of race, he said, what he found "especially refreshing" about *A Promised Land* was the former president's "unsparing observations and honest assessments of race in America and on his administration. . . . Obama summed up the collective exasperation of Black Americans when he wrote that he 'was frus-trated with the constant need to soften for white folks' benefit the blunt truths about race in America.' "[33]

Floyd's death occurred in the midst of the coronavirus (COVID-19) pan-demic that was sweeping the world and killing more than 120,000 victims in the United States by the end of July. It affected especially minorities living in poor neighborhoods and the elderly with preconditions such as diabetes or a history of pneumonia. Obama was incensed by Trump's total lack of leadership in response to the pandemic and his total insensitivity to the BLM movement, even accusing peaceful protestors of being looters and vandals because of random cases of violence and business break-ins immediately fol-lowing Floyd's death. Calling for "law and order," Trump threatened the use of force to suppress the demonstration. As for the coronavirus, Obama was furious that the president even refused to be a role model for the nation, such as by wearing a mask and social distancing. "More than anything, this pan-demic has fully, finally torn back the curtain on the idea that so many of the folks in charge know what they're doing. A lot of them aren't even pretend-ing to be in charge," the former president said of Trump's administration during an online commencement address in May to graduates of historically Black colleges and universities.[34]

"Doing what feels good, what's convenient, what's easy—that's how little kids think," Obama added in a second online speech a week later for gradu-ating US high school students. "Unfortunately, a lot of so-called grown-ups, including some with fancy titles and important jobs, still think that way— which is why things are so screwed up." In a telephone call leaked about the same time, the former president also described the US government's corona-virus response "as an absolute chaotic disaster."[35]

Intending to highlight Trump's lack of leadership during a critical period for the nation, he announced in May his support for his former vice pres-ident, Joe Biden, as the next president of the United States. Despite calls for the former president to assume a more active role during the crowded Democratic primary season, which at several points threatened to divide the party into warring parties, he remained on the sidelines, refusing to endorse anyone even when it appeared that Senator Bernie Sanders, whose political views were to the left of his own, might get the nomination. Only after a strange twist of circumstances, including a strong endorsement by the Black majority leader of the House, James Clyburn, which led in March to Biden's becoming the presumptive Democratic presidential nominee, did Obama publicly endorse him.[36]

Even then the former president waited a month before making his public endorsement. Behind the scenes, however, he worked the phones in an effort to get Sanders and the other Democratic candidates, who had not yet rallied behind Biden, to endorse him publicly. In the twelve-minute video he issued in April endorsing Biden, he had high praise for Sanders, calling him an "American original" and "a man who has devoted his life to giving voice to working people's hopes, dreams and frustrations."[37]

In the video that the *Washington Post* described as "part endorsement and part political blueprint," Obama also called on Americans to have "a great awakening" behind Biden in November. Without mentioning Trump by name, he crafted his endorsement of Biden in a way that was also an attack on the incumbent. "Pandemics have a way of cutting through a lot of noise and spin to remind us of what is real, and what is important," he remarked. "This crisis has reminded us that government matters. It's reminded us that good government matters."[38]

During the campaign, the former president made numerous stops on behalf of the Biden campaign, concentrating especially in Florida and Georgia, where he sought to get Blacks and other people of color to vote in November. Almost everywhere he went, he attacked Trump for his inadequate response to the coronavirus pandemic, taking him to task, for example, for failing to have those attending White House events to mask or practice social distancing and saying that the president had "turned the White House into a hot zone" for the virus. At another campaign stop, he accused the president of being "jealous of COVID's media coverage."[39]

On November 3, Biden won a decisive victory over Trump gaining over 81 million popular votes and 306 electoral college votes to his opponent's 74 million popular votes and 232 electoral college votes. Although he lost in Florida, he won a narrow, upset, victory in Georgia. How much Obama contributed to bringing out the state's large Black vote is impossible to know. Certainly, Stacey Abrams, who lost narrowly in her 2018 bid to be Georgia's first Black governor and the nation's first Black female governor, was instrumental in organizing the Black community. But wherever he went, the highly popular former president attracted large crowds in parking lots, where wearing masks and social distancing were practiced and where the crowds responded repeatedly to his remarks by waving flags and banners and beeping their car horns.[40]

Still only fifty-nine years old as of December 2020, the former president can be expected to have one of the longest postpresidential careers in the nation's history. Although he campaigned actively in Georgia after the November elections in support of the Democratic candidates, Jon Ossoff and Raphael Warnock, in a special January 2021 runoff election for the state's two US Senate seats, he can also be expected to devote much of his time to the work of his foundation. Likewise, he will continue to remain on the lecture circuit, complete his memoirs, write other books, and be involved with his production company, *Higher Grounds Productions*.[41]

How active Obama will remain in politics after January is harder to say, especially since President-Elect Biden has become the new leader of the Democratic Party and the former president's desire since leaving office has been to withdraw from the political scene. Given his popularity and his other activities, however, it is hard to believe that he will be other than a major public figure, at least for the foreseeable future.

Acknowledgments

I dedicate this book to my wife, Jane Bloom, who, for the past five years, has been not only my special partner in life but my personal editor. She read the entire book in early draft form and helped improve the quality of my manuscript through her many recommendations, from changes in words and wording to more substantive changes in terms of issues and ideas.

My children, Scott and Heather, have contributed so much to this book. They read the manuscript, offered their own thoughtful comments and helped in so many other ways as well. My stepdaughters, Ona, Beryl, and Rachel, were especially helpful in providing tech support for an avowed Luddite. I am also grateful to their spouses and special others (Julie, Steve, Glenn, Jim, and Milan). While I have been writing this book, I have had fruitful—sometimes spirited but always friendly—exchanges of ideas with them related to the Obama presidency and the current state of American politics.

I also want to thank Valerie Achilles, my undergraduate summer intern in 2018 and now a graduate of Columbia Law School, who was of great assistance to me in researching newspapers and other primary printed sources, and my editor at Cornell University Press, Michael McGandy, who has been highly supportive and patient while I was writing this book and helped improve its quality substantially. Similarly, the two outside readers for the manuscript offered helpful suggestions for changes that are reflected throughout the volume. One of the readers has remained anonymous. The other,

John Robert Green of Cazenovia College, a highly respected historian of recent American history, who has written numerous books on American politics and politicians, provided a chapter-by-chapter, paragraph-by-paragraph, line-by-line list of recommendations for change. I have incorporated many of his suggestions into the book.

Finally I acknowledge the assistance of such scholars and friends as Martin Quitt, emeritus dean and professor of history at the University of Massachusetts, Boston; Jacob Kipp, former professor of history at Kansas State University and now adjunct professor of history at the University of Kansas's Center for Russian, East European, and European Studies; Burton Melnick, retired head of the English Department at the International School in Geneva, Switzerland; and Donald Marks, retired historian and technology genius. Burt and Jake, in particular, read early draft chapters of the book and made extremely useful suggestions for improvement. I have known all of these scholars and friends for at least fifty years, some for more than sixty years. I want to thank them and the others I have mentioned for the great influence they have had on my scholarship and on my life.

Notes

1. Roots

* For purposes of proper syntax, I have occasionally altered the capitalization of the first letter of a word when quoting from an original document. On no occasion has this changed the meaning of the original document.

1. James T. Patterson, *Grand Expectations: The United States, 1945–1974* (New York: Oxford University Press, 1996), vii–ix, 3–104, and 442–709.

2. Although she grew up being called "Stanley," she preferred to be called "Ann" and used that name in her adult life.

3. Jonathan Martin, "Obama's Mother Known Here as 'Uncommon,'" *Seattle Times*, April 8, 2008, https://www.seattletimes.com/seattle-news/politics/obamas-mother-known-here-as-uncommon/

4. Janny Scott, *A Singular Woman: The Untold Story of Barack Obama's Mother* (New York: Riverhead Books, 2011), 44–54.

5. Martin, "Obama's Mother Known Here as 'Uncommon'"; Scott, *A Singular Woman*, 54–75; Garen Thomas, *Yes We Can: A Biography of President Barack Obama* (New York: Fiewel and Friends, 2008), 14–15; Barack Obama, *Dreams from My Father* (New York: Three Rivers Press, 2004),16 and 122–23; David Maraniss, *Barack Obama: The Story* (New York: Simon and Schuster, 2012), 127–29 and 158; David J. Garrow, *Rising Star: The Making of Barack Obama* (New York: William Morrow, 2017), 50–51.

6. Barack Obama, interview by David Axelrod, Full Transcript for the Axe Files," CNN, December 26, 2016, https://www.cnn.com/2016/12/26/politics/axe-files-obama-transcript; Scott, *A Singular Woman*, 54–75; Maraniss, *Barack Obama: The Story*, 159.

7. Martin, "Obama's Mother Known Here as 'Uncommon'"; Scott, *A Singular Woman*, 44–54; Maraniss, *Barack Obama: The Story*, 69–70.

8. Maraniss, *Barack Obama: The Story*, 4–7.

9. Barack Obama, *A Promised Land* (New York: Crown, 2020), 7–8; Obama, *Dreams from My Father*, 13–15; Maraniss, *Barack Obama: The Story*, 25–32; David Mendell, *Obama: From Promise to Power* (New York: HarperCollins, 2007), 39.

10. Maraniss, *Barack Obama: The Story*, 32–34; Obama, *Dreams from My Father*, 14–15.

11 Maraniss, *Barack Obama: The Story*, 287–88; Obama, *Dreams from my Father*, 16–17; Scott, *A Singular Woman*, 60–61.

12. Obama, *Dreams from My Father*, 21; Maraniss, *Barack Obama: The Story*, 125–26 and 287–88.

13. Maraniss, *Barack Obama: The Story*, 143–44; David Remnick, *The Bridge: The Life and Rise of Barack Obama* (New York: Vintage Books, 2011), 48–49.

14. In *Dreams from My Father*, Obama states that his grandparents may have exaggerated their racial tolerance, especially his grandfather's account of why he left Texas. But he does not dismiss their account entirely. He also recognized his grandparents' progressive racial views. Obama, *Dreams from My Father*, 12–18.

15. Obama, *Dreams from My Father*, 8–10; Maraniss, *Barack Obama: The Story*, 174–78, 182, 206–8.

16. Garrow, *Rising Star*, 43–48, 50–52; Peter Firstbrook, *The Obamas: The Untold Story of an American Family* (New York: Crown Publishers, 2010), 179–80, 210–12, 216–17, 225–26; Scott, *A Singular Woman*, 86–90, 96; Maraniss, *Barack Obama: The Story*, 94–120, and 172–74.

17. Scott, *A Singular Woman*, 101–7; Firstbrook, *The Obamas*, 211–12; Maraniss, *Barack Obama: The Story*, 175–81, 195–201, and 209–11; Garrow, *Rising Star*, 61–64.

18. Janny Scott, "Obama's Young Mother Abroad," *New York Times Magazine*, April 20, 2011, https://www.nytimes.com/2011/04/24/magazine/mag-24Obama-t.html; Maraniss, *Barack Obama: The Story*, 195–201, 210–14; Garrow, *Rising Star*, 57–63.

19. Scott, "Obama's Young Mother Abroad"; Scott, *A Singular Woman*, 113–18, Garrow, *Rising Star*, 63–64; Maraniss, *Barack Obama: The Story*, 214–15, and 234–35.

20. Scott, "Obama's Young Mother Abroad"; Scott, *A Singular Woman*, 118–30; Obama, *Dreams from My Father*, 46–47; Garrow, *Rising Star*, 73, 105 and 118–19.

21. James T. Kloppenberg, *Reading Obama: Dreams, Hope, and the American Political Tradition* (Princeton, NJ: Princeton University Press, 2011), 11. Obama, *Dreams from My Father*, 47–51; Scott, "Obama's Young Mother Abroad"; Scott, *A Singular Woman*, 134–41; Maraniss, *Barack Obama: The Story*, 230–34 and 242.

22. Obama, *A Promised Land*, 9; Scott, "Obama's Young Mother Abroad"; Garrow, *Rising Star*, 64–65; Mendell, *Obama*, 35–38.

23. Scott, *A Singular Woman*, 199–218; Maraniss, *Barack Obama: The Story*, 237–41; Kloppenberg, *Reading Obama*, 11–12.

24. Scott, *A Singular Woman*, 199–218, and 264.

25. Ibid., 138–49; Obama, interview by Axelrod; Maraniss, *Barack Obama: The Story*, 278–79.

26. Obama, *Dreams from My Father*, 35; Jennifer Steinhauer, "Charisma and a Search for Self in Obama's Hawaii Childhood," *New York Times*, March 17, 2007, https://www.nytimes.com/2007/03/17/us/politics/17hawaii.html; Kirsten Scharnberg and Kim Barker, "The Not-So-Simple Story of Barack Obama's Youth," *Chicago Tribune*, March 25, 2007, https://www.chicagotribune.com/chi-070325obama-youth-story-archive-story.html; Scott, *A Singular Woman*, cover, 99, 139, and 148; Maraniss, *Barack Obama: The Story*, 221–22, 241–42; Garrow, *Rising Star*, 66–67.

27. Obama, *Dreams from My Father*, 36–37; Maraniss, *Barack Obama: The Story*, 215–24 and 244; Garrow, *Rising Star*, 65–66; Mendell, *Obama*, 33.

28. Scott, "Obama's Young Mother Abroad"; Maraniss, *Barack Obama: The Story*, 241–42; Mendell, *Obama*, 33–35; Remnick, *The Bridge*, 239; Obama, interview by Axelrod.

29. Obama, *Dreams from My Father*, 24–25.

30. Ibid., 55–56; Maraniss, *Barack Obama: The Story*, 286–87; Mendell, *Obama*, 51.

31. Jackie Calmes, "On Campus, Obama and Memories," *New York Times*, January 2, 2009, https://www.nytimes.com/2009/01/03/us/politics/03Reunion.html; Steinhauer, "Charisma and a Search for Self in Obama's Hawaii Childhood"; Maraniss, *Barack Obama: The Story*, 265 and 287–92; Garrow, *Rising* Star, 84–85; Mendell, *Obama*, 36–37. Obama, *Dreams from My Father*, 55–56.

32. Mendell, *Obama*, 45–46.

33. Obama, *A Promised Land*, 8; Scharnberg and Barker, "The Not-So-Simple Story of Barack Obama"; Obama, *Dreams from My Father*, 78–80; Maraniss, *Barack Obama: The Story*, 283–85; Mendell, *Obama*, 43 and 45.

34. Calmes, "On Campus, Obama and Memories"; Mendell, *Obama*, 45 and 47; Garrow, *Rising Star*, 91–94.

35. Obama, *Dreams from My Father*, 85–89; Obama, *A Promised Land*, 8–9; Maraniss, *Barack Obama: The Story*, 270–71 and 362–63; Garrow, *Rising Star*, 84–86.

36. Obama, *A Promised Land*, 9; Obama, *Dreams from My Father*, 84–85 and 128–29; Kloppenberg, *Reading Obama*, 13–16; Barack Obama, "Barack Obama and Doris Kearns Goodwin: The Ultimate Exit Interview," *Vanity Fair*, December, 2016, https://www.vanityfair.com/news/2016/09/barack-obama-doris-kearns-goodwin-interview; Steinhauer, "Charisma and a Search for Self in Obama's Hawaii Childhood"; Garrow, *Rising Star*, 88–90, 100; Mendell, *Obama*, 41, 43–44, 47 and 51; Remnick, *The Bridge*, 229–32.

37. Punahou School, https://www.punahou.edu/about; Obama, *Dreams from My Father*, 96; Obama, interview by Axelrod.

38. Calmes, "On Campus, Obama and Memories"; Mendell, *Obama*, 55–56.

39. Obama, *Dreams from My Father*, 96.

40. Andy Faught, "School of Barack," *Occidental Magazine*, Winter 2017, https://obamascholars.oxy.edu/news/school-barack; David Maraniss, "Barack Obama: The College Years," *Guardian*, May 25, 2012, https://www.theguardian.com/world/2012/may/25/barack-obama-the-college-years.

41. Obama, *A Promised Land*, 10–11; Maraniss, "Barack Obama: The College Years"; Maraniss, *Barack Obama: The Story*, 366–67.

42. Andrew Ferguson, "Self-Made Man," Free Republic, June 18, 2012, https://freerepublic.com/focus/f-news/2896401/posts; Occidental College, "Boesche Gets Rare 'Drop In' Visit at White House," August 17, 2009, http://www.oxy.edu/news/boesche-gets-rare-drop-visit-white-house; Kloppenberg, *Reading Obama*, 16–22; Maraniss, *Barack Obama: The Story*, 351–65, and 368.

43. Obama, *Dreams from My Father*, 100–101 and 105–7; Obama, *A Promised Land*, 10–11; Margot Mifflin, "Obama at Occidental, *New Yorker*, October 3, 2012, https://www.newyorker.com/news/news-desk/obama-at-occidental; Faught, "School of Barack"; Maraniss, *Barack Obama: The Story*, 364–67 and 374–84; Remnick, *The Bridge*, 241; Garrow, *Rising Star*, 113–22 and 126–28.

44. Obama, *Dreams from My Father*, 86–87; Maraniss, "Barack Obama: The College Years"; Remnick, *The Bridge*, 232–34.

45. Obama, *Dreams from My Father*, 102–3 and 111; Calmes, "On Campus, Obama and Memories"; Maraniss, *Barack Obama: The Story*, 278–79 and 372–73.

46. Obama, *Dreams from My Father*, 115–18; Kloppenberg, *Reading Obama*, 22; Maraniss, *Barack Obama: The Story*, 386–88; Garrow, *Rising Star*, 131–37.

47. Obama, *Dreams from My Father*,121–22; Obama, *A Promised Land*, 11–12; Maraniss, *Barack Obama: The Story*, 420–43, 457–58 and 465–66; Garrow, *Rising Star*, 143–45.

48. Scott, *A Singular Woman*, 223–79; Garrow, *Rising Star*, 139; Maraniss, *Barack Obama: The Story*, 406–13.

49. Obama, *A Promised Land*, 12–13; Scott, *A Singular Woman*, 261–63; Maraniss, *Barack Obama: The Story*, 428–31; Tammerlin Drummond, "Barack Obama, Harvard Law Review Editor, March 19, 1990," *Daily Mirror* (blog), *Los Angeles Times*, September 4, 2008, https://latimesblogs.latimes.com/thedailymirror/2008/09/barack-obama-ha.html.

50. The quotes are from Maraniss, *Barack Obama: The Story*, 452 and 456, and Maraniss, "Barack Obama: The College Years." See also Obama, *Dreams from My Father*, 120.

51. The quotes are from Maraniss, "Barack Obama: The College Years" and Maraniss, *Barack Obama: The Story*, 452–55. See also 484–85.

52. As quoted in Kloppenberg, *Reading Obama*, 23.

53. Scott, *A Singular Woman*, 263; Obama, *Dreams from My Father*, 135–36; Maraniss, *Barack Obama: The Story*, 460–66 and 483–86; Garrow, *Rising Star*, 164–67.

54. David Maraniss, "Becoming Obama," *Vanity Fair*, May 2, 2012, https://www.vanityfair.com/news/politics/2012/06/young-barack-obama-in-love-david-maraniss; Lisa Miller, "Barack Obama's Christian Journey," *Newsweek*, July 11, 2008, https://www.newsweek.com/cover-story-barack-obamas-christian-journey-92611 Maraniss, *Barack Obama: The Story*, 448–49 and 472–90; Remnick, *The Bridge*, 244–45; Garrow, *Rising Star*, 152–53, 156–64, 168–78, 180, and 182–92. In his memoirs, *A Promised Land*, Obama never mentions his relationship with the two women.

55. The quote is from a letter Obama's mother wrote. In fairness, most of BI's clients were countries with significant foreign operations. Scott, *A Singular Woman*, 263. In his memoirs, Obama also compared his job to "a spy behind enemy lines." Obama, *Dreams from My Father*, 135. See also Tamara K. Nopper, "Barack Obama's Community Organizing as New Black Politics," *Political Power and Social Theory* 22 (2008): 61–62; Garrow, *Rising Star*, 169–70.

56. Obama, *Dreams from My Father*, 133–35. Kloppenberg, *Reading Obama*, 24–25.

57. Obama, *Dreams from My Father*, 137–38. Maraniss, *Barack Obama: The Story*, 469–70. See also Garrow, *Rising Star*, 179.

58. Obama, *Dreams from My Father*, 138–41; Edward McClelland, *Young Mr. Obama: Chicago and the Making of a Black President* (New York: Bloomsbury Press, 2010), 11; Garrow, *Rising Star*, 182–90. On Obama's reaction to the lack of response from civil rights organizations to the letters he wrote them, see Nopper, "Barack Obama's Community Organizing as New Black Politics," 57.

59. Obama, *Dreams from My Father*, 141–43. The Kellman quote is from Serge Kovaleski, "Obama's Organizing Years, Guiding Others and Finding Himself," *New York Times*, July 7, 2008; Garrow, *Rising Star*, 191–92. See also Nopper, "Barack Obama's Community Organizing as New Black Politics," 57.

60. Obama, *Dreams from My Father*, 146–48; Obama, *A Promised Land*, 15.

61. Ben Joravsky, "When Obama Needed Public-Access TV to Reach Voters," *Chicago Reader*, January 14, 2014, https://www.chicagoreader.com/chicago/

barack-obama-interviewed-on-public-access-television/Content?oid=12134521; McClelland, *Young Mr. Obama*, 15–16; Obama, *Dreams from My Father*, 155–60.

62. McClelland, *Young Mr. Obama*, 18–19.

63. McClelland, *Young Mr. Obama*, 5; Remnick, *The Bridge*, 165; Obama, *Dreams from My Father*, 164–65; Garrow, *Rising Star*, 30–32.

64. McClelland, *Young Mr. Obama*, 5–6; Remnick, *The Bridge*, 164, and 242–43; Garrow, *Rising Star*, 1–11, 21–22, 200–201.

65. McClelland, *Young Mr. Obama*, 8; Kovaleski, "Obama's Organizing Years, Guiding Others and Finding Himself"; Saul D. Alinsky, *Rules for Radicals: A Pragmatic Primer for Realistic Radicals* (New York: Random House, 1971), esp. xiii–xxvi and 126–27. See also Noam Cohen, "Know Thine Enemy," *New York Times*, August 22, 2009, https://www.nytimes.com/2009/08/23/weekinreview/23alinsky.html; Garrow, *Rising Star*, 198; Kloppenberg, *Reading Obama*, 92–93.

66. Cohen, "Know Thine Enemy"; Nelson Lichtenstein, "It Never Hurts to Have a Few Enemies," *New York Times Book Review*, November 12, 1989, https://www.nytimes.com/1989/11/12/books/it-never-hurts-to-have-a-few-enemies.html; McClelland, *Young Mr. Obama*, 9–10; Obama, *Dreams from My Father*, 168–69; Garrow, *Rising Star*, 39–40.

67. McClelland, *Young Mr. Obama*, 8–10, 13–15; Kloppenberg, *Reading Obama*, 29–30, 33–34.

68. McClelland, *Young Mr. Obama*, 13–15; Kovaleski, "Obama's Organizing Years, Guiding Others and Finding Himself."

69. Kovaleski, "Obama's Organizing Years, Guiding Others and Finding Himself"; McClelland, *Young Mr. Obama*, 11–12; Garrow, *Rising Star*, 201–2.

70. Edward McClelland, "Barack Obama as a Young Man," HuffPost, October 15, 2010, updated May 25, 2011, https://www.huffpost.com/entry/barack-obama-young-man_b_761827; Barack Obama, "Why Organize? Problems and Promise in the Inner City," Illinois Issues, http://gatherthepeople.org/Downloads/WHY_ORGANIZE.pdf.

71. Kovaleski, "Obama's Organizing Years, Guiding Others and Finding Himself"; McClelland, *Young Mr. Obama*, 20–24 and 52–54; Obama, *Dreams from My Father*, 223–26, 274–75, 280, and 290–95; Remnick, *The Bridge*, 169–77; Garrow, *Rising Star*, 36, 255, 258–60.

72. Kovaleski, "Obama's Organizing Years, Guiding Others and Finding Himself"; McClelland, *Young Mr. Obama*, 41–46; Remnick, *The Bridge*, 166–68; Garrow, *Rising Star*, 23–27.

73. Michele Norris, "How Chicago Politics Shaped Obama," NPR, October 16, 2008, https://www.npr.org/templates/story/story.php?storyId=95797455.

74. Obama, "Why Organize? Problems and Promise in the Inner City"; Kovaleski, "Obama's Organizing Years, Guiding Others and Finding Himself"; McClelland, *Young Mr. Obama*, 47–50; Obama, *Dreams from My Father*, 275–76; Kloppenberg, *Reading Obama*, 30–31, 33, 34–36; Garrow, *Rising* Star, 209–12, 219–20, 230–33, 239–44, 248–54, 282–89; Remnick, *The Bridge*, 163–64, 178–81 and 243–44.

75. Garrow, *Rising Star*, 288.

76. Obama, *A Promised Land*, 17–18; Obama, interview by Axelrod; McClelland, *Young Mr. Obama*, 40 and 174–75. Obama, *Dreams from My Father*, 287–89; Remnick,

The Bridge, 160–61 and 178; Garrow, *Rising Star*, 216, 276, 292–94. Washington died suddenly of a heart attack just as Obama was preparing to leave Chicago. Obama, *Dreams from My Father*, 289.

77. The quote is from Obama, *Dreams from My Father*, 276; see also 276–79; Ryan Lizza, "Making It: How Chicago Shaped Obama, "*New Yorker*, July 21, 2008, https://www.newyorker.com/magazine/2008/07/21/making-it; Cassandra Butts, interview by Michael Kirk, "The Frontline Interviews," PBS, July 10, 2008, https://www.pbs.org/wgbh/pages/frontline/government-elections-politics/choice-2012/the-frontline-interview-cassandra-butts/; Kloppenberg, *Reading Obama*, 35–36.

78. Obama, *Dreams from My Father*, 301–2.

79. Ibid., 301–2; Maraniss, *Barack Obama: The Story*, 564: Remnick, *The Bridge*, 245.

80. Obama, *Dreams from My Father*, 309; Maraniss, *Barack Obama: The Story*, 565; Garrow, *Rising Star*, 319–20.

81. Obama, *Dreams from My Father*, 311–15; Maraniss, *Barack Obama: The Story*, 565.

82. Remnick, *The Bridge*, 246–47.

83. Obama, *Dreams from My Father*, 318–20, 333–35.

84. Ibid., 328–31. As previously written, Obama had already begun to think about issues of wealth while a financial writer at BI. See above, section "Collegiate Years."

85. Obama, *Dreams from My Father*, 331–34.

86. Ibid., 347; Maraniss, *Barack Obama: The Story*, 565–66.

87. Maraniss, *Barack Obama: The Story*, 429–30. See also Remnick, *The Bridge*, 247–49.

88. Obama, *Dreams from My Father*, 429–30.

89. Kloppenberg, *Reading Obama*, 8–9.

2. From Organizer to Politician

1. For an account of a typical incoming class (One L) and its experiences at Harvard Law School, see Scott Turow, *One L: What They Really Teach You at Harvard Law School* (New York: Penguin, 1978). Turow went on to become a best-selling novelist and an early backer of Obama in Chicago politics. Although he preceded Obama at Harvard by thirteen years, his experiences were similar to those of first-year students in 1988. See also David J. Garrow, *Rising Star: The Making of Barack Obama* (New York: William Morrow, 2017), 327–28.

2. Ari Shapiro, "Obama Made a Strong First Impression at Harvard," National Public Radio, May 22, 2012, https://www.npr.org/2012/05/22/153214284/obamas-harvard-days-began-with-exclamation-point; See also Cassandra Butts, interview by Michael Kirk, "The Frontline Interviews," PBS, July 10, 2008, https://www.pbs.org/wgbh/pages/frontline/government-elections-politics/choice-2012/the-frontline-interview-cassandra-butts; "Obama First Made History at HLS," *Harvard Law Today*, November 1, 2008, https://today.law.harvard.edu/obama-first-made-history-at-hls/#:~:text=It%20was%20as%20a%20law,in%20the%20spring%20of%201990.

3. Justin Driver, "Obama's Law," *New Republic*, June 9, 2011, https://newrepublic.com/article/89647/obama-legal-philosophy-laurence-tribe. See also David

Remnick, *The Bridge: The Life and Rise of Barack Obama* (New York: Vintage Books, 2011), 192–93.

4. Laurence H. Tribe, "The Curvature of Constitutional Space: What Lawyers Can Learn from Modern Physics," *Harvard Law Review* 103 (November 1989): 1–36. See also James T. Kloppenberg, *Reading Obama: Dreams, Hope, and the American Political Tradition* (Princeton, NJ: Princeton University Press, 2011), 58–62.

5. Driver, "Obama's Law"; Laurence Tribe, "My Most Famous Students: President Obama and Justice Roberts," *Newsweek*, July 9, 2012, https://www.newsweek.com/my-most-famous-students-president-obama-and-justice-roberts-65599; Remnick, *The Bridge*, 194–96. In the one brief published article that Obama wrote for the *Review*, he stated that the way to limit abortions in the United States was not to make abortions illegal but to expand access to prenatal education and health-care facilities. Jeffrey Ressner and Ben Smith, "Exclusive: Obama's Lost Law Review Article," *Politico*, August 2008, https://www.politico.com/story/2008/08/exclusive-obamas-lost-law-review-article-012705; Nora Caplan-Bricker, "The Young Barack Obama Anticipated How 'Fetal Rights' Could Endanger Women," *Slate*, February 9, 2016, https://slate.com/human-interest/2016/02/barack-obama-at-harvard-law-school-anticipated-dangers-to-rights-of-pregnant-women.html.

6. The quote is from Garrow, *Rising Star*, 332. See also Remnick, *The Bridge*, 182–95.

7. Robert W. Gordon, "American Law through English Eyes: A Century of Nightmares and Noble Dreams," *Georgetown Law Journal* 84 (1995–1996): 2215–43; Kloppenberg, *Reading Obama*, 32–55; Remnick, *The Bridge*, 183–86.

8. Kloppenberg, *Reading Obama*, 78–84. For a different view by one of Obama's instructors who later claimed that Obama took a more skeptical view of the possibility of change, see Remnick, *The Bridge*, 185–86.

9. Kloppenberg, *Reading Obama*, xxxiv–xxxvi and 193; Tribe, "My Most Famous Students."

10. Laurence Tribe, "The Steadiness and Grace of President Obama," *Harvard Law and Policy Review*," November 14, 2016, https://harvardlpr.com/2016/11/14/laurence-tribe-the-steadiness-and-grace-of-president-obama/; Tribe, "My Most Famous Students"; Joanna Walters, "Class of '91: Obama and Gorsuch Rubbed Shoulders at Harvard, but Their Paths Split," *Guardian*, February 5, 2010, https://www.theguardian.com/education/2017/feb/05/barack-obama-neil-gorsuch-harvard-law-classmates; Kloppenberg, *Reading Obama*, 62–65.

11. Kloppenberg, *Reading Obama*, 37–39; Remnick, *The Bridge*, 199–200; Garrow, *Rising Star*, 359–60. Interestingly, another member of Obama's class who was able to reach across ideological boundaries was Associate Justice of the Supreme Court, Neil Gorsuch. Walters, "Class of '91."

12. "Obama First Made History at HLS"; Ari Shapiro, "Obama Made a Strong First Impression at Harvard," National Public Radio, May 22, 2012, https://www.npr.org/2012/05/22/153214284/obamas-harvard-days-began-with-exclamation-point; Jodi Kantor, "In Law School, Obama Found Political Voice," *New York Times*, January 28, 2007, https://www.nytimes.com/2007/01/28/us/politics/28obama.html; Remnick, *The Bridge*, 205–6.

13. John B. Judis, "Creation Myth," *New Republic*, September 10, 2008, https://newrepublic.com/article/65874/creation-myth-0; Tammerlin Drummond, "Barack Obama, Harvard Law Review Editor, March 19, 1990," *Daily Mirror* (blog), *Los Angeles Times*, September 4, 2008, https://latimesblogs.latimes.com/thedailymirror/2008/09/barack-obama-ha.html; Fox Butterfield, "First Black Elected to Head Harvard's Law Review," *New York Times*, February 6, 1990, https://www.nytimes.com/1990/02/06/us/first-Black-elected-to-head-harvard-s-law-review.html; Garrow, *Rising Star*, 382–84; Remnick, *The Bridge*, 195.

14. Linda Matchan, "A Law Review Breakthrough," *Boston Globe*, February 15, 1990, http://archive.boston.com/news/politics/2008/articles/1990/02/15/a_law_review_breakthrough/; Remnick, *The Bridge*, 200.

15. Drummond, "Barack Obama, Harvard Law Review Editor"; Garrow, *Rising Star*, 384–85; Remnick, *The Bridge*, 206–7.

16. Quoted in Remnick, *The Bridge*, 207. See also Kantor, "In Law School, Obama Found Political Voice"; Butts, interview by Kirk; Garrow, *Rising Star*, 387–91.

17. Quoted in Drummond, "Barack Obama, Harvard Law Review Editor." See also Butterfield, "First Black Elected to Head Harvard's Law Review"; Elise O'Shaughnessy, "Harvard Law Reviewed: Kicking Down Doors," *Vanity Fair*, June 1990, https://www.vanityfair.com/news/1990/06/obama199006; Garrow, *Rising Star*, 375 and 391–95; Remnick, *The Bridge*, 208 and 217–18.

18. Michelle Obama, *Becoming* (New York: Crown, 2018), 96; Remnick, *The Bridge*, 200; Garrow, *Rising Star*, 348–49 and 350–51.

19. Michelle Obama, *Becoming*, 3–83; Christopher Andersen, *Barack and Michelle: Portrait of an American Marriage* (New York: William Morrow, 2009), 124–25; Craig Robinson, *A Game of Character: A Family Journey from Chicago's Southside to the Ivy League and Beyond* (New York: Gotham Books, 2010), xi; Remnick, *The Bridge*, 202.

20. Andersen, *Barack and Michelle*, 78–80; Robinson, *A Game of Character*, 4–6; Garrow, *Rising Star*, 364.

21. Barack Obama, *A Promised Land* (New York: Crown, 2020), 20–21; Michelle Obama, *Becoming*, 97–107; Andersen, *Barack and Michelle*, 119–23; Garrow, *Rising Star*, 361–63; Remnick, *The Bridge*, 201; David Mendell, *Obama: From Promise to Power* (New York: HarperCollins, 2007), 93–94. See also David Bergen Brophy, *Michelle Obama: Meet the First Lady* (New York: HarperCollins, 2009), 45–49.

22. Robinson, *A Game of Character*, xvi–xxiii; Andersen, *Barack and Michelle*, 126–29; Liza Mundy, *Michelle* (New York: Pocket Star Books, 2009), 15; Mendell, *Obama*, 93–95 and 100–101.

23. Andersen, *Barack and Michelle*, 130–31; Mendell, *Obama*, 99; Butts, interview by Kirk.

24. Michelle Obama, *Becoming*, 122–25; Andersen, *Barack and Michelle*, 132–33; Garrow, *Rising Star*, 381–82.

25. Andersen, *Barack and Michelle*, 145–46.

26. Barack Obama, *A Promised Land*, 23; Michelle Obama, *Becoming*, 152 and 158; Mendell, *Obama*, 104–6; Remnick, *The Bridge*, 219–20; Andersen, *Barack and Michelle*, 128, 138–39 and 160–61; Garrow, *Rising Star*, 429–30 and 465–66.

27. Remnick, *The Bridge*, 208–9; Andersen, *Barack and Michelle*, 137; Garrow, *Rising Star*, 394–401; Kantor, "In Law School, Obama Found Political Voice."

28. The quote is from Drummond, "Barack Obama, Harvard Law Review Editor." For a more critical view of Obama's management of the *Review*, see Garrow, *Rising Star*, 420–31.

29. Drummond, "Barack Obama, Harvard Law Review Editor"; Kantor, "In Law School, Obama Found Political Voice"; Garrow, *Rising Star*, 412–15 and 438–39.

30. Kantor, "In Law School, Obama Found Political Voice"; Garrow, *Rising Star*, 438–43. There was also an essay on the reconstruction theology of Dr. Martin Luther King, but this had to do more with critical legal studies than racial discrimination. The essays and book reviews of the *Harvard Law Review* while Obama was its editor can be found in *Harvard Law Review*, vols. 105–6. See also Kloppenberg, *Reading Obama*, 58–65.

31. Michelle Obama, *Becoming*, 132–35; Mundy, *Michelle*, 166; Garrow, *Rising Star*, 463.

32. Michelle Obama, *Becoming*, 125–29 and 146–51; Mundy, *Michelle*, 165–67; Brophy, *Michelle Obama*, 54–55; Remnick, *The Bridge*, 272–74.

33. Barack Obama, *A Promised Land*, 22-23; Michelle Obama, *Becoming*, 156–57; Garrow, *Rising Star*, 462–64. Some biographers have maintained that there was even a political calculation in Obama's decision to marry Michelle. According to this view, one reason why Obama broke off his earlier relationships with white women was because he felt that if he was going to have a successful political career, he had to marry someone who was Black. Otherwise, too much scandal would be involved in a biracial marriage. On this point, see Garrow, *Rising Star*, 277–78. But according to Cassandra Butts, who knew Barack since their days at Harvard Law School and later served in the White House as deputy counsel, there was no political calculation involved. "It was a very personal connection with Michelle," she later commented. Butts, interview by Kirk; Brophy, *Michelle and Obama*, 59–60. See also Garrow, *Rising Star*, 344–47. On the wedding itself, see Andersen, *Barack and Michelle*, 156–61.

34. Michelle Obama, *Becoming*, 61–65; Andersen, *Barack and Michelle*, 150–52; Mundy, *Michelle*, 180–84; Remnick, *The Bridge*, 268–69; Garrow, *Rising Star*, 489–91.

35. Gretchen Reynolds, "Vote of Confidence," *Chicago Magazine*, January 1, 1993,   http://www.chicagomag.com/Chicago-Magazine/January-1993/Vote-of-Confidence; Garrow, *Rising Star*, 489; Andersen, *Barack and Michelle*, 152–53; Michelle Obama, *Becoming*, 166–69.

36. Remnick, *The Bridge*, 220–21; Andersen, *Barack and Michelle*, 154; John Presta, *Mr. and Mrs. Grassroots: How Barack Obama, Two Bookstore Owners, and 300 Volunteers Did It* (Paoli, PA: Elevator Group, 2010), 16–17; Angie Drobnic Holan, "Project Vote Not 'An Arm of ACORN,'" PolitiFact, October 17, 2008, http:www.politifact.com/truth-o-meter/statements/2008/oct/17/john-mccain/project-vote-not-an-arm-of-acorn/.

37. Reynolds, "Vote of Confidence"; Garrow, *Rising Star*, 471–72; Andersen, *Barack and Michelle*, 150; Remnick, *The Bridge*, 221–22 and 269–70.

38. Reynolds, "Vote of Confidence"; Andersen, *Barack and Michelle*, 154–56; Remnick, *The Bridge*, 222–24; Garrow, *Rising Star*, 472–81.

39. Reynolds, "Vote of Confidence"; Garrow, *Rising Star*, 482.

40. Reynolds, "Vote of Confidence"; Holan, "Project Vote Not 'An Arm of ACORN'"; Remnick, *The Bridge*, 224–25; Ezra Klein, "The Woods Fund," The Prospect,

May 2, 2008, http://prospect.org/article/woods-fund; Judis, "Creation Myth"; Garrow, *Rising Star*, 510–11 and 521–24.

41. Barack Obama, *A Promised Land*, 22; Remnick, *The Bridge*, 225–26 and 260; Garrow, *Rising Star*, 481–82.

42. Saul D. Alinsky, *Rules for Radicals: A Pragmatic Primer for Realistic Radicals* (New York: Vintage Books, 1989), esp. 60–97; Judis, "Creation Myth."

43. Judis, "Creation Myth"; Melinda Henneberger, "Saul Alinsky Would Be So Disappointed: Obama Breaks 'Rules for Radicals,'" *Washington Post*, January 25, 2012, https://www.washingtonpost.com/blogs/she-the-people/post/saul-alinsky-would-so-disappointed-sotu-breaks-rules-for-radicals/2012/01/24/gIQAt1cVPQ_blog.html. See also Frederick C. Harris, *The Price of the Ticket: Barack Obama and the Rise and Decline of Black Politics* (New York: Oxford University Press, 2014), 44; Garrow, *Rising Star*, 372–74, 499–503 and 554–56.

44. Christopher Drew and Mike McIntire, "After 2000 Loss, Obama Built Donor Network from Roots Up," *New York Times*, April 3, 2007, https://www.nytimes.com/2007/04/03/us/politics/03obama.html; Remnick, *The Bridge*, 268–74.

45. Robin I. Mordfin, "From the Green Lounge to the White House," *Record* (University of Chicago Alumni Magazine), Spring 2009, https://www.law.uchicago.edu/news/green-lounge-white-house; Remnick, *The Bridge*, 218–20.

46. Mendell, *Obama*, 105; Remnick, *The Bridge*, 260–61 and 269–70.

47. Barack Obama, *A Promised Land*, 24; Mendell, *Obama*, 108; Remnick, *The Bridge*, 276–88; Andersen, *Barack and Michelle*, 169–72; John Presta, *Mr. and Mrs. Grassroots*, 18; Garrow, *Rising* Star, 507–8, 521–26, 538–42 and 546–47.

48. Barack Obama, *A Promised Land*, 26–30; Remnick, *The Bridge*, 288–90; Garrow, *Rising Star*, 526–27 and 548–54; Mendell, *Obama*, 108–9.

49. Kathleen Henehan and Jeremy Schulman, "CNN Report Accusing Obama of 'Getting a Little Dirty' in Challenging Political Opponents Ignored Facts Undermining Allegations," Media Matters, June 2, 2008, https://www.mediamatters.org/cnn/cnn-report-accusing-obama-getting-little-dirty-challenging-political-opponents-ignored-facts; Remnick, *The Bridge*, 290–92; Mendell, *Obama*, 109.

50. Remnick, *The Bridge*, 291–93; Mendell, *Obama*, 109–10; Garrow, *Rising Star*, 557–58 and 562; Michelle Obama, *Becoming*, 182–84.

51. Janny Scott, *A Singular Woman: The Untold Story of Barack Obama's Mother* (New York, Riverhead Books, 2011), 343–54; Michelle Obama, *Becoming*,184; Remnick, *The Bridge*, 288. Barack Obama, *A Promised Land*, 30–31.

52. Barack Obama, *The Audacity of Hope: Thoughts on Reclaiming the American Dream* (New York: Penguin, 2006), dedication page; Remnick, *The Bridge*, 287–88; Garrow, *Rising Star*, 510 and 547.

53. Barack Obama, *The Audacity of Hope*, 30; Scott, *A Singular Woman*, 281.

54. Barack Obama, *A Promised Land*, 25–26.

55. Barack Obama, interview by David Axelrod, Full Transcript for the Axe Files, CNN, December 26, 2016, http://www.cnn.com/2016/12/26/politics/axe-files-obama-transcript/index.html; David Maraniss, "The 44th President Was His Mother's Son," *Washington Post*, May 11, 2012, https://www.washingtonpost.com/opinions/the-44th-president-was-his-mothers-son/2012/05/11/gIQA6NV1IU_story.html; Stacy Schiff, "Obama's Mother Ann Dunham Shaped His Success," *News-*

week, May 1, 2011, https://www.newsweek.com/obamas-mother-ann-dunham-shaped-his-success-67633; Scott, *A Singular Woman*, 274–77, 326–31, 335–42.

56. Scott, *A Singular Woman*, 104–5 and 362–66; Garrow, *Rising Star*, 421 and 470.

57. Scott, *A Singular Woman*, 354–56; Michelle Obama, *Becoming*, 184; Garrow, *Rising Star*, 549.

58. Jodi Kantor, "Inside Professor Obama's Classroom," *New York Times*, July 30, 2008, https://thecaucus.blogs.nytimes.com/2008/07/30/inside-professor-obamas-classroom; Garrow, *Rising Star*, 488, 497–98, and 575–76.

59. Mordfin, "From the Green Lounge to the White House"; Kantor, "Inside Professor Obama's Classroom"; Tim Phelps, "Barack Obama: President and Lawyer-in-Chief," *U.S. News*, December 29, 2016, https://www.usnews.com/news/national-news/articles/2016-12-29/barack-obama-president-and-lawyer-in-chief; Remnick, *The Bridge*, 262–66; Garrow, *Rising Star*, 488, 497–98, 514–15, 565–66 and 613–15, 673, and 718–19.

60. Kantor, "Inside Professor Obama's Classroom."

61. Ibid.

62. Stacey Marlise Gahagan and Alfred L. Brophy, "Reading Professor Obama: Race and the American Constitutional Tradition," *University of Pittsburgh Law Review* 75 (Summer 2014): 495, https://lawreview.law.pitt.edu/ojs/index.php/lawreview/article/view/342; Kantor, "Inside Professor Obama's Classroom"; Phelps, "Barack Obama: President and Lawyer-in-Chief"; Kloppenberg, *Reading Obama*, 69–71.

63. Kloppenberg, *Reading Obama*, 69–70; Garrow, *Rising Star*, 477–78.

64. John Cook, "Why We're Talking about Barack Obama and Derrick Bell Now," *Gawker*, March 8, 2012, http://gawker.com/5891738/why-were-talking-about-barack-obama-and-derrick-bell-now; David A. Graham, "Breitbart.com's Massive Barack Obama-Derrick Bell Video Fail," *Atlantic*, March 8, 2012, https://www.theatlantic.com/politics/archive//2012/03/breitbartcoms-massive-barack-obama-derrick-bell-video-fall/254213; Tom Cohen, "Obama's Harvard Law Professor Challenged U.S. Racism," CNN Politics, March 9, 2012, https://www.cnn.com/2012/03/09/us/obamas-harvard-law-professor-challenged-u-s-racism; Gahagan and Brophy, "Reading Professor Obama," 496; Ben Shapiro, "Why the Bell-Obama Connection Matters," Townhall, March 14, 2012, https://patriotpost.us/opinion/12890-why-the-bell-obama-connection-matters-2012-03-14; Garrow, *Rising Star*, 409–11; Remnick, *The Bridge*, 211–14 and 262; Kloppenberg, *Reading Obama*, 66 and 70.

65. Gahagan and Brophy, "Reading Professor Obama," 500–505; Kloppenberg, *Reading Obama*, 67–68; Graham, "Breibart.com's Massive Barack Obama-Derrick Bell Video Fail."

66. The quote is in Remnick, *The Bridge*, 284.

67. Ryan Lizza, "Making It: How Chicago Shaped Obama," *New Yorker*, July 21, 2008, https://www.newyorker.com/magazine/2008/07/21/making-it; Chicago Sun-Times, "Springfield Remembers Obama as 'A Chicago Guy . . . an Illinois Guy,'" January 10, 2017, https://chicago.suntimes.com/2017/1/10/18401882/springfield-remembers-obama-as-a-chicago-guy-an-illinois-guy; Mendell, *Obama*, 111.

68. Hank De Zutter, "What Makes Obama Run?" Chicago Reader, December 7, 1995, https://www.chicagoreader.com/chicago/what-makes-obama-run/Content?oid=889221; Mendell, Obama, 110.

69. De Zutter, "What Makes Obama Run?"; Remnick, The Bridge, 294–95.

70. Lizza, "Making It: How Chicago Shaped Obama"; Kenneth T. Walsh, "Obama's Years in Chicago Politics Shaped His Presidential Candidacy," U.S. News, April 11, 2008, https://www.usnews.com/news/campaign-2008/articles/2008/04/11/obamas-years-in-chicago-politics-shaped-his-presidential-candidacy.

71. Edward McClelland, Young Mr. Obama: Chicago and the Making of a Black President (New York: Bloomsbury Press, 2010), 122–26; Remnick, The Bridge, 288–89 and 296–300; Mendell, Obama, 114–15. In A Promised Land, Obama writes about his first term in the state senate in much more positive terms. Barack Obama, A Promised Land, 32.

72. Lizza, "Making It: How Chicago Shaped Obama"; McClelland, Young Mr. Obama, 122–24 and 188–92; Garrow, Rising Star, 597–99.

73. Jodi Kantor, The Obamas (New York: Back Bay Books, 2012), 18; Garrow, Rising Star, 520–21; Barack Obama, A Promised Land, 22.

74. Kantor, The Obamas, 18; Michelle Obama, Becoming, 174–86.

75. Kantor, The Obamas, 18–19; Remnick, The Bridge, 226–27 and 282–83; Michelle Obama, Becoming, 182–83.

76. Barack Obama, A Promised Land, 35.

77. Ibid., 35–36; Michelle Obama, Becoming, 189; Mendell, Obama, 103.

78. Andersen, Barack and Michelle, 162–68; Scott, A Singular Women, 360; Mendell, Obama, 144; Garrow, Rising Star, 489–92 and 530–33; Michelle Obama, Becoming, 169–74. Of the 9,000 copies of Dreams from My Father sold, hundreds of them were bought and given away free during Obama's campaign for state senate in 1996. Presta, Mr. and Mrs. Grassroots, 30.

79. Mendell, Obama, 122–23. See also Tom Purdum, "Raising Obama," Vanity Fair, March 2008, https://www.vanityfair.com/news/2008/03/obama200803; Kloppenberg, Reading Obama, 2; Lizza, "Making It: How Chicago Shaped Obama"; Remnick, The Bridge, 298–99; Garrow, Rising Star, 589–92, and 597–98.

80. Barack Obama, A Promised Land, 32; Lizza, "Making It: How Chicago Shaped Obama"; Remnick, The Bridge, 298–99.

81. Barack Obama, Dreams from My Father (New York: Three Rivers Press, 2004), 223; Purdum, "Raising Obama"; McClelland, Young Mr. Obama, 210–11.

82. Jo Becker and Christopher Drew, "Pragmatic Politics, Forged on the South Side," New York Times, May 11, 2008, https://www.nytimes.com/2008/05/11/us/politics/11chicago.html; Purdum, "Raising Obama"; Mendell, Obama, 123; Harris, The Price of the Ticket, 62–64; Remnick, The Bridge, 299; Garrow, Rising Star, 512.

83. Presta, Mr. and Mrs. Grassroots, 2–3; Dan Shomon, "Dan Shomon Inc.," https://www.danshomon.com/dan-shomon-bio; Barack Obama, A Promised Land, 33 and 40; Harris, The Price of the Ticket, 66–67; Remnick, The Bridge, 299–300.

84. CBS, "Obama's Political 'Godfather' in Illinois," CBS Interactive, April 31, 2008, https://www.cbsnews.com/news/obamas-political-godfather-in-illinois/; Edward McClelland, "Why Emil Jones Jr. Took a Bullet for Obama," June 11, 2010, https://www.nbcchicago.com/blogs/ward-room/The Godfather-Took-a-Hit-for-Obamna-96140239.

html; Garrett M. Graff, "The Legend of Barack Obama," Washingtonian, November 1, 2006, https://www.washingtonian.com/2006/11/01/the-legend-of-barack-obama/. Purdum, "Raising Obama"; Mendell, *Obama*, 124; McClelland, *Young Mr. Obama*, 126–28; Remnick, *The Bridge*, 300–302; Garrow, *Rising Star*, 514, 603, 607–9, 616, 625–31, 644–46, 648–50, 652, 654–59.

85. Ted Kleine, "Is Bobby Rush in Trouble?" Chicago Reader, March 16, 2000, https://www.chicagoreader.com/chicago/is-bobby-rush-in-trouble/Content?oid=901745; Janny Scott, "In 2000, a Streetwise Veteran Schooled a Bold Young Obama," *New York Times*, September 9, 2007, http://www.nytimes.com/2007/09/09/us/politics/09obama.html; Jonathan Kaufman, "For Obama, Chicago Days Honed Tactics," *Wall Street Journal*, April 21, 2008, https://www.wsj.com/articles/SB120873956522230099. See also Harris, *The Price of the Ticket*, 58–59; Barack Obama, *A Promised Land*, 36–37; Michelle Obama, *Becoming*, 193–94; Walsh, "Obama's Years in Chicago Politics Shaped His Presidential Candidacy"; Garrow, *Rising Star*, 645–46, 650–52, 659, 662–63, 669, and 12.

86. Scott, "In 2000, a Streetwise Veteran Schooled a Bold Young Obama"; Kleine, "Is Bobby Rush in Trouble?"; McClelland, *Young Mr. Obama*, 128–35 and 142–45; Garrow, *Rising Star*, 701.

87. The quote is from Kleine, "Is Bobby Rush in Trouble?" See also Scott, "In 2000, a Streetwise Veteran Schooled a Bold Young Obama"; Don Gonyea, "Obama's Loss May Have Aided White House Bid," National Public Radio, September 19, 2007, http://www.npr.org/templates/story/story.php?storyid=14502364; Harris, *The Price of the Ticket*, 41–45 and 60–61; Remnick, *The Bridge*, 316–22; Michelle Obama, *Becoming*, 19–98; Garrow, *Rising Star*, 703–4. On Reynolds, see also Garrow, *Rising Star*, 406–7 and 704.

88. Kleine, "Is Bobby Rush in Trouble?"; Garrow, *Rising Star*, 698.

89. Kleine, "Is Bobby Rush in Trouble?"; McClelland, *Young Mr. Obama*, 14–48; Harris, *The Price of the Ticket*, 60–61, and 659.

90. Scott, "In 2000, a Streetwise Veteran Schooled a Bold Young Obama"; Harris, *The Price of the Ticket*, 61; Barack Obama, *A Promised Land*, 37; Michelle Obama, *Becoming*, 196–97; Remnick, *The Bridge*, 323–31; Garrow, *Rising Star*, 677–78, 687–90, and 699. For an opposite view of who prevailed in the debate by one of Obama's most ardent supporters, see Presta, *Mr. and Mrs. Grassroots*, 39–45.

91. Kleine, "Is Bobby Rush in Trouble?"; Scott, "In 2000, a Streetwise Veteran Schooled a Bold Young Obama"; Remnick, *The Bridge*, 330.

92. The quote is from Graff, "The Legend of Barack Obama." See also Barack Obama, interview by Axelrod; Remnick, *The Bridge*, 330–31.

93. Barack Obama, *A Promised Land*, 37–38; Barack Obama, interview by Axelrod; Remnick, *The Bridge*, 334; Garrow, *Rising Star*, 716–17.

94. Michelle Obama, *Becoming*, 199–200 and 203–7; Remnick, *The Bridge*, 331–32; Garrow, *Rising Star*, 662, 675, 721, and 736–37.

95. Remnick, *The Bridge*, 332–33; Garrow, *Rising Star*, 749–53.

96. Michelle Obama, *Becoming*, 203–13; Barack Obama, interview by Axelrod; Garrow, *Rising Star*, 58–59; Remnick, *The Bridge*, 336.

97. Michelle Obama, *Becoming*, 213; Garrow, *Rising Star*, 758–59; Remnick, *The Bridge*, 336.

3. The Presidential Run and the Earthquake of Iowa

1. John Presta, *Mr. and Mrs. Grassroots: How Barack Obama, Two Bookstore Owners, and 300 Volunteers Did It* (Paoli, PA: Elevator Group, 2010), 23–24.

2. David Remnick, *The Bridge: The Life and Rise of Barack Obama* (New York: Vintage Books, 2011), 317–18.

3. Barack Obama, *A Promised Land* (New York: Crown, 2020), 40–41; Remnick, *The Bridge,* 319.

4. Barack Obama, *A Promised Land,* 41–42.

5. Barack Obama, *A Promised Land,* 42–43 and 46; Remnick, *The Bridge,* 304 and 341–42; Edward McClelland, *Young Mr. Obama: Chicago and the Making of a Black President* (New York: Bloomsbury Press, 2010), 172; David J. Garrow, *Rising Star: The Making of Barack Obama* (New York: HarperCollins, 2017), 754; Hank De Zutter, "What Makes Obama Run?" Chicago Reader, December 7, 1995, https://www.chicagoreader.com/chicago/what-makes-obama-run/Content?oid=889221.

6. Jodi Wilgoren, "Illinois Senator Announces He Won't Seek Re-Election," *New York Times,* April 16, 2003, https://www.nytimes.com/2003/04/16/us/illinois-senator-announces-he-won-t-seek-re-election.html; Remnick, *The Bridge,* 359–60; Garrow, *Rising Star,* 756–57, 791–92, and 814–15.

7. John S. Jackson, "The Making of a Senator: Barack Obama and the 2004 Illinois Senate Race," Simon Review (Occasional Papers of the Paul Simon Public Policy Institute), August 2006, page 6 (Simon Review Papers#4), https://opensiuc.lib.siu.edu/cgi/viewcontent.cgi?article=1004&context=ppi_papers. See also Remnick, *The Bridge,* 367–70.

8. Jackson, "The Making of a Senator," 7; Remnick, *The Bridge,* 375–76.

9. Jackson, "The Making of a Senator," 10–11; Remnick, *The Bridge,* 374–75 and 378–81; Garrow, *Rising Star,* 832–33.

10 Jackson, "The Making of a Senator," 8–10; Remnick, *The Bridge,* 376–77.

11. Ben Wallace-Wells, "Obama's Narrator," *New York Times Magazine,* April 1, 2007, http://www.nytimes.com/2007/04/01/magazine/01axelrod.t.html. Remnick, *The Bridge,* 363–64.

12. David Axelrod, *Believer: My Forty Years in Politics* (New York: Penguin, 2015), 8, 79–81; Wallace-Wells, "Obama's Narrator"; Remnick, *The Bridge,* 365–66.

13. Salzman's quote is in Ryan Lizza, "Making It: How Chicago Shaped Obama," *New Yorker,* July 21, 2008, https://www.newyorker.com/magazine/2008/07/21/making-it. See also Axelrod, *Believer,* 119–20.

14. Axelrod, *Believer,* 119–21 and 137.

15. Ibid., 122.

16. Barack Obama, *A Promised Land,* 43–44; Axelrod, *Believer,* 122–23; Remnick, *The Bridge,* 363–66; Garrow, *Rising Star,* 755–75.

17. Janny Scott, "In 2000, a Streetwise Veteran Schooled a Bold Young Obama," *New York Times,* September 7, 2007, https://www.nytimes.com/2007/09/09/us/politics/09obama.html; Garrow, *Rising Star,* 805–6, and 923.

18. Garrow, *Rising Star,* 777–78; Remnick, *The Bridge,* 365–66 and 404.

19. Quoted in Remnick, *The Bridge,* 337. See also Barack Obama, "President Obama Remarks," C-Span, September 11, 2016, https://www.c-span.org/video/?314973-2/

presidential-remarks-september-11-remembrance-ceremony-pentagon; Garrow, *Rising Star*, 742–43 and 747–48.

20. Barack Obama, *The Audacity of Hope* (New York: Broadway Paperbacks, 2006), 293–95; Axelrod, *Believer*, 129–30; Remnick, *The Bridge*, 344–45; Garrow, *Rising Star*, 777–78.

21. Barack Obama, *A Promised Land*, 46; Axelrod, *Believer*, 129–30; Garrow, *Rising Star*, 778.

22. "Transcript: Obama's Speech against the Iraq War," NPR, October 2, 2009, https://www.npr.org/templates/story/story.php?storyId=99591469; Barack Obama, *The Audacity of Hope*, 293–95; Remnick, *The Bridge*, 346–48; Barack Obama, *A Promised Land*, 47.

23. "Obama Speech against the War, Delivered by Supporters," https://www.youtube.com/watch?v=AUV69LZbCNQ; Garrow, *Rising Star*, 786–87; Remnick, *The Bridge*, 346–49.

24. Axelrod, *Believer*, 130–31.

25. Garrow, *Rising Star*, 797–98, and 860–61.

26. Ibid., 861–63; Remnick, *The Bridge*, 370.

27. William Finnegan, "The Candidate: How the Son of a Kenyan Economist Became an Illinois Everyman," *New Yorker*, May 31, 2004, https://www.newyorker.com/magazine/2004/05/31/the-candidate-5; Monica Davey, "The Speaker: A Surprise Senate Contender Reaches His Biggest Stage Yet," *New York Times*, July 26, 2004, https://www.nytimes.com/2004/07/26/us/the-speaker-a-surprise-senate-contender-reaches-his-biggest-stage-yet.html; Larissa MacFarquhar, "The Conciliator," *New Yorker*, May 2007, https://www.newyorker.com/magazine/2007/05/14/larissa-macfarquhar-the-conciliator; Axelrod, *Believer*, 138–39; Remnick, *The Bridge*, 361–63.

28. Finnegan, "The Candidate"; Remnick, *The Bridge*, 370–71.

29. Barack Obama, *The Audacity of Hope*.

30. Ibid.

31. Barack Obama, *A Promised Land*, 47–49; Finnegan, "The Candidate"; Jackson, "The Making of a Senator"; Peter Slevin, "For Obama, A Handsome Payoff in Political Gambles," *Washington Post*, November 13, 2007, http://www.washingtonpost.com/wp-dyn/content/article/2007/11/12/AR2007111201945.html; Glen Justice, "In Races with One Deep Pocket, the Law Tries to Tailor a Second," *New York Times*, October 17, 2003, https://www.nytimes.com/2003/10/17/us/in-races-with-one-deep-pocket-the-law-tries-to-tailor-a-second.html; Lizza, "Making It"; Finnegan, "The Candidate"; Axelrod, *Believer*, 378–79; Garrow, *Rising Star*, 814 and 845.

32. Debbie Howlett, "Campaign 2004," *USA Today*, March 18, 2004, https://usatoday30.usatoday.com/news/politicselections/nation/2004-03-18-obama-usat_x.htm; Monica Davey, "As Quickly as Overnight, a Democratic Star Is Born," *New York Times*, March 18, 2004, https://www.nytimes.com/2004/03/18/us/as-quickly-as-overnight-a-democratic-star-is-born.html; Finnegan, "The Candidate"; Barack Obama, *A Promised Land*, 49; Remnick, *The Bridge*, 371–83; Axelrod, *Believer*, 142–45; Garrow, *Rising Star*, 872–84, 899, and 906.

33. Jackson, "The Making of a Senator"; Nancy Day, "The Battle for Illinois: Two Law School Alumni Square Off for a Pivotal U.S. Senate Seat," *Harvard Magazine*,

July-August 2004, http://harvardmagazine.com/2004/07/the-battle-for-illinois; Barack Obama, *A Promised Land*, 50; Remnick, *The Bridge*, 388.

34. Finnegan, "The Candidate"; Jackson, "The Making of a Senator"; Remnick, *The Bridge*, 388.

35. Jackson, "The Making of a Senator"; Remnick, *The Bridge*, 388–91; Garrow, *Rising Star*, 894–95 and 924–27.

36. Garrow, *Rising Star*, 926.

37. Alan Keyes, "Alan Keyes Discusses Homosexuality with Sirius OutQ," Alan Keyes Archives, August 31, 2004, http://www.keyesarchives.com/transcript. php?id=340. See also "Mr. Keyes the Carpetbagger," *Washington Post*, August 9, 2004, https://www.washingtonpost.com/archive/opinions/2004/08/09/mr-keyes-the-carpetbagger/ccf8225e-9040-4087-ba11-9dbdd8d08260/; "Keyes Assails Obama's Abortion Views," NBC News, August 9, 2004, https://www.nbcnews.com/id/wbna5654128; Garrow, *Rising Star*, 819, 945–52.

38. `Barack Obama, *A Promised Land*, 53–54; Jackson, "The Making of a Senator"; Garrow, *Rising Star*, 956–57.

39. Jackson, "The Making of a Senator," 20–21.

40. Davey, "As Quickly as Overnight, a Democratic Star Is Born"; Bob Herbert, "A Leap of Faith," *New York Times*, June 4, 2004, http://www.nytimes.com/2004/06/04/opinion/a-leap-of-faith.html; Remnick, *The Bridge*, 384–87; Garrow, *Rising Star*, 902–3 and 928–31.

41. Axelrod, *Believer*, 155; Davey, "As Quickly as Overnight, a Democratic Star Is Born"; Herbert, "A Leap of Faith"; Davey, "The Speaker"; Remnick, *The Bridge*, 391–92.

42. Barack Obama, *A Promised Land*, 51; Axelrod, *Believer*, 155–56; Liza Mundy, "A Series of Fortunate Events," *Washington Post*, August 12, 2007, https://www.washingtonpost.com/wp-dyn/content/article/2007/08/08/AR2007080802038.html.

43. Barack Obama, *A Promised Land*, 51.

44. Ibid., 51; Axelrod, *Believer*, 157; Remnick, *The Bridge*, 393–96.

45. Barack Obama, *A Promised Land*, 51. Axelrod was also concerned that Obama's delivery before the convention would be too wooden and that his audience would soon lose interest in the speech. To remedy that problem, he had Obama practice every day before the convention in order to get him to be more relaxed and his voice less stale. Axelrod, *Believer*, 158–59. See also Remnick, *The Bridge*, 394 and 396; Garrow, *Rising Star*, 936–37.

46. "Transcript: Illinois Senate Candidate Barack Obama," *Washington Post*, July 27, 2004, https://www.washingtonpost.com/wp-dyn/articles/A19751-2004Jul27.html; Aaron Wood, "Great Speeches Analyzed," June 7, 2011, http://speechesanalysed.blogspot.com/2011/06/first-analysis-obamas-2004-dnc-cpeech.html; Michelle Obama, *Becoming* (New York: Crown, 2018), 214; "Speech Analysis of Barack Obama," n.d., https:www.slideshare.net/shreysoni/speech-analysis-of-barack-obama; Remnick, *The Bridge*, 397–98.

47. "Transcript: Illinois Senate Candidate Barack Obama"; Wood, "Great Speeches Analyzed"; "Speech Analysis of Barack Obama."

48. Wood, "Great Speeches Analyzed"; David Welna, "Obama Stresses Hope, Opportunity at Convention," NPR, July 18, 2004, https://www.npr.org/templates/

story/story.php?storyId=3624700; Barack Obama, *A Promised Land*, 52; Remnick, *The Bridge*, 399–400.

49. David A. Frank and Mark Lawrence McPhail, "Barack Obama's Address to the 2004 Democratic National Convention: Trauma Compromise, Consilience, and the (Im)possibility of Racial Reconciliation," *Rhetoric and Public Affairs* 8 (Winter 2005): http://muse.jhu.edu/journals/rap/summary/v008/8.4frank.html; Wood, "Great Speeches Analyzed." See also Ron Walters, "Barack Obama and the Politics of Blackness," *Journal of Black Studies* 38 (September, 2007): https://www.jstor.org/stable/40034399?seq=1; Michelle Obama, *Becoming*, 214–17; Remnick, *The Bridge*, 400–402; Garrow, *Rising Star*, 939–42.

50. Wood, "Great Speeches Analyzed"; Remnick, *The Bridge*, 401.

51. Remnick, *The Bridge*, 403–4.

52. Garrow, *Rising Star*, 903; Remnick, *The Bridge*, 456–57 and 490–91.

53. Barack Obama, *A Promised Land*, 55–58.

54. Ibid., 61–62; Remnick, *The Bridge*, 437–40.

55. Patti Villacora, "Hope(fund) and Change: Breaking the Obama Code," American Thinker, March 16, 2010, https://www.americanthinker.com/articles/2010/03/hopefund_and_change_breaking_t_1.html; Kathy Gill, "Barack Obama: Political Career of Barack Obama," Thought Co., August 8, 2017, https://www.thoughtco.com/barack-obamas-political-career-3368167; David Plouffe, *The Audacity to Win: How Obama Won and How We Can Beat Back the Party of Limbaugh, Beck, and Palin* (New York: Penguin, 2010), 6, 417–20; Remnick, *The Bridge*, 390 and 402–4.

56. Axelrod, *Believer*, 157; Alyssa Mastromonaco, "What I Learned from 10 Years Working with Barack Obama," *Marie Claire*, March 16, 2017, https://www.marieclaire.com/politics/a26023/alyssa-mastromonaco-barack-obama/; Plouffe, *The Audacity to Win*, 5–6.

57. Don Babwin, "Obama Kicks Off Book Tour in Chicago," *Washington Post*, October 1, 2006, https://www.washingtonpost.com/wp-dyn/content/article/2006/10/17/AR2006101700908.html; Remnick, *The Bridge*, 403–4; Barack Obama, *A Promised Land*, 59.

58. Barack Obama, *The Audacity of Hope*, 21, 37, and 201.

59. Ibid., 38–39.

60. Ibid., 63.

61. Michelle Obama, *Becoming*, 220–21; Barack Obama, *A Promised Land*, 62–63. For the destruction of the storm and the Bush administration's response to it, see Douglas Brinkley, *The Great Deluge: Hurricane Katrina, New Orleans, and the Mississippi Gulf Coast* (New York: Harper Perennial), 2006.

62. Axelrod, *Believer*, 157; Plouffe, *The Audacity to Win*, 10: Richard Wolffe, *Renegade: The Making of a President* (New York: Crown, 2009), 25.

63. Wolffe, *Renegade*, 38–40 and 68–69; Remnick, *The Bridge*, 459.

64. Plouffe, *The Audacity to Win*, 10–13; Remnick, *The Bridge*, 459–65.

65. Barack Obama, *A Promised Land*, 65–67.

66. Plouffe, *The Audacity to Win*, 12–13; Axelrod, *Believer*, 192; Wolffe, *Renegade*, 53.

67. Wolffe, *Renegade*, 4–5; Plouffe, *The Audacity to Win*, 10–13.

68. "Barack Obama: How He Did It," *Newsweek*, November 4, 2008, https://www.newsweek.com/barack-obama-how-he-did-it-85083; Garrow, *Rising Star*,

757–59; Remnick, *The Bridge*, 464–65; Plouffe, *The Audacity to Win*, 11–12; Wolffe, *Renegade*, 51.

69. "Barack Obama: How He did It"; Remnick, *The Bridge*, 314–15, 332–33; Plouffe, *The Audacity to Win*, 12–13; Garrow, *Rising Star*, 841–42; Michelle Obama, *Becoming*, 220–25; Barack Obama, *A Promised Land*, 70–71.

70. Michelle Obama, *Becoming*, 222–23; Jodi Kantor, *The Obamas* (New York: Little, Brown, 2012), 26–27; "Barack Obama: How He Did It"; Wolffe, *Renegade*, 52–57.

71. Barack Obama, *A Promised Land*, 71.

72. Michelle Obama, *Becoming*, 225–26; Barack Obama, *A Promised Land*, 71; Kantor, *The Obamas*, 28.

73. Jaime Fuller, "How People Responded to Obama's Presidential Bid in 2007," *Washington Post*, February 20, 2014, https://www.washingtonpost.com/news/the-fix/wp/2014/02/10/how-people-responded-to-obamas-presidential-bid-in-2007/.

74. Plouffe, *The Audacity to Win*, 14–16; Wolffe, *Renegade*, 65–68.

75. Plouffe, *The Audacity to Win*, 14–16; Wolffe, *Renegade*, 65–68.

76. Barack Obama, *A Promised Land*, 47 and 130–31; Plouffe, *The Audacity to Win*, 16–17.

77. Barack Obama, *A Promised Land*, 130–31.

78. Adam Nagourney, "The '08 Campaign: Sea Change for Politics as We Know It," *New York Times*, November 3, 2008, https://www.nytimes.com/2008/11/04/us/politics/04memo.html; Plouffe, *The Audacity to Win*, 15, 21, 23, 33–36, 50, and 77; Axelrod, *Believer*, 176–78; Wolffe, *Renegade*, 75–76 and 80–82.

79. "Barack Obama, How He Did It"; Plouffe, *The Audacity to Win*, 52–53; Wolffe, *Renegade*, 74; Barack Obama, *A Promised Land*, 135–36.

80. Quoted in "Barack Obama: How He Did It." Obama's remarks were on tapes that *Newsweek* obtained and were published in a story about the Obama campaign on election day; Barack Obama, *A Promised Land*, 137–40; Plouffe, *The Audacity to Win*, 3–74; Remnick, *The Bridge*, 403–4.

81. Quoted in "Barack Obama: How He Did It." See also Remnick, *The Bridge*, 404–5; Axelrod, *Believer*, 221–24; Plouffe, *The Audacity to Win*, 46–47, and 56–62; Garrow, *Rising Star*, 837, and 906–8.

82. Betsy Myers, *Take the Lead: Motivate, Inspire, and Bring Out the Best in Yourself and Everyone around You* (New York: Atria Books, 2011), 21–24, 26, 87–88, 186–87, and 195; Plouffe, *The Audacity to Win*, 46–47; Mendell, *Obama*, 377–78; Wolffe, *Renegade*, 95–96; Garrow, *Rising Star*, 1035–36.

83. Lynn Sweet, "Obama, First Lady Michelle, Invite Edith Childs—She Coined 'Fired Up, Ready to Go'—to White House," *Chicago Sun-Times*, December 26, 2009, https://web.archive.org/web/20140330052950/htttp://blogs.suntimes.com/sweet/2009/12/obama_first_lady_michelle_invi.html.

84. Plouffe, *The Audacity to Win*, 110–15; Wolffe, *Renegade*, 87–92.

85. Barack Obama, "Speech at the Jefferson-Jackson Dinner," *American Rhetoric*, November 10, 2007, https://www.americanrhetoric.com/speeches/barackobama/barackobamajeffersonjacksondinner.htm; Plouffe, *Renegade*, 92–93.

86. Crowley's and Frank-Ruta's remarks are in The Daily Dish, "Obama at Jefferson-Jackson," *Atlantic*, November 11, 2007, https://www.theatlantic.com/daily-dish/archive/2007/11/obama-at-jefferson-jackson/223727/; Ana Marie Cox, "Can

Obama Rock the Nomination?" *Time*, November 11, 2007, http://content.time.
com/time/nation/article/0,8599,1682827,00.html. See also Richard Lowry, "Barack
Obama's Jefferson-Jackson Dinner Speech—Then and Now," *National Review*, July 7,
2008, https://www.nationalreview.com/corner/barack-obamas-jefferson-jackson-
dinner-speech-then-and-now-rich-lowry/.

87. Plouffe, *The Audacity to Win*, 108–9.

88. Roger Simon, "Jefferson-Jackson a Warm-Up for Iowa," *Politico*, November 11, 2000, https://www.politico.com/story/2007/11/jefferson-jackson-a-warm-
up-for-iowa-006815; Axelrod, *Believer*, 116; Remnick, *The Bridge*, 480–84; Wolffe. *Renegade*, 91; Plouffe, *The Audacity to Win*, 38 and 121–22.

89. Dan Balz, Anne E. Kornblut, and Shailagh Murray, "Obama Wins Iowa's
Democratic Caucuses," *Washington Post*, January 4, 2008, web page no longer available; Wolffe, *Renegade*, 85.

90. Remnick, *The Bridge*, 493–94.

4. From Iowa to President-Elect

1. "Barack Obama's Caucus Speech," *New York Times*, January 3, 2008, https://
www.nytimes.com/2008/01/03/us/politics/03obama-transcript.html.

2. Richard Wolffe, *Renegade: The Making of a President* (New York: Crown, 2009),
104–19; David Plouffe, *The Audacity to Win: How Obama Won and How We Can Beat
the Party of Limbaugh, Beck, and Palin* (New York: Penguin, 2010), 142–45; John Heilemann and Mark Halperin, *Game Change: Obama and the Clintons, McCain and Palin, and
the Race of a Lifetime* (New York: HarperCollins, 2010), 177–82 and 187–88.

3. David Axelrod claimed later that he was worried from the start about the
outcome in New Hampshire because of the sympathy for Clinton now that she was
no longer the front-runner for the nomination. David Axelrod, *Believer: My Forty
Years in Politics* (New York: Penguin, 2015), 250–51. See also James W. Ceaser, Andrew
E. Busch, and John J. Pitney Jr., *Epic Journey: The 2008 Elections and American Politics*
(Lanham, MD: Rowman and Littlefield, 2009), 114–15; Evan Thomas, *"A Long Time
Coming": The Inspiring, Combative 2008 Campaign and the Historic Election of Barack
Obama* (New York: Public Affairs, 2009), 28–29; Plouffe, *The Audacity to Win*, 145–46.

4. Quoted in Wolffe, *Renegade*, 110. Edwards received 16.9 percent of the vote
and four delegates to the national convention. Axelrod, *Believer*, 252–56; Plouffe, *The
Audacity to Win*, 146–47 and 157; Ceaser, Busch, and Pitney Jr., *Epic Journey*, 115–16;
Heilemann and Halperin, *Game Change*, 183–91 and 201–2.

5. Plouffe, *Audacity to Win*, 157; David Remnick, *The Bridge: The Life and Rise of
Barack Obama* (New York: Vintage, 2011), 496–508; Heilemann and Halperin, *Game
Change*, 202–3, 205–15.

6. Election Center 2008, "Bill Clinton: What Happened in South Carolina a 'Myth,'"
CNN, March 17, 2008, http://edition.cnn.com/2008/POLITICS/03/17/clinton
.bill/index.html; Patrick Healy, "In S. Carolina, It's Obama vs. Clinton. That's Bill
Clinton," *New York Times*, January 22, 2008, https://www.nytimes.com/2008/01/22/
us/politics/22clinton.html; Axelrod, *Believer*, 258–59; Plouffe, *The Audacity to Win*,
157–62; Wolffe, *Renegade*, 110 and 195–99; Remnick, *The Bridge*, 510–12; Heilemann
and Halperin, *Game Change*, 197–98.

7. "Why the Kennedys Went for Obama," *Time*, January 21, 2008, http://content.time.com/time/politics/article/0,8599,1707700,00.html; Heilemann and Halperin, *Game Change*, 218–22; Remnick, *The Bridge*, 508–9; Axelrod, *Believer*, 259–61; Ceaser, Busch, and Pitney Jr., *Epic Journey*, 116–17; Plouffe, *The Audacity to Win*, 117–19, 155, and 165–66; Wolffe, *Renegade*, 94–95, 199–200.

8. Plouffe, *The Audacity to Win*, 164–65; Axelrod, *Believer*, 262–63; Ceaser, Busch, and Pitney Jr., *Epic Journey*, 18; Heileman and Halperin, *Game Change*, 223.

9. Plouffe, *The Audacity to Win*, 167–75; Ceaser, Busch, and Pitney Jr., *Epic Journey*, 118.

10. Adam Nagourney, "Neck and Neck, Democrats Woo Superdelegates," *New York Times*, February 10, 2008, https://www.nytimes.com/2008/02/10/world/americas/10iht-10superdelegates.9899121.html; Adam Nagourney, "Obama's Lead in Delegates Shift Focus of Campaign," *New York Times*, February 14, 2008, https://www.nytimes.com/2008/02/14/us/politics/14delegates.html; Ceaser, Busch, and Pitney Jr., *Epic Journey*, 118; Axelrod, *Believer*, 264–65; Plouffe, *The Audacity to Win*, 179–82; Thomas, *"A Long Time Coming,"* 66; Heilemann and Halperin, *Game Change*, 224–25.

11. Barack Obama, *A Promised Land*, 138–39.

12. Plouffe, *The Audacity to Win*, 164–65.

13. Ron Walters, "Barack Obama and the Politics of Blackness," *Black Studies* 38 (September 2007): 7–29.

14. Quoted in Walters, "Barack Obama and the Politics of Blackness," 14; John Harris and Mike Allen, "Obama Supported by Wilder," *Politico*, August 28, 2007, https://www.politico.com/story/2007/08/obama-supported-by-wilder-005518; "Douglas Wilder on Race, Politics and America," NPR, October 15, 2008, https://www.npr.org/templates/story/story.php?storyId=95739248. See also Jeff Zelany, "When It Comes to Race, Obama Makes His Point with Subtlety," *Chicago Tribune*, June 26, 2005, https://www.chicagotribune.com/news/nationworld/chi-050626obama-race-archive-story.html; Stanley A. Renshon, *Barack Obama and the Politics of Redemption* (New York: Routledge, 2012), 84–87.

15. Remnick, *The Bridge*, 517–19; Obama, *The Audacity of Hope*, 206–7; Ceaser, Busch, and Pitney Jr., *Epic Journey*, 119. On Wright see also Stephen Mansfield, *The Faith of Barack Obama* (Nashville, TN: Thomas Nelson, 2008), 36–43.

16. Obama, *A Promised Land*, 23 and 120; Remnick, *The Bridge*, 520–21; Axelrod, *Believer*, 269–71; Plouffe, *The Audacity to Win*, 207–10.

17. Heilemann and Halperin, *Game Change*, 229–30.

18. Robert Farley, "Obama Served on Board with Ayers," PolitiFact, April 26, 2008, http://www.politifact.com/truth-o-meters/statements/2008/apr/16/hillary-clinton/obama-served-on-board-with-ayers/; Christopher Cooper, "Woods Fund Could Become Obama's 'Swift Boat,'" *Wall Street Journal*, April 18, 2008, https://www.wsj.com/articles/SB120848023736325005; Ezra Klein, "The Woods Fund," *American Prospect*, May 2, 2008, http://prospect.org/article/woods-fund; Drew Griffin and Kathleen Johnston, "Ayers and Obama Crossed Paths on Boards, Record Shows," CNN, October 7, 2008, http://www.cnn.com/2008/POLITICS/10/07/obama.ayers/.

19. Bob Drogin and Dan Morain, "Obama and the Former Radicals," *Los Angeles Times*, April 18, 2008, https://www.latimes.com/archives/la-xpm-2008-apr-18-na-

radicals18-story.html; Ryan Lizza, "Making It: How Chicago Shaped Obama," *New Yorker*, July 21, 2008, https://www.newyorker.com/magazine/2008/07/21/ making-it; Farley, "Obama Served on Board with Ayers"; Cooper, "Woods Fund Could Become Obama's 'Swift Boat.'"

20. Obama, *A Promised Land*, 139–40; Heileman and Halperin, *Game Change*, 231–32; Plouffe, *The Audacity to Win*, 189–203; Axelrod, *Believer*, 266–68; Wolffe, *Renegade*, 203; Ceaser, Busch, and Pitney Jr., *Epic Journey*, 119.

21. Peter Slevin, "Senator Says He Regrets Land Deal with Fund Raiser," LJWorld, December 18, 2006, https://www2.ljworld.com/news/2006/dec/18/ senator_says_he_regrets_land_deal/; Axelrod, *Believer*, 271–72.

22. Christopher Drew and Mike McIntire, "An Obama Patron and Friend until an Indictment," *New York Times*, June 14, 2007, https://www.nytimes.com/2007/06/14/ us/politics/14rezko.html; Robert Farley, "Obama's Rezko Connection," PolitiFact, June 19, 2008, http://politifact.com/truth-o-meter/article/2008/oct/25/obamas-rezko-connection; Slevin, "Obama Says He Regrets Land Deal with Fund Raiser"; Brian Ross and Rhonda Schwartz, "The Rezko Connection: Obama's Achilles Heel?" ABC News, June 2007, https://abcnews.go.com/Blotter/rezko-connection-obamas-achilles-heel/story?id=4111483; Thomas, "A Long Time Coming," 70–71; Remnick, *The Bridge*, 521; Plouffe, *The Audacity to Win*, 196–97.

23. Quoted in "Seven Years Ago Today: Obama's 'A More Perfect Union' Speech," *Constitution Daily* (blog), National Constitution Center, March 18, 2015, https://www. yahoo.com/news/five-years-ago-today-obama-more-perfect-union-102607846. html; Obama, *A Promised Land*, 141. See also Heilemann and Halperin, *Game Change*, 233–35; Wolffe, *Renegade*, 203.

24. Obama, *A Promised Land*, 141–42; Heilemann and Halperin, *Game Change*, 236–37; Remnick, *The Bridge*, 521–22; Plouffe, *The Audacity to Win*, 211–12; Axelrod, *Believer*, 271–73.

25. "Barack Obama's Speech on Race," *New York Times*, March 13, 2008, https://www.nytimes.com/2008/03/18/us/politics/18text-obama.html; Remnick, *The Bridge*, 24; Plouffe, *The Audacity to Win*, 212–13.

26. "Barack Obama's Speech on Race."

27. Ibid.

28. Ibid.

29. Ibid.

30. Ibid.

31. Ibid.; Thomas, "A Long Time Coming," 73–74.

32. "Barack Obama's Speech on Race"; Larissa MacFarquhar, "The Conciliator: Where Is Barack Obama Coming From?" *New Yorker*, May 7, 2007, https://www. newyorker.com/magazine/2007/05/07/the-conciliator; Heilemann and Halperin, *Game Change*, 238.

33. The quote is from "Obama's Speech on Race Draws Diverse Local Reactions," Minnpost, March 3, 2008, https://www.minnpost.com/politics-policy/2008/03/ obamas-speech-race-draws-diverse-local-reactions.

34. The quotes are from Amanda Paulson, "Obama's Speech Opens Up Race Dialogue," *Christian Science Monitor*, March 21, 2008, https://www.csmonitor.com/ USA/Politics/2008/0321/p01s02-uspo.html; "Hardball College Tour at Villanova

University," April 15, 2004, https://www.nbcnews.com/id/wbna24148308. See also Jay Newton-Small, "Reaction to the Obama Speech," *Time Magazine*, March 18, 2008, http://content.time.com/time/politics/article/0,8599,1723442,00.html; Roy Peter Clark, "Why It Worked: A Rhetorical Analysis of Obama's Speech on Race," Poynter, October 20, 2017, https://www.poynter.org/news/why-it-worked-rhetorical-analysis-obamas-speech-race; Remnick, *The Bridge*, 524–27; Plouffe, *The Audacity to Win*, 213–14: Axelrod, *Believer*, 274–75.

35. Marc Ambinder, "Obama's 'Gaffe': Some Perspective," *Atlantic*, April 11, 2008, https://www.theatlantic.com/politics/archive/2008/04/obamas-gaffe-some-perspective/52638/; Allison Keyes, "Obama Catches Flak for Remarks on Working Class," NPR, April 12, 2008, https://www.npr.org/templates/story/story.php?storyId=89588766; Katharine Q. Seelye and Jeff Zeleny, "On the Defensive, Obama Calls His Words Ill-Chosen," *New York Times*, April 13, 2008, https://www.nytimes.com/2008/04/13/us/politics/13campaign.html; Mayhill Fowler, "Obama: No Surprise That Hard-Pressed Pennsylvanians Turn Bitter," HuffPost, April 6, 2008, https://www.huffingtonpost.com/mayhill-fowler/obama-no-surprise-that-ha_b_96188.html; "2008 Democratic Popular Vote," Real Clear Politics, n.d., https://www.realclearpolitics.com/epolls/2008/president/democratic_vote_count.html; Obama, *A Promised Land*, 143–46; Heilemann and Halperin, *Game Change*, 241–42; Plouffe, *The Audacity to Win*, 214–21; Ceaser, Busch, and Pitney Jr., *Epic Journey*, 120–21.

36. Quoted in Remnick, *The Bridge*, 528. See also Plouffe, *The Audacity to Win*, 223–24; Axelrod, *Believer*, 278–79; Heilemann and Halperin, *Game Change*, 245.

37. Quoted in Remnick, *The Bridge*, 530. Obama, *A Promised Land*, 146–47; See also Heilemann and Halperin, *Game Change*, 246–47; Wolffe, *Renegade*, 181–85; Plouffe, *The Audacity to Win*, 224–25.

38. Heilemann and Halperin, *Game Change*, 248–49; Plouffe, *The Audacity to Win*, 230–31.

39. Andy Sullivan, "Democrats in Standoff over Florida, Michigan Votes," Reuters, February 15, 2008, https://www.reuters.com/article/usa-politics-dispute/democrats-in-standoff-over-florida-michigan-votes-idUSN1552334220080215; Michael Luo and John M. Broder, "Delegate Battles Snarl Democrats in Two States," *New York Times*, March 15, 2008, https://www.nytimes.com/2008/03/15/us/politics/15donate.html; John Jackson, "The 2008 Presidential Nominations Process, a Marathon and a Sprint: An Analysis of What Happened and Why," Paul Simon Public Policy Institute, September 7, 2008, https://opensiuc.lib.siu.edu/cgi/viewcontent.cgi?article=1005&context=ppi_papers; Ceaser, Busch, and Pitney Jr., *Epic Journey*, 117; Plouffe, *The Audacity to Win*, 232–33.

40. Michael Falcone, "D.N.C. Cuts Fla., Mich. Votes in Half," *The Caucus* (blog), *New York Times*, May 31, 2008, https://thecaucus.blogs.nytimes.com/2008/05/31/the-dnc-deliberates/?mtrref=www.google.com&gwh=FF73E3F8CD91472B24A5 17735381306B&gwt=pay&assetType=PAYWALL; Jackson, "The 2008 Presidential Nominations Process, a Marathon and a Sprint"; Ceaser, Busch, and Pitney Jr., *Epic Journey*, 117.

41. Remnick, *The Bridge*, 530–31; Plouffe, *The Audacity to Win*, 225–31; Heilemann and Halperin, *Game Change*, 251–59.

42. Wolffe, *Renegade*, 206–7; Plouffe, *The Audacity to Win*, 232–33 and 240–43; Heilemann and Halperin, *Game Change*, 260–61 and 266.

43. "Hillary Clinton Endorses Barack Obama: Transcript," *New York Times*, June 7, 2008, https://www.nytimes.com/2008/06/07/us/politics/07text-clinton.html; "2008 Democratic Popular Vote," Real Clear Politics; Remnick, *The Bridge*, 512–16; Plouffe, *The Audacity to Win*, 233–36 and 243–44; Heilemann and Halperin, *Game Change*, 261–62; Obama, *A Promised Land*, 151.

44. Obama, *A Promised Land*, 150.

45. Ibid., 150.

46. Brooks Jackson, "Obama's Lame Claim about McCain's Money," June 20, 2008, FactCheck.Org, https://www.factcheck.org/2008/06/obamas-lame-claim-about-mccains-money/. See also "The Democratic Debate in Cleveland: Transcript," *New York Times*, February 26, 2008, https://www.nytimes.com/2008/02/26/us/politics/26text-debate.html.

47. Plouffe, *The Audacity to Win*, 247–59; Obama, *A Promised Land*, 152–53; Wolffe, *Renegade*, 211–12; Amy Hollyfield, "McCain Says 'Accept'; Obama Says 'Pursue,'" PolitiFact, March 3, 2008, http://politifact.com/truth-o-meter/statements/2008/mar/03/john-mccain/mccain-says-accept-obama-says-pursue.

48. Plouffe, *The Audacity to Win*, 257–63; Heilemann and Halperin, *Game Change*, 326–27.

49. The full text of Obama's video to his supporters can be found in Jackson, "Obama's Lame Claim about McCain's Money." See also "The Democratic Debate in Cleveland: Transcript."

50. Jackson, "Obama's Lame Claim about McCain's Money." See also "The Democratic Debate in Cleveland: Transcript."

51. In fairness to Obama, his pledge to accept public financing was never absolute. As he later explained, "In February 2007, I proposed a novel way to preserve the strength of the public financing system. My plan requires both major party candidates to agree on a fundraising truce, return excess money from donors, and stay within the public financing system for the general election." In an op-ed in *USA Today* a year later, he used almost exactly the same language in reaffirming his conditional commitment to public financing. "I propose a meaningful agreement in good faith that results in real spending limits," he wrote. "The candidates will have to commit to discouraging cheating by supporters, to refusing fundraising help to outside groups; and to limiting their own parties to legal forms." On the basis of these and other statements, PolitiFacts, which evaluated the truthfulness of candidates' remarks, concluded in March 2008, "It would appear then, from public statements, that Obama and McCain both wanted a publicly funded general election." The point remains, however, that McCain could never accept the terms Obama proposed. Alan Silverlieb, "Analysis: Rejecting Public Funding Won't Hurt Obama," CNN, June 20, 2008, http://www.cnn.com/2008/POLITICS/06/20/obama.financing/;Adam Nagourney and Jeff Zeleny, "Obama Forgoes Public Funds in First for Major Candidate," *New York Times*, June 20, 2008, https://www.nytimes.com/2008/06/20/us/politics/20obamacnd.html; Jackson, "Obama's Lame Claim about McCain's Money"; Plouffe, *The Audacity to Win*.

52. "Public Financing on the Ropes," *New York Times*, June 20, 2008, http://www.nytimes.com/2008/06/20/opinion/20fri1.html; Ewen MacAskill, "Obama Tarnished by Rejecting Public Funds for Election Fight," *Guardian*, June 21, 2008, https://www.theguardian.com/world/2008/jun/21/barackobama.uselections2008; Leslie Wayne, "Obama's Decision Threatens Public Financing System," *New York Times*, June 20, 2008, https://www.nytimes.com/2008/06/20/us/politics/20finance.html; Michael Dobbs, "Obama Reneges on Public Financing," *Washington Post*, June 20, 2009, http://voices.washingtonpost.com/fact-checker/2008/06/obama_reneges_on_public_financ.html; Obama for America Organization, "Sen. Barack Obama-Democratic Nominee for President," n.d., http://p2008.org/cands08/obamamain.html.

53. "Alan Silverleib, "Analysis: Rejecting Public Funding Won't Hurt Obama," CNN, June 20, 2008, http://www.cnn.com/2008/POLITICS/06/20/obama.financing/; Plouffe, *The Audacity to Win*, 237; John K. Wilson, *Barack Obama: This Improbable Quest* (Boulder, CO: Paradigm, 2008), 14–16.

54. Dorothy Wickenden, "What's the Big Idea?" *New Yorker*, June 30, 2008, https://www.newyorker.com/magazine/2008/06/30/whats-the-big-idea; Matthew Mosk, "An Attack That Came Out of the Ether," *Washington Post*, June 2, 2008, http://www.washingtonpost.com/wp-dyn/content/article/2008/06/27/AR2008062703781.html.

55. Barbara Bradley Hagerty, "Obama's Religious Rhetoric Puts Faith in Spotlight," NPR, April 13, 2009, https://www.npr.org/templates/story/story.php?storyId=89598497. See also Wilson, *Barack Obama*, 134–35.

56. "Obama's Speech on Faith and Politics," *New York Times*, June 18, 2006, http://www.nytimes.com/2006/06/28/us/politics/2006obamaspeech.html; Barack Obama, *The Audacity of Hope* (New York: Random House, 2006), 202–4; Lisa Miller, "Barack Obama's Christian Journey," *Newsweek*, July 11, 2008, http://www.newsweek.com/cover-story-barack-obamas—christian-journey-92611.

57. Obama, *The Audacity of Hope*, 204–5; Wilson, *Barack Obama*, 139–40.

58. Mansfield, *The Faith of Barack Obama*, xvi.

59. Jodi Kantor, "Barack Obama's Search for Faith," *New York Times*, April 30, 2007, https://www.nytimes.com/2007/04/30/world/americas/30iht-30obama.5501905.html.

60. Obama, *The Audacity of Hope*, 202 and 206; Wilson, *Barack Obama*, 136.

61. Obama, *The Audacity of Hope*, 206. See also Peniel E. Joseph, "Why the Black Church Has Always Mattered," The Root, June 19, 2015, https://www.theroot.com/why-the-black-church-has-always-mattered-1790860217; Miller, "Barack Obama's Christian Journey."

62. Mansfield, *The Faith of Barack Obama*, 43–47; Kantor, "Barack Obama's Search for Faith"; Wilson, *Barack Obama*, 135–36.

63. Obama, *The Audacity of Hope*, 206–8; Wilson, *Barack Obama*, 138–39; Miller, "Barack Obama's Christian Journey."

64. The text of the speech can be found in "Obama Delivers Speech on Faith in America," *New York Times*, July 1, 2008, https://www.nytimes.com/2008/07/01/us/politics/01obama-text.html. See also Mayhill Fowler, "Obama, God and Governance," HuffPost, July 16, 2008, https://www.huffingtonpost.com/may-

hill-fowler/obamas-faith-based-govern_b_111393.html; Adam Nagourney and Jeff Zeleny, "Obama Takes the Fight to McCain," *New York Times*, August 29, 2008, https://www.nytimes.com/2008/08/29/us/politics/29dems.html; Kantor, "Barack Obama's Search for Faith." For the reaction of skeptics on both the right and the left to Obama's views on faith, see also Wilson, *Barack Obama*, 131–34.

65. Fowler, "Obama, God and Governance."

66. Robert Draper, "The Making (and Remaking) of McCain," *New York Times Magazine*, October 22, 2008, https://www.nytimes.com/2008/10/26/magazine/26mccain-t.html; Ceaser, Busch, and Pitney Jr., *Epic Journey*, 133–34.

67. Inter-University Consortium for Political and Social Research (ICPSR), "Campaign Themes, Strategies, and Developments," n.d., https://www.icpsr.umich.edu/web/pages/instructors/setups2008/campaign-strategies.html; Ceaser, Busch, and Pitney Jr., *Epic Journey*, 135; Remnick, *The Bridge*, 537; Heilemann and Halperin, *Game Change*, 264.

68. Obama, *A Promised Land*, 153–60 and 162–65; Plouffe, *The Audacity to Win*, 271–79; Ceaser, Busch, and Pitney Jr., *Epic Journey*, 135–36; Heilemann and Halperin, *Game Change*, 329–30.

69. Draper, "The Making (and Remaking) of McCain"; Ceaser, Busch, and Pitney Jr., *Epic Journey*, 138.

70. Draper, "The Making (and Remaking) of McCain"; Ceaser, Busch, and Pitney Jr., *Epic Journey*, 138; Jodi Kantor, "A Consistent Yet Elusive Nominee," *New York Times*, August 2, 2008, http://www.nytimes.com/2008/08/28/us/politics/28obamaQM.html; Remnick, *The Bridge*, 542–43.

71. Jennifer Brown, "Obama Accepts Democratic Nomination," *Denver Post*, August 28, 2008, https://www.denverpost.com/2008/08/28/obama-accepts-democratic-nomination/; Ceaser, Busch, and Pitney Jr., *Epic Journey*, 140–41.

72. Obama, *A Promised Land*, 167–68; "Transcript: Barack Obama's Acceptance Speech," NPR, August 28, 2008, https://www.npr.org/templates/story/story.php?storyId=96624326.

73. "Transcript: Barack Obama's Acceptance Speech."

74. Ibid.; Steve Gorman, "Obama Acceptance Speech Believed to Set TV Record," Reuters, August 29, 2008, https://www.reuters.com/article/us-usa-politics-ratings-idUSN2945249120080829. See also Brown, "Obama Accepts Democratic Nomination."

75. Ceaser, Busch, and Pitney Jr., *Epic Journey*.

76. "Evangelicals Energized by McCain-Palin Ticket," *Oklahoman*, August 30, 2008, https://www.oklahoman.com/article/3291041/evangelicals-energized-by-mccain-palin-ticket; "McCain Choose 'Hockey Mom' as Running Mate," *Jackson Free Press*, August 29, 2008, https://www.jacksonfreepress.com/news/2008/aug/29/mccain-chooses-alaska-hockey-mom-as-running-mate/; Toby Harnden, "John McCain Picks Alaska Governor Sarah Palin as Republican Running Mate," *Telegraph*, August 29, 2008, https://www.telegraph.co.uk/news/newstopics/uselection2008/johnmccain/2646415/John-McCain-picks-Alaska-governor-Sarah-Palin-as-Republican-running-mate.html; Draper, "The Making (and Remaking) of McCain"; Ceaser, Busch, and Pitney Jr., *Epic Journey*, 142.

77. "Transcript of Palin's Speech at the Republican National Convention," *New York Times*, September 3, 2008, https://www.nytimes.com/elections/2008/president/conventions/videos/transcripts/20080903_PALIN_SPEECH.html.

78. Obama, *A Promised Land*, 169–70; Michael Calderone, "Media Swoon over Palin's Fiery Speech," *Politico*, September 4, 2008, https://www.politico.com/story/2008/09/media-swoon-over-palins-fiery-speech-013148. See also Mark Halperin, "The Palin Pick: Bold or Disastrous," *Time Magazine*, August 29, 2008, http://content.time.com/time/politics/article/0,8599,1837514,00.html.

79. "Transcript of John McCain's Acceptance Speech," *New York Times*, September 4, 2008, https://www.nytimes.com/elections/2008/president/conventions/videos/transcripts/20080904_MCCAIN_SPEECH.html.

80. Ibid.

81. "Transcript: Barack Obama's Acceptance Speech." See also ICPSR, "Campaign Themes, Strategies, and Developments."

82. "Transcript of John McCain's Acceptance Speech."

83. "Frank Rich Puts Palin in Perspective," September 7, 2008, http://sociologistsforobama.blogspot.com/2008/09/frank-rich-puts-palin-in-perspective.html; John Tolson, "John McCain and Barack Obama: How They Speak to Voters," *U.S. News and World Report*, October 22, 2008, https://www.usnews.com/news/campaign-2008/articles/2008/10/22/mccain-and-obama-how-they-speak-to-voters.

84. John Whitesides, "McCain's Surge: After Convention, He Catches Obama," Reuters, September 3, 2008, https://www.reuters.com/article/us-usa-politics/mccains-surge-after-convention-he-catches-obama-idUSN0847083820080909; Frank Newport, "Republicans' Enthusiasm Jumps after Convention," Gallup, September 8, 2008, https://news.gallup.com/poll/110107/republicans-enthusiasm-jumps-after-convention.aspx; "Gallup Daily: McCain Maintains 5-Point Lead," September 9, 2008, https://news.gallup.com/poll/110143/gallup-daily-mccain-maintains-5point-lead-aspx; "The Palin Phenomenon Drives Campaign Coverage," Pew Research Center, September 8, 2008, http://www.journalism.org/2008/09/08/pej-campaign-coverage-index-september-1-7-2008/; Matthew Mosk, "McCain Gets $7 Million Bounce from Palin Pick," *Washington Post*, August 30, 2008, http://voices.washingtonpost.com/44/2008/08/mccain-gets-7-million-bounce-f.html.

85. Scott Conroy, "Palin's Husband Was Arrested in 1986 for DUI," CBS News, September 2, 2008, https://www.cbsnews.com/news/palins-husband-was-arrested-in-1986-for-dui/; "Is Palin an Evangelical," *Christianity Today*, August 30, 2008, https://www.christianitytoday.com/news/2008/august/is-palin-evangelical.html; Ceaser, Busch, and Pitney Jr., *Epic Journey*, 143. See also Charles Krauthammer, "The Palin Puzzle," *Washington Post*, August 29, 2008, http://voices.washingtonpost.com/postpartisan/2008/08/the_palin_puzzle.html; Ben Smith, "Noonan, Murphy Trash Palin on Hot Mike: It's Over," *Politico*, September 3, 2008, https://www.politico.com/blogs/ben-smith/2008/09/noonan-murphy-trash-palin-on-hot-mike-its-over-011554.

86. Patrick Healy and Michael Luo, "$150,000 Wardrobe for Palin May Alter Tailor-Made Image," *New York Times*, October 22, 2008, https://www.nytimes.com/2008/10/23/us/politics/23palin.html; Michael Joseph Gross, "Sarah Palin's Shopping Spree: Yes, There's More," *Vanity Fair*, October 2010, https://www.vanity

fair.com/news/2010/10/sarah-palin-spending-201010; Jean Cummings, "RNC Shells Out $150K for Palin Fashion," *Politico*, October 21, 2008, https://www.politico.com/story/2008/10/rnc-shells-out-150k-for-palin-fashion-014805; Martin Peretz, "Krauthammer Almost Throws in the Towel," October 3, 2008, https://newrepublic.com/article/44869/krauthammer-almost-throws-the-towel; Katha Pollitt, "The End of Meritocracy," *Guardian*, September 20, 2008, https://www.theguardian.com/commentisfree/cifamerica/2008/sep/29/sarah.palin.feminism.election.

87. Katie Couric, "One on One with Sarah Palin," CBS News, September 24, 2008, https://www.cbsnews.com/news/one-on-one-with-sarah-palin/; "Transcript: Palin and McCain Interview," CBS News, September 30, 2008, https:www.cbsnews.com/news/transcript-palin-and-mccain-interview/; Nico Pitney, "Palin Talks Russia with Katie Couric," Huffington Post, November 3, 2008, https://www.huffingtonpost.com/2008/09/25/palin-talks-russia-with-k_n_129318.html; Tim Mak, "5 Best Couric-Palin Moments," *Politico*, April 2, 2012, https://www.politico.com/story/2012/04/5-best-couric-palin-2008-moments-074735.

88. "Tina Fey as Sarah Palin: Katie Couric SNL Skit," Huffington Post, September 27, 2008, https://www.huffingtonpost.com/2008/09/27/tina-fey-as-sarah-palin-k_n_129956.html.

89. Obama, *A Promised Land*, 170; "Post-Debate: Palin Still Seen as Unqualified, a Bump for Biden," Pew Research Center, October 6, 2008, https://www.pewresearch.org/politics/2008/10/06/post-debate-palin-still-seen-as-unqualified-a-bump-for-biden/; Mary Lu Carnevale, "WSJ/NBC Poll: Voters Doubt Palin's Qualifications to Be President," *Wall Street Journal*, September 24, 2008, https://blogs.wsj.com/washwire/2008/09/24/wsjnbc-poll-voters-doubt-palins-qualifications-to-be-president/.

90. Michael Cooper and Dalia Sussman, "Growing Doubts on Palin Take a Toll, Poll Finds," *New York Times*, October 30, 2008, https://www.nytimes.com/2008/10/31/us/politics/31poll.html. "Michael Palin 'Better Running Mate' Than Sarah Palin," *Telegraph*, September 21, 2008, https://www.telegraph.co.uk/news/worldnews/sarah-palin/3043219/Michael-Palin-better-running-mate-than-Sarah-Palin.html; Eric Gorski, "Younger Evangelicals Split over Palin Choice," Fox News, September 14, 2008, https://www.denverpost.com/2008/09/14/younger-evangelicals-split-over-palin/.

91. John K. Wilson, "Obama Media Bias: Little Evidence for Self-Proclaimed 'Lovefest,'" Fair, September 10, 2008, http://fair.org/extra/the-myth-of-pro-obama-media-bias/; Frank Rich, "The Terrorist Barack Hussein Obama," *New York Times*, October 11, 2008, http:www.nytimes.com/2008/10/11/us/politics/11acorn.html; Jim Rutenberg, "The Man Behind the Whispers about Obama," *New York Times*, October 12, 2008, http://www.nytimes.com/2008/10/13/us/politics/13martin.html; Griffin and Johnston, "Ayers and Obama Crossed Paths on Boards, Records Show"; "Anyone Could Do This in Photoshop," Wikileaks, n.d., https://wikileak.org/wiki/Talk:Obama_1961_birth_announcement_from_. . ._announcement_was_first_posted_online_Summer_2008_-_This_is_not_new; Jack Cashill, "Why Obama Is Mum about Harvard," WorldNetDaily, September 11, 2008, http://www.wnd.com/2008/09/74877/; Rich, "The Terrorist Barack Hussein Obama."

92. Stephanie Strom, "On Obama, ACORN, and Voter Registration," *New York Times*, October 10, 2008, http://www.nytimes.com/2008/10/11/us/

politics/11acorn.html; Angie Drobnic Holan, "Project Vote Not 'An Arm of ACORN,'" PolitiFact, October 17, 2008, http://www.politifact.com/truth-o-meter/statements/2008/oct/17/john-mccain/project-vote-not-an-arm-of-acorn/.

93. David Welna, "McCain and Bush: Common Ground on War, Torture," NPR, June 16, 2008, https://www.npr.org/templates/story/story.php?storyId=91560330; Heilemann and Haleperin, *Game Change*, 316.

94. "Top 10 Conservative Endorsements for Obama," *Common Mistakesblog*, November 2, 2008, http://www.commonmistakesblog.com/2008/11/top-10-conservatives-endorsing-obama.html; Ron Chusid, "Peggy Noonan Makes a Case for Barack Obama," *Liberal Values*, October 31, 2008, http://www.liberalvalues blog.com/2008/10/31/peggy-noonan-makes-a-case-for-barack-obama. See also "Christopher Hitchens on Why He's Voting for Obama," *Fox News*, October 21, 2008, http://www.foxnews.com/story/2008/10/21/christopher-hitchens-on-why-voting-for-obama.html.

95. Heilemann and Halperin, *Game Change*, 377–78; Obama, *A Promised Land*, 181–82.

96. Obama, *A Promised Land*, 173–75.

97. Obama, *A Promised Land*, 176–77; Ron Suskind, *Confidence: Wall Street, Washington, and the Education of a President* (New York: HarperCollins, 2011), 104–5 and 109; Ceaser, Busch, and Pitney Jr., *Epic Journey*, 146; Heilemann and Halperin, *Game Change*, 379.

98. Obama, *A Promised Land*, 180–81; Suskind, *Confidence*, 104–5 and 109; Ceaser, Busch, and Pitney Jr., *Epic Journey*, 146; Heilemann and Halperin, *Game Change*, 379.

99. David Brooks, "Ceding the Center," *New York Times*, October 26, 2008, https://www.nytimes.com/2008/10/26/opinion/26brooks.html; Draper, "The Making (and Remaking) of McCain"; Heilemann and Halperin, *Game Change*, 382–84; Ceaser, Busch, and Pitney Jr., *Epic Journey*, 146; Obama, *A Promised Land*, 184–85.

100. Obama's quote is from Heilemann and Halperin, *Game Change*, 388.

101. Obama, *A Promised Land*, 181–90; Ceaser, Busch, and Pitney Jr., *Epic Journey*, 147.

102. "US Election: Full Text of Barack Obama's Speech on the Economy," *Guardian*, October 13, 2008, https://www.theguardian.com/world/2008/oct/13/uselec tions2008-barackobama.

103. "General Election: McCain vs. Obama," Real Clear Politics, November 2008, https://www.realclearpolitics.com/epolls/2008/president/us/general_election_ mccain_vs_obama-225.html; "Washington Post-ABC News Poll," *Washington Post*, October 13, 2008, https://www.washingtonpost.com/wp-srv/politics/polls/post poll_101308.html; Frederick Weill, "The 2008 Election: Polling and Analysis," n.d., n.p., http://www.fweil.com/Elections/2008/Election2008.html#Post.

104. "Election Results 2008," *New York Times*, November 5, 2008, https://www.nytimes.com/elections/2008/results/president/map.html.

105. Obama, *A Promised Land*, 196–202.

106. Adam Nagourney, "The '08 Campaign: Sea Change for Politics as We Know It," *New York Times*, November 3, 2008, https://www.nytimes.com/2008/11/04/us/politics/04memo.html.

5. Landmark Achievement

1. Adam Nagourney, "Obama Wins Election," *New York Times*, November 4, 2008, https://www.nytimes.com/2008/11/05/us/politics/05campaign.html; Peter Walker, "The World Reacts to the New US President," *Guardian*, November 5, 2008, https://www.theguardian.com/world/2008/nov/05/barackobama-uselec tions2008; Election Center, "Obama's Win Sparks Celebrations outside the White House, CNN, November 5, 2008, http://www.cnn.com/2008/POLITICS/11/05/us.reaction/; "Transcript of Election Night Victory Speech, Grant Park, Illinois," November 4, 2008, http://obamaspeeches.com/E11-Barack-Obama-Election-Night-Victory-Speech-Grant-Park-Illinois-November-4-2008.htm. See also Barack Obama, *A Promised Land* (New York: Crown, 2020), 202; David Remnick, *The Bridge: The Life and Rise of Barack Obama* (New York: Vintage, 2010), 558–59; Evan Thomas, *"A Long Time Coming": The Inspiring, Combative 2008 Campaign and the Historic Election of Barack Obama* (New York: Public Affairs, 2009), 183–84.

2. Barack Obama, "First President-Elect Weekly Transition Address," American Rhetoric, November 8, 2008, https://www.americanrhetoric.com/speeches/barackobama/barackobamaweeklytransition1.htm; Obama, *A Promised Land*, 206–8.

3. Obama, "First President-Elect Weekly Transition Address"; Barack Obama, "Second President-Elect Weekly Transition Address," American Rhetoric, November 15, 2008, https://www.americanrhetoric.com/speeches/barackobama/barackobamaweeklytransition2.htm.

4. Obama, "Second President-Elect Weekly Transition Address"; Stanley A. Renshoon, *Barack Obama and the Politics of Redemption* (New York: Routledge, 2012), 6–8.

5. The literature on the financial crisis in 2008 and 2009 is extensive, but see especially Andrew Ross Sorkin, *Too Big to Fail: The Inside Story of How Wall Street and Washington Fought to Save the Financial System—and Themselves* (New York: Viking, 2009); Ron Suskind, *Confidence Men: Wall Street, Washington, and the Education of a President* (New York: HarperCollins, 2011); Henry M. Paulson Jr., *On The Brink: Inside the Race to Stop the Collapse of the Global Financial System* (New York: Business Plus, 2010); Timothy F. Geithner, *Stress Test: Reflections on Financial Crises* (New York: Broadway, 2014); Ben Bernanke, *The Courage to Act: A Memoir of a Crisis and Its Aftermath* (New York: W. W. Norton, 2015).

6. Suskind, *Confidence Men*, 133–57.

7. Ibid., 133–35; Obama, *A Promised Land*, 212–14.

8. Barack Obama, "Senate Floor Speech in Support of the Wall Street Bailout Bill," American Rhetoric, October 1, 2008, https://americanrhetoric.com/speeches/barackobama/barackobamasenatespeechonbailoutbill.htm.

9. Ibid.

10. "US Election: Full Text of Barack Obama's Speech on the Economy," *Guardian*, October 13, 2008, https://www.theguardian.com/world/2008/oct/13/uselec tions2008-barackobama.

11. Obama, *A Promised Land*, 211–14; Suskind, *Confidence Men*, 133–58.

12. Suskind, *Confidence Men*, 82; Geithner, *Stress Test*, 2–3 and 23–77; Michael Grunwald, *The New New Deal: The Hidden Story of Change in the Obama Era* (New York: Simon and Schuster, 2012), 76–83 and 98–103.

13. Andy Kroll, "Six Ways the Financial Bailout Scams Taxpayers," *Mother Jones*, May 26, 2009, https:///www.motherjones.com//politics//2009/05/six-ways-financial-bailout-scams-taxpayers.

14. James T. Kloppenberg, *Reading Obama: Dreams, Hope, and the American Political Tradition* (Princeton, NJ: Princeton University Press, 2011), 225–28.

15. See chapter 2.

16. David Axelrod, *Believer: My Forty Years in Politics* (New York: Penguin, 2015), 324.

17. "Paul Krugman Interview on American Morning," American Morning, December 3, 2008, http://www.pkarchive.org/economy/CNNAM120308.html; "Paul Krugman on Obama's Economic Priorities," MSNBC, November 7, 2008, https://www.thenation.com/article/paul-krugman-obamas-economic-priorities/; "Transcript: The Rachel Maddow Show," NBC, November 19, 2008, web page no longer available. See also Paul Krugman, "The Obama Agenda," *New York Times*, November 7, 2008, https://www.nytimes.com/2008/11/07/opinion/07krugman.html; Suskind, *Confidence Men*, 153–54; Peter Baker, *Obama: The Call of History* (New York: Callaway, 2017), 22.

18. Obama, *A Promised Land*, 237–39; Grunwald, *The New New Deal*, 58–61; Suskind, *Confidence Men*, 153–54; Baker, *Obama: The Call of History*, 22.

19. Obama, *A Promised Land*, 221.

20. Ibid., 221–23 and 238–39.

21. Carl Hulse, "Obama Is Sworn In as the 44th President," *New York Times*, January 20, 2009, https://www.nytimes.com/2009/01/21/us/politics/20web-inaug2.html; Suskind, *Confidence Men*, 155–56.

22. Barack Obama, "First Presidential Inaugural Address," American Rhetoric, January 20, 2009, https://www.americanrhetoric.com/speeches/barackobama/barackobamainauguraladdress.htm. See also Suskind, *Confidence Men*, 156–57.

23. "Obama's Inaugural Address Draws Some Criticism," Huffington Post, February 21, 2009, https://www.huffpost.com/entry/obamas-inaugural-address_n_159713; Robert Schlesinger, "Expert Reaction to the Obama Inaugural," January 20, 2009, https://www.usnews.com/opinion/blogs/robert-schlesinger/2009/01/20/expert-reaction-to-the-obama-inaugural; Jonathan Raban, "The Golden Trumpet," *Guardian*, January 23, 2009, https://www.theguardian.com/world/2009/jan/24/barack-obama-inauguration-speech-presidency-president-review-jonathan-raban; David E. Sanger, "Rejecting Bush Era, Reclaiming Values," *New York Times*, January 20, 2009, https://www.nytimes.com/2009/01/21/us/politics/21assess.html; Obama, *A Promised Land*, 230.

24. Editorial Board, "President Obama," *New York Times*, January 20, 2009, https://www.nytimes.com/2009/01/21/opinion/21wed1.html; "Mr. Obama's Summons," *Washington Post*, January 21, 2009, http://www.washingtonpost.com/wp-dyn/content/article/2009/01/20/AR2009012003555.html; Susan Salter Reynolds, "Writers Praise Barack Obama's Inaugural Address," *Los Angeles Times*, January 21, 2009, https://www.latimes.com/archives/la-xpm-2009-jan-21-na-inaug-literati21-story.html; Roy Peter Clark, "Obama's Inauguration Speech Relies on the Rhetoric of Responsibility," Poynter, January 20, 2009, https://www.poynter.org/news/obamas-inauguration-speech-relies-rhetoric-responsibility.

25. Obama, *A Promised Land*, 208–9.

26. Ibid., 211, 224–23; Sheryl Gay Stolberg, "Richardson Won't Pursue Cabinet Post," *New York Times*, January 4, 2009, https://www.nytimes.com/2009/01/05/us/politics/05richardson.html; Michael. D. Shear, "Richardson Withdraws Name as Commerce Secretary-Designee," *Washington Post*, January 4, 2009, http://voices.washingtonpost.com/44/2009/01/04//richardson_withdraws_as_commer.html; "Tom Daschle Becomes Latest of President Barack Obama's Cabinet Picks Mired in Minor Scandal," *NY Daily News*, January 31, 2009, http://www.nydailynews.com/news/politics/tom-daschle-latest-president-barack-obama-cabinet-picks-mired-minor-scandal-article-1.366499#; The Politico, "Daschle Withdraws Nomination," CBS News, February 3, 2009, https://www.cbsnews.com/news/daschle-withdraws-nomination/; Jeff Zeleny and David Stout, "Daschle Withdraws as Cabinet Nominee," *New York Times*, February 3, 2009, https://www.nytimes.com/2009/02/04/world/americas/04iht-04obama.19911311.html.

27. "Quotes from Barack Obama in His First 100 Days as President," *South Florida South Sentinel*, April 25, 2009, https://www.sun-sentinel.com/news/politics/sfl-obama-100-042609quotes-story.html.

28. Eric Rauchway, "Neither a Depression nor a New Deal: Bailout, Stimulus, and the Economy," in *The Presidency of Barack Obama: A First Historical Assessment*, ed. Julian E. Zelizer (Princeton, NJ: Princeton University Press, 2018), 42–43; Grunwald, *The New New Deal*, 26–80; Michael D'Antonio, *A Consequential President: The Legacy of Barack Obama* (New York: Thomas Dunne Books, 2016), 18–19 and 29–31.

29. "Obama and Conservatives Break Bread at George Will's House," Huffington Post, January 13, 2009, https://www.huffpost.com/entry/obamas-dinner-with-conser_n_157701; Sheryl Gay Stolberg, "Obama Signs Equal-Pay Legislation," *New York Times*, January 29, 2009, http://www.nytimes.com/2009/01/30/us/politics/30ledbetter-web.html; Heidi Brown, "Equal Payback for Lilly Ledbetter," *Forbes*, April 28, 2009, https://www.forbes.com//2009/04/28/equal-pay-discrimination-forbes-woman-leadership-wages.html; Lilly Ledbetter and Linda Hallman, "For Women, What a Difference a Year Almost Made," Huffington Post, March 31, 2010, https://www.huffpost.com/entry/for-women-what-a-differen_b_436113; Obama, *A Promised Land*, 234.

30. Barack Obama, "First Presidential Weekly Address," American Rhetoric, January 24, 2009, https://americanrhetoric.com/speeches/barackobama/weeklyaddresses/barackobamaweekly1.htm; Barack Obama, "First Presidential Prime Time Press Conference," American Rhetoric, February 9, 2009, https://americanrhetoric.com/speeches/barackobama/barackobamafirstprimetimepressconference.htm.

31. Obama, "First Presidential Prime Time Press Conference," February 9, 2009.

32. Dan Froomkin, "White House Watch: A Missed Opportunity," *Washington Post*, February 10, 2009, http://voices.washingtonpost.com/white-house-watch/financial-crisis/a-missed-opportunity.html; and Anne E. Kornblut and Michael A. Fletcher, "Obama Says Economic Crisis Comes First," *Washington Post*, February 10, 2009, https://www.washingtonpost.com/wp-dyn/content/article/2009/02/09/AR2009020903430.html.

33. Froomkin, "White House Watch: A Missed Opportunity"; Martha Joynt Kumar, "Obama Meets the Press—on His Terms," Real Clear Politics, August 29,

2015, https://www.realclearpolitics.com/articles/2015/08/29/obama_meets_the_press_--_on_his_terms_127907.html.

34. Peter Baker, "Obama Sternly Takes On His Critics," New York Times, February 9, 2009, https://www.nytimes.com/2009/02/10/us/politics/10assess.html.

35. Grunwald, The New New Deal, 298–308.

36. Steven Rattner, Overhaul: An Insider's Account of the Obama Administration's Emergency Rescue of the Auto Industry (Boston: Houghton Mifflin, 2010), 12–47; Steven Rattner, "The Auto Bailout: How We Did It," CNNMoney, October 21, 2009, https://money.cnn.com/2009//10/21/autos/auto_bailout_rattner.fortune/; Obama, A Promised Land, 297–98; Susskind, Confidence Men, 221–27; D'Antonio, A Consequential President, 58–59.

37. Obama, A Promised Land, 297–301; Eugene Robinson, "Eugene Robinson: GOP Senators Were Foolish to Oppose the Detroit Bailout," East Bay Times, December 16, 2008, https://www.eastbaytimes.com/2008/12/16/eugene-robinson-gop-senators-were-foolish-to-oppose-the-detroit-bailout/.

38. Charles Krauthammer, "A Lemon of a Bailout," Washington Post, November 14, 2008, http://washingtonpost.com/wp-dyn/content/article/2008/11/13/AR2008111303348.html.

39. Jim Rutenberg, Peter Baker, and Bill Vlasic, "Early Resolve: Obama Stand in Auto Crisis," New York Times, April 29, 2009, https://www.nytimes.com/2009/04/29/us/politics/29decide.html; Sheryl Gay Stolberg and Bill Vlasic, "President Gives a Short Lifeline to Carmakers," New York Times, March 30, 2009, https://www.nytimes.com/2009/03/31/business/31auto.html; "Special Report with Brit Hume," Fox News, December 19, 2008, https://www.foxnews.com/story/special-report-panel-on-president-bushs-auto-bailout-illinois-defiant-governor; D'Antonio, A Consequential President, 62–63.

40. "Business Issues in the News," PollingReport.com., n.d., http://www.pollingreport.com/business2.htm; "The Unpopular, Successful Auto Bailout," Prospect, May 24, 2011, https://prospect.org/article/unpopular-successful-auto-bailout/.

41. Obama, A Promised Land, 300–301.

42. Kimberly Amadeo, "Auto Industry Bailout: Was the Big Three Bailout Worth It?" The Balance, October 9, 2018, https://www.thebalance.com/auto-industry-bailout-gm-ford-chrysler-3305670; Peter Weber, "The U.S. Auto Bailout Is Officially Over: Here's What America Lost and Gained," The Week, December 10, 2013, https://theweek.com/articles/454749/auto-bailout-officially-over-heres-what-america-lost-gained.

43. Obama, A Promised Land, 301–6 and 387–91; John Nichols, "The Nation: Obama Pick, Sonia Sotomayor, Reflects America," NPR, May 26, 2009, https://www.npr.org/templates//story/story.php?storyid=104534590; Peter Baker and Jeff Zeleny, "Obama Hails Judge as 'Inspiring,'" New York Times, May 26, 2009, https://www.nytimes.com/2009/05/27//us/politics/27court.html; Text: Obama's Remarks on His Choice of Sotomayor," New York Times, May 26, 2009, https://www.nytimes.com/2009/05/26/us/politics/26obama.sotomayor.text.html. On the ARRA, see especially Grunwald, The New New Deal.

44. These books provide the best introduction to the ACA: The Staff of the Washington Post, Landmark: The Inside Story of America's New Health-Care Law—the

Affordable Care Act—and What It Means for Us All (New York: Public Affairs, 2010); and John E. McDonough, *Inside National Health Reform* (Berkeley: University of California Press, 2011). See also Ezekiel J. Emanuel, *Reinventing American Health Care: How the Affordable Care Act Will Improve Our Terribly Complex, Blatantly Unjust, Outrageously Expensive, Grossly Inefficient, Error Prone System* (New York: Public Affairs, 2014); Elizabeth Rosenthal, *An American Sickness: How Healthcare Became Big Business and How You Can Take It Back* (New York: Penguin, 2017). For a critical view of the ACA, see David Goldhill, *Catastrophic Care: How American Health Care Killed My Father—and How We Can Fix It* (New York: Alfred A. Knopf, 2013).

45. Emanuel, *Reinventing American Health Care*; Rosenthal, *An American Sickness*; D'Antonio, *A Consequential President*, 82–87; Maurie Backman, "This Is the No.1 Reason Americans File for Bankruptcy," The Motley Fool, May 1, 2017, https://www.fool.com/retirement//2017/05/01/this-is-the-no-1-reason-americans-file-for-bankrup.aspx.

46. The White House: President Barack Obama, "Improving Health for All Americans," n.d. https://obamawhitehouse.archives.gov/the-record/health-care; Scott Conroy, "Obama Unveils Universal Health Care Plan," CBS News, May 29, 2007, https://www.cbsnews.com/news/obama-unveils-universal-health-care-plan/.

47. "Obama '08: Barack Obama's Plan for a Healthy America"; "Remarks of Senator Barack Obama," *New York Times*, May 29, 2007, https://www.nytimes.com/2007/05/29/us/politics/28text-obama.html.

48. Obama, *A Promised Land*, 382–83; "Obama '08: Barack Obama's Plan for a Healthy America"; "Remarks of Senator Barack Obama."

49. "Remarks of Senator Barack Obama."

50. "Transcript: The Democratic Debate in Cleveland," *New York Times*, February 26, 2008, https://www.nytimes.com//2008//02/26/us/politics/26text-debate.html; Kimberly Amadeo, "Hillarycare, the Health Security Act of 1993: Hillarycare, What It Was and Why It Failed," The Balance, December 11, 2018, web page no longer available. Before dropping out of the race in January, John Edwards also favored an individual mandate. See Michael Cooper, "It Was Clinton vs. Obama on Health Care," *New York Times*, November 16, 2007, https://www.nytimes.com/2007/11/16/us/politics/16facts.html; McDonough, *Inside National Health Reform*, 107–16.

51. Obama, *A Promised Land*, 378–79.

52. The Staff of the *Washington Post, Landmark*, 12; Grunwald, *The New New Deal*, 45; Paul Starr, "Achievement without Credit: The Obama Presidency and Inequality," in *The Presidency of Barack Obama: A First Historical Assessment*, ed. Julian E. Zelizer (Princeton, NJ: Princeton University Press, 2018), 53–54.

53. Obama, *A Promised Land*, 377–78; Richard Wolffe, *Revival: The Struggle for Survival inside the Obama White House* (New York: Broadway Paperbacks, 2011), 54–56 and 96–105.

54. Obama, *A Promised Land*, 380–81.

55. Jonathan Oberlander, "Long Time Coming: Why Health Reform Finally Passed," Health Affairs 29, June 2010, https://doi.org/10.1377/hlthaff.2010.0447; Starr, "Achievement without Credit," 54.

56. Barack Obama, "First Speech to a Joint Session of Congress," American Rhetoric, February 24, 2009, https://www.americanrhetoric.com/speeches/

barackobama/barackobamajointsession2009.htm; David Martin, "Obama Calls for Health-Care Reform in 2009," CNN, February 25, 2009, https://www.cnn.com/2009/POLITICS/02/24/obama.health.care/index.html; Wolffe, *Revival*, 90.

57. "Obama's Remarks at the White House Health Care Forum," *New York Times*, March 5, 2009, https://www.nytimes.com/2009/03/05/us/politics/05obama-text.html.

58. Ibid.

59. Oberlander, "Long Time Coming"; Eggert and Connolly, "Health Industry Voices Support for Health Plan."

60. This coordinated approach contrasted sharply with the divisions in the House that had helped doom Clinton's efforts at health reform. Oberlander, "Long Time Coming."

61. Obama, *A Promised Land*, 392–94; "Why 'HillaryCare' Failed and 'ObamaCare' Succeeded," American Health Line, n.d., https://ahlalerts.wordpress.com/2012/07/03/why-hillarycare-failed-and-obamacare-succeeded-2/; Brian Montopoli, "Washington Unplugged: Coburn, Romer on Health Care Battle," CBSNews, March 6, 2009, https://www.cbsnews.com/news/washington-unplugged-coburn-romer-on-health-care-battle/; Oberlander, "Long Time Coming."

62. Oberlander, "Long Time Coming."

63. Obama, *A Promised Land*, 401–2; Ceci Connolly, "Coming This Spring: Health Care Forums in the States," *Washington Post*, March 6, 2009, http://voices.washingtonpost.com/44/2009/03/06/coming_this_spring_health_care.html.

64. "Transcript of Obama's Health Care Speech to Congress," *New York Times*, September 9, 2009, https://www.nytimes.com/2009/09/10/us/politics/10obama.text.html.

65. "Rep. Wilson Shouts, 'You Lie' to Obama during Speech," CNN, September 9, 2009, https://edition.cnn.com/2009/POLITICS/09/09/joe.wilson/.

66. On the complex history of the health care legislation in the Senate Finance Committee, which had been working on a health-care measure since 2008, see Wolffe, *Revival*, 66–68. See also Axelrod, *Believer*, 376–78; Obama, *A Promised Land*, 392.

67. Obama, *A Promised Land*, 392.

68. Helen A. Halpin and Peter Harbage, "The Origins and Demise of the Public Option," Health Affairs 29, June 2010, https://www.healthaffairs.org/doi/10.1377/hlthaff.2010.0363; Max Fisher, "Why Obama Dropped the Public Option," *Atlantic*, February 4, 2010, https://www.theatlantic.com/politics/archive/2010/02/why-obama-dropped-the-public-option/346546/; Jonathan Chait, "Does Obama Prefer the Public Option?" *New Republic*, February 23, 2010, https://newrepublic.com/article/73303/does-obama-prefer-the-public-option; Steve Benen, "Choice and the Public Option," *Washington Monthly*, August 20, 2009, https://washingtonmonthly.com/2009/08/20/choice-and-a-public-option/; Wolffe, *Revival*, 109–10.

69. Obama, *A Promised Land*, 412; Wolffe, *Revival*, 109–10; Axelrod, *Believer*, 381–82.

70. Obama, *A Promised Land*, 416–18; Wolffe, *Revival*, 52–53, 56, and 73–74; Axelrod, *Believer*, 383–87.

71. Obama, *A Promised Land*, 418; Sheryl Gay Stolberg and Robert Pear, "President Urges Focus on Common Ground," *New York Times*, February 25, 2010, https://

www.nytimes.com/2010//02/26/health/policy/26health.html; Axelrod, *Believer*, 387–88.

72. "Highlights from Obama's Health Care Summit," CNN, February 25, 2010, http://www.cnn.com/2010/POLITICS/02/25/health.care.summit.updates/index. html; Obama, *A Promised Land*, 420–22; Stolberg and Pear, "President Urges Focus on Common Ground"; Wolffe, *Revival*, 121–28.

73. McDonough, *Inside National Health Reform*; Obama, *A Promised Land*, 421–26.

74. Sheryl Gay Stolberg and Robert Pear, "Obama Signs Health Care Overhaul Bill, with a Flourish," *New York Times*, March 23, 2010, https://www.nytimes.com/2010/03/24/health/policy/24health.html.

75. McDonough, *Inside National Health Reform*.

76. Ibid., xiii–xiv, 5, 21–23, and 103–39.

6. Quest for a Common Purpose

1. David M. Herszenhorn and Robert Pear, "Health Vote Is Done, but Partisan Debate Rages On," *New York Times*, March 22, 2010, https://www.nytimes.com/2010/03/23/health/policy/23health.html; David M. Herszenhorn and Robert Pear, "Final Votes in Congress Cap Battle on Health Bill," *New York Times*, March 25, 2010, https://www.nytimes.com/2010/03/26/health/policy/26health.html; "Public Approval of Health Care Law," Real Clear Politics, n.d., https://www.realclearpolitics.com/epolls/other/obama_and_democrats_health_care_plan-1130.html.

2. Herszenhorn and Pear, "Health Vote Is Done, but Partisan Debate Rages On"; Herszenhorn and Pear, "Final Votes in Congress Cap Battle on Health Bill."

3. Barack Obama, *A Promised Land* (New York: Crown, 2020), 261, 271–74, 276–77, and 403–7; Robert Draper, *When the Tea Party Came to Town* (New York: Simon and Schuster, 2012), xi–xviii and 20; Russell Berman, "Gallup: Tea Party's Top Concerns Are Debt, Size of Government," *The Hill*, July 5, 2010, https://thehill.com/blogs/blog-briefing-room/news/107193-gallup-tea-partys-top-concerns-are-debt-size-of-government; "Comments on the Tea Party Movement," April 20, 2010, web page no longer available; Jonathan Alter, *The Promise: President Obama, Year One* (New York: Simon and Schuster, 2010), 263–64; Draper, *When the Tea Party Came to Town*, 20.

4. David Barstow, "Tea Party Lights Fuse for Rebellion on Right," *New York Times*, April 16, 2010, https://archive.nytimes.com/www.nytimes.com/2010/02/16/us/politics/16teaparty.html; Will Bunch, "Karl Rove and the Tea Party: What Really Happened," Huffington Post, September 20, 2010, https://www.huffpost.com/entry/karl-rove-and-the-tea-par_b_732487; "Comments on the Tea Party"; Alter, *The Promise*, 274–75; Obama, *A Promised Land*, 405.

5. Alter, *The Promise*, 274; H. A. Goodman, "Tea Party Hatred of Obama Has Always Been about Race—'War on Whites' Philosophy Confirms This," Huffington Post, August 5, 2014, https://www.huffpost.com/entry/tea-party-hatred-of-obama_b_5650966; Barstow, "Tea Party Lights Fuse for Rebellion on Right"; Gary Gerstle, "Civic Ideals, Race, and the Nation in the Age of Obama," in *The Presidency of Barack Obama: A First Historical Assessment*, ed. Julian E. Zelizer (Princeton, NJ: Princeton University Press, 2018), 272–75.

6. Barstow, "Tea Party Lights Fuse for Rebellion on Right"; Alter, *The Promise*, 276.

7. Obama, *A Promised Land*, 405–7; Barack Obama, interview by Matt Lauer, "Today Show," NBC, March 30, 2010, https://www.presidency.ucsb.edu/documents/interview-with-matt-lauer-nbcs-today-0.

8. "Obama Makes Light of Anti-Tax Protestors," Associated Press, April 15, 2010, https://www.cleveland.com/nation/2010/04/obama_makes_light_of_anti-tax.html; Patrik Jonsson, "Obama's 'Tea Party' Complex," *Christian Science Monitor*, April 17, 2010, https://www.csmonitor.com/USA/Politics/2010/0417/Obama-s-tea-party-complex; Stephanie Condon, "Conservatives Upset with Obama's Reference to 'Tea Baggers,'" "CBS Interactive," CBS News, May 4, 2010, https://www.cbsnews.com/news/conservatives-upset-with-obamas-reference-to-tea-baggers/; Jared Keller, "Obama Calls Tea Partiers 'Tea-Baggers,'" *Atlantic*, May 4, 2010, https://www.theatlantic.com/politics/archive/2010/05/obama-calls-tea-partiers-tea-baggers/340942/; Alter, *The Promise*, 279.

9. Kenneth T. Walsh, "Obama Says Race a Key Component in Tea Party Protests," *U.S. News and World Report*, March 2, 2011, www.usnews.com.

10. John Hinderaker, "Tea Party vs. Obama," *PowerLine* (blog), April 5, 2010, https://www.powerlineblog.com/archives/2010/04/025998.php; Walsh, "Obama Says Race a Key Component in Tea Party Protests."

11. Walsh, "Obama Says Race a Key Component in Tea Party Protests."

12. Sheryl Gay Stolberg, "Disappointed Supporters Question Obama," *New York Times*, September 20, 2010, https://www.nytimes.com/2010//09/21/us/politics/21obama.html.

13. Figures are from the US Bureau of Labor Statistics, https://www.bls.gov/news.release/archives/empsit_02052010.pdf.

14. "Transcript: President Obama Delivers Remarks at Georgetown University," *Washington Post*, April 14, 2009, https://www.washingtonpost.com/wp-srv/politics/documents/Obama_Economy_Georgetown.html.

15. "Obama Hitler Billboard Removed," CBS News, July 14, 2010, https://www.cbsnews.com/news/billboard-linking-obama-to-hitler-lenin-removed/; Richard Wolffe, *Revival: The Struggle for Survival inside the Obama White House* (New York: Broadway Paperbacks, 2011), 193–97.

16. Quoted in Stolberg, "Disappointed Supporters Question Obama."

17. Quoted in Jason Easley, "Obama Sets a Tea Party Trap," PoliticusUSA, September 20, 2010, https://www.politicususa.com/2010/09//20/obama-tea-party.html.

18. Wolffe, *Revival*, 193.

19. Jeremi Suri, "Liberal Internationalism, Law, and the First African American President," in *The Presidency of Barack Obama: A First Historical Assessment*, ed. Julian E. Zelizer (Princeton, NJ: Princeton University Press, 2018), 195.

20. Barack Obama, "First Presidential Inaugural Address," American Rhetoric, January 20, 2009, https://www.americanrhetoric.com/speeches/barackobama/barackobamainauguraladdress.htm.

21. Amy Belasco, "Troop Levels in the Afghan and Iraq Wars, FY2001–FY2012: Costs and Other Potential Issues," *Congressional Research Service*, July 2, 2009, https://

fas.org/sgp/crs/natsec/R40682.pdf; Bob Woodward, *Obama's Wars* (New York: Simon and Schuster, 2010), 3; Barack Obama, "Address to the People of Berlin," American Rhetoric, July 24, 2008, https://americanrhetoric.com/speeches/barackobamaberlinspeech.htm; Obama, *A Promised Land*, 315–19.

22. "Obama, "First Presidential Inaugural Address"; Barack Obama, "Al Arabiya Television Interview with Hisham Melhem," American Rhetoric, January 26, 2009, https://www.americanrhetoric.com/speeches/barackobama/barackobamaalarabiya.htm; George Packer, "The Last Mission: Richard Holbrooke's Plan to Avoid the Mistakes of Vietnam in Afghanistan," *New Yorker*, September 28, 2009, http://www.newyorker.com/magazine/2009/09/28/the-last-mission; Robert M. Gates, *Duty: Memoirs of a Secretary at War* (New York: Alfred A. Knopf, 2014), 337; Alter, *The Promise*, 373–74.

23. Woodward, *Obama's Wars*, 76–98 and 107–10.

24. Ben Rhodes, *The World as It Is: A Memoir of the Obama White House* (New York: Random House, 2018), 65–66; Woodward, *Obama's Wars*, 3; Packer, "The Last Mission"; Alter, *The Promise*, 132–33, 366–67, and 375; Gates, *Duty*, 336–39; Obama, *A Promised Land*, 318.

25. As quoted in Packer, "The Last Mission"; Gates, *Duty*, 340 and 342–43. On the use of drones, see also Daniel Klaidman, *Kill or Capture: The War on Terror and the Soul of the Obama Presidency* (Boston: Mariner Books, 2013), 18–19, 215–20, and 261–65.

26. Barack Obama, "Post G20 Economic Summit Remarks and Press Conference," American Rhetoric, April 2, 2009, https://www.americanrhetoric.com/speeches/barackobama/barackobamag20summitpressconference.htm; Barack Obama, "Address in Strasbourg Town Hall," American Rhetoric, April 3, 2009, https://www.americanrhetoric.com/speeches/barackobama/barackobamastrasbourgspeech.htm; Obama, *A Promised Land*, 346.

27. Barack Obama, "Speech at Hradcany Square in Prague," American Rhetoric, April 5, 2009, https://www.americanrhetoric.com/speeches/barackobama/barackobamapraguespeech.htm; Obama, *A Promised Land*, 346–47; Alter, *The Promise*, 352–55.

28. Barack Obama, "Speech to the Turkish Parliament," American Rhetoric, April 6, 2009, https://www.americanrhetoric.com/speeches/barackobama/barackobamaturkishparliament.htm.

29. "London Summit—Leaders' Statement," April 2, 2009, https://www.imf.org/external/np/sec/pr/2009/pdf/g20_040209.pdf; "The Art of Persuasion at the G-20 Summit," *New York Times*, April 1, 2009, https://www.nytimes.com/2009/04/03/world/europe/03summit.html; Mark Landler and David E. Sanger, "World Leaders Pledge $1.1 Trillion for Crisis," *New York Times*, April 2, 2009, https://www.nytimes.com/2009/04/03/world/europe/03summit.html; Nicholas Watt, "G20: Sarkozy's Empty-Chair Threat Shows EU Fails to Realise Times Have Changed," *Guardian*, April 1, 2009, https://www.theguardian.com/politics/blog/2009/apr/01/sarkozy-obama-eu; Obama, "Post G20 Economic Summit Remarks and Press Conference"; John Vinocur, "Analyzing Obama's European Tour," *New York Times*, April 13, 2009, https://www.nytimes.com/2009/04/14/world/europe/14iht-politicus.html. See also Rhodes, *The World as It Is*," 40–44; Obama, *A Promised Land*, 345–46.

30. Dan Froomkin, "Obama to Europe: No More Excuses," *Washington Post*, April 3, 2009, http://voices.washingtonpost.com/white-house-watch/afghanistan/007obama-to-europe-no-more-excuse.html; Alter, *The Promise*, 132–33.

31. NATO, "Strasbourg/Kehl Summit Declaration," April 4, 2009, https://www.nato.int/cps/en/natolive/news_52837.htm; NATO, "Summit Declaration on Afghanistan," April 4, 2009, https://www.nato.int/cps/en/natolive/news_52836.htm; "Obama on Afghan Initiative," *Washington Post*, April 3, 2009, https://www.washingtonpost.com/wp-dyn/content/article/2009/04/02/AR2009040203727.html.

32. Packer, "The Last Mission"; Obama, *A Promised Land*, 314–15.

33. Quoted in Alter, *The Promise*, 364. See also Gates, *Duty*, 343–44; Obama, *A Promised Land*, 320–21.

34. Obama, *A Promised Land*, 357–63; Rhodes, *The World as It Is*, 51–53; Jeff Zeleny and Helene Cooper, "Rival Messages as Obama Lands in the Middle East," *New York Times*, June 3, 2009. https://www.nytimes.com/2009/06/04/world/middleeast/04prexy.html.

35. Obama, "First Presidential Inaugural Address"; Obama, "Al Arabiya Television Interview with Hisham Melhem"; David E. Sanger, "Rejecting Bush Era, Reclaiming Values," *New York Times*, January 20, 2009, https://www.nytimes.com/2009/01/21/us/politics/21assess.html; Rhodes, *The World as It Is*, 53–59; Robert Draper, "Barack Obama's Work in Progress," *New York Times*, June 3, 2009, web page no longer available.

36. Barack Obama, "A New Beginning: Speech at Cairo University," American Rhetoric, June 4, 2009, https://www.americanrhetoric.com/speeches/barackobama/barackobamacairouniversity.htm; Nazila Fathi, "Iran to Sign Inspection Pact On Atomic Sites," *New York Times*, December 18, 2003, https://www.nytimes.com/2003/12/18/world/iran-to-sign-inspection-pact-on-atomic-sites.html; "Iran Signs Nuclear Inspection Treaty," *Guardian*, December 18, 2003, https://www.theguardian.com/world/2003/dec/18/iran.

37. Obama, "A New Beginning: Speech at Cairo University"; Hauser and Fathi, "Iran Signs Pact Allowing Inspection of Its Nuclear Sites."

38. Obama, "A New Beginning: Speech at Cairo University."

39. Editors, "What Obama Said, What the Mideast Heard," *New York Times*, June 4, 2009, https://roomfordebate.blogs.nytimes.com/2009/06/04/what-obama-said-what-the-mideast-heard/; Obama, *A Promised Land*, 366–67.

40. Obama, "A New Beginning: Speech at Cairo University."

41. Woodward, *Obama's Wars*, 159; Obama, *A Promised Land*, 432–33; Alter, *The Promise*, 363.

42. Woodward, *Obama's Wars*, 202–380, but see especially, 324–33; Obama, *A Promised Land*, 433; Alter, *The Promise*, 369–94.

43. "The Nobel Peace Prize for 2009," *Norwegian Nobel Committee*, October 9, 2009, https://www.nobelprize.org/prizes/peace/2009/press-release/; Steven Erlanger and Sheryl Gay Stolberg, "Surprise Nobel for Obama Stirs Praise and Doubts," *New York Times*, October 9, 2009, https://www.nytimes.com/2009/10/10/world/10nobel.html.

44. Obama, *A Promised Land*, 439–40; Huma Khan, Yunji de Nies, and Karen Travers, "Obama on Nobel Prize Win: 'This Is Not How I Expected to Wake Up This

Morning,'" ABC News, October 9, 2009, https://abcnews.go.com/Politicd/presi dent-obama-wins-nobel-peace-prize/story?id=8788973.

45. Jeffrey A. Bader, *Obama and China's Rise: An Insider's Account of America's Asia Strategy* (Washington, DC: Brookings Institution Press, 2012), 48–69.

46. "Remarks by President Barack Obama at Suntory Hall," *Office of the Press Secretary, The White House,* November 14, 2009, https://obamawhitehouse. archives.gov/the-press-office/remarks-president-barack-obama-suntory-hall; Obama, *A Promised Land,* 477–78; Sheila Smith, Joshua Kurlantzick, Elizabeth Economy, and Scott Snyder, "President Obama Tours Asia," Council on Foreign Relations, November 3, 2009, https://www.cfr.org/expert-roundup/president-obama-tours-asia.

47. Bader, *Obama and China's Rise,* 1–17 and 94–96; Obama, *A Promised Land,* 479.

48. Quoted in Meg Jacobs, "Obama's Fight against Global Warming," in *The Presidency of Barack Obama: A First Historical Assessment,* ed. Julian E. Zelizer (Princeton, NJ: Princeton University Press, 2018), 62–67.

49. Tom Cohen, "Obama to Seek Stronger Ties on Asian Trip," CNN, November 10, 2009, https://www.cnn.com/2009/POLITICS/11/10/obama.asia.trip/index.html.

50. Michael Auslin, Michael Green, Victor Cha, et al., "Foreign Policy Specialists Assess Obama's Trip to Asia," *Washington Post,* November 22, 2009, https://www. washingtonpost.com/wp-dyn/content/article/2009/11/20/AR2009112003594. html.

51. Bader, *Obama and China's Rise,* 48–52.

52. Ibid., 48 and 54–56; Helene Cooper, "China Holds Firm on Major Issues in Obama's Visit," *New York Times,* November 17, 2009, https://www.nytimes. com/2009/11/18/world/asia/18prexy/html; Helene Cooper, Michael Wines, and David E. Sanger, "China's Role as Lender Alters Obama's Visit," *New York Times,* November 14, 2009, https://www.nytimes.com/2009/11/15/world/asia/15china. html.

53. Bader, *Obama and China's Rise,* 57–60.

54. Cooper, "China Holds Firm on Major Issues."

55. Rhodes, *The World as It Is,* 72–81; "Hu Jintao and Barack Obama, Remarks on Their Meetings and Joint Statement," USC US-China Institute, November 17, 2009, https://china.usc.edu/hu-jintao-and-barack-obama-remarks-their-meetings-and-joint-statement-nov-17-2009; "U.S.-China Joint Statement," *Office of the Press Secretary, The White House,* November 18, 2009, https://obamawhitehouse.archives.gov/the-press-office/2011/01/19/us-china-joint-statement. See also Obama, *A Promised Land,* 479–48.

56. "Full Transcript: President Obama's Speech on Afghanistan," ABC News, December 1, 2009, https://abcnews.go.com/Politics/full-transcript-president-obamas-speech-afghanistan-delivered-west/story?id=9220661.

57. Ibid.

58. Ibid.

59. Ibid.

60. Ibid.

61. Obama, *A Promised Land,* 444–45.

62. Jeff Zeleny, "Analyzing Obama's Afghan Speech," *New York Times*, December 1, 2009, https://thecaucus.blogs.nytimes.com/2009/12/01/live-blogging-obamas-afghan-speech/; Gregg Miller, Julian E. Barnes, and Christi Parsons, "'Our Security Is at Stake,' Obama Says in Ordering Surge to Afghanistan," *Chicago Tribune*, December 12, 2009, https://www.chicagotribune.com/news/ct-xpm-2009-12-02-chi-obama-afghan-1202dec02-story.html; "Sarah Palin's Response to Obama's Speech at West Point," Sarah Palin's Facebook page, December 2, 2009.

63. "Full Transcript: President Obama's Speech on Afghanistan."

64. Rhodes, *The World as It Is*, 80–82; Obama, *A Promised Land*, 445–46.

65. David Brooks, "Obama, Gospel and Verse," *New York Times*, April 26, 2007, https://www.nytimes.com/2007/04/26/opinion/26brooks.html. See also Krista Tippett, David Brooks, and E. J. Dionne, "Obama's Theologian: Reinhold Niebuhr and the American President," On Being, August 13, 2009, https://onbeing.org/programs/david-brooks-and-e-j-dionne-obamas-theologian-reinhold; Fred Kaplan, "Obama's War and Peace: How the President Accepted the Nobel While Sending More Troops to Fight in Afghanistan," *Slate*, December 10, 2009, https://slate.com/news-and-politics/2009/12/how-obama-accepted-the-nobel-peace-prize-while-esca-lating-the-war-in-afghanistan.html.

66. Barack Obama, "Nobel Peace Prize for Peace Lecture," American Rhetoric, December 10, 2009, www.americanrhetoric.com/speeches/barackobama/barackobamanobelprizespeech.htm.

67. Ibid.

68. Ibid.

69. Ibid.

70. Ibid.

71. Ibid.

72. Ibid.

73. Ibid.

74. Chris Herlinger and Ecumenical News International, "Obama's Peace Prize Speech Prompts Debate on Ethics of War," *Anglican Journal*, December 11, 2009, https://www.anglicanjournal.com/obamas-peace-prize-speech-prompts-debate-on-ethics-of-war-8852/amp/; Kaplan, "Obama's War and Peace: How the President Accepted the Nobel While Sending More Troops to Fight in Afghanistan"; "Reaction to Obama's Nobel Speech," "All Things Considered," NPR, December 10, 2009, https://www.npr.org/templates/story/story.php?storyId=121304855. See also John Blake, "How Obama's Favorite Theologian Shaped His First Year in Office," CNN, February 5, 2010, http://www.cnn.com/2010/POLITICS/02/05/Obama.theologian/index.html. For an exception to the influence of Niebuhr on Obama, see "Niebuhr and Obama," *Policy Review*, April and May 2009, https://www.hoover.org/research/niebuhr-and-obama.

75. Obama, *A Promised Land*, 590–92.

76. Peter Roff, "Measuring the Size of Election 2010 Republican Sweep," *U.S. News and World Report*, November 20, 2010, https://www.usnews.com/opinion/blogs/peter-roff/2010/11/05/measuring-the-size-of-election-2010s-republican-sweep.

77. "US Midterm Election Results Herald Political Era as Republicans Take House," *Guardian*, November 5, 2010, https://www.theguardian.com/world/2010/nov/03/us-midterm-election-results-tea-party.

78. Quoted in Roff, "Measuring the Size of Election 2010 Republican Sweep."

79. Barack Obama, "Press Conference Following 2010 Congressional Election," American Rhetoric, November 3, 2010, https://www.americanrhetoric.com/speeches/barackobama/barackobamamidtermpresser.htm.

80. Ibid.

81. Ibid.

82. Ibid.

83. Ibid.

84. Paul Starr, "Achievement without Credit: The Obama Presidency and Inequality," in The Presidency of Barack Obama: A First Historical Assessment, ed. Julian E. Zelizer (Princeton, NJ: Princeton University Press, 2018), 59–61; Alter, The Promise, 267–90; William A. Galston, "President Barack Obama's First Two Years: Policy Accomplishments, Political Difficulties," Brookings, November 4, 2010, https://www.brookings.edu/research/president-barack-obamas-first.

85. Obama, A Promised Land, 576–77; Paul Kane and Ben Pershing, "Pelosi Rejects Tax Proposal to Pay for Afghan War," Washington Post, December 3, 2009, http://voices.washingtonpost.com/capitol-briefing/2009/12/pelosi_rejects_tax_proposal_to.html; Woodward, Obama's Wars, 307.

86. Barack Obama, "Address to the Troops in Afghanistan," American Rhetoric, March 28, 2010, https://www.americanrhetoric.com/speeches/barackobama/barackobamatroopsafghanistan.htm; Michael Hastings, "The Runaway General: The Profile That Brought Down McChrystal, Rolling Stone, June 22, 2010, https://www.rollingstone.com/politics/politics-news/the-runaway-general-the-profile-that-brought-down-mcchrystal-192609/; "US Afghan Commander Stanley McChrystal Fired by Obama," BBC, June 24, 2010, https://www.bbc.com/news/10395402; Helene Cooper and David E. Sanger, "Obama Says Afghan Policy Won't Change after Dismissal," New York Times, June 23, 2010, https://www.nytimes.com/2010/06/24/us/politics/24mcchrystal.html. On the firing of McChrystal, see also Obama, A Promised Land, 578–80; Woodward, Obama's Wars, 371–73; Gates, Duty, 487–92; Rhodes, The World as It Is, 83–85.

7. The Comeback President

1. McConnell later claimed that his remarks were taken out of context. Mitch McConnell, The Long Game: A Memoir (New York: Sentinel, 2016), 202–3.

2. Robert Draper, When the Tea Party Came to Town (New York: Simon and Schuster, 2012), 224–27; Barack Obama, A Promised Land (New York: Crown, 2020), 670.

3. Kimberly Amadeo, "Obama Tax Cuts Facts and Consequences: Why Did Obama Extend the Bush Tax Cuts?" The Balance, February 13, 2019, https://www.thebalance.com/obama-tax-cuts-3306330; David M. Herszenhorn and Jackie Calmes, "Tax Deal Suggests New Path for Obama," CNBC, December 7, 2010, https://www.cnbc.com/id/40545954; Montgomery, Murray, and Branigan, "Obama Signs Bill to Extend Bush-Era Tax Cuts for Two More Years."

4. Dan Baltz, "For President Obama, Signing Tax-Cut Bill Makes for a Good Day," Washington Post, December 18, 2010, web page no longer available.

5. Quoted in Baltz, "For President Obama, Signing Tax-Cut Bill Makes for a Good Day"; Timothy Stewart-Winter, "The Gay Rights President," in *The Presidency of Barack Obama: A First Historical Assessment*, ed. Julian E. Zelizer (Princeton, NJ: Princeton University Press, 2018), 97–99; Barack Obama, *A Promised Land*, 591, 603 and 609–10; David Corn, *Showdown: The Inside Story of How Obama Fought Back against Boehner, Cantor, and the Tea Party* (New York: HarperCollins, 2012) 79–82.

6. Stewart-Winter, "The Gay Rights President," 97–99.

7. Stewart-Winter, "The Gay Rights President," 103–6; Corn, *Showdown*, 82–85. On the selection of Rick Warren to deliver the invocation at Obama's inaugural, see, for example, Sally Quinn, "Was Obama's Selection an Inspired Choice or a Blunder?" *Washington Post*, January 9, 2009, http:washingtonpost.com/wp-dyn/content/article/2009/01/19/AR2009011902374.html; Tobin Harshaw, "Invoking Rick Warren," *New York Times*, January 20, 2009, https://opinionator.blogs.nytimes.com/2009/01/20/invoking-rick-warren/.

8. Barack Obama, *A Promised Land*, 608–11.

9. Christine Simmons, "Gays Question Obama 'Don't Ask, Don't Tell' Pledge," *Seattle Times*, October 11, 2009, https://www.seattletimes.com/seattle-news/politics/gays-question-obama-dont-ask-dont-tell-pledge/; Josh Gerstein, "President Obama Offers Little New in Speech to Gay Rights Activists at HRC Dinner," *Politico*, October 10, 2009, http:www.politico.com/news/stories/1009/28156.html.

10 Barack Obama, "First Presidential State of the Union Address," American Rhetoric, January 27, 2010, https://americanrhetoric.com/speeches/stateoftheunion2010.htm; "Obama Calls for 'Don't Ask, Don't Tell' Repeal," CNN, January 27, 2010, http://www.cnn.com/2010/POLITICS/01/27/obama.gays.military/index.html; Barack Obama, *A Promised Land*, 611–14; Corn, *Showdown*, 82–84.

11. Robert Gates, *Duty: Memoirs of a Secretary at War* (New York: Alfred A. Knopf, 2014), 433–36; Corn, *Showdown*, 85–92; Stewart-Winter, "The Gay Rights President," 105–6.

12. John Schwartz, "Judge Orders U.S. Military to Stop 'Don't Ask, Don't Tell,'" *New York Times*, October 12, 2010, https://www.nytimes.com/2010/10/13/us/13military.html; Charlies Savage, "Obama Seeks Stay on Don't Ask, Don't Tell Ruling," *New York Times*, October 14, 2010, https://www.nytimes.com/2010/10/15/us/politics/15military.html; "'Don't Ask, Don't Tell' Policy Ruled Unconstitutional," CNN, September 10, 2010, www.cnn.com/2010/US/09/09/dont.ask.dont.tell/index.html; Ben Smith, "Federal Judge Overturns 'Don't Ask, Don't Tell,'" *Politico*, September 9, 2009, https://www.politico.com/blogs/ben-smith/2010/09/federal-judge-overturns-dont-ask-dont-tell-029123.

13. The quote is from Corn, *Showdown*, 92–93. See also Stewart-Winter, "The Gay Rights President,"105–6.

14. Carl Hulse, "Senate Repeals Ban against Openly Gay Military Personnel," *New York Times*, December 18, 2010, https://www.nytimes.com/2010/12/19/us/politics/19cong.html; "Military Lays Out Plan to Implement Gay Ban Repeal," USA Today, January 29, 2011, https://usatoday30.usatoday.com/news/military/2011-01-29-repeal-implementation_N.htm.

15. Peter Baker and Dan Bilefsky, "Russia and U.S. Sign Nuclear Arms Reduction Pact," *New York Times*, April 8, 2010, https://www.nytimes.com/2010/04/09/

world/europe/09prexy.html; Mark Tran, "Barack Obama Signs Nuclear Treaty with Russia," *Guardian*, April 8, 2010, https://www.theguardian.com/world/2010/apr/08/barack-obama-nuclear-treaty-russia; "Obama, Russian President Sign Arms Treaty," CNN, April 8, 2010, www.cnn.com/2010/POLITICS/04/08/obama.russia.treaty/index.html.

16. "Remarks by President Obama and President Medvedev of Russia at New START Treaty Signing Ceremony and Press Conference," *Office of the Press Secretary, The White House*, April 8, 2010, https://obamawhitehouse.archives.gov/the-press-office/remarks-president-obama-and-president-medvedev-russia-new-start-treaty-signing-cere; Corn, *Showdown*, 104–5.

17. Julian Borger and Ewen MacAskill, "Barack Obama Pledges to Push Nuclear New Start Treaty through Congress," *Guardian*, November 14, 2010, https://www.theguardian.com/world/2010/nov/14/barack-obama-nuclear-treaty-congress; Corn, *Showdown*, 102–4.

18. Barack Obama, "Remarks by the President at a Meeting on the New START Treaty," *Office of the Press Secretary, The White House*, November 10, 2010, https://obamawhitehouse.archives.gov/the-press-office/remarks-president-obama-and-president-medvedev-russia-new-start-treaty-signing-cere; Borger and MacAskill, "Barack Obama Pledges to Push Nuclear New Start Treaty through Congress."

19. "US Senate Approves Nuclear Arms Control Treaty with Russia," *Guardian*, December 22, 2010, https://www.theguardian.com/world/2010/dec/22/us-senate-new-start-approved; "Senate Approves Nuclear Arms Pact with Russia," CBS/AP, December 22, 2010, https://www.cbsnews.com/news/senate-approves-nuclear-arms-pact-with-russia; Barack Obama, *A Promised Land*, 608; Corn, *Showdown*, 106–14.

20. David Lightman and William Douglas, "Obama Wins 67–27 Senate Vote Ensures START Ratification," *McClatchy Newspapers*, December 21, 2010, https://www.mcclatchydc.com/news/politics-government/article24605254.html; "Senate Approves Nuclear Arms Pact with Russia"; Corn, *Showdown*, 114–20.

21. Barack Obama, *A Promised Land*, 603, 609–10, and 618–19.

22. Mary Beth Sheridan and William Branigin, "Senate Ratifies New U.S.-Russia Nuclear Weapons Treaty," *Washington Post*, December 22, 2010, www.washingtonpost.com/wp-dyn/content/article/2010/12/21/AR2010122104371.html; Corn, *Showdown*, 102–3.

23. Mark Memmott, "START Ratification Could Be 'Defining Moment for Obama,'" NPR Newscast, December 21, 2010, https://www.npr.org/sections/thetwo-way/2010/12/21/132228871/start-treaty-ratification-could-be-defining-moment-for-obama; Corey Dade, "Obama: Do You Like Me Yet," NPR Newscast, December 21, 2010, https://www.npr.org/2010/12/22/132235761/obama-do-you-like-me-yet; Corn, *Showdown*, 104–5 and 121.

24. Barack Obama, *A Promised Land*, 619.

25. Kimberly Amadeo, "US Budget Deficit by President," The Balance, March 14, 2019, https://www.thebalance.com/deficit-by-president-what-budget-deficits-hide-3306151; Kimberly Amadeo, "U.S. Budget Deficit by Year, Compared to GDP, Debt Increase and Events," The Balance, n.d., https://www.thebalance.com/us-deficit-by-year-3306306.

July 3, 2013, https://www.cnn.com/2013/07/03/world/meast/egypt-protests/index.html.

51. The quote is from Landler and Cooper, "Obama Seeks a Course of Pragmatism in the Middle East."

52. US Energy Information Administration, "Today in Energy," EIA, March 21, 2011, https://www.eia.gov/todayinenergy/detail.php?id=590; Corey Flintoff, "Where Does America Get Oil? You May Be Surprised," NPR, April 12, 2012, https://www.npr.org/2012/04/11/150444802/where-does-america-get-oil-you-may-be-surprised; Barack Obama, "Remarks on the Historic Revolution in Egypt," American Rhetoric, February 11, 2011, https://americanrhetoric.com/speeches/barackobama/barackobamaegyptrevolution.htm.

53. Barack Obama, "Statement on the 15th Anniversary of the Genocide in Rwanda," in *Public Papers of the Presidents of the United States: Barack Obama* (Washington, DC: Office of the Federal Register, 2008), 464, https://www.presidency.ucsb.edu/documents/statement-the-15th-anniversary-the-genocide-rwanda; Evan Buxbaum, "Tears Mark 15th Anniversary of Rwanda Genocide," CNN, April 7, 2009, http://edition.cnn.com/2009/WORLD/africa/04/07/rwanda.genocide/; Samantha Power, *A Problem from Hell: America and the Age of Genocide* (New York: Basic Books, 2002), esp. 329–89; Barack Obama, "Address on Libya," American Rhetoric, March 18, 2011, https://www.americanrhetoric.com/speeches/barackobama/barackobamalibyawarning.htm; Sanger, *Confront and Conceal*, 337–43; Corn, *Showdown*, 202 and 205–8; Lizza, "The Consequentialist."

54. Eric Schmitt, "U.S. Gives Its Air Power Expansive Role in Libya," *New York Times*, March 28, 2011, https://www.nytimes.com/2011/03/29/us/29military.html; Jennifer Steinhauer, "House Spurns Obama on Libya, but Does Not Cut Funding," *New York Times*, June 24, 2011, https://www.nytimes.com/2011/06/25/us/politics/25powers.html; "Libya Profile—Timeline," BBC News, July 13, 2017, https://www.bbc.com/news/world-africa-13755445.

55. Kareem Fahim, Anthony Shahid, and Rick Gladstone, "Violent End to an Era as Qaddafi Dies in Libya," *New York Times*, October 20, 2011, https://www.nytimes.com/2011/10/21/world/africa/qaddafi-is-killed-as-libyan-forces-take-surt.html.

56. Schmitt, "U.S. Gives Its Air Power Expansive Role in Libya"; Steinhauer, "House Spurns Obama on Libya, but Does Not Cut Funding"; Lizza, "The Consequentialists." See also Gates, *Duty*, 515–16 and 520; Leon Panetta, *Worthy Fights: A Memoir of Leadership in War and Peace* (New York: Penguin, 2014), 310 and 380–82; Corn, *Showdown*, 209–16.

57. Sanger, *Confront and Conceal*, 357.

58. Barack Obama, "Address to the Nation on Libya," American Rhetoric, March 28, 2011, https://www.americanrhetoric.com/speeches/barackobama/barackobamalibyanationspeech.htm; Chris Cillizza, "President Obama's Libya Speech: First Thoughts," *Washington Post*, March 28, 2011, https://www.washingtonpost.com/blogs/the-fix/post/president-obamas-libya-speech-first-thoughts/2011/03/28/AFlfa5qB_blog.html; Corn, *Showdown*, 218–20.

59. Sanger, *Confront and Conceal*, 357–58.

60. Ibid., 358–60.

61. Ibid., 361–63.

62. Ibid., 361.

63. Brian Michael Jenkins, "The 1970s and the Birth of Contemporary Terrorism," *The Hill*, July 30, 2015, https://thehill.com/blogs/pundits-blog/homeland-security/249688-the-1970s-and-the-birth-of-contemporary-terrorism; Peter Bergen and Courtney Schuster, "The Golden Age of Terrorism," CNN, August 21, 2015, https://www.cnn.com/2015/07/28/opinions/bergen-1970s-terrorism/index.html; Simon Rogers, "Four Decades of US Terror Attacks Listed and Detailed," *Guardian*, April 17, 2013, https://www.theguardian.com/news/datablog/2013/apr/17/four-decades-us-terror-attacks-listed-since-1970.

64. David Klaidman, *Kill or Capture: The War on Terror and the Soul of the Obama Presidency* (Boston: Mariner Books, 2013), 18–19, 215–20, 241–47, and 261–65.

65. Ibid., 32 and 43; Charlie Savage, *Power Wars: Inside Obama's Post-9/11 Presidency* (New York: Little, Brown, 2015), 60–67.

66. Klaidman, *Kill or Capture*, 39–43; Savage, *Power Wars*, 67–88.

67. Savage, *Power Wars*, 25–35.

68. Klaidman, *Kill or Capture*, 245–47. Since bin Laden's death a number of books and articles have been written, mostly by journalists, including Carlotta Gall, the bureau chief in Afghanistan for the *New York Times*, and the highly respected investigative reporter Seymour Hersh, disputing the official account of what took place both before and after the raid at Abbottabad. They argue that Pakistan knew about, and was complicit in, killing bin Laden. They even claim that the leader of Al-Qaeda had been under protective custody of the powerful Inter-Services Intelligence (ISI), the intelligence arm of the Pakistani military, which controlled the Taliban and wanted to destabilize the Kabul government because of its close relationship with India. See Carlotta Gall, *The Wrong Enemy: America in Afghanistan, 2001–2014* (New York: Mariner Books, 2014) and Seymour Hersh, *The Killing of Osama bin Laden* (New York: Verso, 2016). At a press conference, White House Press Secretary Josh Earnest denied Hersh's claims, stating that the book was "riddled with inaccuracies and outright falsehoods." Other security analysts rejected Hersh's account. See transcript of Amy Goodman, "Seymour Hersh's New Book Disputes U.S. Account of Bin Laden Killing," Democracy Now, April 26, 2010, https://www.democracynow.org/2016/4/25/part_2_seymour_hershs_new_book; "Pakistan Helped Lead US to Bin Laden," Australian Associated Press, May 3, 2011, web page no longer available. This account is based on my own reading of the pertinent literature, including former president Barack's latest memoirs, *A Promised Land*, 676–700.

69. Barack Obama, *A Promised Land*, 677.

70. The quote is from Mark Bowden, "The Hunt for Geronimo," *Vanity Fair*, October 12, 2012, https://www.vanityfair.com/news/politics/2012/11/inside-osama-bin-laden-assassination-plot. See also Panetta, *Worthy Fights*, 289–92; Nicholas Schmidle, "Getting Bin Laden: What Happened That Night in Abbottabad," *New Yorker*, August 1, 2011, https://www.newyorker.com/magazine/2011/08/08/getting-bin-laden.

71. Massimo Calabresi, "CIA Chief: Pakistan Would Have Jeopardized bin Laden Operation," Forum, May 3, 2011, https://www.ocregister.com/2011/05/03/massimo-calabresi-pakistan-would-have-jeopardized-bin-laden-raid/; Sanger, *Confront and Conceal*, 241–43; Schmidle, "Getting Bin Laden."

72. The quote is from Bowden, "The Hunt for Geronimo"; Panetta, *Worthy Fights*, 294–300, 307–20; Jonathan Alter, *The Center Holds: Obama and His Enemies* (New York: Simon and Schuster, 2013), 144–48; Michelle Obama, *Becoming* (New York: Crown, 2018), 346–47 and 362–64; Barack Obama, *A Promised Land*, 691–92.

73. Schmidle, "Getting Bin Laden"; Alter, *The Center Holds*, 149–50.

74. Schmidle, "Getting Bin Laden"; Alter, *The Center Holds*, 152.

75. Barack Obama, *A Promised Land*, 692; Schmidle, "Getting Bin Laden"; Alter, *The Center Holds*, 151 and 153–55.

76. Adam Rubin, "Phillies Crowd Erupts in 'U-S-A' Cheers," ESPN, May 3, 2011, https://www.espn.com/new-york/mlb/news/story?id=6463361; Alter, *The Center Holds*, 154–57.

77. Mark Halperin and John Heilemann, *Double Down: Game Change 2012* (New York: Penguin, 2013), 23; Alter, *The Center Holds*, 154.

78. Barack Obama, *A Promised Land*, 699.

79. Dan Baltz, *Collision 2012: Obama vs. Romney and the Future of American Elections in America* (New York: Viking, 2013), 35–50; Alter, *The Center Holds*, 174–75.

80. Barack Obama, "Announces Candidacy for 2012 Presidency," American Rhetoric, April 26, 2011, https://www.americanrhetoric.com/speeches/barackobama/barackobama2012prescandidacy.htm.

81. Halperin and Heilemann, *Double Down*, 15–18; Baltz, *Collision 2012*, 41–42; Alter, *The Center Holds*, 14–17.

82. "President Obama Job Approval," Real Clear Politics, January 2017, https://www.realclearpolitics.com/epolls/other/president_obama_job_approval-1044.html; Dan Kopf, "Obama's Approval Rating from His First Day to His Last, in Charts," Quartz, January 20, 2017, https://qz.com/889644/obamas-approval-rating-from-his-first-day-to-his-last-in-charts/; Michael Barbaro, "Donald Trump Clung to 'Birther' Lie for Years, and Still Isn't Apologetic," *New York Times*, September 16, 2016, https://www.nytimes.com/2016/09/17/us/politics/donald-trump-obama-birther.html; Benjy Sarlin, "With Drudge Report's Help, Birthers Latch onto Phony Forgery Theory," April 29, 2011, https://talkingpointsmemo.com/dc/with-drudge-report-s-help-birthers-latch-onto-phony-forgery-theory; "Arpaio: Birth Certificate a Fraud," Associated Press, July 17, 2012, https://www.politico.com/story/2012/07/arpaio-birth-certificate-a-fraud-078645; Victor Zapanta, "Rep. Jean Schmidt Tells Birther: 'I Agree with You,'" ThinkProgress, September 8, 2009, https://archive.thinkprogress.org/rep-jean-schmidt-tells-birther-i-agree-with-you-9a073cb91cdf/; Halperin and Heilemann, *Double Down*, 10–12 and 17–21; Jeffrey M. Jones, "Obama's Job Approval Average Slides to New Low in 11th Quarter," *Gallup*, October 21, 2011, https://news.gallup.com/poll/150230/obama-job-approval-average-slides-new-low-11th-quarter.aspx; Baltz, *Collision 2012*, 42; Alter, *The Center Holds*, 34–35.

83. Barbaro, "Donald Trump Clung to 'Birther' Lie for Years"; Mark Steyn: "Eternally Shifting Sand of Obama's Biography," *Orange County Register*, May 21, 2012, https://www.ocregister.com/2012/05/21/mark-steyn-eternally-shifting-sands-of-obamas-biography/; Bob Unruh, "Mark Steyn Jumps into Obama Eligibility Debate," October 27, 2014, https://www.wnd.com/2014/10/media-star-jumps-into-obama-eligibility-debate/; Alter, *The Center Holds*, 39–40.

84. Barack Obama, "Address on Release of Official Certification of Birth," American Rhetoric, April 27, 2011, https://americanrhetoric.com/speeches/barackobama/barackobamabirthcertificatespeech.htm.

85. Alter, *The Center Holds*, 179; Molly Ball, "Was Mitt Romney a Good Governor," *Atlantic*, May 31, 2012, https://www.theatlantic.com/politics/archive/2012/05/was-mitt-romney-a-good-governor/257942/; Balz, *Collision 2012*, 28–34.

86. James Joyner, "Mitt Romney 2012 GOP Favorite," Outside the Beltway, April 11, 2010, https://www.outsidethebeltway.com/mitt_romney_2012_gop_favorite/; "2012 Republican Presidential Nomination," Real Clear Politics, n.d., https://www.realclearpolitics.com/epolls/2012/president/us/republican_presidential_nomination-1452.html; Alter, *The Center Holds*, 179–90 and 220–22; Baltz, *Collision 2012*, 87–238.

87. Barack Obama, "Address on the Economy at Osawatomie High School," American Rhetoric, December 6, 2011, https://www.americanrhetoric.com/speeches/barackobama/barackobamaosawatomieeconomy.htm; Ken Thomas, "In Osawatomie Speech, Obama Embracing Roosevelt's Middle-Class Appeal," AP, December 6, 2011, https://www.newsmax.com/US/Obama/2011/12/06/id/420043; Alter, *The Center Holds*, 235–36.

88. Barack Obama, "Address on the Economy at Osawatomie High School."

89. Barack Obama, "Address on the Economy at Osawatomie High School"; Benjamin Soskins, "New Republic: Are We Misreading Obama's Speech," NPR, December 2, 2011, https://www.npr.org/2011/12/07/143258671/new-republic-are-we-misreading-obamas-speech.

90. Barack Obama, "Address on the Economy at Osawatomie High School."

91. Ibid.

92. Barack Obama, "Third Presidential State of the Union Address," American Rhetoric, January 24, 2012, https://americanrhetoric.com/speeches/stateofthe union2012.htm.

93. Ibid.

94. Alter, *The Center Holds*.

95. Matt Bai, "Did Barack Obama Save Ohio," *New York Times Magazine*, September 5, 2012, https://www.nytimes.com/2012/09/09/magazine/ohio-economy.html.

96. "Transcript: Michelle Obama's Convention Speech," NPR, September 4, 2012, https://www.npr.org/templates/story/story.php?storyId=93963863; Richard Adams, "Michelle Obama Speaks to the Democratic National Convention—as It Happened," *Guardian*, September 4, 2012, https://www.theguardian.com/world/2012/sep/04/michelle-obama-democratic-convention-live; Tina Daunt, "2012 Democratic Convention: Michelle Obama Receives Rapturous Response during Speech," September 4, 2012, https://www.hollywoodreporter.com/news/general-news/michelle-obama-democratic-national-convention-367983/; Rebecca Shapiro, "Michelle Obama Media Reactions: Pundits Swoon over First Lady's DNC Speech," September 5, 2012, https://www.huffpost.com/entry/michelle-obama-media-reactions-dnc-speech_n_1856453; Tim Mak, "Reviews: Flotus Hits It out of the Park," *Politico*, September 5, 2012, https://www.politico.com/story/2012/09/

reviews-michelle-hits-it-out-of-park-080738; Halperin and Heilemann, *Double Down*, 34–36; Michelle Obama, *Becoming*, 336–39, 347–48, 365–66, and 371–76.

97. Baltz, *Collision 2012*, 340–41; Alter, *The Center Holds*, 206–18.

98. Josh Vorhees and Daniel Politi, "Romney Camp Had No Idea Clint Eastwood Was Going to Talk to a Chair," *Slate*, September 1, 2012, https://slate.com/news-and-politics/2012/09/ann-romney-on-clint-eastwood-his-rnc-speech-was-unique.html; M. J. Lee, "Eastwood's Rambling RNC Speech," *Politico*, August 31, 2012, https://www.politico.com/story/2012/08/clint-eastwoods-rambling-gop-speech-080498; Toby Harnden, "Clint Eastwood Wowed Republican Delegates," *Daily Mail*, August 31, 2012, https://www.dailymail.co.uk/news/article-2196201/Clint-Eastwoods-speech-steals-GOP-2012-convention.html; Mackenzie Weinger, "Paul: I'm an 'Undecided' Voter," *Politico*, August 28, 2012, https://www.politico.com/story/2012/08/ron-paul-im-an-undecided-voter-080301.

99. "Transcript: Mitt Romney's Acceptance Speech," NPR, August 30, 2012, https://www.npr.org/2012/08/30/160357612/transcript-mitt-romneys-accep tance-speech; Jennifer Rubin, "Mitt Romney's Acceptance Speech," *Washington Post*, August 30, 2012, https://www.washingtonpost.com/blogs/right-turn/post/mitt-romneys-acceptance-speech/2012/08/30/f51a3e1c-f2fb-11e1-adc6-87dfa8eff430_blog.html.

100. Scot Lehigh, "Democrats Pay Tribute to Ted Kennedy," *Boston Globe*, September 4, 2012, https://www.bostonglobe.com/news/politics/2012/09/04/democrats-pay-tribute-ted-kennedy-video-montage-democrats-pay-tribute-ted-kennedy-democrats-pay-tribute-ted-kennedy-video-montage/YtWLEe0GhhXzYEMbCF1OxN/story.html; Michael A. Memoli, "Dems Recall Ted Kennedy Defeating Mitt Romney in Senate Race," *Los Angeles Times*, September 4, 2012, https://www.latimes.com/politics/la-xpm-2012-sep-04-la-pn-ted-kennedy-romney-dnc-20120904-story.html.

101. "Transcript of Bill Clinton's Speech to the Democratic National Convention," *New York Times*, September 5, 2012, https://www.nytimes.com/2012/09/05/us/politics/transcript-of-bill-clintons-speech-to-the-democratic-national-convention.html; "'The Man Is Cool on the Outside . . . but He Burns for America Inside': Bill Clinton Heaps Praise on Obama as He Tears into Republicans," *Daily Mail*, September 6, 2012, https://www.dailymail.co.uk/news/article-2198703/Bill-Clintons-speech-heaps-praise-Obama-tears-Republicans-Democratic-National-Convention-2012.html.

102. Barack Obama, "Second Democratic Presidential Nomination Acceptance Speech," American Rhetoric, September 6, 2012, https://www.americanrhetoric.com/speeches/convention2012/barackobama2012dnc.htm; Helene Cooper and Peter Baker, "Obama Makes Case for 2nd Term: 'Harder' Path to 'Better Place,'" *New York Times*, September 6, 2012, https://www.nytimes.com/2012/09/07/us/politics/obama-in-democratic-convention-speech-asks-for-more-time.html; Richard Adams and Adam Gabbatt, "Barack Obama's Speech to the Democratic National Convention—as It Happened," *Guardian*, September 6, 2012, https://www.theguardian.com/world/2012/sep/06/barack-obama-dnc-speech-live; Baltz, *Collision 2012*, 295.

103. Molly Moorhead, "Mitt Romney Says 47 Percent of Americans Pay No Income Tax," PolitiFact, September 18, 2012, https://www.politifact.com/fact-

checks/2012/sep/18/mitt-romney/romney-says-47-percent-americans-pay-no-income-tax/; Dashiell Bennett, "Who Are Mitt Romney's 47%,"*Atlantic*, September 18, 2012, https://www.theatlantic.com/politics/archive/2012/09/who-are-47/323536/.

104. Moorhead, "Mitt Romney Says 47 Percent of Americans Pay No Income Tax"; Bennett, "Who Are Mitt Romney's 47%"; Michael Cooper, "A Closer Look at the 47 Percent," *New York Times*, September 17, 2012, https://theagenda.nytimes.com/post/31758381202/a-closer-look-at-the-47-percent.

105. On this latter point see Chris Cillizza, "Why Romney's '47 Percent' Comment Was So Bad," *Washington Post*, March 4, 2013, https://www.washingtonpost.com/news/the-fix/wp/2013/03/04/why-mitt-romneys-47-percent-comment-was-so-bad/.

106. Adam Nagourney, Ashley Parker, Jim Rutenberg, and Jeff Zeleney, "How a Race in the Balance Went to Obama," *New York Times*, November 7, 2012, https://www.nytimes.com/2012/11/08/us/politics/obama-campaign-clawed-back-after-a-dismal-debate.html; Maeve Reston, "When Romney Trounced," CNN Politics, September 26, 2016, https://www.cnn.com/2016/09/25/politics/obama-debate-election-2012/index.html; Alter, *The Center Holds*, 83–110 and 226; Baltz, *Collision 212*, 326–27; Halperin and Heilemann, *Double Down*, 28.

107. Baltz, *Collision 2012*, 276–78; Alter, *The Center Holds*, 201–6, and 233–35.

108. "Transcript and Audio-First Obama-Romney Debate," NPR, October 3, 2012, https://www.npr.org/2012/10/03/162258551/transcript-first-obama-romney-presidential-debate; Nagourney et al., "How a Race in the Balance Went to Obama"; Ewen MacAskill, "Mitt Romney Comes Out on Top as Obama Stumbles in First Debate," *Guardian*, October 4, 2012, https://www.theguardian.com/world/2012/oct/04/romney-obama-first-presidential-debate.

109. "Transcript and Audio-First Obama-Romney Debate"; Nagourney et al., "How a Race in the Balance Went to Obama"; Jeff Zeleny and Jim Rutenberg, "Obama and Romney, in First Debate, Spar over Fixing the Economy," *New York Times*, October 3, 2012, https://www.nytimes.com/2012/10/04/us/politics/obama-and-romney-hold-first-debate.html; MacAskill, "Mitt Romney Comes Out on Top as Obama Stumbles in First Debate." On Obama's disdain for sound bites, see Alter, *The Center Holds*, 116–20.

110. Anup Kaphie, "Timeline: How the Benghazi Attacks Played Out," *Washington Post*, June 17, 2014, https://www.washingtonpost.com/world/national-security/timeline-how-the-benghazi-attack-played-out/2014/06/17/a5c34e90-f62c-11e3-a3a5-42be35962a52_story.html; Baltz, *Collision 2012*, 312–15.

111. The administration's best defense of the steps taken to defend the American compound in Benghazi is Hillary Clinton, *Hard Choices* (New York: Simon and Schuster Paperbacks, 2014), 316–39. See also Panetta, *Worthy Fights*, 428–30; Baltz, *Collision 2012*, 316–17; Nagourney et al., "How a Race in the Balance Went to Obama"; Dakshayani Shankar, "Five Best Moments from Obama and Romney's 2012 Second Debate," NBC News, October 9, 2016, https://www.nbcnews.com/storyline/2016-presidential-debates/five-best-moments-obama-romney-s-2012-second-debate-n662121.

112. "October 22, 2012 Debate Transcript," Commission on Presidential Debates, October 22, 2012, https://www.debates.org/voter-education/debate-transcripts/

october-22-2012-the-third-obama-romney-presidential-debate/; Tim Dickinson, "The Final Presidential Debate: Four Punches That Knocked Out Mitt Romney," *Rolling Stone*, October 23, 2012, https://www.rollingstone.com/politics/politics-news/the-final-presidential-debate-four-punches-that-knocked-out-mitt-romney-241491/.

113. Nagourney et al., "How a Race in the Balance Went to Obama"; Baltz, *Collision 2012*, 328–29, 345; Alter, *The Center Holds*, 121–33.

114. Nagourney et al., "How a Race in the Balance Went to Obama"; Baltz, *Collision 2012*, 331–32.

115. Baltz, *Collision 2012*, 318–34.

116. Halperin and Heilemann, *Double Down*, 4–6; Baltz, *Collision 2012*, 297–98, 335, and 338; Alter, *The Center Holds*, 95–97.

117. Baltz, *Collision 2012*, 338.

118. Robert Barnes, "Justice Kennedy, the Pivotal Swing Vote on the Supreme Court, Announces His Retirement," *Washington Post*, June 17, 2018, https://www.washingtonpost.com/politics/courts_law/justice-kennedy-the-pivotal-swing-vote-on-the-supreme-court-announces-retirement/2018/06/27/a40a8c64-5932-11e7-a204-ad706461fa4f_story.html.

119. Baltz, *Collision 2012*, 338.

8. Dysfunctional Government

1. Mary Ball, "Republican Wave Sweeps the Midterm Elections," *Atlantic*, November 5, 2014, https://www.theatlantic.com/politics/archive/2014/11/republicans-sweep-the-midterm-elections/382394/; "Republicans Rule House and Senate for First Time in 8 Years," NBC News, November 4, 2014, https://www.nbcnews.com/politics/elections/republicans-rule-house-senate-first-time-8-years-n241126; Dan Pfeiffer, *Yes We (Still) Can: Politics in the Age of Obama, Twitter, and Trump* (New York: Twelve, 2018), 191–92; Ben Rhodes, *The World as It Is: A Memoir of the Obama White House* (New York: Random House, 2018), 361–64; David Axelrod, *Believer: My Forty Years in Politics* (New York: Penguin, 2015), 486–87.

2. Jennifer Steinhauer, "Divided House Passes Tax Deal in End to Latest Fiscal Standoff," *New York Times*, January 1, 2013, https://www.nytimes.com/2013/01/02/us/politics/house-takes-on-fiscal-cliff.html.

3. The quote is from ibid. See also Lori Montgomery and Rosalind S. Helderman, "Congress Approves 'Fiscal Cliff' Measure," *Washington Post*, January 1, 2013, https://www.washingtonpost.com/business/economy/house-members-meet-to-review-senate-passed-cliff-deal/2013/01/01/6e4373cc-5435-11e2-bf3e-76c0a789346f_story.html; Peter Baker, *Obama: The Call of History* (New York: Callaway, 2017), 153.

4. "Transcript of President Obama's News Conference," *New York Times*, November 14, 2012, https://www.nytimes.com/2012/11/14/us/politics/running-transcript-of-president-obamas-press-conference.html.

5. "Transcript of President Obama's News Conference."

6. The comments on Rice's qualification to serve as secretary of state are in Scott Wilson, "Obama Faces Array of Questions at White House News Conference," *Washington Post*, November 14, 2012, https://www.washingtonpost.com/politics/obama-faces-array-of-questions-at-white-house-news-conference/2012/11/14/abac87de-2e7f-11e2-beb2-4b4cf5087636_story.html.

7. Simon Rogers, "Four Decades of US Terror Attacks Listed and Detailed," *Guardian*, April 17, 2013, https://www.theguardian.com/news/datablog/2013/apr/17/four-decades-us-terror-attacks-listed-since-1970.

8. "Just Like Anyone Else's Kids—The Obama Years," History Channel, n.d., https://www.history.com/the-obama-years/newtown.html; Megan Slack, "President Obama Speaks on the Shooting in Connecticut," *Press Office, The White House*, December 14, 2012, https://obamawhitehouse.archives.gov/blog/2012/12/14/president-obama-speaks-shooting-connecticut; Jodi Kantor, "Change Comes after 4 Years, Friends See Shifts in the Obamas," *New York Times*, January 19, 2013, https://www.nytimes.com/2013/01/20/us/politics/after-4-years-friends-see-shifts-in-obamas.html.

9. "President Obama's Speech at Prayer Vigil for Newtown Shooting Victims (Full Transcript)," *Washington Post*, December 16, 2012, https://www.washingtonpost.com/politics/president-obamas-speech-at-prayer-vigil-for-newtown-shooting-victims-full-transcript/2012/12/16/f764bf8a-47dd-11e2-ad54-580638ede391_story.html.

10. "Just Like Anyone Else's Kids—The Obama Years."

11. Barack Obama, "Second Presidential Inaugural Address," American Rhetoric, January 21, 2013, https://americanrhetoric.com/speeches/barackobama/barackobamasecondinauguraladdress.htm; Barack Obama, "Fourth Presidential State of the Union Address," American Rhetoric, February12, 2013, https://americanrhetoric.com/speeches/stateoftheunion2013.htm; Carney's quote is from William A. Galston, "Reaction and Analysis to President Obama's State of the Union," Brookings, February 12, 2013, https://www.brookings.edu/blog/up-front/2013/02/12/reaction-and-analysis-to-president-obamas-2013-state-of-the-union/.

12. United States Senate, "Roll Call Vote 113th Congress—1st Session," April 17, 2013, https://www.senate.gov/legislative/LIS/roll_call_lists/roll_call_vote_cfm.cfm?congress=113&session=1&vote=00004); Jonathan Weisman, "Senate Blocks Drive for Gun Control," *New York Times*, April 17, 2013, https://www.nytimes.com/2013/04/18/us/politics/senate-obama-gun-control.html; Ed O'Keefe and Phillip Rucker, "Gun Control Overhaul Is Defeated in Senate," *Washington Post*, April 17, 2013, https://www.washingtonpost.com/politics/gun-control-overhaul-is-defeated-in-senate/2013/04/17/57eb028a-a77c-11e2-b029-8fb7e977ef71_story.html.

13. John Eligon and Michael Cooper, "Blasts at Boston Marathon Kill 3 and Injure 100," *New York Times*, April 15, 2013, https://www.nytimes.com/2013/04/16/us/explosions-reported-at-site-of-boston-marathon.html; Masha Gessen, "In the Boston Marathon, a Verdict, but Few Answers," *New York Times*, April 8, 2015, https://www.nytimes.com/2015/04/09/opinion/in-the-boston-marathon-bombing-dzhokhar-tsarnaev-verdict-but-few-answers.html.

14. Plouffe's remark can be found in "Just Like Anyone Else's Kids—The Obama Years"; "Obama's Remarks after Senate Gun Votes," *New York Times*, April 17, 2013, https://www.nytimes.com/2013/04/18/us/politics/obamas-remarks-after-senate-gun-votes.html. See also Dan Roberts, "Gun Control: Barack Obama Condemns 'Shameful' Failure to Pass Reform," *Guardian*, April 18, 2013, https://www.theguardian.com/world/2013/apr/18/obama-condemns-senate-gun-reform.

15. Kantor, "Change Comes after 4 Years."

16. Ibid.

17. Only years later would it be disclosed that the IRS also looked at liberal groups seeking tax-exempt status. Peter Baker, *Obama: The Call of History*, new ed. (New York: Callaway Arts and Entertainment, 2019), 238; Micah Cohen, "I.R.S. Approved Dozens of Tea Party Groups Following Congressional Scrutiny," *New York Times*, May 6, 2013, https://fivethirtyeight.com/features/i-r-s-approved-dozens-of-tea-party-groups-following-congressional-scrutiny/; Alan Rappeport, "In Targeting Political Groups, I.R.S. Crossed Party Lines," *New York Times*, October 5, 2017, https://www.nytimes.com/2017/10/05/us/politics/irs-targeting-tea-party-liberals-democrats.html.

18. Gerhard Peters and John T. Woolley, "Barack Obama, Remarks at the White House Correspondents' Association Dinner," *The American Presidency Project*, April 27, 2013, https://www.presidency.ucsb.edu/node/304052; Peter Baker, "Onset of Woes Casts Pall over Obama's Policy Aspirations," *New York Times*, May 15, 2013, https://www.nytimes.com/2013/05/16/us/politics/new-controversies-may-undermine-obama.html Baker, *Obama*, new ed., 240–41; Maureen Dowd, "No Bully in the Pulpit," *New York Times*, April 20, 2013, https://www.nytimes.com/2013/04/21/opinion/sunday/dowd-president-obama-is-no-bully-in-the-pulpit.html.

19. Barack Obama, "Address to the People of Northern Ireland," American Rhetoric, June 17, 2013, https://www.americanrhetoric.com/speeches/barackobama/barackobamanorthernireland.htm; Barack Obama, "Brandenburg Gate Address," American Rhetoric, June 19, 2013, https://americanrhetoric.com/speeches/barackobama/barackobamabrandenburggate.htm; Barack Obama, "University of Cape Town Address," American Rhetoric, June 30, 2013, https://www.americanrhetoric.com/speeches/barackobama/barackobamacapetownuniversity.htm; Louise Boyle, "Obama Braves Blistering Berlin Heat to Make Speech before Invite-Only Crowd of 4,500 (That's 195,500 FEWER Than Last Time He Was in Germany)," *Daily Mail*, June 19, 2013, https://www.dailymail.co.uk/news/article-2344442/Obama-makes-historic-speech-Brandenburg-Gate-Berlin.html.

20. Harriet Sherwood, "Barack Obama Visits Israel in Effort to Boost Relations with Netanyahu," *Guardian*, March 20, 2013, https://www.theguardian.com/world/2013/mar/20/barack-obama-visits-israel; Mark Landler and Jodi Rudoren, "In Israel, Obama Seeks to Offer Reassurance of 'Unbreakable Bonds,'" *New York Times*, March 20, 2013, https://www.nytimes.com/2013/03/21/world/middleeast/obama-arrives-in-israel-for-two-day-trip.html.

21. "Historic Visit Comes to Close, Obama Departs Israel," *Jerusalem Post*, March 22, 2013, https://www.jpost.com/Diplomacy-and-Politics/Obama-to-visit-Herzl-Rabin-graves-as-Israel-trip-concludes-307391; Landler and Rudoren, "In Israel, Obama Seeks to Offer Reassurance of 'Unbreakable Bonds'"; Colleen Curtis, "On Third Day of Middle East Trip, President Obama Visits Jewish and Christian Landmarks," Obama White House Archives, March 22, 2013, https://obamawhitehouse.archives.gov/blog/2013/03/22/third-day-middle-east-trip-president-obama-visits-jewish-and-christian-landmarks.

22. Michael Martinez, "5 Things to Know about Obama's Presidential Visit to Israel," CNN Politics, May 20, 2013, https://edition.cnn.com/2013/03/20/politics/obama-mideast-five-things/index.html; Sherwood, "Barack Obama Visits Israel in

Effort to Boost Relations with Netanyahu"; Curtis, "On Third Day of Middle East Trip, President Obama Visits Jewish and Christian Landmarks."

23. Barack Obama, "Address at the Jerusalem International Convention Center," American Rhetoric, March 21, 2013. https://americanrhetoric.com/speeches/barackobama/barackobamajerusalemconventioncenter.htm; Robert Tait, "Barack Obama Turned Israel's Narrative Back on Them," Telegraph, March 21, 2013, https://www.telegraph.co.uk/news/worldnews/barackobama/9947184/Barack-Obama-turned-Israels-narrative-back-on-them.html.

24. "A Corker of a Speech," Pomegranate (blog), Economist, March 21, 2013, https://www.economist.com/pomegranate/2013/03/21/a-corker-of-a-speech; Tait, "Barack Obama Turned Israel's Narrative Back on Them." See also Landler and Rudoren, "In Israel, Obama Seeks to Offer Reassurance of 'Unbreakable Bonds'"; "Remarks by President Obama and Prime Minister Netanyahu of Israel in Joint Press Conference," Office of the Press Secretary, The White House, March 20, 2013, https://obamawhitehouse.archives.gov/the-press-office/2013/03/20/remarks-president-obama-and-prime-minister-netanyahu-israel-joint-press-; Landler and Rudoren, "In Israel, Obama Seeks to Offer Reassurance of 'Unbreakable Bonds'"; Julie Pace, "Obama, Netanyahu Show Solidarity on Iran and the Mideast," Associated Press, March 20, 2013, https://news.yahoo.com/obama-netanyahu-show-solidarity-iran-234329024--politics.html.

25. David Remnick, "Obama in Israel: A President at Large," New Yorker, March 21, 2013, https://www.newyorker.com/news/daily-comment/obama-in-israel-a-president-at-large; Josh Ruebner, "Obama's Legacy on Israel/Palestine," Institute for Palestinian Studies 46 (2016–2017), https://oldwebsite.palestine-studies.org/jps/fulltext/207365.

26. Daniel Klaidman, Kill or Capture: The War on Terror and the Soul of the Obama Presidency (Boston: Mariner Books, 2013), 21–22, 32, and 42–43.

27. "Obama's Speech on Drone Policy," New York Times, March 24, 2013, https://www.nytimes.com/2013/05/24/us/politics/transcript-of-obamas-speech-on-drone-policy.html.

28. Ibid.

29. Ibid.

30. The quotes can be found in Lesley Clark and Jonathan S. Landay, "Obama Speech Suggests Possible Expansion of Drone Killings," McClatchy, May 23, 2013, https://www.mcclatchydc.com/news/politics-government/white-house/article24749398.html. See also Tom McCarthy, "Obama Speech: 'Perpetual War Will Prove Self-Defeating'—as It Happened," Guardian, May 23, 2013, https://www.theguardian.com/world/2013/may/23/obama-drones-guantanamo-speech-live; Karen DeYoung and Greg Miller, "Obama: U.S. at 'Crossroads' in Fight against Terrorism," Washington Post, May 23, 2013, https://www.washingtonpost.com/politics/obama-outlines-new-rules-for-drones/2013/05/23/1b5918e6-c3cb-11e2-914f-a7aba60512a7_story.html; Danya Greenfield, "Obama's Drone Speech Misses the Mark," Foreign Policy, June 4, 2013, https://foreignpolicy.com/2013/06/04/obamas-drone-speech-misses-the-mark/.

31. Barack Obama, "Remarks by the President to the White House Press Corps," Office of the Press Secretary, The White House, August 20, 2012, https://obamawhite-

house.archives.gov/the-press-office/2012/08/20/remarks-president-white-house-press-corps; Peter Baker, "Off-the-Cuff Obama Line Put U.S. in Bind on Syria," *New York Times*, May 4, 2013, https://www.nytimes.com/2013/05/05/world/middleeast/obamas-vow-on-chemical-weapons-puts-him-in-tough-spot.html.

32. Barack Obama, "Address to the 113th Convention of the Veterans of Foreign Wars," American Rhetoric, July 23, 2012, https://www.americanrhetoric.com/speeches/barackobama/barackobama113vfw.htm. See also "Full Transcript: President Obama's Press Conference with Swedish Prime Minister Fredrik Reinfeldt in Stockholm," *Washington Post*, September 4, 2013, https://www.washingtonpost.com/politics/full-transcript-president-obamas-press-conference-with-swedish-prime-minister-fredrik-reinfeldt-in-stockholm/2013/09/04/35e3e08e-1569-11e3-804b-d3a1a3a18f2c_story.ht.

33. On this point, see Rhodes, *The World as It Is*, 223–40. For a different view, however, see Glenn Kessler, "President Obama and the 'Red Line' on Syria's Chemical Weapons," *Washington Post*, September 6, 2013, https://www.washingtonpost.com/news/fact-checker/wp/2013/09/06/president-obama-and-the-red-line-on-syrias-chemical-weapons/.

34. Patrice Taddonio, " 'The President Blinked': Why Obama Changed Course on the 'Red Line' in Syria," "Frontline," PBS, May 25, 2015, https://www.pbs.org/wgbh/frontline/article/the-president-blinked-why-obama-changed.

35. Alex Lockie, "Inside the Most Embarrassing Foreign Policy Failure of Obama's Presidency—the Syrian 'Red Line,' " *Business Insider*, June 4, 2018, https://www.businessinsider.com/ben-rhodes-on-obamas-syrian-red-line-foreign-policy-failure-2018-6; John Dickerson, "Obama's War of Words," *Slate*, August 28, 2013, https://slate.com/news-and-politics/2013/08/barack-obamas-red-line-the-pres idents-foreign-policy-rhetoric-on-syria-has-closed-his-options.html; Rhodes, *The World as It Is*, 230–31; Ben Rhodes, "Inside the White House during the Syrian 'Red Line' Crisis," *Atlantic*, June 3, 2018, https://www.theatlantic.com/international/archive/2018/06/inside-the-white-house-during-the-syrian-red-line-crisis/561887/.

36. Barack Obama, "On the Use of Chemical Weapons by the Syrian Government," American Rhetoric, August 31, 2013, https://www.americanrhetoric.com/speeches/barackobama/barackobamasyriachemicalweapons.htm; Taddonio, " 'The President Blinked' "; Derek Chollett, "Obama's Red Line, Revisited," *Politico*, July 19, 2016, https://www.politico.com/magazine/story/2016/07/obama-syria-foreign-policy-red-line-revisited-214059/; Peter Baker and Jonathan Weisman, "Obama Seeks Approval by Congress for Strike in Syria," *New York Times*, August 31, 2013, https://www.nytimes.com/2013/09/01/world/middleeast/syria.html; Susan Rice, *Tough Love: My Story of the Things Worth Fighting For* (New York: Simon and Schuster, 2019), 362–64; Rhodes, *The World as It Is*, 233–37.

37. Lockie, "Inside the Most Embarrassing Foreign Policy Failure of Obama's Presidency"; Rhodes, "Inside the White House during the Syrian 'Red Line' Crisis."

38. Chollett, "Obama's Red Line, Revisited"; Baker, *Obama*, new ed., 257–58.

39. Geoff Dyer, "John Kerry and Sergei Lavrov Meet UN Syria Envoy," *Financial Times*, September 13, 2013, https://www.ft.com/content/73efd592-1bd9-11e3-b678-00144feab7de; Patrick J. McDonnell, "Syria Backs Russian Proposal for Regime to Hand Over Chemical Weapons," *Los Angeles Times*, September 9, 2013, https://

www.latimes.com/world/worldnow/la-fg-wn-syria-russia-chemical-weapons-20130909-story.html.

40. Barack Obama, "Address to the Nation on U.S. Military Action in Syria," American Rhetoric, September 10, 2013, https://www.americanrhetoric.com/speeches/barackobama/barackobamasyrianation.htm; Jim Newell, "Barack Obama Address on Syria Weapons Plan—as It Happened," *Guardian*, September 10, 2013, https://www.theguardian.com/world/2013/sep/10/barack-obama-tv-address-syria-chemical-weapons; Alia Dastagir, "Obama's Syria Speech: 10 Things You Need to Know," USA Today, September 10, 2013, https://www.usatoday.com/story/news/world/2013/09/10/obama-syria-speeches/2796333.

41. Obama, "Address to the Nation on U.S. Military Action in Syria"; Newell, "Barack Obama Address on Syria Weapons Plan."

42. Anthony Deutsch, "Exclusive: Syria Begins Destruction of Chemical Weapons Facilities," Reuters, January 19, 2013, https://www.reuters.com/article/us-syria-crisis-chemicalweapons-idUSKBN0KS1GY20150119.

43. John Bolton, "Obama Put America in a Red-Line Box on Syria," *Wall Street Journal*, April 28, 2013, https://www.wsj.com/articles/SB10001424127887323528404578450561574249892. Pavel is quoted in Peter Baker, Mark Landler, David E. Sanger, and Anne Barnard, "Off-the-Cuff Obama Line Put U.S. in Bind on Syria," *New York Times*, May 4, 2013, https://www.nytimes.com/2013/05/05/world/middleeast/obamas-vow-on-chemical-weapons-puts-him-in-tough-spot.html; Shibley Telhami, "President Obama's Confused Logic on Syria," Brookings, September 10, 2013, https://www.brookings.edu/opinions/president-obamas-confused-logic-on-syria/.

44. Barack Obama, "On Strengthening the Economy for the Middle Class," American Rhetoric, February 15, 2013, https://www.americanrhetoric.com/speeches/barackobama/barackobamamiddleclasseconomy.htm.

45. "U.S. Violence against Women Act Renewed," Human Rights Watch, February 28, 2013, https://www.hrw.org/news/2013/02/28/us-violence-against-women-act-renewed.

46. Obama, "Fourth Presidential State of the Union Address"; "The Council on Women and Girls: Violence against Women Accomplishments," Obama White House Archives, June 2016, https://obamawhitehouse.archives.gov/sites/whitehouse.gov/files/documents/Women%20and%20Girls_VAW.pdf.

47. Obama is quoted in Jennifer Bendery, "VAWA Vote: Senate Overwhelmingly Passes Violence against Women Act," Huffington Post, February 12, 2013, https://www.huffpost.com/entry/vawa-vote_n_2669720; "Senate Approves Anti-Violence against Women Act," Associated Press, February 12, 2013, https://news.yahoo.com/senate-approves-anti-violence-against-women-act-201051981--politics.html; Rosalind S. Helderman, "Violence against Women Act Passed by House, Sent to Obama for Signature," *Washington Post*, February 28, 2013, https://www.washingtonpost.com/politics/violence-against-women-act-passed-by-house-sent-to-obama-for-signature/2013/02/28/c540f058-81b4-11e2-b99e-6baf4ebe42df_story.html.

48. "Remarks by the President and Vice President at Signing of the Violence against Women Act," *Office of the Press Secretary, The White House*, March 7, 2013, https://obamawhitehouse.archives.gov/the-press-office/2013/03/07/remarks-president-and-vice-president-signing-violence-against-women-act.

49. Suzy Khimm, "The Sequester Explained," *Washington Post*, September 14, 2012, https://www.washingtonpost.com/news/wonk/wp/2012/09/14/the-seques ter-explained/; Suzy Khimm, Ezra Klein, Dylan Matthews, and Brad Plumer, "The Fiscal Cliff: Absolutely Everything You Could Possibly Need to Know, in One FAQ," *Washington Post*, November 27, 2012, https://www.washingtonpost.com/news/ wonk/wp/2012/11/27/absolutely-everything-you-need-to-know-about-the-fiscal-cliff-in-one-faq/; Dylan Matthews, "Can a Possible Government Shutdown Save Us from the Sequester?" *Washington Post*, February 27, 2013, https://www.washington post.com/news/wonk/wp/2013/02/27/can-a-possible-government-shutdown-save-us-from-the-sequester/.

50. Khimm, "The Sequester Explained."

51. "Statement by the President on the Sequester," *Office of the Press Secretary, The White House*, March 1, 2013, https://obamawhitehouse.archives.gov/the-press-office/2013/03/01/statement-president-sequester.

52. Richard Cowan and David Lawder, "Republicans Unveil 10-Year Plan to Shrink Deficit," Reuters, March 11, 2013, https://www.reuters.com/article/us-usa-fiscal-ryan-idUSBRE92B02E20130312; Kristina Peterson, "Democrats' Budget Equally Lifts Taxes, Cuts Spending," *Wall Street Journal*, March 3, 2013, https://www.wsj.com/articles/SB10001424127887324392804578358760519778702.

53. Lori Montgomery, "Obama Releases a Budget Plan with a Simple Goal: Ending the Debt Standoff," *Washington Post*, April 10, 2013, https://www.wash-ingtonpost.com/business/economy/obama-to-unveil-377-trillion-spending-plan/2013/04/10/843adef4-a18d-11e2-82bc-511538ae90a4_story.html; Sharon Par-rott, Joel Friedman, Richard Kogan, and Paul N. Van De Water, "President Obama's Deficit-Reduction Package and Other Proposals in the 2014 Budget," Center on Bud-get and Policy Priorities, April 11, 2013, https://www.cbpp.org/research/president-obamas-deficit-reduction-package-and-other-proposals-in-the-2014-budget.

54. Tod Lindberg, "Do Republicans Oppose Everything Obama Does? Here's a Test," *New Republic*, August 8, 2013, https://newrepublic.com/article/114206/ republican-obstructionism-ideological-or-partisan; "Cantor Says GOP Efforts to Oppose ACA Will Continue after Recess," California Healthline Daily Edition, August 26, 2013, https://californiahealthline.org/morning-breakout/cantor-says-gop-efforts-to-oppose-aca-will-continue-after-recess/.

55. Jonathan Weisman, "House G.O.P. Raises Stakes in Debt-Ceiling Fight," *New York Times*, September 26, 2013, https://www.nytimes.com/2013/09/27/us/politics/ house-gop-leaders-list-conditions-for-raising-debt-ceiling.html; Burgess Everett and Jake Sherman, "Shutdown: Congress Sputters on CR," *Politico*, October 13, 2013, https:// www.politico.com/story/2013/09/house-senate-government-shutdown-097557.

56. Elizabeth Landau and Caleb Hellerman, "5 Things That Have Happened Since Obamacare Launched," CNN Health, October 19, 2013, https://www.cnn. com/2013/10/19/health/obamacare-enrollment-launch-overview/index.html; Thomas B. Edsall, "The Obamacare Crisis," *New York Times*, November 19, 2013, https://www.nytimes.com/2013/11/20/opinion/edsall-the-obamacare-crisis.html.

57. David Frum, "The Obamacare Ripoff: More Money for Less Insurance," Daily Beast, October 29, 2013, https://www.thedailybeast.com/the-obamacare-ripoff-more-money-for-less-insurance.

58. Barack Obama, "Statement on the U.S. Government Shutdown," American Rhetoric, October 2, 2013, https://www.americanrhetoric.com/speeches/baracko bama/barackobamagovernmentshutdown.htm.

59. Ian Hill, Margaret Wilkinson, and John Holahan, "The Launch of the Afford-able Care Act in Selected States: The Problem of Provider Capacity," Urban Institute, March 2014, http://www.urban.org/sites/default/files/publication/22361/413043-The-Launch-of-the-Affordable-Care-Act-in-Eight-States-The-Problem-of-Provider-Capacity.PDF.

60. "Full Transcript: President Obama's Oct. 8 News Conference on the Shut-down and Debt Limit," *Washington Post*, October 8, 2013, https://www.washington post.com/politics/transcript-president-obamas-oct-8-news-conference-on-the-shut down-and-debt-limit/2013/10/08/866088c0-3038-11e3-8906-3daa2bcde110_story. html.

61. Ibid.

62. Lori Montgomery and Rosalind S. Helderman, "Congress Sends Obama Bill to End Shutdown," *Washington Post*, October 17, 2013, https:// www.washingtonpost.com/politics/house-effort-to-end-fiscal-crisis-col lapses-leaving-senate-to-forge-last-minute-solution/2013/10/16/1e8bb150-36 4d-11e3-be86-6aeaa439845b_story.html; Jonathan Weisman and Ashley Parker, "Republicans Back Down, Ending Crisis over Shutdown and Debt Limit," *New York Times*, October 16, 2013, https://www.nytimes.com/2013/10/17/us/con gress-budget-debate.html.

63. Montgomery and Helderman, "Congress Sends Obama Bill to End Shut-down"; Weisman and Parker, "Republicans Back Down."

64. "Senate Nears Shutdown Endgame While House Support Remains in Ques-tion," PBS News Hour, October 15, 2013, https://www.pbs.org/newshour/politics/ senate-nears-shutdown-endgame-while-house-support-remains-in-question; Weis-man and Parker, "Republicans Back Down"; Montgomery and Helderman, "Con-gress Sends Obama Bill to End Shutdown"; Alexander Bolton and Pete Kasperowicz, "Shutdown Ends; Obama Signs Deal," *The Hill*, October 17, 2013, https://thehill. com/blogs/floor-action/house/328989-congress-approves-deal-to-end-shutdown-raise-debt-ceiling.

65. The first quote is from Montgomery and Helderman, "Congress Sends Obama Bill to End Shutdown." The second is from Weisman and Parker, "Republi-cans Back Down."

66. "Transcript: President Obama's Oct. 17 Remarks on the Budget Deal," *Washington Post*, October 17, 2013, https://www.washingtonpost.com/politics/ transcript-president-obamas-oct-17-remarks-on-shutdown-deal/2013/10/17/3eff02 b6-3738-11e3-8a0e-4e2cf80831fc_story.html.

67. Ibid.

68. Ibid.; Jonathan Weisman and Ashley Parker, "House Approves Higher Debt Limit without Conditions," *New York Times*, February 11, 2014, https://www. nytimes.com/2014/02/12/us/politics/boehner-to-bring-debt-ceiling-to-vote-without-policy-attachments.html; Jake Sherman, "House Passes Clean Debt Ceiling Bill," *Politico*, February 11, 2014, https://www.politico.com/story/2014/02/house-gop-debt-limit-plan-103370.

69. Wesley Lowery, "Congress Approves Increase in Debt Limit after Dramatic Vote," *Washington Post*, February 12, 2014, https://www.washingtonpost.com/news/post-politics/wp/2014/02/12/senate-to-vote-on-debt-limit-increase-vote-early-this-afternoon/; Sherman, "House Passes Clean Debt Ceiling Bill."

70. Sherman, "House Passes Clean Debt Ceiling Bill."

71. Barack Obama, "Fifth Presidential State of the Union," January 28, 2014, American Rhetoric, https://www.americanrhetoric.com/speeches/stateoftheunion2014.htm.

72. Ibid.; Peter Baker, "In State of the Union Address, Obama Vows to Act Alone on the Economy," *New York Times*, January 24, 2014, https://www.nytimes.com/2014/01/29/us/politics/obama-state-of-the-union.html.

73. Baker, "In State of the Union Address, Obama Vows to Act Alone on the Economy."

74. "Text and Video of the G.O.P. Response to Obama's Speech," *New York Times*, January 27, 2014, https://www.nytimes.com/2014/01/29/us/politics/text-of-the-gop-response-to-obamas-speech.html; William A. Galston, "SOTU 2014: Reaction to President Obama's State of the Union," Brookings, January 28, 2014, https://www.brookings.edu/blog/fixgov/2014/01/28/sotu-2014-reaction-to-president-obamas-state-of-the-union/.

75. Rice, *Tough Love*, 398; James Clapper, *Facts and Fears: Hard Truths from a Life in Intelligence* (New York: Viking, 2018), 257–61; Mark Landler, Annie Lowrey, and Steven Lee Myers, "Obama Steps Up Russia Sanctions in Ukraine Crisis," *New York Times*, March 20, 2014, https://www.nytimes.com/2014/03/21/us/politics/us-expanding-sanctions-against-russia-over-ukraine.html.

76. Clapper, *Facts and Fears*, 257–61; Landler, Lowrey, and Myers, "Obama Steps Up Russia Sanctions in Ukraine Crisis."

77. Rice, *Tough Love*, 398–401; "Transcript: Obama Announces Sanctions after Crimea Referendum, *Washington Post*, March 20, 2014, https://www.washingtonpost.com/world/transcript-obama-announces-sanctions-after-crimea-referendum/2014/03/17/b000e574-ade4-11e3-9627-c65021d6d572_story.html; Landler, Lowrey, and Myers, "Obama Steps Up Russia Sanctions in Ukraine Crisis."

78. Barack Obama, "Statement on the Downing Malaysia Airlines Flight 17," American Rhetoric, July 18, 2014, https://www.americanrhetoric.com/speeches/barackobama/barackobamaflightmh17.htm; Aliyah Frumin, "Obama's Dilemma: How to Push Putin without Causing More Problems," MSNBC, July 21, 2014, https://www.msnbc.com/msnbc/obamas-dilemma-how-push-putin-without-causing-more-problems-msna373631; Michael E. O'Hanlon, "Obama the Carpenter: The President's National Security Legacy," Brookings, May 2015, https://www.brookings.edu/research/obama-the-carpenter-the-presidents-national-security-legacy/; Baker, new ed., *Obama*, 265–67.

79. Rice, *Tough Love*, 404 and 418–23.

80. Rhodes, *The World as It Is*, 291; Rice, *Tough Love*, 358–61 and 418–19. Clapper tried later to defend himself for the poor intelligence on the Iraqi army remarking that while intelligence analysis was "very good at evaluating capabilities," it lacked "clairvoyance" and found it "frustratingly difficult" to assess "the will to fight," as proven by its underestimation of the Vietcong and its overestimation of the South

Vietnamese army during the Vietnam War. Clapper, *Facts and Fears*, 257–59 and 264. See also Rice, *Tough Love*, 418–19.

81. Spencer Ackerman, "Obama: Murder of James Foley 'Shocks the Conscience of the Entire World,'" *Guardian*, August 20, 2014, https://www.theguardian.com/world/2014/aug/20/james-foley-isis-video-authenticated-us-government; "James Foley: Islamic State Militants 'Behead Reporter,'" BBC, August 20, 2014, https://www.bbc.com/news/world-middle-east-28862268; "Outrage over ISIS Beheading of US Journalist James Foley—Live Updates," *Guardian*, April 20, 2014, https://www.theguardian.com/world/live/2014/aug/20/iraq-crisis-outrage-over-isis-beheading-of-us-journalist-james-foley-live-updates; Erin Banco, "Muslim World Reacts to Isis Brutal Tactics, Beheading of U.S. Journalist James Foley," *International Business Times*, August 22, 2014, https://www.ibtimes.com/muslim-world-reacts-isis-brutal-tactics-beheading-us-journalist-james-foley-1665792.

82. "Transcript: President Obama's Remarks on the Execution of Journalist James Foley by Islamic State," *Washington Post*, August 20, 2014, https://www.washingtonpost.com/politics/transcript-president-obamas-remarks-on-the-execution-of-journalist-james-foley-by-islamic-state/2014/08/20/f5a63802-2884-11e4-8593-da634b334390_story.html.

83. "Ibid.; Zeke Miller, Erin Dooley, and Arlette Saenz, "'World Appalled' by James Foley Beheading, Obama Says," ABC News, August 20, 2014, https://abcnews.go.com/Politics/world-appalled-james-foley-beheading-obama/story?id=25052699.

84. Julie Pace, "US Mission to Rescue Hostages in Syria Failed," Military.com, August 21, 2014, web page no longer available; Karen DeYoung, "The Anatomy of a Failed Hostage Rescue Deep in Islamic State Territory," *Washington Post*, February 14, 2015, https://www.washingtonpost.com/world/national-security/the-anatomy-of-a-failed-hostage-rescue-deep-into-islamic-state-territory/2015/02/14/09a5d9a0-b2fc-11e4-827f-93f454140e2b_story.html.

85. DeYoung, "The Anatomy of a Failed Hostage Rescue Deep in Islamic State Territory"; Shiv Malik, "John Cantlie Speaks about Failed US Attempt to Rescue Hostages in ISIS Video," *Guardian*, November 21, 2014, https://www.theguardian.com/world/2014/nov/21/john-cantlie-failed-us-attempt-rescue-isis-hostages-raqqa-video.

86. The quotes can be found in "Full Transcript of BuzzFeed News Interview with President Barack Obama," BuzzFeed News, February 11, 2015, https://www.buzzfeednews.com/article/buzzfeednews/full-transcript-of-buzzfeed-news-interview-with-president; and in DeYoung, "The Anatomy of a Failed Hostage Rescue Deep in Islamic State Territory." See also Thomas L. Friedman, "Obama on the World," *New York Times*, August 8, 2014, https://www.nytimes.com/2014/08/09/opinion/president-obama-thomas-l-friedman-iraq-and-world-affairs.html.

87. Friedman, "Obama on the World." See also Benjamin Haddad and Alina Polyakova, "Don't Rehabilitate Obama on Russia," Brookings, March 5, 2018, https://www.brookings.edu/blog/order-from-chaos/2018/03/05/dont-rehabilitate-obama-on-russia/; Baker, new ed., *Obama*, 268.

88. Rhodes, *The World as It Is*, 340–41; O'Hanlon, "Obama the Carpenter"; Fred Kaplan, "Obama's Way: The President in Practice," *Foreign Affairs*, January/Febru-

ary 2016, https://www.foreignaffairs.com/articles/2015-12-07/obamas-way; Haddad and Polyakova, "Don't Rehabilitate Obama on Russia."

89. Ball, "The Republican Wave Sweeps the Midterm Elections"; "Republicans Rule House and Senate for First Time in 8 Years," https://www.nbcnews.com/politics/elections/republicans-rule-house-senate-first-time-8-years-n241126.

90. Quoted in Ball, "The Republican Wave Sweeps the Midterm Elections."

91. Ibid.

92. "Transcript: President Obama's Nov. 5 News Conference on Midterm Election Results," *Washington Post*, November 5, 2014, https://www.washingtonpost.com/politics/transcript-president-obamas-remarks-on-midterm-election-results/2014/11/05/491a02b2-6524-11e4-9fdc-d43b053ecb4d_story.html.

93. Ball, "The Republican Wave Sweeps the Midterm Elections"; "Republicans Rule House and Senate for First Time in 8 Years."

94. Rhodes, *The World as It Is*," 304.

9. A Second Recovery

1. Barack Obama, "Address to the Nation on Redressing U.S. Immigration Policy," American Rhetoric, November 20, 2014, http://www.americanrhetoric.com/speeches/barackobama/barackobamaimmigrationnationalpolicy.htm.

2. Susan R. Coleman, "A Promise Unfulfilled, an Imperfect Legacy: Obama and Immigration Policy," in *The Presidency of Barack Obama: A First Historical Assessment*, ed. Julian E. Zelizer (Princeton, NJ: Princeton University Press, 2018), 184–85; Serena Marshall, "Obama Has Deported More People Than Any Other President," ABC News, August 29, 2016, https://abcnews.go.com/Politics/obamas-deportation-policy-numbers/story?id=41715661; Justin Salhani, "Will 44th President Be Remembered as Deporter in Chief or Dreamer?" Washington Diplomat, October 30, 2016, https://washdiplomat.com/will-44th-president-be-remembered-as-deporter-in-chief-or-dreamer/; A. J. Vicens, "The Obama Administration's 2 Million Deportations Explained," *Mother Jones*, April 4, 2014, https://www.motherjones.com/politics/2014/04/obama-administration-record-deportations/.

3. Coleman, "A Promised Unfulfilled, an Imperfect Legacy," 185.

4. Obama, "Address to the Nation on Redressing U.S. Immigration."

5. Ibid.

6. Kate M. Manuel, "The Obama Administration's November 2014 Immigration Initiatives: Questions and Answers," *Congressional Research Service*, November 24, 2014, https://fas.org/sgp/crs/homesec/R43798.pdf; Ian Gordon, "3 Ways Obama's Immigration Executive Action Changes Everything (and One Way It Doesn't)," *Mother Jones*, November 14, 2014, https://www.motherjones.com/politics/2014/11/obama-executive-action-immigration-reform/. See also Jerry Weissman, "Obama Pulls Out 5 Rhetorical Stops in Immigration Speech," *Forbes*, November 21, 2014, https://www.forbes.com/sites/jerryweissman/2014/11/21/obama-pulls-out-five-rhetorical-stops/?sh=6c3eabd34791.

7. Obama, "Address to the Nation on Redressing U.S. Immigration." For ongoing criticism of Obama's immigration policies, including even expansion of the DACA program, by proimmigration advocates, see Marcia Zug, "The Mirage of

Immigration Reform: The Devastating Consequences of Obama's Immigration Policies," *Kansas Law Review*, May 1, 2015, http://law.ku.edu/sites/law.drupal.ku.edu/files/docs/law_review/v63/7-Zug%20Final%20EIC.pdf.

8. Barack Obama, "Cuba Policy Changes Address," American Rhetoric, December 17, 2014, https://www.americanrhetoric.com/speeches/barackobama/barackobamacubapolicychanges.htm.

9. Quoted in Ben Rhodes, *The World as It Is: A Memoir of the Obama White House* (New York: Random House, 2018), 12.

10. Rhodes, *The World as It Is*, 209–17; Peter Baker, "U.S. to Restore Full Relations with Cuba, Erasing a Last Trace of Cold War Hostility," *New York Times*, December 17, 2014, https://www.nytimes.com/2014/12/18/world/americas/us-cuba-relations.html; Dan Pfeiffer, *Yes We (Still) Can* (New York: Hachette Book Group, 2018), 72–74.

11. Rhodes, *The World as It Is*, 307; Susan Rice, *Tough Love: My Story of the Things Worth Fighting For* (New York: Simon and Schuster, 2019), 407–10.

12. Obama, "Cuba Policy Changes Address."

13. Ibid.

14. Baker, "U.S. to Restore Full Relations with Cuba, Erasing a Last Trace of Cold War Hostility." See also "Obama's Cuban Détente," *Wall Street Journal*, December 14, 2014, https://www.wsj.com/articles/obamas-cuban-detente-1418862551; Igor Bobic, "GOP Opposes Diplomatic Relations with Cuba, but Not Other Human Rights Abusers," Huffington Post, December 17, 2014, https://www.huffpost.com/entry/marco-rubio-torture-cuba_n_6343248.

15. Barack Obama, "Sixth Presidential State of the Union Address," American Rhetoric, January 21, 2015, https://www.americanrhetoric.com/speeches/stateoftheunion2015.htm.

16. Ibid.; Pfeiffer's remarks are in Peter Baker, "Analysis of Obama's State of the Union Address," *New York Times*, January 20, 2015, https://www.nytimes.com/2016/01/13/us/politics/final-state-of-the-union-address.html. See also David Nakamura, "Obama, in 2015 State of the Union, Says Crisis Has Passed and Takes Credit," *Washington Post*, January 21, 2015, https://www.washingtonpost.com/politics/president-is-expected-to-deliver-an-assertive-state-of-the-union-speech/2015/01/20/6fef7846-a0ec-11e4-9f89-561284a573f8_story.html; Rebecca Kaplan, "Obama Declares Turning Point for the Nation in His State of the Union," CBS News, January 20, 2015, https://www.cbsnews.com/news/obama-declares-turning-point-for-the-nation-in-his-state-of-the-union/.

17. Obama, "Sixth Presidential State of the Union Address"; Peter Baker, "Bold Call to Action in Obama's State of the Union Even If No Action Is Likely," *New York Times*, January 20, 2015, https://www.nytimes.com/2015/01/21/us/politics/state-of-the-union-speech-leaves-questions-about-usefulness-of-unlikely-goals.html; Nakamura, "Obama, in 2015 State of the Union, Says Crisis Has Passed"; Kaplan, "Obama Declares Turning Point for the Nation."

18. Baker, "Analysis of Obama's State of the Union Address."

19. Ibid.

20. See chapter 6, section "Foreign Policy."

21. Rice, *Tough Love*, 264–69; Rhodes, *The World as It Is*, 248.

22. Rice, *Tough Love*, 411–12; Rhodes, *The World as It Is*, 248.

23. Rhodes, *The World as It Is*, 248; John Kerry, *Every Day Is Extra* (New York: Simon and Schuster, 2018), 487–94; Rice, *Tough Love*, 412.

24. Rhodes, *The World as It Is*, 249–50.

25. Rhodes, *The World as It Is*, 250–51; Kerry, *Every Day Is Extra*, 487–509; Rice, *Tough Love*, 412.

26. Barack Obama, "Statement on Historic Nuclear Agreement with Iran," American Rhetoric, April 2, 2015, https://www.americanrhetoric.com/speeches/barackobama/barackobamairannuclearagreement.htm; Peter Baker, "President Obama Calls Preliminary Iran Nuclear Deal 'Our Best Bet,'" *New York Times*, April 5, 2015, https://www.nytimes.com/2015/04/06/world/middleeast/obama-strongly-defends-iran-nuclear-deal.html; Rhodes, *The World as It Is*, 252–53; Rice, *Tough Love*, 413–15.

27. Thomas L. Friedman, "Iran and the Obama Doctrine," *New York Times*, April 5, 2015, https://www.nytimes.com/2015/04/06/opinion/thomas-fried-man-the-obama-doctrine-and-iran-interview.html; "The Complete Transcript of Netanyahu's Address to Congress," *Washington Post*, March 3, 2015, https://www.washingtonpost.com/full-text-netanyahus-address-to-congress; Krishnadev Calamur, "Netanyahu Blasts 'A Very Bad Deal' with Iran," NPR, March 3, 2015, https://www.npr.org/sections/thetwo-way/2015/03/03/390250986/netanyahu-to-outline-iran-threats-in-much-anticipated-speech-to-congress; Rice, *Tough Love*, 413–15. In responding to Netanyahu's appearance before Congress, which many Democrats viewed as a political stunt by the Republican leadership on Capitol Hill, Obama pointed out that the Israeli prime minister was speaking prematurely since an agreement with Iran had yet to be concluded. He also remarked that, without an agreement, the threat against Israel and the Middle East would be far greater since it would be harder to keep the Tehran government from developing a nuclear weapon. Barack Obama, "On Ash Carter Briefing, Iran and PM Netanyahu's Address," American Rhetoric, March 3, 2015, https://www.americanrhetoric.com/speeches/barackobama/barackobamairanpmnetanyahucongressspeech.htm. See also Bernard Avishai, "Netanyahu's Speech," *New Yorker*, March 3, 2015, https://www.newyorker.com/news/news-desk/netanyahu-speech-congress. See also Kerry, *Every Day Is Extra*, 504–5 and 510.

28. Friedman, "Iran and the Obama Doctrine"; Mortimer B. Zuckerman, "Obama's Unforgivable Betrayal: The President's Nuclear Accommodation of Radical Islamist Theocrats Threatens Israel's Survival," *U.S. News and World Report*, April 17, 2015, https://www.usnews.com/opinion/articles/2015/04/17/obamas-iran-nuclear-deal-is-an-unforgivable-betrayal-of-israel.

29. Friedman, "Iran and the Obama Doctrine"; Pamela Engel, "Obama Explains the 'Doctrine' That Underlies His Foreign Policy," Business Insider, April 6, 2018, https://www.businessinsider.com/the-obama-doctrine-is-now-clear-2015-4. See also Baker, "President Obama Calls Preliminary Iran Nuclear Deal 'Our Best Bet.'"

30. Friedman, "Iran and the Obama Doctrine."

31. Ibid.

32. Barack Obama, "Iran Nuclear Accord Announcement," American Rhetoric, July 14, 2015, https://www.americanrhetoric.com/speeches/barackobama/barack

obamairannucleardealfinal.htm; Julian Borger, "Iran Nuclear Deal: World Powers Reach Historic Agreement to Lift Sanctions," *Guardian*, July 14, 2015, https://www. theguardian.com/world/2015/jul/14/iran-nuclear-programme-world-powers-historic-deal-lift-sanctions. On Obama's position on releasing $100 billion of Iranian assets, see Kerry, *Every Day Is Extra*, 518–20.

33. Obama, "Iran's Nuclear Accord Announcement."

34. Barack Obama, "Post Iran Nuclear Accord Announcement Press Conference," American Rhetoric, July 15, 2015, https://www.americanrhetoric.com/speeches/barackobama/barackobamairannuclearaccordfinalpresser.htm; Rhodes, *The World as It Is*, 322–25.

35. Barack Obama, "Address on Iran at American University," American Rhetoric, August 5, 2015, https://www.americanrhetoric.com/speeches/barackobama/barackobamairanamericanuniversity.htm; Rhodes, *The World as It Is*, 323–30; Kerry, *Every Day Is Extra*, 511; Lesley Clark and Jonathan S. Landay, "Obama Launches Fierce Defense of Iran Nuclear Deal," McClatchy News, August 5, 2015, https://www.bnd.com/news/nation-world/national/article30019119.html.

36. Rhodes, *The World as It Is*, 330–33; Kerry, *Every Day Is Extra*, 513–17; Rice, *Tough Love*, 415–16; Carl Huse and David M. Herszenhorn, "Coordinated Strategy Brings Obama Victory on Iran Nuclear Deal," *New York Times*, September 2, 2015, https://www.nytimes.com/2015/09/03/world/obama-clinches-vote-to-secure-iran-nuclear-deal.html.

37. Obama is quoted in Patrick Zengerle and Richard Cowan, "Senate Democrats Block Effort to Kill Iran Nuclear Deal," Reuters, September 10, 2015, https://www.reuters.com/article/us-iran-nuclear-congress/senate-democrats-block-effort-to-kill-iran-nuclear-deal-idUKKCN0RA20P20150911; Huse and Herszenhorn, "Coordinated Strategy Brings Obama Victory on Iran Nuclear Deal."

38. Gideon Rose, "What Obama Gets Right: Keep Calm and Carry the Liberal Order On," *Foreign Affairs* 94 (September-October 2015), https://www.foreignaffairs.com/articles/2017-07-05/what-obama-gets-right; Ash Carter, *Inside the Five-Sided Box: Lessons from a Lifetime of Leadership in the Pentagon* (New York: Dutton, 2019), 281–83.

39. Jeffrey A. Bader, *Obama and China's Rise: An Insider's Account of America's Asia Strategy* (Washington, DC: Brookings Institution Press, 2012), 3–8, 23–39, 48–52, 54, 69–71, and 109; David E. Sanger, *Confront and Conceal: Obama's Secret Wars and Surprising Use of American Power* (New York: Broadway Paperbacks, 2012), 373–75; Rice, *Tough Love*, 434–36; Jeremi Suri, "Liberal Internationalism, Law, and the First African American President," in *The Presidency of Barack Obama: A First Historical Assessment*, ed. Julian E. Zelizer (Princeton, NJ: Princeton University Press, 2018), 202–3. See also Paul Starobin, "Q&A: *Confront and Conceal* Author David Sanger," *Columbia Journalism Review*, July 2, 2012, https://archives.cjr.org/critical_eye/qa_confront_and_conceal_author.php.

40. Sanger, *Confront and Conceal*, 263–64, 370, 389; J. Bader, *Obama and China's Rise*, 79–93; James Clapper, *Facts and Fears: Hard Truths from a Life in Intelligence* (New York: Viking, 2018).

41. Hillary Clinton, *Hard Choices* (New York: Simon and Schuster Paperbacks, 2014), 65–70; Sanger, *Confront and Conceal*, 412–13; Rice, *Tough Love*, 242–43 and 436–41.

On Clinton's confrontational relationship with China up to 2010, see also Bader, *Obama and China's Rise*, 96–108, 112–29, and 140–44.

42. Obama's quotes can be found in Clinton, *Hard Choices*, 69; and Barack Obama, "Trans-Pacific Trade Pact Address at Nike Headquarters," American Rhetoric, May 8, 2015, https://www.americanrhetoric.com/speeches/barackobama/barackobamatradenike.htm.

43. Clinton, *Hard Choices*, 70–71; Rhodes, *The World as It Is*, 164–65; Jeffrey J. Schott, "Overview: Understanding the Trans-Pacific Partnership," Peterson Institute for International Economics, n.d., piie.com/bookstore/understanding-trans-pacific-partnership; Carter, *Inside the Five-Sided Box*, 285. See also John Kerry, "Speech on Trans-Pacific Trade Pact," American Rhetoric, May 19, 2015, https://www.americanrhetoric.com/speeches/johnkerrytranspacifictradepact boeing.htm.

44. "Remarks by President Barack Obama in Meeting with Trans-Pacific Partnership," Office of the United States Trade Representative, November 12, 2011, https://ustr.gov/about-us/policy-offices/press-office/speeches/transcripts/2010/november/remarks-president-barack-obama-meeting-tran; Rhodes, *The World as It Is*, 165–66.

45. Jackie Calmes, "Obama and Asian Leaders Confront China's Premier," *New York Times*, November 19, 2011, https://www.nytimes.com/2011/11/20/world/asia/wen-jiabao-chinese-leader-shows-flexibility-after-meeting-obama.html; "Obama Meets with Asian Leaders," Voice of America, November 17, 2011, https://www.voanews.com/east-asia/obama-meets-asian-leaders; "Obama, Wen Meet on Sidelines of Bali Summit," Reuters, November 18, 2011, https://cn.reuters.com/article/us-usa-china-obama/obama-wen-meet-on-sidelines-of-bali-summit-idUS-TRE7AI05Q20111119.

46. "Remarks by President Obama at the University of Yangon," *Office of the Press Secretary, The White House*, November 19, 2012, https://obamawhitehouse.archives.gov/the-press-office/2012/11/19/remarks-president-obama-university-yangon; Rhodes, *The World as It Is*, 164–65.

47. Jane Perlez, "Cancellation of Trip by Obama Plays to Doubts of Asia Allies," *New York Times*, October 4, 2013, https://www.nytimes.com/2013/10/05/world/asia/with-obama-stuck-in-washington-china-leader-has-clear-path-at-asia-conferences.html.

48. Ibid.; "Handover of U.S. Command of South Korean Troops Still under Debate," *Washington Post*, September 29, 2013, https://www.washingtonpost.com/world/national-security/handover-of-us-command-of-south-korean-troops-still-under-debate/2013/09/29/25a73374-28fb-11e3-83fa-b82b8431dc92_story.html.

49. "Tpp: What Is It and Why Does It Matter?" BBC, January 23, 2017, https://www.bbc.com/news/business-32498715; Deborah Gleeson, Joel Lexchin, Ruth Lopert, and Burcu Kilic, "The Trans Pacific Partnership Agreement, Intellectual Property and Medicines: Differential Outcomes for Developed and Developing Countries," Sage Publications, October 13, 2017, https://doi.org/10.1177/1468018117734153; "Reconsidering the Trans-Pacific Partnership and Impact on Intellectual Property," Baker McKenzie, April 22, 2018, lexology.com/library/detail.aspx?g=f9ba8dbe-44c4-4a61-9145-a6463e04db58; "Analysis of August 2015 Leaked TPP Text on Copyright,

ISP and General Provisions," *ARL Policy Notes* (blog), Association of Research Libraries, August 2015, https://policynotes.arl.org/?m=201508.

50. Obama is quoted in Adam Behsudi, "Obama Puts Congress on Notice: TPP Is Coming," *Politico*, August 12, 2016, https://www.politico.com/story/2016/08/obama-congress-trade-warning-226952. See also Gail Ablow, "Why Is Obama Pushing the TPP?" Bill Moyers, September 1, 2016, https://billmoyers.com/story/obamas-push-tpp/; Jeffrey Rothfeder, "Why Obama Is Still Trying to Pass the T.P.P.," *New Yorker*, September 18, 2016, https://www.newyorker.com/business/currency/why-obama-is-still-trying-to-pass-the-t-p-p; Alan Wolff, "Obama Still Has a Shot at Passing the TPP," *Fortune*, August 17, 2016, https://fortune.com/2016/08/17/obama-tpp-congress-lame-duck-trade/.

51. Behsudi, "Obama Puts Congress on Notice"; "Trans-Pacific Partnership Agreement: What Was the Trans-Pacific Partnership Agreement (TPP)?" Electronic Frontier Foundation, n.d., https://www.eff.org/issues/tpp.

52. Carter, *Inside the Five-Sided Box*, 280–81.

53. "The President's Climate Action Plan," *Executive Office of the President*, June 2013, https://obamawhitehouse.archives.gov/sites/default/files/image/president27sclimateactionplan.pdf; H. Josef Hebert, "Congress Begins Tackling Climate Issues," CBS Evening News, January 29, 2007, web page no longer available; "A Historic Commitment to Protecting the Environment and Addressing the Impacts of Climate Change," White House Archives, n.d., https://obamawhitehouse.archives.gov/the-record/climate; Meg Jacobs, "Obama's Fight against Global Warming," in *The Presidency of Barack Obama: A First Historical Assessment*, ed. Julian E. Zelizer (Princeton, NJ: Princeton University Press, 2018), 62–65; Clinton, *Hard Choices*, 417–18.

54. Clinton, *Hard Choices*, 419–21.

55. Ibid., 421–22; Kerry, *Every Day Is Extra*, 560; Scott Kaufman, *The Environment and International History* (New York: Bloomsbury Academic, 2018), 147.

56. Darren Samuelsohn, "Obama Negotiates 'Copenhagen Accord' with Senate Climate Fight in Mind," *New York Times*, December 21, 2009, https://archive.nytimes.com/www.nytimes.com/cwire/2009/12/21/21climatewire-obama-negotiates-copenhagen-accord-with-senat-6121.html; Lisa Lerer, "Obama's Dramatic Climate Meet," *Politico*, December 18, 2009, https://www.politico.com/story/2009/12/obamas-dramatic-climate-meet-030801; "Barack Obama's Speech Disappoints and Fuels Frustration at Copenhagen," *Guardian*, December 18, 2009, https://www.theguardian.com/environment/2009/dec/18/obama-speech-copenhagen; Jacobs, "Obama's Fight against Global Warming," 66–69; Kerry, *Every Day Is Extra*, 363.

57. Jacobs, "Obama's Fight against Global Warming," 64–66.

58. Ibid., 67–69; Kerry, *Every Day Is Extra*, 363–66. On the BP oil spill see also Barack Obama, "Remarks and Press Conference on the Gulf Oil Spill Disaster," American Rhetoric, May 27, 2010, https://www.americanrhetoric.com/speeches/barackobama/barackobamagulfoilspillpresser.htm; Barack Obama, "Grand Isle Briefing on the Gulf Oil Spill Disaster," American Rhetoric, May 28, 2010, https://www.americanrhetoric.com/speeches/barackobama/barackobamagrandeisleoilspillbriefing.htm; Andrew Clark, "BP Will 'Pay Every Dime Owed' for Gulf Oil Spill, Obama Warns," *Guardian*, May 27, 2010, https://www.theguardian.com/environment/2010/may/27/gulf-oil-spill-bp-obama; John M. Broder, "Report Slams Administration

for Underestimating Gulf Spill," *New York Times*, October 6, 2010, https://www.nytimes.com/2010/10/07/science/earth/07spill.html.

59. Barack Obama, "Oval Office Address to the Nation on BP Oil Spill Disaster," American Rhetoric, June 15, 2010, https://www.americanrhetoric.com/speeches/barackobama/barackobamabpoilspillovaloffice.htm.

60. Michael D'Antonio, *A Consequential President: The Legacy of Barack Obama* (New York: St. Martin's Press, 2016), 104–31; Jacobs, "Obama's Fight against Global Warming," 70–71.

61. "Statement by the President on the Keystone XL Pipeline," *Office of the Press Secretary, The White House*, January 18, 2012, https://obamawhitehouse.archives.gov/the-press-office/2012/01/18/statement-president-keystone-xl-pipeline; Suzanne Goldenberg, "Keystone XL Oil Pipeline," *Guardian*, January 31, 2014, https://www.theguardian.com/environment/2014/jan/31/keystone-xl-oil-pipeline-everything-you-need-to-know; Juliet Eilperin and Steven Mufson, "Obama Administration Rejects Keystone XL Pipeline," *Washington Post*, January 18, 2012, https://www.washingtonpost.com/national/health-science/obama-administration-to-reject-keystone-pipeline/2012/01/18/gIQAPuPF8P_story.html.

62. Barack Obama, "Second Presidential Inaugural Address," American Rhetoric, January 21, 2013, https://www.americanrhetoric.com/speeches/barackobama/barackobamasecondinauguraladdress.htm; Barack Obama, "Fourth Presidential State of the Union Address," American Rhetoric, February 12, 2013, https://www.americanrhetoric.com/speeches/stateoftheunion2013.htm.

63. "The President's Climate Action Plan"; Clinton, *Hard Choices*, 422–23.

64. Brad Plumer, "The Keystone XL Pipeline Is Dead. Here's Why Obama Rejected It," Vox, November 7, 2015, https://www.vox.com/2015/11/6/9681340/obama-rejects-keystone-pipeline; Coral Davenport, "Nations Approve Landmark Climate Accord in Paris," *New York Times*, December 12, 2015, https://www.nytimes.com/2015/12/13/world/europe/climate-change-accord-paris.html; Suzanne Goldenberg, John Vidal, Lenore Taylor, Adam Vaughan, and Fiona Harvey, "Paris Climate Deal: Nearly 200 Nations Sign In End of Fossil Fuel Era," *Guardian*, December 12, 2015, https://www.theguardian.com/environment/2015/dec/12/paris-climate-deal-200-nations-sign-finish-fossil-fuel-era.

65. "Paris Agreement," United Nations Framework Convention on Climate Change, December 12, 2015, https://unfccc.int/process-and-meetings/the-paris-agreement/the-paris-agreement; "The Paris Agreement Summary," Climate Focus, December 28, 2015, https://www.climatefocus.com/sites/default/files/20151228%20COP%2021%20briefing%20FIN.pdf.

66. Kerry, *Every Day Is Extra*, 561; Tim Boersma, "U.S.-China Joint Announcement on Climate Change Is a Big Deal," Brookings, November 13, 2014, https://www.brookings.edu/blog/planetpolicy/2014/11/13/u-s-china-joint-announcement-on-climate-change-is-a-big-deal/; Davenport, "Nations Approve Landmark Climate Accord in Paris."

67. Kerry, *Every Day Is Extra*, 564.

68. "U.S.-China Joint Announcement on Climate Change," *Office of the Press Secretary, The White House*, November 11, 2014, https://obamawhitehouse.archives.gov/the-press-office/2014/11/11/us-china-joint-announcement-climate-change.

See also "Remarks by President Obama and President Xi Jinping in Joint Press Conference," *Office of the Press Secretary, The White House*, November 11, 2014, https://obamawhitehouse.archives.gov/the-press-office/2014/11/12/remarks-president-obama-and-president-xi-jinping-joint-press-conference; Mark Lander, "Fruitful Visit by Obama Ends with a Lecture from Xi," *New York Times*, November 12, 2014, https://www.nytimes.com/2014/11/13/world/asia/china-us-xi-jinping-obama-apec.html; "Fact Sheet: Advancing the Rebalance to Asia and the Pacific," *Office of the Press Secretary, The White House*, November 16, 2015, https://obamawhitehouse.archives.gov/the-press-office/2015/11/16/fact-sheet-advancing-rebalance-asia-and-pacific.

69. Coral Davenport, "Obama's Strategy on Climate Change, Part of Global Deal, Is Revealed," *New York Times*, March 31, 2015, https://www.nytimes.com/2015/04/01/us/obama-to-offer-major-blueprint-on-climate-change.html.

70. The quotes are from Davenport, "Nations Approve Landmark Climate Accord in Paris." See also "Statement by the President on the Paris Climate Agreement," *Office of the Press Secretary, The White House*, December 12, 2015, https://obamawhitehouse.archives.gov/the-press-office/2015/12/12/statement-president-paris-climate-agreement; Martin Pengelly, "Obama Praises Paris Climate Deal as 'Tribute to American Leadership,'" *Guardian*, December 12, 2015, https://www.theguardian.com/us-news/2015/dec/12/obama-speech-paris-climate-change-talks-deal-american-leadership. See also Tanya Somanader, "President Obama: The United States Formally Enters the Paris Agreement," *Office of the Press Secretary, The White House*, September 3, 2016, https://obamawhitehouse.archives.gov/blog/2016/09/03/president-Obama-United-states-formally-enters-Paris-agreement.

71. Somanader, "The United States Formally Enters the Paris Agreement." See also, "Remarks by the President on the Paris Agreement," *Office of the Press Secretary, The White House*, October 5, 2016, https://obamawhitehouse.archives.gov/the-press-office/2016/10/05/remarks-president-paris-agreement#:~:text=THE%20PRESIDENT%3A%20Good%20afternoon%2C%20everybody,on%20a%20low%2Dcarbon%20course.

72. Jacobs, "Obama's Fight against Global Warming," 74–75.

73. Ibid., 76–77.

74. Greg Botelho, "What Happened the Night Trayvon Martin Died," CNN, May 23, 2012, https://www.cnn.com/2012/05/18/justice/florida-teen-shooting-details/index.html; Michael Eric Dyson, *The Black Presidency: Barack Obama and the Politics of Race in America* (Boston: Houghton Mifflin Harcourt, 2016), 186–87.

75. Botelho, "What Happened the Night Trayvon Martin Died"; Lizette Alvarez and Cara Buckley, "Zimmerman Is Acquitted in Trayvon Martin Killing," *New York Times*, July 13, 2013, https://www.nytimes.com/2013/07/14/us/george-zimmerman-verdict-trayvon-martin.html.

76. Monica Potts, "Barack Obama, Trayvon Martin, and the Presidency," *Vogue*, December 22, 2016, https://www.vogue.com/article/barack-obama-trayvon-martin-presidency; Jeff Mason and Daniel Trotta, "Obama Gets Personal over Killing of Black Florida Teenager," Reuters, March 23, 2012, https://www.reuters.com/article/us-florida-shooting-obama/obama-gets-personal-over-killing-of-black-florida-teenager-idUSBRE82M0QF20120323.

77. As quoted in Jackie Calmes and Helene Cooper, "A Personal Note as Obama Speaks on Death of Boy," *New York Times*, March 23, 2012, https://www.nytimes.com/2012/03/24/us/politics/obama-talks-of-tragedy-not-race-in-florida-killing.html.

78. As quoted in Calmes and Cooper, "A Personal Note as Obama Speaks on Death of Boy"; Mason and Trotta, "Obama Gets Personal over Killing of Black Florida Teenager"; Star Parker, "Racial Divide Worse under Obama," *Washington Examiner*, November 3, 2012, https://www.washingtonexaminer.com/racial-divide-worse-under-obama; "Remarks by the President on Trayvon Martin," *Office of the Press Secretary, The White House*, July 19, 2013, https://obamawhitehouse.archives.gov/the-press-office/2013/07/19/remarks-president-trayvon-martin.

79. "Remarks by the President on Trayvon Martin."

80. Ibid. See also Ta-Nahisi Coates, *We Were Eight Years in Power: An American Tragedy* (New York: One World, 2017), 309–29 and 354–55; Peter Wallstein, "Obama Struggles to Balance African Americans' Hopes with Country's as a Whole," *Washington Post*, October 28, 2012, https://www.washingtonpost.com/politics/decision2012/obama-after-making-history-has-faced-a-high-wire-on-racial-issues/2012/10/28/d8e25ff4-1939-11e2-bd10-5ff056538b7c_story.html.

81. Ann Althouse, "Why Obama Won't Give the Ferguson Speech His Supporters Want," *AltHouse* (blog), August 19, 2014, https://althouse.blogspot.com/2014/08/why-obama-wont-give-ferguson-speech-his.html.

82. Eliott C. McGlaughlin, "What We Know about Michael Brown's Shooting," CNN, August 15, 2014, https://www.cnn.com/2014/08/11/us/missouri-ferguson-michael-brown-what-we-know/index.html.

83. David Hudson, "President Obama Issues a Statement on the Death of Michael Brown," *Office of the Press Secretary, The White House*, August 12, 2014, https://obamawhitehouse.archives.gov/blog/2014/08/12/president-obama-issues-statement-death-michael-brown; Heather MacDonald, "Obama's Assault on the Police," *Commentary*, March 2016, https://www.commentary.org/articles/heather-macdonald/obamas-assault-police/.

84. Hudson, "President Obama Issues a Statement on the Death of Michael Brown."

85. Erik Eckholm and Matt Apuzzo, "Darren Wilson Is Cleared of Rights Violations in Ferguson Shooting, *New York Times*, March 4, 2015, https://www.nytimes.com/2015/03/05/us/darren-wilson-is-cleared-of-rights-violations-in-ferguson-shooting.html.

86. "Transcript: Obama's Remarks on Ferguson Grand Jury Decision," *Washington Post*, November 24, 2014, https://www.washingtonpost.com/politics/transcript-obamas-remarks-on-ferguson-grand-jury-decision/2014/11/24/afc3b38e-744f-11e4-bd1b-03009bd3e984_story.html; Matthew Larotonda and Chris Good, "Obama Says 'We May Never Know What Happened' in Ferguson, but Defends DOJ," ABC News, March 6, 2015, https://abcnews.go.com/Politics/obama-happened-ferguson-defends-doj/story?id=29441456; David Nather, "Obama on Ferguson: 'They Weren't Just Making It Up,'" *Politico*, March 6, 2015, https://www.politico.com/story/2015/03/obama-ferguson-reaction-doj-115839.

87. "Transcript: Obama's Remarks on Ferguson Grand Jury Decision"; Althouse, "Why Obama Won't Give the Ferguson Speech His Supporters Want"; Mychal Denzel Smith, "How President Obama Failed Black Lives," *Washington Post*, July 21, 2016, https://www.washingtonpost.com/posteverything/wp/2016/07/21/how-president-obama-failed-black-lives-matter/; Jonathan Chait, "Obama, Ferguson, and the Torments of Liberalism," *Intelligencer*, November 25, 2014, https://nymag.com/intelligencer/2014/11/obama-ferguson-and-the-torments-of-liberalism.html; Larotonda and Good, "Obama Says 'We May Never Know What Happened' in Ferguson"; Nather, "Obama on Ferguson."

88. Alan Rappeport, "Democratic Speechwriters See Obama's Selma Address as 'Among His Very Best,'" *New York Times*, March 9, 2009, https://www.nytimes.com/politics/first-draft/2015/03/09/obamas-selma-speech-considered-among-his-very-best; "Obama's Selma Speech Ranks among Best," Herald, March 7, 2015, https://www.heraldonline.com/opinion/editorials/article13984940.html; Matt Ford, "Why President Obama's Speech Matters," *Atlantic*, March 7, 2015, https://www.theatlantic.com/politics/archive/2015/03/obama-at-selma-ferguson-exceptionalism/387169/.

89. Barack Obama, "Address on the 50th Anniversary of the Selma, Alabama, March," American Rhetoric, March 7, 2015, https://www.americanrhetoric.com/speeches/barackobama/barackobamaselma50anniversarymarch.htm.

90. Ibid.

91. Ibid; Adam Liptak, "Supreme Court Invalidates Key Part of Voting Rights Act," *New York Times*, June 25, 2013, https://www.nytimes.com/2013/06/26/us/supreme-court-ruling.html; Stephen Dinan, "Supreme Court Says Voting Rights Act of 1965 Is No Longer Relevant," *Washington Times*, June 25, 2013, https://www.washingtontimes.com/news/2013/jun/25/court-past-voting-discrimination-no-longer-held/.

92. Barbara Reynolds, "I Was a Civil Rights Activist in the 1960s. But It's Hard for Me to Get Behind Black Lives Matter," *Washington Post*, August 24, 2015, https://www.washingtonpost.com/posteverything/wp/2015/08/24/i-was-a-civil-rights-activist-in-the-1960s-but-its-hard-for-me-to-get-behind-black-lives-matter/; Shannon Luibrand, "How a Death in Ferguson Sparked a Movement in America," CBS News, August 7, 2015, https://www.cbsnews.com/news/how-the-black-lives-matter-movement-changed-america-one-year-later/; Janell Ross, "How Black Lives Matter Moved from a Hashtag to a Real Political Force," *Washington Post*, August 19, 2015, https://www.washingtonpost.com/news/the-fix/wp/2015/08/19/how-black-lives-matter-moved-from-a-hashtag-to-a-real-political-force/.

93. Patrisse Cullors, "Obama Says Black Lives Matter. But He Doesn't Ensure They Do," *Guardian*, July 16, 2016, https://www.theguardian.com/commentisfree/2016/jul/16/obama-black-lives-matter-doesnt-ensure-they-do. See also Dyson, *The Black Presidency*, 193–99; Peniel E. Joseph, "Barack Obama and the Movement for Black Lives: Race, Democracy, and Criminal Justice in the Age of Ferguson," in *The Presidency of Barack Obama: A First Historical Assessment*, ed. Julian E. Zelizer (Princeton, NJ: Princeton University Press, 2018), 137–38; Maya Rhodan, "President Obama Defends Stance on Police, Black Lives Matter," *Time Magazine*, July 14, 2016, https://time.com/4407362/president-obama-police-black-lives-matter-town-hall/.

94. Motoko Rich, "Obama to Report Widening of Initiative for Black and Latino Boys," *New York Times*, July 20, 2014, https://www.nytimes.com/2014/07/21/education/obamas-my-brothers-keeper-education-program-expands.html.

95. "Remarks by the President on 'My Brother's Keeper' Initiative," *Office of the Press Secretary, The White House*, February 27, 2014, https://obamawhitehouse.archives.gov/the-press-office/2014/02/27/remarks-president-my-brothers-keeper-initiative. See also "Jonathan Capehart on His Interview with President Obama: 'He Has Hope for This Country,'" https://www.msnbc.com/deadline-white-house/watch/jonathan-capehart-on-his-interview-with-president-obama-he-has-hope-for-this-country-96328773767.

96. "Remarks by the President on 'My Brother's Keeper' Initiative."

97. Ibid.; Barack Obama, *A Promised Land* (New York: Crown, 2020), xiv.

98. Matt Ford and Adam Chandler, "'Hate Crime': A Mass Killing at a Historic Church," *Atlantic*, June 2015, https://www.theatlantic.com/national/archive/2015/06/shooting-emanuel-ame-charleston/396209/. Debbie Elliott, "How a Shooting Changed Charleston's Oldest Black Church," NPR, June 8, 2016, https://www.npr.org/sections/codeswitch/2016/06/08/481149042/how-a-shooting-changed-charlestons-oldest-black-church; Jason Horowitz, Nick Corasaniti, and Ashley Southall, "Nine Killed in Shooting at Black Church in Charleston," *New York Times*, June 17, 2015, https://www.nytimes.com/2015/06/18/us/church-attacked-in-charleston-south-carolina.html.

99. Elliott, "How a Shooting Changed Charleston's Oldest Black Church"; Horowtiz, Corasaniti, and Southall, "Nine Killed in Shooting at Black Church in Charleston."

100. "Full Text: Obama's Remarks on Fatal Shooting in Charleston, S.C.," *Washington Post*, June 18, 2015, https://www.washingtonpost.com/news/post-politics/wp/2015/06/18/full-text-obamas-remarks-on-fatal-shooting-in-charleston-s-c/.

101. "Remarks by the President on the Supreme Court Decision on Marriage Equality," *Office of the Press Secretary, The White House*, June 26, 2015, https://obamawhitehouse.archives.gov/the-press-office/2015/06/26/remarks-president-supreme-court-decision-marriage-equality; Ed Pilkington, "Obama Gives Searing Speech on Race in Eulogy for Charleston Pastor," *Guardian*, June 26, 2015, https://www.theguardian.com/us-news/2015/jun/26/obama-charleston-eulogy-pinckney-amazing-grace; Valerie Jarrett, *Finding My Voice: My Journey to the West Wing and the Path Forward* (New York: Viking, 2019), 273–74.

102. "Full Text: Obama's Remarks on Fatal Shooting in Charleston, S.C."

103. Ibid.; Adam Chandler, "A Eulogy in Charleston: President Obama Traveled to South Carolina to Speak at Clementa Pinckney's Funeral," *Atlantic*, June 26, 2015, https://www.theatlantic.com/national/archive/2015/06/a-eulogy-in-charleston/396998/.

104. "Full Text: Obama's Remarks on Fatal Shooting in Charleston, S.C."

105. Ibid.; Peter Manseau, "Obama's Graceful Pause in Charleston," *Atlantic*, June 30, 2015, https://www.theatlantic.com/politics/archive/2015/06/obamas-graceful-pause-in-charleston/397223/; Jordan Phelps, "The Story behind President Obama Singing 'Amazing Grace' at Charleston Funeral," ABC News, July 7, 2015,

https://abcnews.go.com/Politics/story-president-obama-singing-amazing-grace-charleston-funeral/story?id=32264346.

106. The quotes are from Pilkington, "Obama Gives Searing Speech on Race in Eulogy for Charleston Pastor"; Clarissa-Jan Lim, "This Was the Most Moving Moment of Obama's Presidency, According to George Clooney," APlus, January 11, 2017, https://staging.aplus.com/a/george-clooney-obama-amazing-grace?no_monetization=true; Michiko Kakutani, "Obama's Eulogy, Which Found Its Place in History," *New York Times*, July 3, 2015, https://www.nytimes.com/2015/07/04/arts/obamas-eulogy-which-found-its-place-in-history.html; Phelps, "The Story behind President Obama Singing 'Amazing Grace' at Charleston Funeral"; Jarrett, *Finding My Voice*, 274–75.

107. Carol E. Lee and Colleen McCain Nelson, "Obama Has a Good Week," *Wall Street Journal*, June 25, 2015, https://www.wsj.com/articles/obama-has-a-good-week-1435253458.

108. Chris Cillizza, "This Was the Best Week of Obama's Presidency," *Washington Post*, June 26, 2015, https://www.washingtonpost.com/news/the-fix/wp/2015/06/26/this-was-the-best-week-of-obamas-presidency/; "Face the Nation Transcript June 28, 2015: Gowdy, Ryan, Cummings," CBS News, June 28, 2015, https://www.cbsnews.com/news/face-the-nation-transcript-june-28-2015; Hal Boedeker, "Barack Obama: Race Central to Legacy," *Orlando Sentinel*, June 30, 2015, https://www.orlandosentinel.com/entertainment/tv-guy/os-barack-obama-race-central-to-legacy-20150630-post.html.

10. The Shock of Donald J. Trump's Election

1. Barack Obama, "Final Presidential State of the Union Address," American Rhetoric, January 12, 2016, https://www.americanrhetoric.com/speeches/stateoftheunion2016.htm; Favreau's quote is in Peter Baker, "State of the Union Speech Is One Half of Nation's Political Split Screen," *New York Times*, January 12, 2016, https://www.nytimes.com/2016/01/13/us/politics/final-state-of-the-union-address.html; Peter Baker, "In the Final State of the Union Address, Obama Aims to Set Tone for '16 Campaign," *New York Times*, January 10, 2016, https://www.nytimes.com/2016/01/11/us/politics/obama-last-state-of-the-union.html; Liz Scheltens, Carlos Waters, and Sarah Turbin, "Obama's 2016 State of the Union, in 4 Minutes," Vox, January 13, 2016, https://www.vox.com/2016/1/13/10759146/obama-2016-state-of-the-union-video.

2. Barack Obama, "Final Presidential State of the Union Address."

3. Psaki is quoted in Baker, "In the Final State of the Union Address."

4. Ben Rhodes, *The World as It Is: A Memoir of the Obama White House* (New York: Random House, 2018), 123–24. See also Susan Rice, *Tough Love: My Story of the Things Worth Fighting For* (New York: Simon and Schuster, 2019), 453; Dan Pfeiffer, *Yes We (Still) Can: Politics in the Age of Obama, Twitter, and Trump* (New York: Twelve, 2018), 113–26; Lymari Morales, "Obama's Birth Certificate Convinces Some, but Not All, Skeptics," Gallup, May 13, 2011, https://news.gallup.com/poll/147530/obama-birth-certificate-convinces-not-skeptics.aspx; Barack Obama, "Final Presidential State of the Union Address"; Julie Hirschfeld Davis and Michael D. Shear,

"Obama Confronts Americans' Fears in State of the Union Speech," *New York Times*, January 12, 2016, https://www.nytimes.com/2016/01/13/us/politics/obama-state-of-the-union.html.

5. Barack Obama, "Final Presidential State of the Union Address"; Davis and Shear, "Obama Confronts Americans' Fears in State of the Union Speech."

6. "6th Republican Debate Transcript, Annotated: Who Said What," *Washington Post*, January 14, 2016, https://www.washingtonpost.com/news/the-fix/wp/2016/01/14/6th-republican-debate-transcript-annotated-who-said-what-and-what-it-meant/; Eric Bradner, "6 Takeaways from the Republican Presidential Debate," CNN Politics, January 15, 2016, https://www.cnn.com/2016/01/15/politics/republican-debate-2016-recap/index.html; Paoli Chavez, "Best Lines of the First Republican Debate of 2016," ABC News, January 14, 2016, https://abcnews.go.com/Politics/best-lines-republican-debate/story?id=36296985; Lela Moore, "Readers React to Obama's Final State of the Union Address," *New York Times*, January 13, 2016, https://www.nytimes.com/2016/01/14/us/readers-react-to-obamas-final-state-of-the-union-address.html?.?mc=aud_dev&ad-keywords=auddevgate&gclid=CjwKCAjw55-HBhAHEiwARMCszlP1OwhY2aprSQIMtnsGhCl2dIP-gT0jVNp99wEqN9l3KVQ_vwpoJhoCCdgQAvD_BwE&gclsrc=aw.ds.

7. Helene Cooper and David E. Sanger, "Iran Seizes U.S. Sailors amid Claims of Spying," *New York Times*, January 12, 2016, https://www.nytimes.com/2016/01/13/world/middleeast/iran-holds-us-navy-boats-crew.html; Michael S. Schmidt, "9 in Navy Disciplined over Iran's Capture of Sailors," *New York Times*, June 30, 2016, https://www.nytimes.com/2016/07/01/world/middleeast/us-navy-iran.html; Meghann Myers, "Navy Punishes Four Sailors Who Were Detained by Iran," *Navy Times*, July 14, 2016, https://www.navytimes.com/news/your-navy/2016/07/15/navy-punishes-four-sailors-who-were-detained-by-iran/.

8. Quoted in Andrew Glass, "President Obama Visits Havana," *Politico*, March 20, 2019, https://www.politico.com/story/2019/03/20/obama-havana-cuba-1224370. See also Carmen Sesin, John Brecher, and Sandra Lilley, "In Cuba and U.S., Expectations Are Mixed on Obama's Historic Trip," NBC News, March 20, 2016, https://www.nbcnews.com/news/latino/cuba-u-s-expectations-are-mixed-obama-s-historic-trip-n541986; Rhodes, *The World as It Is*, 352–54.

9. Barack Obama, "Joint Press Conference with Raul Castro," American Rhetoric, March 21, 2016, https://americanrhetoric.com/speeches/barackobama/barackobamaraulcastropresser.htm; Barack Obama, "Address to the Entrepreneurs of Cuba," American Rhetoric, March 21, 2016, https://americanrhetoric.com/speeches/barackobama/barackobamacubaentrepreneurs.htm; Barack Obama, "Address to the People of Cuba," American Rhetoric, March 22, 2016, https://www.americanrhetoric.com/speeches/barackobama/barackobamacubapeoplespeech.htm; Frances Robles, "Cuban Dissidents Praise 'Closeness and Trust' after Meeting with Obama," *New York Times*, March 22, 2016, https://www.nytimes.com/2016/03/23/world/americas/cuban-dissidents-meeting-with-obama.html; Rhodes, *The World as It Is*, 354–55.

10. Barack Obama, "Joint Press Conference with Raul Castro."

11. Ibid.

12. Ibid.

13. Ibid.; Rhodes, *The World as It Is*, 356–59.

14. Barack Obama, "Address to the People of Cuba"; Tom Gjeltin, "Obama Praises and Challenges Cubans in Speech in Havana," NPR, March 22, 2016, https://www.npr.org/sections/thetwo-way/2016/03/22/471515401/obama-praises-and-challenges-cubans-in-speech-in-havana.

15. Barack Obama, "Address to the People of Cuba"; Gjeltin, "Obama Praises and Challenges Cubans in Speech in Havana."

16. Jon Lee Anderson, "Cuba after Obama Left," *New Yorker*, April 1, 2016, https://www.newyorker.com/news/daily-comment/cuba-after-obama-left; see also Lizette Alvarez, "Reaction to Obama Trip Reflects Change in Cuban-Americans," *New York Times*, March 21, 2016, https://www.nytimes.com/2016/03/22/world/americas/reaction-to-obama-trip-reflects-change-in-cuban-americans.html; Dan Roberts, "Obama Lands in Cuba as First US President to Visit in Nearly a Century," *Guardian*, March 21, 2016, https://www.theguardian.com/world/2016/mar/20/barack-obama-cuba-visit-us-politics-shift-public-opinion-diplomacy.

17. Alvarez, "Reaction to Obama Trip Reflects Change in Cuban-Americans"; Robles, "Cuban Dissidents Praise 'Closeness and Trust' after Meeting with Obama."

18. Pfeiffer, *Yes We (Still) Can*, 192–93; Jonathan Rauch, "How American Politics Went Insane," *Atlantic*, June-July, 2016, https://www.theatlantic.com/magazine/archive/2016/07/how-american-politics-went-insane/485570/; Jonathan Chait, "Why American Politics Really Went Insane," *New York Magazine*, June 22, 2016, https://nymag.com/intelligencer/2016/06/why-american-politics-really-went-insane.html.

19. Rishi Iyengar, "What to Know about President Obama's Visit to Vietnam and Japan," *Time Magazine*, May 23, 2016, https://time.com/4344515/obama-asia-trip-vietnam-japan-embargo-hiroshima/; Gardiner Harris, "Obama in Vietnam Will Focus on Future, Rather Than the Past," *New York Times*, May 15, 2016, https://www.nytimes.com/2016/05/16/us/politics/obama-in-vietnam-will-focus-on-future-rather-than-the-past.html; Gardiner Harris, "Arriving in Vietnam, Obama Aims to Lure It Away from China," *New York Times*, May 22, 2016, https://www.nytimes.com/2016/05/23/world/asia/vietnam-obama-china.html; Kristin Donnelly, "President Obama Arrives in Vietnam for Historic Asia Trip," NBC News, May 22, 2016, https://www.nbcnews.com/news/world/president-obama-arrives-vietnam-historic-asia-trip-n578251; David Brown, "Obama in Hanoi: The United States and Vietnam Move Closer Together," *Foreign Affairs*, May 17, 2016, https://www.foreignaffairs.com/articles/vietnam/2016-05-17/obama-hanoi.

20. Leigh Ann Caldwell, "Benghazi: A Timeline," NBC News, October 22, 2015, https://www.nbcnews.com/politics/congress/benghazi-timeline-n448776; David M. Herszenhorn, "House Benghazi Report Finds No New Evidence of Wrongdoing by Hillary Clinton," *New York Times*, June 28, 2016, https://www.nytimes.com/2016/06/29/us/politics/hillary-clinton-benghazi.html; David Samuels, "The Aspiring Novelist Who Became Obama's Foreign-Policy Guru," *New York Times Magazine*, May 5, 2016, https://www.nytimes.com/2016/05/08/magazine/the-aspiring-novelist-who-became-obamas-foreign-policy-guru.html; Carlos Lozada, "Why the Ben Rhodes Profile in the New York Times Magazine Is Just Gross," *Washington Post*, May 6, 2015, https://www.washingtonpost.com/news/book-party/

wp/2016/05/06/why-the-ben-rhodes-profile-in-the-new-york-times-magazine-is-just-gross/; Natasha Bertrand, "Obama's 'Foreign-Policy Guru' Gave a Shockingly Blunt Interview to the New York Times," Yahoo, May 6, 2016, https://finance.yahoo.com/news/obamas-foreign-policy-guru-gave-154200198.html; David Samuels, "Through the Looking Glass with Ben Rhodes," New York Times, May 13, 2016, https://www.nytimes.com/2016/05/12/magazine/through-the-looking-glass-with-ben-rhodes.html.

21. Rhodes, The World as It Is, 372.

22. Yuval Noah Harari, Sapiens: A Brief History of Humankind (New York: HarperCollins, 2015); Rhodes, The World as It Is, 372.

23. Rhodes, The World as It Is, 374–75.

24. Harris, "Arriving in Vietnam, Obama Aims to Lure It Away from China"; Jane Perlez, "Obama's Vietnam Trip Follows Controlled Parliamentary Elections," New York Times, May 20, 2016, https://www.nytimes.com/2016/05/21/world/asia/obama-vietnam-general-assembly.html; Barack Obama, "Address in Vietnam on Entrepreneurship and Business Development," American Rhetoric, May 24, 2016, https://americanrhetoric.com/speeches/barackobama/barackobamavietnambusinessdevelopment.htm.

25. Barack Obama, "Address in Vietnam on Entrepreneurship and Business Development."

26. Gardiner Harris, "Vietnam Arms Embargo to Be Fully Lifted, Obama Says in Hanoi," New York Times, May 23, 2016, https://www.nytimes.com/2016/05/24/world/asia/vietnam-us-arms-embargo-obama.html; Agence France-Presse, "Barack Obama in Vietnam as US Seeks to Turn Former Enemy into Major Trade Market," Guardian, May 22, 2016, https://www.theguardian.com/world/2016/may/23/barack-obama-in-vietnam-as-us-seeks-to-turn-former-enemy-into-major-trade-market.

27. Harris, "Vietnam Arms Embargo to Be Fully Lifted, Obama Says"; Matt Spetalnick and Martin Petty, "Obama Prods Vietnam on Rights after Activists Stopped from Meeting Him," Reuters, May 23, 2016, https://www.reuters.com/article/us-vietnam-obama/obama-prods-vietnam-on-rights-after-activists-stopped-from-meeting-him-idUSKCN0YE2RX; "Remarks Following a Meeting with Civil Society Leaders in Hanoi, Vietnam," The American Presidency Project, May 24, 2016, https://www.presidency.ucsb.edu/documents/remarks-following-meeting-with-civil-society-leaders-hanoi-vietnam; "On Human Rights, Obama Finds Vietnam a Work in Progress," Chicago Tribune, May 24, 2016, https://www.chicagotribune.com/nation-world/ct-obama-vietnam-20160524-story.html.

28. Barack Obama, "Press Conference with Prime Minister Shinzo Abe," American Rhetoric, May 25, 2016, https://www.americanrhetoric.com/speeches/barackobama/barackobamashinzoabepresser.htm.

29. Elise Labott, "Here's Why Obama Decided to Go to Hiroshima," CNN, May 26, 2016, https://www.cnn.com/2016/05/26/politics/hiroshima-obama-visit-why-he-made-the-decision/index.html.

30. Justin McCurry, David Smith, and Alan Yuhas, "Obama Visit to Hiroshima Should Not Be Viewed as an Apology, White House Says," Guardian, May 10, 2016, https://www.theguardian.com/us-news/2016/may/10/obama-hiroshima-japan-

visit-second-world-war; David Nakamura, "Obama to Make Historic Visit to Hiroshima," *Washington Post*, May 10, 2016, https://www.washingtonpost.com/news/post-politics/wp/2016/05/10/obama-to-make-historic-visit-to-hiroshima/.

31. Nakamura, "Obama to Make Historic Visit to Hiroshima"; McCurry, Smith, and Yuhas, "Obama Visit to Hiroshima Should Not Be Viewed as an Apology, White House Says."

32. Barack Obama, "Address at the Hiroshima Peace Memorial," American Rhetoric, May 27, 2016, https://www.americanrhetoric.com/speeches/barackobama/barackobamahiroshimaspeech.htm; Elise Hu and Camila Domonoske, "Obama Makes Historic Visit to Hiroshima Memorial Peace Park," NPR, May 27, 2016, https://www.npr.org/sections/thetwo-way/2016/05/27/479691439/president-obama-arrives.

33. Barack Obama, "Address at the Hiroshima Peace Memorial"; Gardiner Harris, "At Hiroshima Memorial, Obama Says Nuclear Arms Require 'Moral Revolution,'" *New York Times*, May 27, 2016, https://www.nytimes.com/2016/05/28/world/asia/obama-hiroshima-japan.html; Daniel Sneider, "President Obama's Hiroshima Speech: An Assessment," Nippon News, August 5, 2016, https://www.nippon.com/en/currents/d00233/; David Smith, "'Start of Moral Awakening': Obama's Historic Hiroshima Visit Bittersweet," *Guardian*, May 27, 2016, https://www.theguardian.com/us-news/2016/may/27/barack-obama-japan-hiroshima-reaction; Hu and Domonoske, "Obama Makes Historic Visit to Hiroshima Memorial Peace Park."

34. On these points, see especially Sneider, "President Obama's Hiroshima Speech." But see also David French, "The Hiroshima Bombing Was Right and Necessary," *National Review*, May 27, 2016, https://www.nationalreview.com/2016/05/barack-obama-hiroshima-speech-was-wrong; Drew Richard, "Why Obama Is Shinzo Abe's Enabler," *New York Times*, May 31, 2016, https://www.nytimes.com/2016/06/01/opinion/why-obama-is-shinzo-abes-enabler.html; Smith, "'Start of Moral Awakening.'"

35. Quoted in Smith, "'Start of Moral Awakening.'" See also Sneider, "President Obama's Hiroshima Speech."

36. Lizette Alvarez and Richard Pérez-Peña, "Orlando Gunman Attacks Gay Nightclub, Leaving 50 Dead," *New York Times*, June 12, 2016, https://www.nytimes.com/2016/06/13/us/orlando-nightclub-shooting.html; Ralph Ellis, Ashley Frantz, Faith Karimi, and Eliott C. McLaughlin, "Orlando Shooting: 49 Killed, Shooter Pledged ISIS Allegiance," CNN, June 13, 2016, https://www.cnn.com/2016/06/12/us/orlando-nightclub-shooting/index.html.

37. Barack Obama, "Statement on the Orlando, Florida, Shootings," American Rhetoric, June 12, 2016, https://americanrhetoric.com/speeches/barackobama/barackobamaorlandoshootings.htm.

38. "President Obama's Remarks on 'Radical Islam' after Orlando Shooting,'" *Washington Post*, June 14, 2016, https://www.washingtonpost.com/news/post-politics/wp/2016/06/14/president-obamas; Jenna Johnson, "Donald Trump Seems to Connect President Obama to Orlando Shooting," *Washington Post*, June 13, 2016, https://www.washingtonpost.com/news/post-politics/wp/2016/06/13/donald-trump-suggests-president-obama-was-involved-with-orlando-shooting/.

39. "President Obama's Remarks on 'Radical Islam.'"

40. Barack Obama, "Address to the Community of Orlando, Florida, after Meeting Privately with Families of the Victims," American Rhetoric, July 16, 2016, https://www.americanrhetoric.com/speeches/barackobama/barackobamaorland-ocommunitystmt.htm.

41. Ibid.

42. "Obama's Speech: Read the Full Text," USA Today, September 10, 2014, https://www.usatoday.com/story/news/politics/2014/09/10/obama-speech-full-text/15415287/; Mark Landler, "Obama, in Speech on ISIS, Promises Sustained Effort to Rout Militants," New York Times, September 10, 2014, https://www.nytimes.com/2014/09/11/world/middleeast/obama-speech-isis.html; "Obama Announces Expanded Air Strikes against ISIS in Iraq and Syria—Speech Live Updates," Guardian, September 10, 2014, https://www.theguardian.com/world/live/2014/sep/10/obama-speech-strategy-destroy-isis-iraq-syria.

43. Obama's remarks can be found in John Parkinson and Erin Dooley, "President Obama Says 'We Don't Have a Strategy Yet' to Bomb ISIS in Syria," ABC News, August 28, 2014, https://abcnews.go.com/Politics/president-obama-strategy-fight-isis/story?id=25164105. See also Russell Berman, "Obama Says 'We Don't Have a Strategy Yet' in Syria," originally published in Atlantic, n.d., https://www.yahoo.com/entertainment/news/obama-says-dont-strategy-yet-syria-210240683.html; John Kerry, Every Day Is Extra (New York: Simon and Schuster, 2018), 542–48; Josh Rogin and Eli Lake, "Why Obama Backed Off More ISIS Strikes: His Own Team Couldn't Agree on a Strategy," Daily Beast, April 14, 2017, https://www.thedaily-beast.com/why-obama-backed-off-more-isis-strikes-his-own-team-couldnt-agree-on-a-syria-strategy.

44. Parkinson and Dooley, "President Obama Says 'We Don't Have a Strategy Yet' to Bomb ISIS in Syria"; Berman, "Obama Says 'We Don't Have a Strategy Yet' in Syria."

45. Helene Cooper and Eric Schmitt, "Airstrikes by U.S. and Allies Hit ISIS Targets in Syria," New York Times, September 22, 2014, https://www.nytimes.com/2014/09/23/world/middleeast/us-and-allies-hit-isis-targets-in-syria.html; Patrick Wintour, "Russia and US 'Planning Military Coordination against ISIS in Syria,'" Guardian, March 30, 2016, https://www.theguardian.com/world/2016/mar/30/russia-and-us-planning-military-coordination-against-isis-in-syria; Kerry, Every Day Is Extra, 542–48.

46. "Obama Announces Expanded Air Strikes against ISIS in Iraq and Syria—Speech Live Updates"; Ivan Eland, "U.S. Response to Syrian Civil War and Refugee Crisis Is Telling," Common Dreams, September 9, 2015, https://www.common-dreams.org/views/2015/09/09/us-response-syrian-civil-war-and-refugee-crisis-telling.

47. Manjana Pecht, "International Responses to Isis (and Why They Are Failing)," SIPRI, January 29, 2016, https://www.sipri.org/commentary/essay/2016/international-responses-isis-and-why-they-are-failing; David Frum, "The Disappointment of Barack Obama," Atlantic, March 10, 2016, https://www.theatlantic.com/international/archive/2016/03/obama-doctrine-goldberg-disappointment/473172/.

48. Quoted in Jeffrey Goldberg, "Obama's Former Middle East Adviser: We Should Have Bombed Assad," Atlantic, April 20, 2016, https://www.theatlantic.com/

international/archive/2016/04/philip-gordon-barack-obama-doctrine/479031/; Frum, "The Disappointment of Barack Obama."

49. Andrew Blake, "George Soros: Obama Was 'My Greatest Disappointment,'" *Washington Times*, July 18, 2018, https://www.washingtontimes.com/news/2018/jul/18/george-soros-obama-was-my-greatest-disappointment/.

50. Jeffrey Goldberg, "The Obama Doctrine," *Atlantic*, April 2016, https://www.theatlantic.com/magazine/archive/2016/04/the-obama-doctrine/471525/.

51. Ibid. See also David Brooks, "Obama, Gospel and Verse," *New York Times*, April 26, 2007, https://www.nytimes.com/2007/04/26/opinion/26brooks.html.

52. Goldberg, "The Obama Doctrine."

53. Ibid.

54. Ibid.; see also Frum, "The Disappointment of Barack Obama."

55. Goldberg, "The Obama Doctrine"; Frum, "The Disappointment of Barack Obama."

56. Goldberg, "The Obama Doctrine."

57. Ibid.

58. Ibid.

59. Richard Fausset, Richard Pérez-Peña, and Campbell Robertson, "Alton Sterling Shooting in Baton Rouge Prompts Justice Dept. Investigation," *New York Times*, July 6, 2016, https://www.nytimes.com/2016/07/06/us/alton-sterling-baton-rouge-shooting.html; Mitch Smith, "Minnesota Officer Acquitted in Killing of Philando Castile," *New York Times*, June 16, 2017, https://www.nytimes.com/2017/06/16/us/police-shooting-trial-philando-castile.html; Larry McShane, "Philando Castile Stopped by Cops in Minnesota 52 Times in Past 14 Years for a Slew of Misdemeanors," *New York Daily News*, July 9, 2016, https://www.nydailynews.com/news/national/philando-castile-stopped-cops-52-times-14-years-article-1.2705348; Richard Fausset, "Baton Rouge Officer Is Fired in Alton Sterling Case as Police Release New Videos," *New York Times*, March 30, 2018, https://www.nytimes.com/2018/03/30/us/baton-rouge-alton-sterling.html; Eric Levenson, "Baton Rouge Police Chief Apologizes for Hiring the Officer Who Killed Alton Sterling," CNN, August 1, 2019, https://www.cnn.com/2019/08/01/us/alton-sterling-baton-rouge-police; Peniel E. Joseph, "Barack Obama and the Movement for Black Lives: Race, Democracy, and Criminal Justice in the Age of Ferguson," in *The Presidency of Barack Obama: A First Historical Assessment*, ed. Julian E. Zelizer (Princeton, NJ: Princeton University Press, 2018), 140.

60. Manny Fernandez, Richard Pérez-Peña, and Jonah Engel-Bromwich, "Five Dallas Officers Were Killed as Payback, Police Chief Says," *New York Times*, July 8, 2016, https://www.nytimes.com/2016/07/09/us/dallas-police-shooting.html; "Full Transcript of President Obama's Speech at Dallas Police Memorial," ABC News, July 12, 2016, https://abcnews.go.com/Politics/full-transcript-president-obamas-speech-dallas-police-memorial/story?id=40521153.

61. "President Obama on the Fatal Shootings of Alton Sterling and Philando Castile," *The White House*, July 7, 2016, https://obamawhitehouse.archives.gov/blog/2016/07/07/president-obama-fatal-shootings-alton-sterling-and-philando-castile; Emma Ockerman, "President Obama on Alton Sterling and Philando Castile Shootings: 'All Americans Should Be Deeply Troubled,'" *Time Magazine*, July 7, 2016,

https://time.com/4397070/president-obama-alton-sterling-philando-castile-shootings-statement/; Joseph, "The Movement for Black Lives," 140; "Full Transcript of President Obama's Speech at Dallas Police Memorial."

62. "Full Transcript of President Obama's Speech at Dallas."

63. Ibid.

64. Ibid.

65. Ibid.

66. Ibid.; Maya Rhodan, "President Obama Defends Stance on Police, Black Lives Matter," *Time Magazine*, July 14, 2016, https://time.com/4407362/president-obama-police-black-lives-matter-town-hall.

67. As it was, Obama's address was criticized by both those who thought he had gone too far in defending BLM and by others who believed he did not go far enough in recognizing the institutional nature of racism and that the purpose of policing was to uphold hierarchies. See, for example, Rhodan, "President Obama Defends Stance on Police, Black Lives Matter"; Mychal Denzel Smith, "How President Obama Failed Black Lives Matter," *Washington Post*, July 21, 2016, https://www.washingtonpost.com/posteverything/wp/2016/07/21/how-president-obama-failed-black-lives-matter/.

68. Risa Goluboff and Richard Schragger, "Obama's Court?" in *The Presidency of Barack Obama: A First Historical Assessment*, ed. Julian E. Zeliger (Princeton, NJ: Princeton University Press, 2018), 92–93; Peter Baker, *Obama: The Call of History* (New York: Callaway, 2017), 337; David G. Savage, "The Congress Filled the Fewest Judgeships since 1952," *Los Angeles Times*, December 31, 2016, https://www.latimes.com/politics/la-na-judges-trump-senate-20161231-story.html.

69. Goluboff and Schragger, "Obama's Court?" 92–93; Baker, *Obama*, 337.

70. Ron Elving, "What Happened with Merrick Garland in 2016 and Why It Matters Now," NPR, June 29, 2018, https://www.npr.org/2018/06/29/624467256/what-happened-with-merrick-garland-in-2016-and-why-it-matters-now; Goluboff and Schragger, "Obama's Court?" 92–93; Baker, *Obama*, 337.

71. Elving, "What Happened with Merrick Garland in 2016 and Why It Matters Now."

72. Elving, "What Happened with Merrick Garland in 2016 and Why It Matters Now"; Sarah Lyall, "Liberals Are Still Angry, but Merrick Garland Has Reached Acceptance," *New York Times*, February 19, 2017, https://www.nytimes.com/2017/02/19/us/politics/merrick-garland-supreme-court-obama-nominee.html; Christian Farias, "Merrick Garland's Supreme Court Nomination Just Died with the Old Congress," Huffington Post, January 3, 2017, https://www.huffpost.com/entry/merrick-garland-supreme-court-nomination-dead_n_586be633e4b0d e3a08f9a8f2; Lyall, "Liberals Are Still Angry, but Merrick Garland Has Reached Acceptance."

73. "2016 Presidential Election Results," *New York Times*, November 9, 2016, https://www.nytimes.com/elections/2016/results/president; "2016 Election Results, CNN, November 9, 2016, https://www.cnn.com/election/2016/results; Gregory Krieg, "How Did Trump Win? Here Are 24 Theories," CNN, November 10, 2016, https://www.cnn.com/2016/11/10/politics/why-donald-trump-won/index.html; Anthony Zurcher, "US Election 2016 Results: Five Reasons

Donald Trump Won," BBC, November 9, 2016, https://www.bbc.com/news/election-us-2016-37918303.

74. Amy Chozick, Patrick Healey, and Yamiche Alcindor, "Bernie Sanders Endorses Hillary Clinton, Hoping to Unify Democrats," *New York Times*, July 12, 2016, https://www.nytimes.com/2016/07/13/us/politics/bernie-sanders-hillary-clinton.html.

75. Edward-Isaac Dovere, "Obama's 2016 Warning: Trump Is a 'Fascist,' " *Atlantic*, January 25, 2020, https://www.theatlantic.com/politics/archive/2020/01/obama-2016-trump-fascist/605488/.

76. Barack Obama, "2016 Democratic National Convention Address," American Rhetoric, July 27, 2016, https://americanrhetoric.com/speeches/convention2016/barackobamadnc2016.htm.

77. Ibid.

78. Ibid.

79. Michelle Obama, "Democratic National Convention Address," American Rhetoric, July 25, 2016, https://www.americanrhetoric.com/speeches/convention2016/michelleobamadnc2016.htm.

80. Brian Stellar, "Convention Ratings: Democrats Beat Republicans, and Cable Tops Broadcast," CNN, July 27, 2016, https://money.cnn.com/2016/07/27/media/democratic-convention-night-two-ratings; Stephen Battaglio, "TV Viewership for Hillary Clinton's Acceptance Speech Is Smaller than Donald Trump's," *Los Angeles Times*, July 29, 2016, https://www.latimes.com/entertainment/envelope/cotown/la-et-ct-dnc-ratings-20160729-snap-story.html; Brian Stellar, "Trump Prevails over Clinton in Convention Speech Ratings Race," CNN, July 30, 2016, https://money.cnn.com/2016/07/29/media/democratic-convention-night-four-ratings.

81. David Brooks, "I Miss Barack Obama," *New York Times*, February 9, 2016, https://www.nytimes.com/2016/02/09/opinion/i-miss-barack-obama.html; Sophia Tesfaye, "Now He Says He'll Miss Obama, but Here Are 7 of David Brooks' Worst," Salon, February 9, 2016, https://www.salon.com/2016/02/09/now_he_says_hell_miss_obama_but_here_are_7_of_david_brooks_worst_critiques_of_the_president/; Ryu Spaeth, "David Brooks and Barack Obama: A Love Story," *New Republic*, March11, 2016, https://newrepublic.com/article/131453/david-brooks-barack-obama-love-story.

82. Kevin Liptak, "Obama: 'I Really, Really, Really Want to Elect Hillary Clinton,' " CNN, September 13, 2016, https://www.cnn.com/2016/09/13/politics/obama-campaign-trail-2016-election/index.html.

83. Ibid.; Anne Gearan and Phillip Rucker, "Obama Blasts Trump as a Phony Champion of the Working Class," *Washington Post*, September 13, 2016, https://www.washingtonpost.com/politics/obama-blasts-trump-as-a-phony-champion-of-the-working-class/2016/09/13/4a97be98-79c9-11e6-ac8e-cf8e0dd91dc7_story.html; Baker, *Obama*, 348–50.

84. De Elizabeth, "President Obama Just Delivered His Most Passionate Speech EVER," *Teen Vogue*, September 18, 2016, https://www.teenvogue.com/story/president-obama-just-delivered-his-most-passionate-speech-ever; Ian Schwartz, "Obama: I Will Consider It an Insult to My Legacy If You Do Not Vote: Want to Give Me a Good Send Off? Go Vote," Real Clear Politics, September 17, 2016, https://www.

realclearpolitics.com/video/2016/09/17/obama_i_will_consider_it_an_insult_to_
my_legacy_if_you_do_not_vote_want_to_give_me_a_good_send_off_go_vote.
html. "Obama Says If African-Americans Do Not Vote, It Will Be a 'Personal Insult,' "
PBS News Hour, September 18, 2016, https://www.pbs.org/newshour/politics/
obama-african-american-vote.

85. Mark Landler and Ashley Parker, "Obama Tells Trump: Stop 'Whining' and
Trying to Discredit the Election," *New York Times*, October 18, 2016, https://www.
nytimes.com/2016/10/19/us/politics/obama-donald-trump-election.html; Kan-
yakrit Vongkiatkajorn, "President Obama Just Gave His Last Campaign Speech for
Hillary and It Was Amazing," *Mother Jones*, November 8, 2016, https://www.moth
erjones.com/politics/2016/11/obama-speech-philadelphia/.

86. Philip Bump, "4.4 Million 2012 Obama Voters Stayed Home in 2016—More
Than a Third of Them Black," *Washington Post*, March 12, 2018, https://www.wash
ingtonpost.com/news/politics/wp/2018/03/12/4-4-million-2012-obama-voters-
stayed-home-in-2016-more-than-a-third-of-them-black/; "What Does Voter Turnout
Tell Us about the 2016 Election?" PBS News Hour, November 20, 2016, https://www.
pbs.org/newshour/politics/voter-turnout-2016-election; Phillip Louis Casiano,
"Michelle Obama Says These Americans Responsible for Trump's 2016 Victory,"
Fox News, May 4, 2017, https://www.foxnews.com/politics/michelle-obama-says-
these-americans-responsible-trump-2016-victory; Baker, *Obama*, 364–65 and 369–70.

87. Rhodes, *The World as It Is*, 404; Barack Obama "Presidential Election Outcome Address," American Rhetoric, November 9, 2016, https://www.americanrhet-
oric.com/speeches/barackobama/barackobama2016presidentialelectionoutcome.
htm. See also Baker, *Obama*, 365–66.

88. "Barack Obama: Presidential Election Outcome Address"; Jelani Cobb,
"Barack Obama in Defeat," *New Yorker*, November 10, 2016, https://www.newy
orker.com/news/news-desk/barack-obama-in-defeat.

89. Barack Obama, "Remarks on First Meeting with President-Elect Donald
Trump," American Rhetoric, November 10, 2016, https://www.americanrheto
ric.com/speeches/barackobama/barackobamadonaldtrumpmeeting.htm; Barack
Obama, "Press Conference Post 2016 Presidential Election," American Rhetoric,
November 14, 2016, https://www.americanrhetoric.com/speeches/barackobama/
barackobamapostelectionpresser.htm.

90. Rhodes, *The World as It Is*, 390–95 and 406–11; Baker, *Obama*, 356–57.

91. Tucker Higgins, "Obama Response to 2016 Russian Election Meddling
Had 'Many Flaws,' Senate Report Finds," CNBC, February 6, 2020, https://www.
cnbc.com/2020/02/06/obama-response-to-2016-russian-meddling-had-many-
flaws-senate-report.html; Rice, *Tough Love*, 441–49; Baker, *Obama*, 358–64 and
372–73.

92. Simon Tisdall, "Obama Sets Off on Farewell Trip to Europe in Shadow
of President-Elect," *Guardian*, November 14, 2016, https://www.theguardian.
com/us-news/2016/nov/14/barack-obama-faces-awkward-task-on-sad-farewell-
visit-to-europe; "In Europe to Calm Anxious Allies, Obama Warns against 'Crude'
Nationalism," CBS News, November 16, 2016, https://www.cbsnews.com/news/
obama-acropolis-greece-europe-worry-donald-trump-paris-agreement-climate-
change/.

93. Barack Obama, "Address to the People of Greece," American Rhetoric, November 16, 2016, https://www.americanrhetoric.com/speeches/barackobama/barackobamagreecepeople.htm.

94. Barack Obama, "Joint Press Conference with Chancellor Angela Merkel," American Rhetoric, November 17, 2016, https://www.americanrhetoric.com/speeches/barackobama/barackobamaangelamerkelpresser2016.htm.

95. "Press Conference by President Obama in Lima, Peru," *Office of the Press Secretary, The White House*, November 20, 2016, https://obamawhitehouse.archives.gov/the-press-office/2016/11/20/press-conference-president-obama-lima-peru.

96. Gardiner Harris and Keith Bradsher, "China's Influence Grows in Ashes of Trans-Pacific Trade Pact," *New York Times*, November 19, 2016, https://www.nytimes.com/2016/11/20/business/international/apec-trade-china-obama-trump-tpp-trans-pacific-partnership.html; Phillip Corey, "Labor Wants a Better Deal for Workers in Trade Deals," *Australian Financial Review*, November 15, 2016, web page no longer available; "Obama Snubbed at APEC Conference," *The Night Wind* (blog), November 23, 2016, https://nightwind777.blogspot.com/2016/11/obama-snubbed-at-apec-conference.html.

97. Harris and Bradsher, "China's Influence Grows in Ashes of Trans-Pacific Trade Pact"; Corey, "Labor Wants a Better Deal for Workers in Trade Deals"; "Obama Snubbed at APEC Conference"; Andrea Zarate, "Protests Erupt in Peru Ahead of Asia-Pacific Economic Meeting," *New York Times*, November 18, 2016, https://www.nytimes.com/2016/11/19/world/americas/peru-protests-apec.html.

98. Rice, *Tough Love*, 423.

99. Mark Landler and Michael D. Shear, "Obama's Farewell Address: 'Yes, We Did,'" *New York Times*, January 10, 2017, https://www.nytimes.com/2017/01/10/us/politics/obama-farewell-address-president.html; Maya Rhodan, "In His Farewell Speech, President Obama Returns to His Roots as a Community Leader," *Time Magazine*, January 10, 2017, https://time.com/4631089/barack-obama-farewell-speech-analysis/.

100. Barack Obama, "Presidential Farewell Address," American Rhetoric, January 10, 2017, http://www.americanrhetoric.com/speeches/barackobama/barackobamafarewelladdress.htm; Claire Cain Miller, "A Darker Theme in Obama's Farewell: Automation Can Divide Us," *New York Times*, January 12, 2017, https://www.nytimes.com/2017/01/12/upshot/in-obamas-farewell-a-warning-on-automations-perils.html.

101. Barack Obama, "Presidential Farewell Address."

102. Barack Obama, "Final Presidential Press Conference," American Rhetoric, January 18, 2017, https://www.americanrhetoric.com/speeches/barackobama/barackobamafinalpressconference.htm; David Smith, "Barack Obama's Final Press Conference Pep Talk," *Guardian*, January 18, 2017, https://www.theguardian.com/us-news/2017/jan/18/barack-obama-final-press-conference-press-sasha-malia-trump; John Cassidy, "Obama's Not-So-Final Goodbye," *New Yorker*, January 19, 2017, https://www.newyorker.com/news/john-cassidy/obamas-not-so-final-goodbye.

103. Barack Obama, "Final Presidential Press Conference"; Smith, "Barack Obama's Final Press Conference Pep Talk"; Cassidy, "Obama's Not-So-Final Goodbye"; "Barack Obama Uses Final Press Conference as US President to Defend Slashing

Chelsea Manning's Sentence," ABC News, January 19, 2017, https://www.abc.net.
au/news/2017-01-19/barack-obama-final-press-conference-as-president/8193092.

. 104. Barack Obama, "Final Presidential Press Conference"; Smith, "Barack
Obama's Final Press Conference Pep Talk"; Cassidy, "Obama's Not-So-Final Goodbye"; "Barack Obama Uses Final Press Conference as US President to Defend Slashing Chelsea Manning's Sentence."

11. The Postpresidency

1. Burton I. Kaufman, *The Post-Presidency from Washington to Clinton* (Lawrence:
University Press of Kansas, 2012).

2. Ibid., 395, 435–36, and 516.

3. "All Five Former Presidents Appeared Together at a Concert to Raise Money
for Hurricane Relief," *Business Insider*, October 21, 2017, https://www.businessin-
sider.com/all-5-former-presidents-texas-hurricane-relief-concert-2017-10-2.

4. Barack Obama, "Final Presidential Press Conference," American Rhetoric,
January 18, 2017, https://www.americanrhetoric.com/speeches/barackobama/
barackobamafinalpressconference.htm.

5. Aimee Picchi, "Obama after the Presidency: He'll Do Fine," CBS News,
May 31, 2016, https://www.cbsnews.com/news/obama-after-the-presidency-hell-
do-fine; Sam Dangremond, "What Malia Obama Is Doing During Her Gap Year,"
Town and Country Magazine, January 25, 2017, https://www.townandcountrymag.
com/society/news/a5588/malia-obama-harvard; Katherine Skiba, "Obama's Post-
Presidential Life Beginning to Take Shape," *Chicago Tribune*, January 16, 2017, https://
www.chicagotribune.com/news/ct-obamas-after-white-house-met-20170116-story.
html; Amy Davidson Sorkin, "Obama's Life Post-Presidency," *New Yorker*, May 15,
2017, https://www.newyorker.com/magazine/2017/05/15/obamas-life-post-presi-
dency.

6. Skiba, "Obama's Post-Presidential Life Beginning to Take Shape"; Kate
Andersen Brower, *Team of Five: The President's Club in the Age of Trump* (New York:
HarperCollins, 2020), 22.

7. Adam Edelman, "Life after the White House: How Obama Spent His First
Year out of Office," NBC News, January 20, 2018, https://www.nbcnews.com/
politics/barack-obama/life-after-white-house-how-obama-spent-his-first-year-
n838951; "Here's What Barack Obama Is Doing Now," *Town and Country*, June 24,
2019, https://www.townandcountrymag.com/society/politics/news/a9694/what-
barack-obama-is.

8. Megan Friedman, "Read the Full Text Transcript of President Obama's First
Public Speech since Leaving Office," *Elle*, April 24, 2017, https://www.elle.com/
news/a44738/president-obama-university-chicago-transcript.

9. Edelman, "Life after the White House."

10. Kriston Capps, "Why the Case against the Obama Presidential Center Is
So Important," Bloomberg News, February 21, 2019, https://www.bloomberg.
com/news/articles/2019-02-21/chicago-battle-over-obama-presidential-center-
goes-on; Lolly Bowean, "Federal Judge Tosses Suit Seeking to Stop Obama Center in Jackson Park, Compares Project to Soldier Field," Chicago Tribune, June 12,

https://www.chicagotribune.com/news/breaking/ct-met-obama-library-decision-20190611-story.html.

11. "What's behind Trump's Charge That Obama Ordered Trump Tower Wiretap?" PBS News Hour, March 6, 2017, https://www.pbs.org/newshour/show/whats-behind-trumps-charge-obama-ordered-trump-tower-wiretap; Matthew Nussbaum, "Justice Department: No Evidence Obama Wiretapped Trump Tower," *Politico*, September 2, 2017, https://www.politico.com/story/2017/09/02/obama-trump-tower-wiretap-no-evidence-242284; "DOJ: No Evidence Trump Tower Was Wiretapped," Fox News, September 2, 2017, https://www.foxnews.com/politics/doj-no-evidence-trump-tower-was-wiretapped.

12. The quotes are in Brower, *Team of Five*, 18–19.

13. Edelman, "Life after the White House"; Tom McCarthy, "Obama's Post-Presidential Life: What Does His Second Act Have in Store?" *Guardian*, December 25, 2017, https://www.theguardian.com/us-news/2017/dec/25/obama-post-presidential-life-trump.

14. The full transcript of Obama's remarks can be found in Vann R. Newkirk II, "Obama: This Bill Will Do You Harm," *Atlantic*, June 22, 2017, https://www.theatlantic.com/politics/archive/2017/06/this-is-the-obamacare-speech-obama-never-gave/531330/; McCarthy, "Obama's Post-Presidential Life"; Edelman, "Life after the White House"; Charlotte Gao, "A Closer Look at Obama's Trip to China," Diplomat, December 4, 2017, https://thediplomat.com/2017/12/a-closer-look-at-obamas-trip-to-china.

15. "Here's What Barack Obama Is Doing Now"; McCarthy, "Obama's Post-Presidential Life"; Edelman, "Life after the White House."

16. "John McCain Funeral: Barack Obama Eulogy Transcript," CBS News, September 1, 2018, https://www.cbsnews.com/news/john-mccain-funeral-barack-obama-eulogy-transcript. See also "John McCain Funeral: Obama's Eulogy Denounces 'Insult and Bombast' in Politics," *Guardian*, September 1, 2018, https://www.theguardian.com/us-news/2018/sep/01/john-mccain-funeral-obamas-eulogy-denounces-insult-and-bombast-in-politics; Peter Baker, "In McCain Memorial Service, Two Presidents Offer Tribute, and Contrast to Trump," *New York Times*, September 1, 2018, https://www.nytimes.com/2018/09/01/us/politics/john-mccain-funeral.html.

17. "Obama's Full Speech on the State of American Democracy," CBS News, September 7, 2012, https://www.cbsnews.com/news/barack-obama-speech-full-transcript-2018-09-07/. See also Peter Baker, "Obama Lashes Trump in Debut 2018 Speech. President's Response: 'I Fell Asleep,'" *New York Times*, September 7, 2019, https://www.nytimes.com/2018/09/07/us/politics/obama-2018-campaign-trump.html; Edward-Isaac Dovere, "Obama Delivers Full-Throated Rebuke of Trump's Presidency," *Politico*, September 7, 2018, https://www.politico.com/story/2018/09/07/obama-says-trump-has-pushed-america-to-a-pivotal-moment-810650.

18. "Obama's Full Speech on the State of American Democracy"; Baker, "Obama Lashes Trump in Debut 2018 Speech"; Dovere, "Obama Delivers Full-Throated Rebuke of Trump's Presidency."

19. "Obama's Full Speech on the State of American Democracy."

20. Ibid.

21. Ibid.

22. Alexi McCammond, "Where the Obamas Are Hitting the Campaign Trail in 2018," Axios, September 15, 2018, https://www.axios.com/obamas-campaign-trail-2018-midterms-9cffb339-fcea-4cb0-9156-dfa0339d51e7.html.

23. Erin Durkin, "Democrats Secure 218 Seats in Midterms to Win Control of House—as It Happened," *Guardian*, November 7, 2018, https://www.theguard-ian.com/us-news/live/2018/nov/06/us-midterms-elections-2018-latest-live-polls-news-updates-donald-trump-republicans-democrats?page=with:block-5be29c2be4b0e3827e155d14; "U.S. Senate Election Results 2018," *New York Times*, November 6, 2018, https://www.nytimes.com/interactive/2018/11/06/us/elections/results-senate-elections.html; "U.S. House Election Results 2018," *New York Times*, November 6, 2018, https://www.nytimes.com/interactive/2018/11/06/us/elections/results-house-elections.html.

24. Barack Obama, *A Promised Land* (New York: Crown, 2020); "Here's What Barack Obama Is Doing Now," *Town and Country*, June 24, 2019, https://www.townandcountrymag.com/society/politics/news/a9694/what-barack-obama-is-doing-now/.

25. "Welcome to the Obama Foundation," Obama Foundation, n.d., https://obama.org.

26. "Obama Foundation Scholars," Obama Foundation, n.d., https://www.obama.org/scholars; "Obama Foundation Scholars Program," Scholarships for Development, March 19, 2018, https://www.scholars4dev.com/21843/obama-foundation-scholars-program; Gospel Chinonso, "Obama Foundation Scholars Program 2021–2022 (Fully Funded)," Columbia University, January 6, 2021, https://www.academicrelated.com/obama-foundation-scholars-program.

27. "Obama Foundation Scholars"; "Obama Foundation Scholars Program"; "Obama Foundation Scholars Program 2021–2022 (Fully Funded)."

28. See chapter 9, "Racial Crisis." See also Scott Horsley, "Obama's Post-White House Plans Include My Brother's Keeper Effort," NPR, December 26, 2016, https://www.npr.org/2016/12/26/507021405/obamas-post-white-house-plans-include-my-brothers-keeper-effort; "About My Brother's Keeper Alliance," Obama Foundation, n.d., https://www.obama.org/mbka/about-mbka/.

29. Horsley, "Obama's Post-White House Plans Include My Brother's Keeper Effort"; "About My Brother's Keeper Alliance."

30. "Obama Defends Black Lives Matter Movement," PBS News Hour, October 23, 2015, https://www.pbs.org/newshour/politics/obama-defends-black-lives-matter-movement; "President Obama Defends Black Lives Matter Movement," CBS News, October 23, 2015, https://www.cbsnews.com/news/president-barack-obama-defends-black-lives-matter-movement.

31. Sam Levine, "Obama Praises Black Lives Matter, but Says Activists Must Compromise," Huffington Post, April 23, 2016, https://www.huffpost.com/entry/obama-black-lives-matter_n_571b9414e4b0d4d3f7238bb6.

32. Maggie Astor, "What Trump, Biden and Obama Said about the Death of George Floyd," *New York Times*, May 29, 2020, https://www.nytimes.com/2020/05/29/us/politics/george-floyd-trump-biden-obama.html; "Read: Barack Obama's Statement on George Floyd's Death," *U.S. News*, May 29, 2020, https://www.usnews.

com/news/national-news/articles/2020-05-29/read-barack-obamas-statement-on-george-floyds-death.

33. Jonathan Capehardt, "Obama's Raw Recollections on Race in 'A Promised Land,'" *Washington Post*, November 27, 2020, https://www.washingtonpost.com/opinions/2020/11/27/obamas-raw-recollections-race-promised-land/.

34. Alexandra Svokos, "Former President Barack Obama Issues Statement on George Floyd," ABC News, May 29, 2020, https://abcnews.go.com/Politics/president-barack-obama-issues-statement-george-floyd/story?id=70954996; "Barack Obama Attacks Trump Administration's Response to Coronavirus Pandemic," *Guardian*, May 17, 2020, https://www.theguardian.com/us-news/2020/may/16/barack-obama-coronavirus-donald-trump-criticism-speech-covid-19; Peter Wade, "Obama Torches Trump on COVID-19: 'A Lot of Them Aren't Even Pretending to Be in Charge,'" *Rolling Stone*, May 16, 2020, https://www.rollingstone.com/politics/politics-news/obama-torches-trump-coronavirus-commencement-address-1001041/.

35. "Barack Obama Attacks Trump Administration's Response to Coronavirus Pandemic."

36. Maggie Astor and Katie Glueck, "Barack Obama Endorses Joe Biden for President," *New York Times*, April 14, 2020, https://www.nytimes.com/2020/04/14/us/politics/obama-endorses-biden.html; Sean Sullivan, Anne Linskey, and Michael Scherer, "Biden's Endorsement Rollout Has One Goal: To Show Him as the Leader of a Newly Unified Party," *Washington Post*, April 14, 2020, https://www.washingtonpost.com/politics/former-president-barack-obama-to-announce-support-for-joe-biden-his-former-vice-president/2020/04/14/99a49a56-7e57-11ea-8013-1b6da0e4a2b7_story.html; "Obama Endorses Biden for President in an Attempt to Unite Democratic Party," *Guardian*, April 14, 2020, https://www.theguardian.com/us-news/2020/apr/14/barack-obama-endorse-joe-biden-2020-election-democrats.

37. Astor and Glueck, "Barack Obama Endorses Joe Biden for President"; Sullivan, Linskey, and Scherer, "Biden's Endorsement Rollout Has One Goal"; "Obama Endorses Biden for President in an Attempt to Unite Democratic Party."

38. Astor and Glueck, "Barack Obama Endorses Joe Biden for President"; Sullivan, Linskey, and Scherer, "Biden's Endorsement Rollout Has One Goal"; "Obama Endorses Biden for President in an Attempt to Unite Democratic Party."

39. "First Thing Election Special: Barack Obama Is Back on the Campaign Trail," *Guardian*, October 22, 2020, https://www.theguardian.com/us-news/2020/oct/22/first-thing-election-special-barack-obama-is-back-on-the-campaign-trail; "Watch: Obama Campaigns for Biden in Orlando," PBS News Hour, October 27, 2020, https://www.pbs.org/newshour/politics/watch-live-barack-obama-campaigns-for-joe-biden-in-orlando; Melissa Quinn, "Campaigning in Florida, Obama Says Trump Is 'Jealous of COVID's Media Coverage,'" CBS News, October 27, 2020, https://www.cbsnews.com/news/obama-drive-in-rally-orlando-florida-biden-campaign-watch-live-stream-today-2020-10-27; Iyani Hughes, "President Obama Campaigns in Georgia One Day Ahead of Elections," CNN, November 2, 2020, https://www.cbs46.com/news/president-obama-campaigns-in-georgia-one-day-ahead-of-election/article_fada6044-1d12-11eb-b514-f3251ebe24af.html.

40. "U.S. Presidential Election Results 2020: Biden Wins," NBC News, December 18, 2020, https://www.nbcnews.com/politics/2020-elections/president-results;

Erin Delmore, "Stacey Abrams Is 2020's Election Star—Can She Turn Georgia Blue Again, in 2021?" NBC News, November 18, 2020, https://www.nbcnews.com/know-your-value/feature/stacey-abrams-2020-s-election-star-can-she-turn-georgia-ncna1248104; Jazz Tangcay, "Stacey Abrams Hailed as a 'Game Changer' by Documentarians Who Chronicled Her," *Variety*, November 9, 2020, https://variety.com/2020/politics/news/stacey-abrams-2020-election-all-in-documentaries-1234826048/.

41. See, for example, "Obama Appears in Three Digital Campaign Ads for Georgia's Raphael Warnock," CNN, December 18, 2020, https://www.cnn.com/2020/12/18/politics/obama-warnock-senate-ad/index.html.

SELECTED BIBLIOGRAPHY

Barack Obama's three autobiographies—*Dreams from My Father: A Story of Race and Inheritance* (New York: Three Rivers Press, 1996); *The Audacity of Hope: Thoughts on Reclaiming the American Dream* (New York: Broadway Paperbacks, 2006); and *A Promised Land* (New York: Crown, 2020)—offer a map of his life through the assassination of Osama bin Laden in 2011. They also spotlight how he came to make the decisions he did both before and during his presidency. First Lady Michelle Obama's bestselling autobiography, *Becoming* (New York: Crown, 2018), provides additional insights into Barack Obama's personality and mind. It also reveals Michelle's dislike of politics and the stresses and strains of her marriage to Barack.

Other members of the Obama administration have also published books that cover their years as part of his presidency and offer considerable insight about the forty-fourth president and the inner workings of his presidency. Among the most important of these are: David Axelrod, *Believer: My Forty Years In Politics* (New York: Penguin Press, 2016); Jeffrey A. Bader, *Obama and China's Rise: An Insider's Account of America's Asia Strategy* (Washington, DC: Brookings Institution Press, 2012); Ben S. Bernanke, *The Courage to Act: A Memoir of a Crisis and Its Aftermath* (New York: W. W. Norton, 2015); Ash Carter, *Inside the Five-Sided Box: Lessons from a Lifetime of Leadership in the Pentagon* (New York: Dayton, 2019); Hillary Rodham Clinton, *Hard Choices* (New York: Simon and Schuster, 2014); Hillary Rodham Clinton, *What Happened* (New York: Simon and Schuster, 2017); Robert M. Gates, *Duty: Memoirs of a Secretary of War* (New York: Alfred A. Knopf, 2014); Timothy F. Geithner, *Stress Test: Reflections on Financial Crises* (New York: Broadway Books, 2014); Valerie Jarrett, *Finding My Voice: My Journey to the West Wing and the Path Forward* (New York: Viking, 2019); John Kerry, *Every Day Is Extra* (New York: Simon and Schuster, 2018); Leon Panetta, *Worthy Fights: A Memoir of Leadership in War and Peace* (New York: Penguin Books, 2014); Dan Pfeiffer, *Yes We (Still) Can: Politics in the Age of Obama, Twitter and Trump* (New York: Twelve, 2018); David Plouffe, *The Audacity to Win: How Obama Won and How We Can Beat the Party of Limbaugh, Beck, and Palin* (New York: Penguin Books, 2010); Steven Rattner, *Overhaul: An Insider's Account of the Obama Administration's Emergency Rescue of the Auto Industry* (Boston: Houghton Mifflin Harcourt, 2010); Susan Rice, *Tough Love: My Story of the Things Worth Fighting For* (New

York: Simon and Schuster, 2019); and Ben Rhodes, *The World As It Is: A Memoir of the Obama White House* (New York: Random House, 2018).

Also important are the memoirs of President George Bush's treasury secretary during the economic crisis in 2008, Henry M. Paulson Jr., *On the Brink: Inside the Race to Stop the Collapse of the Global Financial System* (New York: Business Plus, 2010). On Republican Senate leader Mitch McConnell's determination to make Barack Obama a one-term president, see also Mitch McConnell, *The Long Game: A Memoir* (New York: Penguin, 2016).

Many of Obama's major speeches as president can be found in *President Barack Obama's Speeches* (n.p.: American Rhetoric, 2009–2017). Other major addresses are in *Obama White House Archives* (Washington D.C.: Office of the Press Secretary, The White House, 2009–2017).

Full transcripts of Obama's other addresses routinely appear in such newspapers as the *New York Times, Washington Post, Wall Street Journal*, and *Guardian*. I have also relied heavily on these and other newspapers, such as the *Chicago Tribune, Chicago Sun-Times, Washington Times, Rolling Stone*, and *Los Angeles Times* for important background material.

The secondary literature on various aspects of Obama's life and presidency is already large. What follows is a select list of these books.

Secondary Sources

Alinsky, Saul D. *Rules for Radicals: A Practical Primer for Realistic Radicals*. New York: Vintage Books, 1989.

Allen, Jonathan, and Amie Parnes. *Shattered: Inside Hillary Clinton's Doomed Campaign*. New York: Crown, 2017.

Alter, Jonathan. *The Center Holds: Obama and His Enemies*. New York: Simon and Schuster, 2013.

Alter, Jonathan. *The Promise: President Obama: Year One*. New York: Simon and Schuster, 2010.

Andersen, Christopher. *Barack and Michelle: Portrait of an American Marriage*. New York: William Morrow, 2009.

Baker, Peter, *Obama: The Call of History*. New York: Callaway, 2017.

Balz, Dan. *Collision 2012: Obama vs. Romney and the Future of Elections in America*. New York: Penguin, 2013.

Belcher, Cornell. *A Black Man in the White House: Barack Obama and the Triggering of America's Racial-Aversion Crisis*. Healdsburg, CA: Water Street Press, 2016.

Brill, Steven. *America's Bitter Pill: Money, Politics, Backroom Deals, and the Fight to Fix Our Broken Health Care System*. New York: Random House, 2015.

Brophy, David. *Michelle Obama: Meet the First Lady*. New York: Collins, 2009.

Chait, Jonathan. *Audacity: How Barack Obama Defied His Critics and Created a Legacy That Will Prevail*. New York: Harper Collins, 2017.

Chezick, Amy. *Chasing Hillary: Ten Years, Two Presidential Campaigns, and One Intact Glass Ceiling*. New York: Harper Collins, 2018.

Coates, Ta-Nehisi. *We Were Eight Years in Power: An American Tragedy*. New York: One World, 2017.

Corn, David. *Showdown: The Inside Story of How Obama Battled the GOP to Set Up the 2012 Election*. New York: William Morrow, 2012.

D'Antonio, Michael. *The Legacy of Barack Obama: A Consequential President*. New York: St. Martin's Press, 2016.

Draper, Robert. *When the Tea Party Came to Town*. New York: Simon and Schuster, 2012.

Dyson, Michael Eric. *The Black Presidency: Barack Obama and the Politics of Race in America* Boston: Houghton Mifflin Harcourt, 2016.

Emmanuel, Ezekial, Jr. *Reinventing American Health*. New York: Public Affairs, 2014.

Garrow, David J. *Rising Star: The Making of Barack Obama* (New York: HarperCollins, 2017).

Gerges, Fawaz A. *Obama and the Middle East: The End of America's Moment?* New York: Palgrave Macmillan, 2012.

Grunwald, Michael. *The New New Deal: The Hidden Story of Change in the Obama Era*. New York: Simon and Schuster, 2012.

Halperin, Mark, and John Heilemann. *Double Down: Game Change 2012*. New York: Penguin Press, 2013.

Harris, Frederick E. *The Price of the Ticket: Barack Obama and the Rise and Decline of Black Politics* (New York: Oxford University Press, 2014).

Heilemann, John, and Mark Halperin. *Game Change: Obama and the Clintons, McCain and Palin and the Race of a Lifetime*. New York: Harper Collins, 2018.

Jacobs, Sally H. *The Other Barack: The Bold and Reckless Life of President Obama's Father*. New York: Public Affairs, 2011.

Kantor, Jodi. *The Obamas*. New York: Back Bay Books, 2012.

Klaidman, Daniel. *Kill or Capture: The War on Terror and the Soul of the Obama Presidency*. New York: Houghton Mifflin Harcourt, 2012.

Kloppenberg, James T. *Reading Obama: Dreams, Hopes, and the American Political Traditions*. Princeton, NJ: Princeton University Press, 2011.

Landler, Mark. *Alter Egos: Hillary Clinton, Barack Obama, and the Twilight Struggle over American Power*. New York: Random House, 2016.

Mann, James. *The Obamians: The Struggle inside the White House to Redefine American Power*. New York: Penguin Group, 2012.

Mann, Thomas E., and Norman J. Ornstein. *It's Even Worse Than It Looks: How the American Constitutional System Collided with the Politics of Extremism*. New York: Basic Books, 2012.

Maraniss, David. *Barack Obama: The Story*. New York: Simon and Schuster, 2012.

McClelland, Edward. *Young Mr. Obama: Chicago and the Making of a Black President*. New York: Bloomsbury Press, 2010.

Mendell, David. *Obama: From Promise to Power*. New York: Harper Collins, 2007.

Mundy Liza, *Michelle: A Biography*. New York: Simon and Schuster, 2008.

O'Rourke, P. J. *How the Hell Did This Happen? The Election of 2016* (New York: Atlantic Monthly Press, 2017).

Posner, Richard A. *A Failure of Capitalism: The Crisis of '08 and the Descent into Depression*. Cambridge, MA: Harvard University Press, 2009.

Remnick, David. *The Life and Rise of Barack Obama*. New York: Vintage Books, 2011.

Rosenthal, Elisabeth. *An American Sickness: How Healthcare Became Big Business and How You Can Take It Back*. New York: Penguin Press, 2017.

Sanger, David E. *Confront and Conceal: Obama's Secret Wars and Surprising Use of American Power*. New York: Broadway Paperbacks, 2013.

Sanger, David E. *The Inheritance: The World Obama Confronts and the Challenges to American Power*. New York: Harmony Books, 2009.

Savage, Charlie. *Power Wars: Inside Obama's Post-9/11 Presidency*. New York: Little, Brown, 2015.

Scheiber, Noam. *The Escape Artists: How Obama's Team Fumbled the Recovery*. New York: Simon and Schuster, 2011.

Scott, Janey. *A Singular Woman: The Untold Story of Barack Obama's Mother*. New York: Riverhead Books, 2011.

Sorkin, Andrew Ross. *The Big Fail: The Inside Story of How Wall Street and Washington Fought to Save the Financial System and Themselves*. New York: Viking, 2009.

Suskind, Ron. *Confidence Men: Wall Street, Washington, and the Education of a President*. New York: Harper Collins, 2011.

Suskind, Ron. *The One Percent Doctrine: Deep Inside America's Pursuit of Its Enemies since 9/11*. New York: Simon and Schuster, 2006.

Wolffe, Richard. *Renegade: The Making of a President*. New York, Crown Publishers, 2009.

Wolffe, Richard. *Revival: The Struggle for Survival inside the Obama White House*. New York: Crown, 2010.

Woodward, Bob. *Obama's Wars*. New York: Simon and Schuster, 2011.

Woodward, Bob. *The Price of Politics*. New York: Simon and Schuster, 2012.

Zelizer, Julian E., ed. *The Presidency of Barack Obama*. Princeton, NJ: Princeton University Press, 2018.

INDEX